The Bloomsbury Reader in Religion, Sexuality, and Gender

ALSO AVAILABLE FROM BLOOMSBURY

The Crisis of Islamic Masculinities, Amanullah De Sondy
The Bloomsbury Reader on Islam in the West, edited by Edward E. Curtis IV
Religions and Environments: A Reader in Religion, Nature and Ecology,
edited by Richard Bohannon

The Bloomsbury Reader in Religion, Sexuality, and Gender

EDITED BY
DONALD L. BOISVERT AND
CARLY DANIEL-HUGHES

Bloomsbury Academic
An imprint of Bloomsbury Publishing Plc

BLOOMSBURY
LONDON · OXFORD · NEW YORK · NEW DELHI · SYDNEY

Bloomsbury Academic

An imprint of Bloomsbury Publishing Plc

50 Bedford Square	1385 Broadway
London	New York
WC1B 3DP	NY 10018
UK	USA

www.bloomsbury.com

BLOOMSBURY and the Diana logo are trademarks of Bloomsbury Publishing Plc

First published 2017

British Library Cataloguing-in-Publication Data
A catalogue record for this book is available from the British Library.

ISBN: HB: 978-1-4742-3779-6
PB: 978-1-4742-3778-9
ePDF: 978-1-4742-3780-2
ePub: 978-1-4742-3781-9

Library of Congress Cataloging-in-Publication Data
Names: Boisvert, Donald L., 1951- editor.
Title: The Bloomsbury reader in religion, sexuality, and gender / edited by
Donald L. Boisvert and Carly Daniel-Hughes.
Description: New York: Bloomsbury, 2016. | Includes index.
Identifiers: LCCN 2016018830 (print) | LCCN 2016033772 (ebook) | ISBN
9781474237796 (hardback) | ISBN 9781474237789 (pbk.) | ISBN 9781474237802
(epdf) | ISBN 9781474237819 (epub)
Subjects: LCSH: Sex–Religious aspects. | Gender identity–Religious aspects.
Classification: LCC BL65.S4 B63 2016 (print) | LCC BL65.S4 (ebook) | DDC
200.81–dc23
LC record available at https://lccn.loc.gov/2016018830

Cover design by Dani Leigh
Cover illustration © Saint Wilgefortis the Bearded by Alana Kerr/alana-kerr.com

Typeset by Deanta Global Publishing Services, Chennai, India
Printed and bound in Great Britain

To Our Concordia University Students
Past, Present and Future

Contents

Permissions

The following were reproduced with kind permission. The publishers have made every effort to trace copyright holders and to obtain permission to reproduce extracts. This has not been possible in every case, however, any omissions brought to our attention will be remedied in future editions.

Acknowledgments

A work such as this is never the product of a single person's effort, even though there are two of us in this case. We want to extend our thanks to the staff at Bloomsbury for their support and patience, especially Lalle Pursglove and Lucy Carroll, and to all the publishers and authors who graciously granted permissions. We are also grateful to our colleagues in the "Women, Gender, and Sexuality" area in the Department of Religion at Concordia University for the conversations and suggestions that nourished this reader. Finally, but by no means least, we thank our spouses, Gaston and Brandon, for their support, and Carly especially wants to single out her son, Silas, as well. Needless to say, all errors and omissions are entirely ours.

DLB & CDH

Introduction to the Volume

In the fifteenth century, European Christians recounted the remarkable story of Saint Wilgefortis. A young daughter of a Portuguese king, she faced a terrible predicament. Her uncompromising father was forcing her to marry a pagan king. She was desperate about her devotion to Christ and her vow of virginity was now under peril. Throwing herself into passionate prayer, Wilgefortis beseeched the Lord to come to her aid, to somehow stop the marriage. He answered her supplications, but in a novel fashion: suddenly the girl's face sprouted a beard. Horrified by the appearance of the hairy-faced, young woman, Wilgefortis' father had his own daughter crucified. Artistic imagery adorning medieval churches tells us, however, that many medieval Christians saw Wilgefortis' hirsute countenance differently. They thought it sublime. Indeed, her name may derive from the Old German *heilige Vartez*, which means "holy face."

Wilgefortis' image adorns the cover of this reader because her story offers a compelling example of how religion and sexuality intersect. It reveals, first, how sexuality regularly infuses religious devotion and identification. Wilgefortis' religious devotion was expressed through her commitment to virginity and it was placed under threat because of an impending marriage. But there is something more here that solicits our interest in this saint's story. For it indicates that holiness or sacredness may itself be "queer." Here we take queer not as an identity (something that Wilgefortis has), but rather as a description of how her story unsettles normative binaries, such as male/female and human/divine. Holy figures, like Christian saints, are often queer in this way. They traverse boundaries. They move between heaven and earth, the infinite and finite. Routinely holy figures move between genders too. They often exist at the margins of masculinity and femininity, incorporating elements of both genders, or destabilizing hegemonic constructions of these altogether.

Early Christians, for instance, told stories of other cross-dressing saints, such as Pelagia of Antioch, who dressed as a man so that she could enjoy the monastic life. So convincing was her drag performance that those who venerated her thought that she was man. In her own lifetime she was known as the monk, Pelagios. We can interpret Wilgefortis and Pelagia as "transfigures" with bodies that broadcast the signs of masculinity, even as the tradition remembers them as female saints. Their stories remind us too that people whose gender performances do not conform to hegemonic norms are often under the threat of erasure or violence. Pelagia must pass as a man to sustain her monastic life. Wilgefortis, in the end, is killed. Their stories tell us that the connections between religion and sexuality are complex. At once religions constrain and make possible variety and difference when it comes to sexuality and gender. By establishing certain norms of behavior and desire as transcendent values, religions regulate expressions of sexuality and gender. But this is only part of the story, for religions are also sites for queer performances that strain against and challenge such norms. Religions can and have sustained various forms and expressions of erotic desire and sexual identities, including those that fall outside of hegemonic definitions.

The study of sexuality and religion

This reader introduces students to the fascinating study of religion and sexuality. It would seem that the *stuff* of religion (texts, concepts, practices) should be central to any examination of sexuality (historical or contemporary) because religious phenomena deeply shape how people experience and understand their erotic lives and interpret the lives of others. Further, as we have noted, religious institutions produce and maintain norms of sexuality and gender and routinely enforce them. Yet it is only in the last two decades that religion and sexuality has become a robust area of scholarly interest. In what follows, we provide some context for how this interest developed and the questions and presumptions that have guided the study of religion and sexuality in recent years. Our aim in so doing is twofold: (1) to provide suggestions for further reading in religion and sexuality and (2) to orient instructors and students to the discussions that they will encounter in this reader.

Beginning in the 1970s and 1980s, scholars became more attentive to the dense connections between sexuality, gender, and religion. This interest registered the social transformations that took place particularly in North America a decade or two earlier in the feminist, civil, and gay rights movements. Together these movements made visible the disenfranchisement of women, "homosexuals," and people of color in social and political life. The gay rights movement, born in the years after the 1969 Stonewall riots, additionally helped to shift cultural perceptions of homosexuality as pathological or deviant, enabling people to openly identify as gay and lesbian. People within these movements called for systemic changes to social policies and institutional structures, including religious institutions, to address sexism, racism, and heterosexism. Sometimes communities banded together in their efforts to bring about social transformation, but at other points, there have existed tensions and points of difference among them. Calls for change made themselves heard in the academy too. The marginalization of women, people of color, and gay and lesbian people began increasingly to inform the study of religious communities and histories as well, opening up new sets of questions and approaches about gender and sexuality in these contexts.

Feminist studies: Women's experience and representations of the female body

Feminist scholars pioneered some of the first impactful studies of sexuality and gender in religion. The majority of these scholars were writing from North America, and early studies often focused on Christian and Jewish traditions, as well as neo-paganism, but the 1980s saw the increasing production of work on traditions well outside of these. Feminist scholars produced a series of influential studies that demonstrated the systematic exclusion of women in the religious symbols, texts, and religious institutions. Notable here is Mary Daly's *Beyond God the Father: Toward a Philosophy of Women's Liberation* (1971), which explored masculine language and symbols for God as that which supports patriarchy and the oppression of women. Scholars such as Judith Plaskow paid careful attention to the exclusion of Jewish women from critical aspects of ritual life and highlighted potentially inclusive aspects of the Jewish tradition as well. Feminist scholars also identified the presence of women's voices and experiences that had been buried or marginalized in religious traditions.

When feminist scholars addressed questions about sexuality, they did so to highlight women's embodied experiences in these traditions, and to show how male experiences and bodies were usually treated as normative. Many feminist studies have additionally shown how religious traditions represented women's bodies as defiling, polluting, and in need of management, with implications for how their sexuality was understood and treated. Catholic theologian, Rosemary Radford Ruether, argued in *Sexism and God-Talk* (1983) that the dualism of mind and body pervaded Western thought and had, therefore, made the body a problem to be controlled in the Christian tradition. Identifying women in terms of the material body, the tradition, she argued, had cut off the radical potential of its theological claim that all human beings, men and women, are made in the image of God.

Whether the negative assessment of the body resides only in the Western tradition is unclear however. In her more recent study, *Charming Cadavers: Horrific Figurations of the Feminine in Indian Buddhist Hagiographic Literature* (1996), Liz Wilson examined images of women's dead, decaying, and repulsive bodies that populate Buddhist hagiographies from India and South Asia in the first millennium C.E. In these texts, asserts Wilson, women's bodies are identified with the traps and temptations of *samsara* (the cycle of birth, death, and rebirth) and used to inspire male readers to be celibate and avoid the allure of sexual desire. We might put Wilson's study into conversation with other work on religion and the body, like the collection edited by Howard Eilberg-Schwartz, *People of the Body: Jews and Judaism from an Embodied Perspective* (1992), from which the Chava Weissler selection in this reader is drawn, or the medievalist Caroline Walker Bynum's *Fragmentation and Redemption: Essays on Gender and the Human Body in Medieval Religion* (1991), which emphasizes the somatic nature of medieval women's devotion to Christ. Read together, studies on religion and the body suggest that the body often occupies an ambivalent and potent place in religious traditions, both powerful and dangerous (a fear that is often located onto female bodies, though not exclusively so). The body is at once the mechanism by which practitioners engage with the divine or transcendent, and that which can limit or prohibit such possibilities.

Already in the 1980s feminist studies of religious traditions extended beyond the scope of Judaism and Christianity. The publication of an edited volume by Nancy Auder

Falk and Rita Gross entitled, *Unspoken Worlds: Women's Lives in Non-Western Cultures* (1980), offers an important example for it explored women's lives in diverse contexts, such as Japanese Buddhism, Iranian Islam, and indigenous traditions in East Africa and Australia. Karen McCarthy Brown's treatment of Haitian Vodou in this volume comes from this expansive collection, one that is important for showcasing the manifold experiences of women in their religious communities. *Unspoken Worlds* offered a nuanced understanding of how religions provide meaning, structure, and value to their lives and embodied experiences including issues such as childbirth, marriage, and erotic attachments.

Critical as well to the development of feminist analyses of religion and sexuality have been the interventions by feminists of color, such as African-American (womanist) and Latina (mujerista) scholars, among others. They have shown that too often white feminists were inattentive to how race and class informed and shaped women's experiences of oppression, including that of sexuality. One illustrative study is Delores William's *Sisters in the Wilderness: The Challenge of Womanist God-Talk* (1993). In it, womanist theologian Williams draws parallels between the experience of African-American women under slavery and the biblical figure, Hagar, the slave of the patriarch, Abraham, who served as a sexual surrogate for him and his barren wife Sarah. Williams envisions a powerful message of survival for African-American women in the figure of Hagar. At the same time, she richly elaborates the connections between race, class, gender, and sexual exploitation that shape the lives of African-American women, themes that resonate with the selection in this volume from Kelly Brown Douglas' *Sexuality and the Black Church* (1999).

Feminist scholars from non-Western contexts echoed the sentiments of feminists of color when they argued that Western feminists often reduplicated colonialist logic and rhetoric in their representation of non-Western women. For instance, Leila Ahmed in her *Women and Gender in Islam: Historical Roots of a Modern Debate* (1992) noted that Western feminists have treated women's veiling as evidence of oppression, in particular as a sign of their sexual servitude, and so too, of the primitive nature of Islam. This representation of veiling still holds sway in Western secular contexts, like France, revealing the intersections between religion and sexuality in Western secularism—a topic that the Mayanthi Fernando reading in this volume addresses.

Shifting landscapes: The emergence of queer and gender theory

Until the 1990s the study of gender and women's experience in religious contexts existed separately from discussions of sexuality. At that time the writings of Michel Foucault on sexuality facilitated something of the convergence of what had been separate lines of query, feminist, gay/lesbian studies, and critical gender theory (more below), in a new theoretical idiom, queer theory. Before Foucault's work made its impact on scholars in North America, however, some scholars were asking questions about sexual orientation, identity, and religion, particularly Christianity. In 1980 Yale historian John Boswell published a study entitled *Christianity, Social Tolerance, and Homosexuality: Gay People in Western Europe from the Beginning of the Christian Era to the Fourteenth Century* that reached audiences in the academy and well beyond. Boswell's thesis held that for much of Christian history there was tolerance for rather than persecution of homosexuality. While some scholars charged him with being an "essentialist," his claim that the condemnation of homoeroticism was not in fact timeless exposed the recent history of homophobia in the Christian tradition and, further, suggested that ancient sources give evidence of homoerotic relationships and experiences.

Bernadette Brooten's *Love Between Women: Early Christian Responses to Homoeroticism* (1996) might be read as an extension of Boswell's thesis in that it shows how a history of female homoeroticism can be written from ancient sources. Brooten's careful historical work challenged Boswell's thesis, even as it was sympathetic to his politics. She did not find tolerance for homoeroticism in early Christian writings, as Boswell did, but rather condemnations of it. Yet she concluded that these denunciations were based on pervasive knowledge of its practice among ancient women.

Engagement with the work of Michel Foucault, particularly his three volumes on *The History of Sexuality* (the first published in English in 1978), ultimately incited more and deeper analyses of sexuality and desire in religious contexts, regularly in combination with feminist, gender, and queer theoretical approaches. The way Foucault framed sexuality as a discourse with a history offered immense possibilities for scholars of religion. A short way of stating Foucault's main point in his opening volume of *The History of Sexuality* is that there is no transcendent ideal of sexuality that we can find across time and place. To examine sexuality, instead, is to analyze how cultures and societies articulate norms and ascribe meaning to sexually differentiated bodies, erotic practices, and desires. Foucault's historical approach claims that we should anticipate other social logics, sexual politics, and constructions of sex/gender when we look at communities elsewhere, whether in the past or in other places.

Queer theory has played a critical role in the study of religion and sexuality as well. Interacting with and responding to Foucault's insights about sexuality as well as feminist accounts of gender oppression, queer theory refers to disparate approaches and strategies that have as their goal to identify and unsettle the social processes that produce and sustain normalized identities. Queer theory takes sexuality and gender into account so closely because they are ways in which such identities are routinely regularized. Queer theorists have pointed out how sexuality (defined as erotic behaviors and desires), sex (as nature), and gender (as culture) are often conflated—what the philosopher Judith Butler calls the "heteronormative matrix"— so that heterosexuality is made coherent and given cultural privilege. Sex and gender, that is male/female and masculine/feminine, shore up heterosexuality's normative status by indicating there are but two sorts of people resulting from the fact of two sorts of bodies.

For activist scholars, queer approaches have been groundbreaking because they invite the possibility of change, with potentially dramatic consequences for LGBTIQ people who have been systematically marginalized in Western societies and religious communities. In terms of studying religion and sexuality, queer theorists have shown how gender is intimately connected to sexuality and desire. The study of sexuality cannot, they argue, be divorced from it in any easy way. This insight bears itself out in the title of this volume: *The Bloomsbury Reader in Religion, Sexuality, and Gender*.

The insights of queer theorists have been felt in religious studies, at times in happy combination with feminist approaches, as represented by Marcella Althaus-Reid's *Indecent Theology: Theological Perversions in Sex, Gender, and Politics* (2001), which brings questions of sexuality to the center of Christian liberation theology, along with poverty and global politics. But at other times, these theoretical orientations, feminist and queer, are at odds with one another. This is the case when the former is grounded in the assertion of "woman" as an enduring identity and the latter challenges the politics of identity itself. It is important to note too that critical gender studies, which in important ways facilitated the emergence of queer theories, has made an indelible impact on recent studies of sexuality and religion. Taking insights from feminist theory, gender analyses have looked beyond constructions of femininity and female identities to masculinity and male identities and have explored how these are instilled and performed. As a result, masculinity studies of this kind open up new vistas for thinking about the ways gender and sexual difference shape not only women's lives, but men's as well.

In religious studies, these various approaches, feminist, gender, and queer theories, can be understood to complement each other, but they might also stand in tension with one another. How scholars use and understand these theories shape the questions they ask of their research subjects and topics, and the kinds of conclusions they draw, just as they are informed by the audience to whom their analyses are directed. This reader does not resolve these theoretical issues. Instead, we think it is more productive to present students with readings that undertake and differently combine theoretical approaches, feminist, gender critical, and queer (among others).

Studies in religion and sexuality

The study of sexuality and gender in Christian contexts has perhaps the longest tenure, in part as a response to Foucault's placement of it in his book *The History of Sexuality*, where he argues that confession was a precedent to modern technologies for studying sex, such as psychology. Yet Foucault also noted something else about premodern Christianity that did not anticipate the Victorian "science of sex" that he traced in his opening volume of *The History of Sexuality*: sexual asceticism. In practicing asceticism, ancient Christians implied that the true self was constituted through escaping sexuality. In other words, sex was exactly what was being denied. This concept stood at odds with Foucault's claim that in modern Western societies the true self was located in it.

This tension has been provocatively elaborated and explored by Virginia Burrus' queer reading of ancient Christian hagiography in her *The Sex Lives of the Saints: An Erotics of Ancient Hagiography* (2004).

While scholars have not always confirmed Foucault's interpretations, the fact that he addressed sexuality in premodern Christianity helped animate studies of sexuality in ancient Christian contexts, such as Peter Brown's foundational text, *The Body and Society: Men, Women, and Sexual Renunciation in Early Christianity* (1988). The work of other scholars, such as Stephen Moore's *God's Beauty Parlor: And Other Queer Spaces in and around the Bible* (2001), showcases the rich convergence of discussions of queer and critical gender theory. Dale Martin's *Sex and the Single Savior: Gender and Sexuality in Biblical Interpretation* (2006) raises critical questions about the roles that interpretation plays in the production and maintenance of hegemonic sexualities. Today, the study of sexuality in Christianity occupies scholars working across this tradition, as reflected in recent titles like Amy DeRogatis' *Saving Sex: Sexuality and Salvation in American Evangelicalism* (2014).

Already in the mid-1990s, the study of sexuality in Judaism was well established. Here we highlight critical studies that address not only sexuality, such as David Biale's *Eros and the Jews: From Biblical Israel to Contemporary America* (1992) (a selection of which appears in this volume) or Daniel Boyarin's *Carnal Israel: Reading Sex in Talmudic Culture* (1995), but also constructions of masculinity, such as Howard Eilberg-Schwartz's *God Phallus: And Other Problems for Men and Monotheism* (1995) and Boyarin's *Unheroic Conduct: The Rise of Heterosexuality and the Invention of the Jewish Man* (1997). The proximity both historically and professionally of scholars working in Jewish and Christian materials has meant that scholars working on masculinity in these two traditions are commonly in dialogue—a fact that is on display in titles such as *Men and Masculinities in Christianity and Judaism: A Critical Reader*, edited by Björn Krondorfer (2009). Lest we be tempted into thinking that these two traditions have emphasized, or even fetishized masculinity, titles like John Powers' study *A Bull of Man: Images of Masculinity, Sex, and the Body in Indian Buddhism* (2009) (also in this volume), reminds us of the potency of masculinity in other religious contexts, and the different configurations it can take.

At present, the study of religion and sexuality flourishes across a host of traditions, time periods, and geographical localities. *Buddhism, Sexuality, and Gender*, edited by José Ignacio Cabezón in 1992 (from which the essay by Paul Schalow in this reader is drawn) offered one of the first studies to examine these intersecting concepts across a variety of Buddhist materials, highlighting especially understudied evidence of same-sex desire in them. Other titles, such as Will Roscoe and Stephen O'Murray's edited collection, *Islamic Homosexualities: Culture, History, and Literature* (1997), Bernard Faure's *The Red Thread: Buddhist Approaches to Sexuality* (1998), Joseph Alter's *Gandhi's Body: Sex, Diet, and the Politics of Nationalism* (2000) or the volume edited by Kathryn Babayan and Afsaneh Najmabadi, *Islamicate Sexualities: Translations across Temporal Geographies of Power* (2008) offered critical correctives to what was in danger of being a Eurocentric subfield.

Texts like Kecia Ali's *Sexual Ethics in Islam: Feminist Reflections on the Qur'an, Hadith, and Jurisprudence* (2006), as well as the study by Martin (above), show keen interest on the part of scholars to empower readers with accessible and challenging treatments of sexuality within critical texts. Scott Siraj al-Haqq Kugle's *Homosexuality in Islam: Critical Reflections on Gay, Lesbian, and Transgender Muslims* (2010) demonstrates a desire for sexual and gender minorities to speak about their own experiences within their cultures and religious traditions. Increasingly insights drawn from postcolonial and critical race theories shape the study of religion, sexuality, and gender. Scholars are more attentive to the impact of cultural representation, migration and dislocation, nationalism, and politics on religious communities and their histories.

Today questions about how religion, gender, and sexuality inform each other; how they impact the lives of individuals and communities; how they shape societies and cultures animate studies of religious communities, worldviews, and texts. It is little wonder that colleges and universities regularly offer courses on religion and sexuality. Yet until now there have not been good pedagogical materials targeted at beginning college and university students. This reader aims to fill that gap.

About the reader: What to expect, and how to utilize it

We begin with a caution. This reader is not:

- A comprehensive survey of religion and sexuality.
- Designed for advanced or graduate students.

It is, however, ideal for undergraduate students in introductory-level lecture and seminar courses. The reader provides a compelling starting point to the examination of religion, sexuality, and gender with selections that will expand students' curiosity about these subjects as well as the horizons of their thinking and reflection about them. To this end, it does not provide students with readings devoted in equal measure to different religious traditions. But it does offer diversity in terms of traditions, communities, periods, and geographic localities represented—to name some examples: rabbinic writings from ancient Judaism, *hijras* in modern South India, contemporary Satanism in North America, and Christianity in colonial Mexico. We envision that this reader will be utilized largely in North American and Western European contexts. Readings lean toward subjects either familiar to these students or which have bearing on their histories. We have likewise selected topically diverse readings, and identified a number of selections that complicate a heteronormative understanding of sexuality and gender. Key readings from theorists who have informed the study of sexuality and gender are incorporated as well. In these selections, students will encounter topics such as childbirth, racial and colonial bodies, bodily purity and impurity, same-sex desire, autoeroticism, erotic fantasy, gender identity and performance, disability, bodily modification, and sexual asceticism.

The reader is organized into three sections: "Bodies," "Desires," and "Performances." Together they consider the ways in which people have made sense of their religious and sexual experiences, the ways they imagine and talk about gender, sex, and the sacred, and the multiple meanings they ascribe to them. The first section, "Bodies," does so by looking closely at how the body is represented and interpreted in various religious traditions, and so, too, how embodied experience shapes religious life. "Desires" explores connections between religious life, practice, and the erotic. "Performances" considers the intersections between gender and sexuality, and the ways in which religious life can enable people to transgress normative views of these. Each section begins with a short introduction, orienting students to some of the bigger questions posed by the readings in it. Every reading additionally contains a brief introduction that provides students with relevant context and highlights issues that can frame their engagement with the selection. No footnotes or endnotes appear in the selections. We have removed these for pedagogical reasons, in order that the authors' main argument be the focus of students' attention. Each section ends with a series of discussion questions for use as assignments or as in-class exercises to facilitate deeper comprehension and reflection. The reader includes a glossary to provide students with relevant terminology as well. It is our hope that this volume solicits and supports productive engagements with the study of religion, sexuality, and gender in a variety of college and university classrooms.

PART ONE

Bodies

1

Introduction

In a number of North American indigenous communities, there existed what was called a third sex or gender: men who inhabited male bodies but who performed traditional female tribal roles, and women who inhabited female bodies but who performed traditional male tribal roles. They would often be partnered with members of their own sex, but live with them as members of the opposite sex, and this was generally accepted by the community. Because of their ability to transcend normative patterns of gender, these persons were seen as being especially powerful in a spiritual sense. In Western anthropological literature, such individuals were often given the pejorative name of *berdache* by missionaries and scholars, a word meaning something like "rent boy." Modern-day indigenous activists prefer the term "two-spirited," which more accurately reflects the sense of a dual spiritual identity. What the existence of such a two-spirited tradition teaches us is that human bodies remain perennial sites of religious malleability across cultures.

This section on "Bodies" explores how religious traditions construct understandings of the human body in relation to gender and sexuality. While religious people often speak of the body as natural and given, in fact it has been understood differently over time and place. We sometimes hear that a given religion is "body-affirming" while another is "body-denying," but such affirmations are false and misleading. Scholars challenge such a simple dichotomy, and they have considered the importance of the body to religious life and identity across diverse types of communities. The body mediates human experience, particularly experiences of the erotic; it plays a profound symbolic role in religious systems; and it serves critically in the regulation of communities and in the organization of social and ritual life. The regulation and control of the body have been significant in the oppression of women and other marginalized groups, such as lesbian, gay, and transgendered persons, who are often reduced to their bodies. Readings in this section highlight how various religious communities conceptualize the body, gender, and sexuality, as well as how they have attempted to normalize and regulate their perspectives. The readings also move beyond simply identifying normative or commonly held views within these religious communities in order to focus on diversity among them, and to address how such views have been challenged or have shifted. Human bodies are ever-changing sites of charged religious symbolism and meaning.

By far the most common attitude of religions when it comes to the human body is that of ambivalence. Is the body a source of goodness or an amalgamation of evil tendencies? Are gender differences between women and men—or, even more problematic, the challenges posed by non-gender-conforming persons—divinely ordained and sanctioned, meant to be severely upheld and policed, or perhaps punished? How far does the biological or sexed body define and construct the religious body? Can the body be used as an instrument of worship, or is it rather an impediment to true enlightenment and spiritual fulfillment? Should heterosexuality be seen as the dominant, if not exclusive, religious paradigm, or can same-sex desire also be spiritually meaningful? In many cases, it is binary thinking that structures the debate: the body is either this or that; it can be nothing else. The problem, of course, is that bodies are essentially "messy" things; they are rarely fixed and constant. They remain inherently unpredictable and in flux. Human bodies are also sites of deep symbolic meaning. On them can be projected any number of cultural anxieties but also distinctive identities, such as in the case of circumcision for Jews. Regulating the human body becomes a compelling challenge for many religious practitioners.

It is undoubtedly women who have suffered the most from the manifold ways in which institutionalized religions have defined and tried to control human bodies. In some traditions, such as Roman Catholicism, this continues to the present, where women remain barred from ordained ministry, due primarily to their gender. Most religions, because of their patriarchal nature, retain an array of prohibitions and taboos surrounding women's bodies. Some of these remain rigidly enforced, while others are more like cultural practices. There are a number of reasons why women's bodies might be understood as being somehow religiously problematic, and therefore necessitating special regulation. Male power and privilege undoubtedly account for a significant part of this. The unique ability of women to control fertility and birth can also be seen as something especially powerful and enigmatic, perhaps even threatening, and therefore requiring elaborate rules and directives. In many cultures, including our own, rigid gender roles, often seen as biologically or religiously indispensable, continue to delineate our understandings of how women's and men's bodies are to be socially and culturally constructed, very often to the detriment of women. Some religious traditions are, in fact, quite affirming of particular features of female bodies, as outlined in the reading on the Church of Satan.

Other sorts of bodies can also raise issues and concerns for some religious traditions or practitioners: the lesbian, gay, or transgendered body, the disabled body, the sexually uncertain body, or the body of the person of color. Most often, these sorts of bodies may be perceived and understood as divergent, incomplete, menacing, or somehow, religiously suspect. Very often, the religious concept of sin or depravity, usually in a Christian context, may be attached to them. These nonnormative bodies—which are less conventional because of their obvious divergence from the typical white, male, heterosexual, abled body and the inherent cultural power attached to it—can become sources of acute anxiety and unease for religious institutions and believers. Their response to the alleged challenges posed by such bodies can be wide-ranging, running the gamut from ostracism to severe chastisement, including the possibility of capital punishment. On the other hand, some religious traditions value and welcome sexed and gendered bodily differences, which are perceived as divinely sanctioned attributes or sources of spiritual power and authority. Once again, ambivalence characterizes the general attitude of religions toward the body. The human body remains a recurring source of religious reflection and action.

The following selection of readings on religion and the body explores different aspects of this theme of ambivalence. The texts by Kelly Brown Douglas, Lynne Gerber, Paula Sanders, and Chava Weissler examine questions of race, sin, hermaphroditism, and childbirth in different religious traditions, and how such issues emerge as sites for the expression and playing-out of religious norms and prohibitions about human bodies. In these readings, control and regulation of what bodies do are of particular concern, especially as regards women. A similar interest in rules is found in Janet Gyatso's piece on how Buddhist monastic bodies should behave in sexual situations. In a somewhat different register, Cimminnee Holt's excerpt discusses the potent qualities of female bodily fluids in modern Satanism. Here, women's bodies become privileged sites of empowerment. The reading by Robert Orsi offers a nuanced and engaging reflection on the intersections between disability and the Catholic ethos of salvific bodily suffering. Finally, the excerpt from John Powers raises questions of normative religious masculinity with respect to the figure of the Buddha. In all these texts, the human body remains under question; its contours ever in religious flux.

Religious ambivalence and regulation need not be seen as inherently problematic or even oppressive of the human body. Because our bodies are the primary means for us to engage with the world, it makes sense that they should be critically significant to religions. We are religious and spiritual beings with, in, and through our bodies. Religions have a vested interest in how we use our bodies for religious purposes. The real danger lies in when religious regulation becomes a source of unwarranted oppression and coercion. It is then that human bodies need to rebel.

2

Stereotypes, False Images, Terrorism:

The White Assault upon Black Sexuality

Kelly Brown Douglas

Kelly Brown Douglas is a leading womanist theologian and ordained Episcopalian priest. Her study Sexuality and the Black Church: A Womanist Perspective *examines the history of negative attitudes about sex in African-American communities in order to challenge and transform them. This excerpt considers stereotypes of black female and male bodies that emerged in institutional slavery in the United States. In 1619, the first African slaves were brought to the colony in Jamestown, Virginia, establishing the practice of slavery throughout the colonies. By the nineteenth century, slavery was exclusive to the American South and finally abolished in the 13th Amendment in 1865. Yet the legacy of slavery continues in the United States with African-Americans routinely disenfranchised by unfair policies of segregation, conditions of poverty, and multiple forms of violence. These concerns fueled the civil rights movement of the 1960s and continue to negatively impact African-Americans today. Douglas examines stereotypes born out of slavery. Her study argues that these stereotypes continue to burden the Black church and community, negatively shaping their responses to various sexual issues, such as homophobia and the HIV/AIDS epidemic.*

Carnal, passionate, lustful, lewd, rapacious, bestial, sensual — these are just some of the many terms that come to mind when thinking of the ways in which White culture has depicted Black people's sexuality. This practice of dehumanizing Black people by maligning their sexuality has been a decisive factor in the exercise of White power in America. So crucial is the exploitation of Black sexuality to White dominance that White culture has left almost no stone unturned in its violation of Black bodies and intimacy. This violation has been grounded in numerous sexually charged stereotypes. These stereotypes have been critical to the achievement of unprincipled racist power. By disguising and mystifying objective reality, they have been indispensable to the maintenance of the social, political, and economic status quo in America. They have functioned to make White supremacy appear not only necessary but also "natural, normal and an inevitable part of everyday life." At the same time, these sexual stereotypes have impacted Black lives in such a way as to render sexuality a virtually taboo topic for the Black church and community.

The Jezebel

One of the most prominent stereotypes has characterized the Black female as "a person governed almost entirely by her libido." She has been described as having an insatiable sexual appetite, being extraordinarily passionate, and being sexually aggressive and cunning. Such stereotyping has produced the paramount image for Black womanhood in White culture — the Jezebel image. "Jezebel" has come to symbolize an evil, scheming, and seductive woman. This symbol no doubt owes its meaning to the ninth-century Phoenician princess and wife of the Israelite king Ahab, who was accused of destroying the kingdom with her idolatrous practices and otherwise diabolical ways (1 Kings 16:29–22:53).

Though the Jezebel image in relation to Black women would come to fruition during slavery, like White cultural stereotypes and images of Black people in general, it is rooted in European travels to Africa. Travelers often interpreted African women's sparse dress — dress appropriate to the climate of Africa — as a sign of their lewdness and lack of chastity. White explains: "The idea that black women were exceptionally sensual first gained credence when Englishmen went to Africa to buy slaves. Unaccustomed to the requirements of tropical climate, Europeans mistook seminudity for lewdness." Indeed, the warm climate came to be associated with "hot constition'd Ladies" possessed of a temper "hot and lascivious."

If the habits, way of life, and living conditions of the African woman gave birth to the notion that Black women were Jezebels, then the conditions and exigencies of slavery brought it to maturity. The life situation of the enslaved woman encouraged the idea that she was a Jezebel, even as the Jezebel image served to justify the life situation she was forced to endure. Essentially, the very institution that the Jezebel image served to guard gave credence to the idea that Black women were in fact Jezebels.

For instance, the institution of slavery forced Black women to display their bodies in a manner that was considered contrary to antebellum notions of moral, chaste, and decent women. This was an era when a "proper" lady was marked not only by her innocence, her attention to her home, and the moral upbringing of her children, but also by her manner of dress. Clothing signified one's moral status as well as class. A "respectable" White woman was thus "adorned" in layers of clothing. By contrast, the enslaved female was often given barely enough clothing to cover her body. In addition, the enslaved woman's work in the fields often required her to raise her dress above her knees. Even house servants often had to pull their skirts up to polish and wash floors. Their sparse covering coupled with working in a manner that required that they were even more exposed all fed the sentiment that the Black female was a wanton, loose creature.

Further supporting the Jezebel image was the public display of nudity that slavery often required. Like Sarah Bartmann, enslaved females' bodies were often stripped bare as they were closely examined, poked, and prodded during slave auctions and sales. Numerous slave testimonies witness to this fact. One enslaved person recalled in an interview:

> Each slave, whether female or male, is brought up to the block, and sometimes stripped entirely of all clothing, that the buyer may examine as to any bodily defect, and their persons are handled like oxen or horses, and each is sold separately to the highest bidder.

A person enslaved in Missouri remembered, "Right here in St. Louis men and women have been stripped stark naked and examined by the critical eyes of prospective purchasers as though they were dumb driven cattle." Lu Perkins said, "I'members when they put me on the auction block. They pulled my dress down over my back to my waist, to show I ain't gashed and slashed up."

Adding to the degradation of public nudity, Black females were sometimes taken to a space where their sexual organs could be closely examined by their prospective buyer so that he (sometimes she) could determine her suitability for breeding. Again, such exigencies of slavery only catered to the notion that Black women were Jezebels. Certainly, in the irrational logic of White culture, no self-respecting woman would allow herself to be put on display in such a manner.

In addition to the conditions of dress and bodily display, the Jezebel image was also reinforced because the reproductive capacity of enslaved women was often a topic of public conversation. With the disruption of the slave trade, the growth of the enslaved population was dependent upon the fertility of the already enslaved. This meant that some masters "encouraged" — by a variety of despicable means — frequent pregnancies of the enslaved women.

Many Black females were bought and sold based on their reproductive potential. As Willie Coffer recalls, "A good young breedin' 'oman brung two thousand dollars easy, 'cause all de marsters wanted to see plenty of strong healthy chillun comin' on, all de time." Most damaging to the Black woman's reputation were articles that appeared discussing her reproductive capacity. These articles would speculate on the best conditions for the proper breeding of slaves. They also marveled at the fertility of enslaved women. Reinforcing this "breeder" mystique was the fact that enslaved women were often forced back into the fields only days, sometimes hours, after delivering. They were also expected to get pregnant as often as possible. Deborah Gray White poignantly captures the Black females' dilemma, "Once [enslaved women's] reproduction became a topic of public conversation, so did the slave woman's sexual activities. People accustomed to speaking and writing about the bondwoman's reproductive abilities could hardly help associating her with licentious behavior."

Black women were helplessly trapped in the mythology of being Jezebels by the very institution that demanded them to be precisely that. The more entrenched the Jezebel image became, the easier it was to justify treating Black women in inhumane ways. Once enslaved females were considered Jezebels, then all manner of treatment of them was deemed appropriate. They could be worked brutally in the fields, displayed on public auction blocks like cattle, and exploited as breeders.

Adding to the persistence of the Jezebel imagery was the fact that this image was necessary to ideas of White male and female privilege and superiority. The Black woman as a Jezebel was a perfect foil to the White, middle-class woman who was pure, chaste, and innocent. As White notes: "In every way Jezebel was the counterimage of the mid-nineteenth-century ideal of the Victorian lady. She did not lead men and children to God; piety was foreign to her. She saw no advantage in prudery, indeed domesticity paled in importance before matters of the flesh."

One of the practical consequences of this counterimage was that it allowed White men to sexually exploit Black women while still protecting the innocence of White women.

By distorting Black women's sexuality, the Jezebel image protected the White slavocracy and fostered the exercise of tyrannical White power. Yet as significant as the Jezebel image was to the slavocracy and White power in general, it was effective only inasmuch as it functioned in conjunction with another powerful and tenacious image foisted upon Black women — that of Mammy.

Mammy

It would not do in the White, racist, patriarchal world of slavery for Black women to be *only* Jezebels. White households could not be entrusted to the care of Jezebels. Such morally reprehensible creatures were certain to damage the moral upbringing of White children and to be an improper influence upon innocent White women. Moreover, if all Black women were Jezebels, then White men would be truly overwhelmed by the presence of so many seductive creatures. The "gentility" of the southern slavocracy demanded the image of Mammy. As historian Patricia Morton observes, "the more [the Black woman] was treated and viewed as a Jezebel, the more essential Mammy became as the counterimage of slavery's racial imagery." This image served to "calm Southern fears of moral slippage and 'mongrelization,' or man's fears of woman's emasculating sexual powers." But who, exactly, was Mammy?

While southern lore paints Mammy as the perfect female slave, obedient and completely loyal to the master's family, sometimes even to the point of being disloyal to other enslaved people, the reality of Mammy is more ambiguous. Testimony suggests a much more complex figure.

If Mammy was a trustful caretaker of her master's and mistress's children, it was not at the expense of her own children's care. She oftentimes found a way to take care of both, even when her slaveholders demanded total devotion to their own children. Typically, Mammy was an older female and thus conformed to the image of being maternal and asexual. Yet she was sometimes young and attractive, thus frequently victimized by the White males of the household. Sometimes Mammy may have been a trusted confidante of the White mistress. But oftentimes she was perceived as a sexual threat and was the victim of her mistress's violent tirades. If her duties as domestic servant were less strenuous than those of a field hand, being in the master's house meant that she was on twenty-four-hour call. If, as a domestic servant, Mammy received better clothing and more food, being in the master's house also meant she was more subject to his whims of violence, sexual or otherwise. So if Mammy appeared docile and subservient, it may have been only a ruse for surviving when living in such close quarters with the master and mistress. If Mammy was a trusted confidante of the mistress, she was also a friend on the inside for the other enslaved persons.

Clearly Mammy is one of the more complex and elusive figures of enslavement. That there were Black female house servants is indisputable. The prevalence of them and the nature of their work are more difficult to determine. There is simply not a single picture that can be painted of the life or labor of the enslaved female domestic. Yet while the actual role and life of these women may be unclear, the significance of the Mammy image to White, racist, patriarchal culture is most clear. Whether the "perfect" Mammy existed in the minds of the slavocracy or was real is less significant than how this role — the household female servant/Mammy — preserved White female and male prestige and privilege.

By acting as a surrogate mother, Mammy allowed White women to maintain their Victorian role as perfect mothers. While White women may have handed down certain moral and religious values to their children, Mammy performed the more mundane and physical tasks of rearing children, even to the point of nursing White infants. Despite being labeled asexual, Mammy still performed the kind of functions that reflected Black women's so-called sensual nature.

Notwithstanding Mammy's importance to reinforcing the role of woman as perfect mother, Mammy was most notable as an alternative to the Jezebel image. For its own survival, the White patriarchal slavocracy needed White culture to portray a convincing image of an enslaved female that was more domesticated than Jezebel. Mammy was the answer. For some, she symbolized the "civilizing" potential of slavery. (In this regard Mammy was the female counterpart to the Black male "Sambo" image, as they were both portrayed as happy, docile, domesticated slaves.) This image pointed to the opportunity slavery provided for training and uplifting Black women. Mammy meant that it was possible for Black women to become something other than Jezebels. The logic of White culture implied that with the help of slavery Black women could actually come close — through their care of White children — to personifying the Victorian image of women as happy homemakers.

The significance of Jezebel and Mammy to the institution of slavery, and more especially to White patriarchal power, shows why these images are so central to White culture and thus so persistent and abiding. By distorting the sexuality of Black women, White culture effectively dehumanized them. Such dehumanization made them most vulnerable to rape by White men. The weapon of rape provided an effective means of control. In essence, the Jezebel and Mammy images crafted in White culture allowed White people to cruelly exploit Black female bodies with relative impunity. Such exploitation is a linchpin to the survival of White hegemony. For this reason, these stereotypic images have endured and even, as we shall see later, reappear in various forms in contemporary society.

Violent bucks

These images of Black womanhood provided a gateway to the dehumanization of Black men. The Jezebel character in particular has provided an excuse for the sexual degradation of these males. That Black women were considered sexual reprobates provided White culture with the fundamental proof of the inevitable nature of Black men's sexual perversion. That Black women were Jezebels meant that Black men had no choice but to be passionate and lascivious, if for no other reason than to fulfill the sexual desires of the "hot" Black woman. One southern female writer put it bluntly in a popular nineteenth-century periodical: "They [black women] are evidently the chief instruments of the degradation of the men of their race." In order to complement the unrestrained Black woman, White culture portrayed Black men as wild, bestial, violent bucks.

Black men were regarded, like their female counterparts, as highly sexualized, passionate beings. They were considered lewd, lascivious, and also quite sexually proficient. Black male sexual prowess has become almost legend in the stereotypic logic of White culture. The idea that Black men possess an unusually large penis has only reinforced notions of their sexual aggressiveness and mastery. According to Winthrop Jordan, the ideas about Black male genitalia predate the settlement of America and possibly even the Portuguese explorations of the West African coast. To be sure, Jordan says, "By the final quarter of the eighteenth century the idea that the Negro's penis was larger than the white man's had become something of a commonplace in European scientific circles." Exemplifying the persistence of these myths, novelist Richard Wright remembered a time when two White employees questioned the size of his penis, goading him to "spin around on it like a top." These beliefs surrounding the Black man's sexual temperament and physical attributes no doubt contributed to the White cultural image of the Black man as a buck.

As a buck, the enslaved male was quite useful to the slavocracy. He was deemed a powerful animal not only in terms of his abilities to produce work, but also in terms of his ability to breed offspring. Yet, as indispensable as this image of the Black buck was to the institution of slavery, it also posed a potential threat to the peace and sanctity of the White world. For if being a Jezebel meant that Black women were seducers, then being a buck meant that Black men were sexual predators. Even more threatening to White existence was the idea that the common prey of bucks was White women. Having painted Black women in such a vile manner, White culture then had to accept the notion that these women would not be attractive even to their own men. As is so aptly explained by Paula Giddings (using the words of Philip A. Bruce, a nineteenth-century Virginia aristocrat and historian known for his White supremacist views), the discomfiting logic of White culture suggested that "it was the white women's qualities, so profoundly missing in black women, that made black men find white women irresistible and 'strangely alluring and seductive.'" One Black man eloquently refuted this notion, however, by pointing the finger back at the White man. In an 1866 Emancipation Day speech, Henry Turner said: "We have as much beauty as they; *all we ask of the white man is to let our ladies alone,* and they need not fear us. The difficulty has heretofore been *our ladies were not always at our disposal.*"

Finally, the "wisdom" of White culture advised that a passionate, unrestrained Black buck was also by nature feral. This meant that the Black buck posed a danger to the very lives of White men and women.

White culture seemed trapped by its own insidiously racist logic. The Jezebel was not a desired sexual partner for the Black buck, so he was compelled toward White women. The superpotency and virility of the Black male might also mean that White women were erotically attracted to him. It certainly indicated that the Black male was governed by passion and was thus naturally violent. Ironically, this portrait of the Black buck challenged what it was contrived to protect — the notion of White male superiority. The buck imposed upon White women, impugned White manhood, and threatened White lives.

Castration

Yet, despite the implied power of the Black buck, White culture was relentless in its portrayal. Instead of reconfiguring the images painted of Black people to escape the inevitable conclusions of racist logic, it sanctioned the tools necessary to keep the virile, fiery Black man in his place. Black male bodies were attacked and dismembered with impunity. Castration, though objected to by some Englishmen and abolitionists, became a punishment meted out to Black men. It was initially used as a penalty for running away, plotting insurrection, or similar offenses in the eyes of the slaveholding class. With continued outcry from abolitionists and others about its practice, by the eighteenth century it became a punishment primarily in accusations of rape. By definition rape could only happen to White women. No such crime as rape of a Black woman existed. Such a crime would be ludicrous since Black women "were said to give themselves willingly, even wantonly, to white men." Yet slave-masters often castrated those enslaved males whom they believed to be barriers to their own vile desires to ravish a particular Black woman.

Lynching

As odious as castration was, no crime against the Black man more clearly indicated the White male fear of Black male sexuality or power than lynching. The phenomenon of lynching clearly exemplifies Foucault's understanding of the relationship between sexual discourse and the exercise of power. Through careful deployment of discourse about Black male sexuality, White society was able to easily embrace lynching as a necessary means for protection against such a passionate animal.

Even as lynching was clearly a sexually directed and motivated attack against Black male bodies, it was a primary weapon employed to control Black men and women socially, economically, and politically. Lynching is thus a classic example of the tools used to enforce and uphold White patriarchal hegemony. Lynching rose in popularity after emancipation. With the nominal end of slavery, there was no clear way to control the movement or perceived threat of thousands of once enslaved people turned loose on White society. In an effort to maintain control, White society made certain that the old stereotypes that supported the slavocracy would continue in effect. Black women remained vulnerable to rape — as they were still thought of as little more than Jezebels. Herbert Gutman describes the plight of the emancipated female this way: "Ex-slave women everywhere dealt with a legacy that viewed them as dependent sexual objects." White poignantly comments: "Black women continued to be perceived by white America as individuals who desired promiscuous relationships, and this perception left them vulnerable to sexual crimes. . . . As far as the Jezebel image was concerned, the Thirteenth Amendment freed no black woman."

If the Black woman was most vulnerable to rape, the emancipated male — still thought of as a violent buck — was vulnerable to being lynched. Indeed, almost three thousand Black people were reportedly lynched between 1889 and 1918. Some fifty were women, and thus the overwhelming number were Black men. While lynchings were justified by the claim that the man hanged had violated a White woman, it was more often simply "rumors of rape" that led to such lynchings. The real threat to White male supremacy probably rested in the knowledge that some White women were actually attracted to Black men and voluntarily entered into a relationship with them. As Gutman has shown, "There is also scattered evidence indicating sexual contact and even marital connections between southern white women and slave and ex-slave men." Ida B. Wells bluntly states, "White men lynch the offending Afro-American not because he is a despoiler of virtue, but because he succumbs to the smiles of white women." Again, it would seem that the discourse surrounding the Black man's virility was so effective that it backfired in terms of protecting the purity of White women and hence of the White race.

But, again, the perceived threat to White male supremacy went beyond Black men's real or imagined sexual contact with White women. Lynching was not simply utilized as a remedy for an imagined sexual crime; it was a response to social, political, and economic challenges that White men felt from Black males. Essentially, it was a reaction to a perceived threat to White supremacy. Litwack puts the matter plainly: "Victims of lynch mobs, more often than not, had challenged or unintentionally violated the prevailing norms of white supremacy, and these ranged from the serious offenses (in the eyes of whites) to the trivial."

The terror of rape, castration, and lynching as well as the caricatures that fueled this terror provide incontrovertible evidence of how Black people's sexuality has been a pawn in White culture's efforts to secure White patriarchal hegemony in American society. The abuse and defilement of Black sexuality are embedded in the very core of White culture. They are as natural to White culture as the very air we breathe. As long as White culture exists, attacks upon Black sexuality will persist. This point is made poignantly clear by the continued presence of the most salient sexual stereotypes.

Mammy to matriarch: The Moynihan Report

The portrait of Black women as Mammy lasted long after slavery largely because the jobs most available to Black women have been as domestic workers in White households. Deborah Gray White intuits, "Surely there is some connection between the idea of Mammy, the service and domestic jobs readily offered to black women, and their near-exclusion from other kinds of work." As a Mammy or domestic worker, Black women were exploited for the economic advantage of White society. While Mammy provided free labor, the grossly underpaid domestic worker provided cheap labor. Like Mammy, these Black domestic workers cared for the house and reared the White children. However, as domestic workers Black women performed the mundane duties of White motherhood that allowed White women to take their places not on Victorian pedestals, but with White men in the workplace.

The idea of the Black woman as a powerful matriarch, most commonly referred to in stereotypic language as Sapphire, was cemented in White culture by a 1965 report on the "Negro family" by Daniel P. Moynihan, who at the time was assistant secretary of labor and director of the Office of Policy Planning and Research in the Johnson administration. The report opens by presenting the "deterioration of the Negro family" as the "fundamental source of the weakness of the Negro community." It goes on to argue that the Negro family is at the heart of a "tangle of pathology" that perpetuates poverty and antisocial behavior within the Black community. Essentially, Moynihan identified family "disorganization" as the major source of weakness for the Black community. In so doing, he clearly named the Black woman as the culprit. She was considered the root cause for the "tangle of pathology" that ensnared the Black family. She, Moynihan argued, was the center of a "black matriarchy" that was the core of the problem, imposing "a crushing burden on the Negro male."

It is important to note at this point the significance of the Black family to the White cultural attack upon Black sexuality. If the family is the source of communicating values and ways of behaving to a people, then to suggest a "deviant" family is to imply the handing down of deviant values and standards. To stigmatize the family is to stigmatize the entire race of people. Paul Gilroy explains, "The family is not just the site of cultural reproduction; it is also identified as the mechanism for reproducing the cultural dysfunction that disables the race as a whole." The Moynihan Report therefore perpetuated the perception of Black people as deviant, especially as Moynihan attacked the Black family by means of Black sexuality.

Because Black women could often find work while Black men could not, the Moynihan Report blamed Black women for depriving Black men of their masculine right to provide for their families and, as he said, "to strut" like a "bantam rooster" or "four star general." By blaming Black women for the plight of Black men and hence the plight of the Black family, the report directed attention away from the social, economic, and political structures — all of them racist and patriarchal — that actually deprived Black men of work and relegated Black women to domestic labor.

The Moynihan Report also strongly implied that Black women were responsible for the failure of Black children to achieve. According to Moynihan, Black boys in female-led homes were in particular jeopardy. Lacking strong Black male role models, the boys were destined to be sexually confused, to demonstrate various antisocial behaviors, and to become welfare dependent. The overall effect was that Black families would remain in poverty, because Black men would be so emasculated by Black women that they would never be able to contribute to the uplift and economic well-being of Black families. Moreover, Black children, especially boys, would not acquire the skills for climbing out of the poverty cycle. In actuality, the Moynihan Report perpetuated the myth that "the crisis of black politics and social life [is] a crisis solely of black masculinity. . . . It is to be repaired by instituting appropriate forms of masculinity and male authority, intervening in the family to rebuild the race."

The ultimate coup of the Moynihan Report, however, was the way it shrewdly manipulated Black female sexuality. Moynihan shamelessly identified "Black women's failure to conform to the cult of true woman-hood . . . as one fundamental source of Black cultural deficiency." If Mammy in the White home is a de-sexed figure, then Mammy as matriarch in the Black home is an oversexed figure. "The matriarch represents the sexually aggressive woman, one who emasculates Black men because she will not permit them to assume roles as Black patriarchs."

By skillfully transforming the image of Mammy into that of matriarch, White culture has continued to demean Black women and disparage their sexuality to make it appear that White male hegemony is natural and normal, if not inevitable. The "overachieving" Black woman becomes the scapegoat for the so-called emasculation of Black men. Such emasculation is seen as the basis for these men's lack of success in the social, political, and economic marketplace. In the reasoning of White culture, it is because of the Black matriarch that Black men are unable to exercise political, economic, or social power, and thus the Black community fails to thrive. Audre Lorde clarifies the issue: "[T]he myth of the Black matriarchy as a social disease was presented by racist forces to redirect our attentions away from the real sources of Black oppression."

Jezebel to welfare queen

If the slavocracy's Mammy became contemporary society's matriarch, then Jezebel became the foundation for the idea of the Black woman as a welfare mother/queen. The Black welfare mother/queen is portrayed as one who, like Jezebel, is most suited for breeding children. Welfare mothers are characterized as promiscuous unmarried women who sit around, collect government checks, and give birth to a lot of children. While the offspring of the Jezebels were beneficial to the economy, the offspring of the welfare mothers are seen as detrimental. Therefore, just as White society attempted to regulate the reproductive capacity of enslaved woman, it too has attempted to intervene in the reproductive capacities of the welfare mother. Collins observes, "The image of the welfare mother thus provides ideological justification for the dominant group's interest in limiting the fertility of Black mothers who are seen as producing too many economically unproductive children." Most significantly, however, the Black woman as welfare mother remains essential to White hegemony because the White culture blames the woman for her impoverished condition and again deflects attention away from White, racist, patriarchal structures. In essence, the welfare mother "represents a woman of low morals and uncontrolled sexuality, factors identified as the cause of her impoverished state."

That the welfare mother/queen image continues to be an effective means for seizing and maintaining power in a racist, patriarchal society is illustrated by Supreme Court Justice Clarence Thomas's quest for power. While still a congressional aide, Thomas shamelessly attacked the character of his sister, Emma Mae Martin. In front of a 1980 San Francisco conference sponsored by Black Republicans, he depicted Ms. Martin as a quintessential welfare queen. He painted a false picture of her as the stereotypic Black breeder woman who shirks responsibilities for her children by going on welfare and consequently models this slothful behavior to her sons and daughters. He announced to laughter that his sister "gets mad when the mailman is late with her welfare check. That's how dependent she is. What's worse is that now her kids feel entitled to the check, too. They have no motivation for doing better or for getting out of that situation."

In his portrayal, Thomas unwittingly disclosed more about himself than about his sister. He revealed that he had been so indoctrinated by White culture that he shared the contempt of Black women found in that culture. Reflective of White cultural animus, he grossly and crudely distorted the truth and maligned a Black woman (his own sister), attacking her character through her sexuality, as a means to support his place in White patriarchal hegemony. His sister became for him a perfect foil to his "meteoric ride" out of the poverty of Pinpoint, Georgia.

As harmful as the Jezebel image has been in its contribution to the image of the Black woman as welfare mother/queen, it has affected Black women even more directly. Black women, even today, are thought of as Jezebels. As Nell Painter has astutely pointed out, "The oversexed-black-Jezebel is more likely than not still taken at face value." This fact was made personally clear to me during my sophomore year at Denison University. It happened one early spring evening when my Black female roommate and I were returning from selecting our dorm room for the next school year. As we entered one of the residential quadrangles, we noticed a crowd of excited White students in a circle who were obviously being entertained by something in the center. We both walked over to see what was causing such uproarious behavior. When we looked into the center of the circle, we were shocked and horrified by what we saw. One of the fraternities was conducting one of its rites of spring by enacting a drama. Central to this drama was a White male in blackface, costumed as an African woman (with a grass skirt and spear in hand), prancing around the circle in a stereotypic, tribal-like fashion. As I stood in pained shock, I heard shouted words, "Hey, get down, you African wench." The words deepened the pain, while also making crystal clear to me that I as a Black woman was nothing more than a "wench," a Jezebel to many on that campus. The wider significance of that incident became clear to me only after I left Denison. I later understood that as long as there was a White patriarchal hegemony in America, so fervently protected by White culture, Black women — regardless of our successes — would forever be branded as Jezebels.

3

Sin

Lynne Gerber

L ynne Gerber is an ethnographer and scholar of Christianity as well as a fat activist. *Her book* Seeking the Straight and Narrow: Weight Loss and Sexual Reorientation in Evangelical America *examines two evangelical ministries,* First Place, *a weight loss program, and* Exodus International, *an ex-gay ministry. In* First Place *members are given food and diet guidelines along with biblical studies and other devotional materials. This ministry holds that a strong relationship with Christ enables members to confront their life struggles in ways that sustain their weight loss and physical health. For nearly 37 years, Exodus International offered counseling, small group support, and reparative therapies to help its Christian members confronting same-sex desire (the ministry closed in 2013). In her study Gerber draws out connection between fat and sexuality in these ministries' efforts to change members' bodies and desires. The following excerpt considers how the language of sin operates productively in the self-understanding of those participating in them.*

Disordered desires

Disordered desire has been a central concern in Christian thought and practice, generating efforts to redirect desire away from the body and toward the divine. The regulation of eating and of sexuality and the closely related issues of body size and same-sex eroticism have been two ongoing foci of that concern. The apostle Paul wrote on both issues when instructing the fledgling Christian community at Corinth on right Christian living, warning them of the dangers of eating food consecrated to idols and instructing them on the sexual compromise of Christian marriage. According to scholars, because of the bodily interface with the outside world inherent in eating and sex, both were seen as potential sites for boundary transgression and thus important sites for regulation.

The association of gluttony with fatness per se was effected by a range of cultural forces much closer to our own era.

Sins related to sexuality, including those involving same-sex eroticism, have a more complicated history and carried much heavier weight in terms of moral approbation and ecclesial and civic punishment. *Luxuria* was one of the earliest categories to contain homosexual sin. Used in early Latin translations of the Bible to indicate excesses of food, drink, and sexual pleasure, by the medieval era it was more closely associated with "venereal things." Aquinas cataloged sexual transgression with members of one's own sex under this category, its placement in his text and moderate level of attention making it seem a minor problem. Yet in commenting on *luxuria,* he stated that "sins against nature"—theoretically any sin but rhetorically linked to "Sodomitic vice"—are "an injury done to God himself," and thus, *luxuria* was a transgression of a greater magnitude than its location in his catalog would suggest. Despite the ambiguity in Aquinas's own thinking, the linking of a "sin against nature" and homoerotic activity gained considerable power in Christian thought.

One of the most important modern rivals to religion in terms of cultural authority is consumer capitalism. A consumption-based economy requires indulgence to thrive, and the burgeoning capitalist marketplace of the modern era gave Americans a plethora of opportunities to do so. The traditional religious virtues of restraint, self-reliance, and hard work were increasingly confronted with competing cultural messages urging indulgence, self-creation, and expression via consumption. This confrontation generated anxieties over the moral meaning of the market's pleasures, anxieties that could not be engaged directly if that market was to grow. Historian Peter Stearns writes that until the mid-nineteenth century, religion and religious jeremiads provided a cultural means to temper fears raised by mandates for consumption. But by the 1870s Protestant culture began taking a more permissive approach toward consumption, and other restraints were called on to contain modern excesses. Diet and homosexual sex, he argues, were two foci for such restraints.

The moralization of homosexuality has been a major stake in symbolic struggles both within religious traditions and between religion and secular society. Within Protestant Christianity, the question of whether and how homosexuality should be understood in moral terms has been deeply fraught, leading to divisions in many Protestant denominations. Those taking a more liberal position argue that homosexuality is not a sin and that the ethics of homosexual relationships are best thought within existing frameworks of Christian sexual ethics. Some even suggest that homosexuality gives Christians a valuable opportunity to test those frameworks and rethink aspects of Christian sexual teachings that cannot encompass ethical homosexuality. More conservative Christians insist on homosexuality's sinfulness on both biblical and traditional grounds. Identifying authentic Christian faith with a literalist biblical hermeneutic, they argue that biblical passages condemning homosexuality cannot be ignored, and compassion for those struggling with homosexuality, while possibly laudable, cannot be extended to the point of condoning sin.

Religious conservatives' conversation about the moral status of homosexuality is not limited to intrachurch conversations. Homosexuality has been an important point of distinction for them in their engagement with American culture writ large. For evangelicals in particular, insistence on the sinfulness of homosexuality has allowed religious leaders to depict themselves as guardians of and warriors for vital moral truths, fighting the licentious secularism that, in their view, eschews moral truth for bodily pleasure. Some with political interests have used popular discomfort with homosexuality to formulate a Christian social politics defined largely by opposition to it. Indeed, opposition to homosexuality has become a core component of identity for many evangelical individuals and institutions—an example of evangelicals engaging with salient cultural issues and developing an increasingly distinctive subcultural identity.

In the case of food and diet, the search for constraints that could compensate for the indulgences of the modern marketplace fueled the growing obsession with weight loss and food regulation and the stigmatization of the fat body and fat people. By the turn of the twentieth century, gluttony became synonymous with fat. With the decline of religious resistance to consumer capitalism, issues of food and diet took on quasi-religious dimensions, with body size serving as an indicator of character. "Fat became a secular sin," writes Stearns, "and an obvious one at that."

Efforts at weight loss in the United States and the kind of moral capital they generate straddle the religious and the secular in varied ways. Commercial weight loss programs have developed largely in secular contexts, but many observers, both popular and scholarly, have noted the ways in which dieting takes on certain religious qualities. Moralism in relation to fat and body size bridges differences that homosexuality tears asunder, with leaders at every point on the political spectrum agreeing that fat is bad and fat people need to be restrained. Even when pursued in secular environments, questions of eating, body size, and weight loss are infused with the gravity of the moral and the power of the sacred.

But religion itself, especially Protestant religion, has also played a significant part in the moralization of fat and the sacralization of weight loss. Historian R. Marie Griffith has documented the ways in which Protestant religiosity, particularly the New Thought movement, influenced the development of weight loss culture by propagating beliefs in the perfectible body and practices to help the believer attain it. In one of the first Christian weight loss books, Charlie Shedd's 1957 *Pray Your Weight Away*, the fat body itself, rather than gluttony, is depicted as sinful, beginning a discursive association that has gained strength over the last fifty years. Evangelical weight loss culture has been a very profitable enterprise, with best-selling Christian diet books bolstering the growing Christian book market, an example of the commingling of religiosity, consumerism, and weight loss. While some, like Stearns, argue that dieting and weight loss have filled a cultural void of moral restraint left by secularization, it may be an example of the secularization of a long-standing Protestant concern, one that ceased to be marked as religious but maintained its power in part through its intimate relationship to dominant religious and moral sensibilities. Christian weight loss programs, then, may be an example of an evangelical effort at engaging with cultural issues for the purposes of exemplifying dominant values rather than distinguishing the subculture from them.

Is it a sin?

"Sin" is a high-stakes designation in evangelical culture. Evangelicals come to faith by coming to understand that each person, themselves included, is a sinner in need of a savior. The act of conversion is centered on this recognition in oneself, confessing one's irredeemable sinfulness to Jesus, and accepting the gift of salvation that Christ offers to flawed humans unable to achieve it by their own efforts. Part of the process of conversion, then, is identification as a sinner—and being a sinner becomes integral to evangelical identity. Yet, Christians are forgiven their sins, and some believe that through the gift of salvation one sins no more. For ministry members there was a sense that calling something a sin risked placing people who struggled with it outside the Christian community: that one could not be both a sinner and a Christian. The designation "sin" is therefore used with care.

Whether or not the language of sin was appropriate for the issue at hand was a problem that gripped both ministries. Members and leaders were concerned with the moral weight that sin invokes and worked hard to understand their issue through an appropriate moral and theological framework. They argued over whether or not their issue is rightly understood as sin, and if so, what that meant both for ministry participants and for the Christian community. In each case there was considerable ambivalence about how this highly charged language is best deployed, but for very different reasons. First Place struggled with whether or not sin was the appropriate category for an issue that carries strong moral charge but is rarely thought to put the believer's status as a Christian into question. Exodus International clearly designated homosexuality a sin—that affirmation was necessary to maintain legitimacy as an evangelical organization—but sensitivity to how sin language has been used to expel homosexuals from the Christian community informed debates about what sin signifies and what it does not. Members of both ministries drew on a common set of scriptural sources, theological ideas, and subcultural understandings to develop and nuance their approaches to this problem.

What does sin mean?

The potential stakes of sin in terms of community membership, combined with ambiguity about those stakes, generate the caution with which ministries and their members talk about sin. For First Place this is reflected in the ongoing conversation about whether or not the issues they address, while strongly felt, are quite grave enough to merit the designation. In the case of Exodus, the careful parsing of which aspects of homosexuality are sinful and which are not reflects the harm that has resulted from the intensity with which the Christian tradition has infused this particular sin, especially its power to expel. For different reasons, then, both groups attempt to soften the blow of calling something sin. They do this, in part, through an understanding of sin that is considerably gentler than the fire-and-brimstone harshness that characterizes other Christian approaches. It is also accomplished by democratizing sins, making them rhetorically equivalent, which levels the playing field of sin and makes the designation malleable enough to serve each ministry's distinctive purposes.

The ministry members I spoke with understood sin in different ways. The mildest rendition was perhaps the most common: sin as a falling short of God's best. Jacqui, the director of an East Coast Exodus ministry, explained it to me this way: "Sin is—people say it's missing the mark. So it's just not quite being who God created you to be. It's not even that you maliciously set out to do something wrong. It's like—I believe that there's somebody that God created us to be. Somebody specific. And when we're not that person, we're missing the mark. So I think the word 'sin' has this awful connotation that it really wasn't ever meant to have." Rather than a deep mark of shame, failure, or willful disobedience, sin, in this version, is the common, forgivable flaw of not getting things quite right in God's eyes. Christians should make every effort to more fully become who God intends them to be, but no one ever succeeds completely, and for Jacqui, no one need feel inordinate shame, horror, or guilt for falling short. It is also an extremely broad category. Falling short of God's intention can mean a wide range of things and could, theoretically, mean different things for different people if God created them for different purposes. When this understanding of sin is operative, sin's moral weight is lightened by a capaciousness that is large enough to encompass almost anything, from the seemingly benign to the recognizably serious.

For others, sin signifies the consequences one must face when disobeying God's commands, flouting God's will, or denying God's intention. Betsy, an ex-lesbian, was introduced to evangelical Christianity, and to Exodus ministries, by her former lesbian lover. When they started their relationship, she had no moral problem with homosexuality. But in the course of their relationship, she changed her view. Her current position is the following:

> It is sin. It is not God's intention. The tree in the garden [of Eden], it was like: "I've given you everything, but there's one place you need to stay away from." Well, they chose not to stay away from it. Well, this is a consequence if you do. "Not because I don't want you to have fun or because I don't want you to eat of all of the trees of the fruit of the garden. I've given you lots of fruit." Same thing in sexuality, I think. People tend to think, "If I follow after what God says in marriage only, I'm missing out." Same thing as with the fruit of the tree. "I'm giving you everything and you have this sanctity in marriage to have sexual relationship. If you choose to go outside of it, there's still going to be consequences. For your detriment, not 'cause I don't want you to have great things."

While this perspective relies on a more traditional notion of sin as the rejection of God's rule, understanding sin as a set of consequences also softens its blow, as well as allays God's character. What one suffers as a result of sin is not because of God's vengeance, animosity, opposition to sex, or pleasure in human suffering. Rather, sin triggers a set of responses that are part of sin's very mechanism. The concept of sin is eased because it becomes mechanistic; it sets a series of consequences into motion that are practically beyond God's control and that he almost regrets. God's attitude toward the sinner is not rage or wrathful condemnation but a kind of resignation that makes sin more like the tripping of an unfortunate set of cosmic mechanisms than an evil act that renders the actor flawed at the core. This neutralizes the emotive charge of sin to some extent by rendering it somehow distant from God's will or desire and thus less about the fundamental relationship between God and people than about cosmic mechanisms that, once triggered, proceed in a detached way.

But the most common way members of both ministries talked about sin did not refer to sin's meaning, use, or feeling tone. Rather, it concerned sin's weight. The most frequent comment I heard about sin from members of both ministries was "a sin is a sin," meaning that all sins have equal weight and, in theory, cannot and should not be distinguished by differences in moral gravity. "Sin is sin in God's eyes," Mark, a West Coast Exodus leader, told me. When I asked Celeste, a First Place member, if she thought there was a difference between sexual and food-related sins, she said, "I would say, 'A sin is a sin.' It's the same as if you were to murder someone. If you truly repent, you will be forgiven, I think." This democratization of sins has a number of discursive consequences. By equating all sins, it levels the playing ground between sins, intensifying those deemed minor and defusing those deemed serious. It also generates a sense of identification among sinners by emphasizing the commonality in their transgressions, and it democratizes those transgressions by making them interchangeable in terms of gravity and appropriate remedy. But it also serves particular purposes in each ministry, purposes which reflect the felt differences in moral weight that ministry members experience.

Democratizing sins helps ex-gay ministries in one of their most central tasks: destigmatizing homosexuality. Exodus groups have the paradoxical tasks of insisting on homosexuality's sinfulness while creating a space where Christian gays and lesbians feel comfortable talking about sexuality. Part of that work is creating an evangelical context in which the intensity of moral charge frequently associated with homosexuality is defused enough that people who struggle with this issue will actually participate in their programs. The notion that sins are virtually interchange-able is useful for this purpose. Many Exodus members used this idea to critique the perceived error Christians make when putting homosexuality into a sin class of its own. Betsy, for example, said, "I'm sorry that if I say homosexuality is a sin and it hurts your feelings, but it's true. But I'm not saying you're any worse than whatever else is going on." Louis talked about it in terms of the democratic possibilities of redemption:

> People have not handled the message of love and redemption appropriately. We've singled out a group of people and said, "You know what? You've got to get your

act together before you can receive the benefits of the kingdom." And that's never been a part of God's design. He says, "Come ye unto me who are heavy laden and burden. I'll give you rest and shelter." It says, "God so loved the world"; his extension of love and salvation is for everyone. And once they come in, we expect to be transformed.

In this account, those who assign homosexuality special moral weight violate a central tenet of Christianity. Other sinners need not change before becoming Christian, he argues, and homosexuals are not exceptions. For both Louis and Betsy, the notion that sins are basically indistinguishable means that homosexuality and, by extension, homosexuals cannot and should not be singled out for particular condemnation.

This moral diffusion is also achieved by using the logic of democratized sins to equate homosexual sin with heterosexual sin. Exodus members use "a sin is a sin" to argue that homosexual sin is no different from heterosexual sin and that the rules for sexual morality are, theoretically, the same for straight people and gay people: any sex outside marriage is morally suspect. This perspective was reflected in the structure of a daylong seminar I attended on sexual purity. The day was facilitated by two male pastors, one heterosexual and married and one ex-gay and celibate. The plenary sessions alternated between the two, who addressed heterosexual and homosexual immorality as two complementary faces of sexual sin. One of the facilitators, the ex-gay man, explained this view in the following way:

> What do we know about homosexuality? We know that we're created beings and we were created with a certain intent. If you dismiss Genesis one and two, God's blueprint for human sexuality, [you dismiss God's] divine intent for human sexuality. His divine intent is fulfilled in covenanted, monogamous, heterosexual union. Man and woman—the two become one. Never step over God's boundary line. What if you're single? If you're single, you don't have sex, period. I've been a Christian for twenty years, single the whole time, and I can tell you that if you don't have sex, you won't blow up.

In this view, heterosexual marriage is the undisputed ideal; there is no other context in which sexual activity is acceptable. Any transgression against that ideal is a transgression; homosexual and heterosexual ones are in the same moral category. This treatment of sex and singleness tries to equate heterosexuals and homosexuals who are unmarried in terms of their moral obligations and the weight of their moral transgressions, ignoring the blatant difference that homosexuals have no legitimized opportunity to express their sexual desire and thus experience these rules in very different ways.

This equation of homosexuality and heterosexuality is also reflected in comments made by Exodus members. Stephanie, the wife of an ex-gay man, said, "Sin's scale is not on one to ten and homosexuality's thirteen. Excuse me, it's not. Any sex before or outside of marriage I think is not proper and . . . homosexuality is not any more a sin than living wrong heterosexually." According to Alex:

As I read the Bible I understand that God has created sexuality to be expressed through a specific kind of relationship between a man and a woman which we would call marriage. That it's been ordained to be experienced through a marriage that is begun with the understanding that it's for a lifetime between two people. Now, having said that—of course, people screw that up a lot. And I believe that's true for everybody. That's true for—no matter how your sexual orientation plays itself out—that's equally true for heterosexual people, homosexual people, bisexual people, whatever sexual people you apply yourself.

By appealing to human fallenness as a state that homosexuals and heterosexuals share, Alex shows how the democratization of sins can make homosexuality more understandable and less foreign to heterosexual Christians. It also helps people struggling with homosexuality see themselves as more like heterosexual people than they might have previously thought. Since the ultimate goal of these ministries is to facilitate heterosexual identification, this can be an important effect, making the distance between sexual orientations appear shorter.

The equation of homosexual and heterosexual sin, and the rhetoric of democratized sins more generally, also give Exodus ministries the opportunity to call Christian communities to task for hypocrisy regarding homosexuality and to speak out against injustices committed toward gays and lesbians in their midst. This is reflected in Mark's comments on the difference between how the Christian community treats homosexuality versus divorce:

Homosexuality should not be treated any differently than any other human condition. Scripturally speaking, there's no basis for it. The whole concept of homosexuality as being the worst sin, there's no biblical basis for that. One of my things is, okay, I'll know when the church is serious about dealing with sin when they start to address the whole issue of divorce and remarriage. Because Christ is very clear: if you get married and you divorce for any other reason than infidelity and remarry you are in an adulterous relationship. The church is full of divorced people that are remarried! And when they begin to deal with that with the same consistency and zeal that they deal and approach the homosexual issue, then I'll know it's God.

By asserting the equivalence of sins in God's eyes, Mark is able to point out and criticize discrepancies in the ways the church has treated them. As his tone made apparent, this frame is useful for channeling ex-gay frustration at how they have been treated by the church. Many Exodus members I spoke with experienced homophobia in church, and while they no longer wish to identify as homosexual, the wounds of that treatment are not easily healed. Democratizing sin helps Exodus participants call their communities to account for the harm they experienced without having to identify as homosexuals. It also allows Exodus to present itself as a legitimate defender of people struggling with same-sex attraction, if not of self-accepting gays and lesbians. Critiquing Christian hypocrisy enables Exodus to self-present as more compassionate regarding homosexuality than the church at large and as a space that will protect and defend strugglers against the cruelties they face there.

First Place participants, as we have seen, face a different set of challenges in framing their project's moral stakes, yet they also find a democratized understanding of sins useful. The issues they address—food, eating, and body size—while very strongly felt, are as likely to be trivialized as singled out for particular stigma. The notion that a sin is a sin in this context elevates their seemingly mundane issue to something serious enough to be considered a legitimate part of the Christian conversation about sin and redemption. In a community where identification as a sinner is an important element of Christian identity, framing food issues and weight as sins gives members legitimate entry into Christian discourse. This may be particularly useful for those whose transgressions are relatively mild and who are not able to depict anything else they do in such grand terms, or for those who may not wish to discuss more serious transgressions in the public ways that sin is discussed in the evangelical world.

Because issues of eating and weight are so common and so widely felt, they also become the sin that people fall back on in talking about their struggles with sin. Their ubiquity makes them serve as the lowest common denominator sin, one that guarantees entry into the discourse of sinfulness at a relatively low price. One of the most striking things about participating in the First Place group was how ardently members insisted upon their sinfulness when confessing their meanderings from the program's commitments. One First Place leader likened lying on one's commitment record (a record of eating that members fill out weekly) to "going around and shooting somebody." This emphasis on sinfulness was also commented on by two ex-gay ministry participants. When I told Stacy, a leader in a West Coast Exodus ministry, that I was also looking at Christian weight loss programs, she joked that those are the ministries people go to after they have dealt with all their other issues. "Everyone ends up dealing with their food issues," she said, "because even when other things are under control, we're always probably sinning with food." Melissa told me that losing weight and getting into better physical shape were her next big spiritual project: "I wouldn't engage sexually with my body outside of marriage. But now in my physical person, to be quite blunt, I'm the heaviest I've ever been in my life and I don't like that. I don't feel as well. And I want to try to get in shape. And I'm on the cusp of forty, so if I don't do something now—I can only handle like one life goal at a time, so for years it was overcoming lesbianism . . . and so my next life goal is my physical person." In a context where all sin is equated, issues such as eating and weight loss are salient enough to be experienced as moral transgressions, ubiquitous enough to be used by a wide range of people, cheap enough to ease the price of identification with sin, and mild enough to render other, more charged sins mundane by comparison.

A convincing sinner identity also gives people a way to enter into conversation with other Christians on shared terms. Because sins are indistinguishable, people with issues as seemingly benign as overeating can identify with those with issues as seemingly grave as sexual transgression. That identification puts their own sin, and the sins of others, into a different perspective. Some Exodus members, like Melissa above, explicitly drew on the equation of fatness and homosexuality to make their struggle more mundane and less freighted. Tessa, a leader of the First Place group I attended, used her identification with sin in her struggle with weight loss as a way to understand and develop compassion for homosexuals:

> I try not to judge people and, of course, we all do, but I try not to. And when I hear other people judging people like, let's say, homosexuals or something like that, I say, "Well, what are *you*?" It's a judgment of a sin, and to God all sins are created equal. No one is greater than the other. So homosexuality is a sin just as gluttony is a sin. So I don't, like, ostracize homosexuals or whatever because I am not God and I am not one to judge. It's not my place. And so one of the things I remember is gluttony is a sin. I think many of us can be accused of gluttony.

In her case, identification with gluttony, and thus as a sinner, gives her a position from which to rightfully engage in other questions of sin. As a self-confessed glutton, she can enter the dialogue with homosexuals as one sinner to another. That dialogue is shaped by the other sin that is central to both ministries' discourses: judgment.

4

Blood, Sweat, and Urine:

The Scent of Feminine Fluids in Anton Szandor LaVey's *The Satanic Witch*

Cimminnee Holt

*C*imminnee Holt is completing her doctoral research on an ethnography of the Church of Satan, an international modern-day new religious movement whose beliefs are codified in The Satanic Bible. Members of the Church of Satan do not literally worship the figure of Satan, but consider themselves to be "skeptical atheists." This excerpt, taken from a longer article, explores how the major founder of modern Satanism, Anton Szandor LaVey (1930–97), framed the ritual power and effectiveness of female bodily fluids. It also touches upon the important anthropological work of Mary Douglas, author of Purity and Danger and Natural Symbols, on the symbolism of the body and its marginal points of entry and exit, and on questions of the pure and the impure. Douglas' contributions to the study of religion and sexuality are significant because she was among the first to consider ways in which religious worldviews impact upon pollution taboos.

> *I am a witch; I have power over men!*
> — A SUGGESTED PROCLAMATION FOR WOMEN,
> ANTON SZANDOR LAVEY, *THE SATANIC WITCH*, 1970

*T*he Satanic Witch, written by Anton Szandor LaVey and originally published under the title The Complete Witch: Or What to do When Virtue Fails in 1970, is a book aimed at providing female Satanists (or satanic Witches) helpful tools of manipulation to achieve their goals. LaVey recommends methods of orchestration through dress, speech, mannerisms, and scent applied to a target for seduction, influence, and control. LaVey calls these methods "lesser magic"; that is, "basic psychology, glamour, non-ritual manipulative magic". The book is directed at women, often disregarded by male Satanists, and virtually ignored by scholars. The current High Priestess of the Church of Satan, Peggy Nadramia, writes in its introduction:

> I'm often surprised by how many [male Satanists] let the wisdom of The Satanic Witch just slip through their fingers. There are men of the Satanic persuasion who peruse its pages and then shelve it, figuring they'll wait for The Satanic Warlock to come along and until then, take their fashion cues from heavy metal videos and vampire comics. Tsk, tsk, gentlemen; the parade is passing you by.

Nadramia insists that it is also useful for men; the same ideas can easily be inverted or adapted and applied for particular purposes, as the ultimate goal is a manifestation of desires (professional or personal) by whatever means are under the reader's command. This manifestation of the will is deemed effective magical practice; magicians (male and female) applying various tools (through ceremonial magic or everyday manipulation) to achieve desired ends are considered skilled in the arts of enchantment.

The Satanic Witch places a strong emphasis on the materiality of the human body. LaVey's methods to activate certain emotions, such as empathy, lust, and generosity, from a desired target are based on physiological, psychological, and aesthetic tools. One of the more fascinating means to manipulation within the book is LaVey's suggestion for strategically using the scent of feminine fluids—blood, sweat, and urine—to stimulate lust in prospective partners. His use of bodily fluids is a variation on the notion of a love potion, as he claims that shamans, medicine men, and magicians from different cultures use semen, urine, and blood, among other fluids, from both human and non-human animals alike, for virility and fertility rites. Jesper Aagaard Petersen notes that LaVey sanitizes satanic imagery through secularization and "satanizes" the secular. LaVey expresses his ideas through the language of occultism and mysticism, continuously straddling the divide between rationalistic and esoteric positions. In The Satanic Witch, LaVey's foundational carnal premise is enveloped in the syntax of seduction and magic, lending a theatrical hint and playfulness to some (at times) basic techniques of social interaction.

LaVey's discussion on bodily fluids not only echoes the discourse of esoteric knowledge, but also of the sexual liberation movement of the politically turbulent American society of his time. The 1960s and 1970s saw many changes and upheavals of traditional worldviews: student protests, assassinated politicians, hippies, anti-war sentiment, birth control, sexual politics and feminism, drug culture, the civil rights movement, new age philosophies and religions, and rock/folk protest music, all reflecting a general critique of the status quo in public discourse. To a reserved 1950s society—at least on the surface—they were shocking, causing questions and concerns regarding the shift in social frameworks. Middle-class values, where divorce, pre-marital sex, interracial couples, and autonomous women were taboo, were being challenged by new ideologies. LaVey is firmly rooted within this social context.

This article demonstrates that LaVey's treatment of feminine fluids in *The Satanic Witch* and select publications functions twofold: as an extension of and emphasis on his claim of a solely carnal human condition, and a response to the contemporary socio-historical discourses of America in the 1960s and 1970s such as feminism and occultism. Throughout the essay I use a variety of texts to contrast and compare with LaVey's notion of feminine fluids: Mary Douglas's *Purity and Danger,* which addresses our notions of contagion, dirt, and taboo; feminist rhetoric on 1960s and 1970s feminine hygiene products and their putative cleansing of natural feminine scent; and finally, the use of sexual fluids in the esoteric magical practices of Aleister Crowley. LaVey's ideas are a commentary on all these discourses, as he is emerging from and responding to the overarching discussions of his time.

The Satanic Witch outlines LaVey's notion of female sexual empowerment. In the prologue he states that, "many will feel it to be a treatise on mancatching". He then claims this to be an incomplete understanding of the book. He clarifies:

> Whether or not a witch needs any man other that the one she has currently chosen is relatively unimportant. What is important, however, lies in the fact that if a woman wants anything in life, she can obtain it easier through a man than another woman, despite woman liberationists' bellows to the contrary. The truly "liberated" female is the compleat witch, who knows both how to use and enjoy men. She will find the energies she expends in her quixotic cause would be put to more rewarding use, where she to profit by her womanliness by manipulating the men she holds in contempt, while enjoying the ones she finds stimulating.

In essence, LaVey notes that, because women are perceived objects of men's lust, then they can exploit it to achieve their goals. Even though much of the book is written in a hetero-normative perspective, he claims that a "true witch," being an orchestrator of her own destiny, can also bewitch women and homosexual men, regardless of her own sexual preference. Playing on medieval notions of alleged witchcraft, LaVey states, "In order to be a successful witch, one *does* have to make a pact with the devil, at least symbolically". By this he means that the potential witch must take pride in her ego and acknowledge that the arts of enchantment are meant to enhance her life and pleasure. The "pact" is a commitment to herself to release any feelings of guilt or shame in regards to her sexuality. Lesser magic, then, is the idea of recognizing a woman's sexual nature, harnessing this (perceived) power, and applying it to a witch's advantage.

The rest of the book details how to maximize on a witch's natural attributes in order to enhance her visual appeal. LaVey advocates rejecting popular fashion fads in dress and body type, instead focusing on how a woman can project an image that features her natural physique. He notes that a thin woman with dark hair could create the persona of a "vamp"; an older woman can adopt the mystique of "crone"; a full-figured woman becomes the cuddly, nurturing type. He emphasizes that embracing a woman's body type (especially if it runs counter to the popular standards of beauty) means that one will attract mates that respond specifically to that body type. As an example, if you are naturally prone to weight gain, do not attempt drastic weight loss as you will attract men expecting you to be thin. Instead, embrace your "bulges" so as to attract men that respond to the Rubenesque. LaVey, with a known predilection for voluptuous blonds, proclaims: "you need starve yourself no longer".

Aside from aesthetics (such as wearing garters and stockings), a witch employs voice, mannerisms, touch, and the "Law of the Forbidden" (which suggests that greater stimulation is achieved by exposure to the clandestine, such as cleavage through an unbuttoned blouse, or soiled underwear) with chapters devoted to each, in her reserve of sorcery. The most relevant means to achieve one's goals for the purposes of this essay are LaVey's suggestions for the deliberate and strategic use of natural odors in feminine bodily fluids: blood, sweat, and urine.

The bibliography of *The Satanic Witch* indicates that these techniques of manipulation are derived from psychological, biological, social scientific, neurological, physiological, as well as magical and occult texts and manuals, old and new. Various fields of study dealing with human behavior and interaction employ the theories listed and detailed within. LaVey uses the examinations on human behavior in the biological and psychological texts and presents them in the language of the occult and magical. He claims that all human behavior is animal behavior, quantifiable and predictable by scientific method, and thus malleable to the educated and clever. One of his methods is a "Personality Synthesizer Clock," which is a guide to determining core personality types based on physical traits. It is meant to provide useful hints at categorizing people (and oneself) as a tool for improved manipulation. This manipulability of human behavior is how LaVey defines the notion of "lesser magic": to realize ones desired goals through careful maneuvering, and the scent found in feminine fluids is a prime means to achieve this type of influence.

Mary Douglas' *Purity and Danger: An Analysis of Concepts of Pollution and Taboo*, originally published in 1966, examines the notions of dirt and contagion. She posits that, although the details of what is considered dirt vary from culture to culture, "dirt is essentially disorder". By this, Douglas explains that our notions of dirt are the product of a twofold system: organization and classification, and the subversion of those categories and classes. Douglas elaborates using examples of basic household items:

> Shoes are not dirty in themselves, but it is dirty to place them on the dining-table; food is not dirty in itself, but it is dirty to leave cooking utensils in the bedroom, or food bespattered on clothing; similarly, bathroom equipment in the drawing room; clothing lying on chairs. . .In short, our pollution behaviour is the reaction which condemns any object or idea likely to confuse or contradict the cherished classifications.

Dirt, then, is not independent; it is a concept relative to the social systems in place, where convention is disrupted, and this disruption labeled as a pollutant or taboo. "Where there is dirt there is a system," writes Douglas. In the chapter "External Boundaries," Douglas continues: "pollution fears do not seem to cluster round contradictions which do not involve sex. The answer may be that no other social pressures are potentially so explosive as those which constrain sexual relations". Douglas is referring to the taboos around sexual contact and fluids; which behaviors are tolerated, celebrated, exalted, condemned, and ignored, and what these classifications reveal about a culture's values, fears, and concerns.

For example, Douglas notes that all systems of classification and convention are vulnerable, especially at their margins. These points of vulnerability are then symbolized in the margins of the body—where it secretes, bleeds, sweats, and voids, or, conversely, where it ingests and inhales or is penetrated. For instance, the Israelites saw blood as the divine force of life when contained inside the human body; but blood must be ritualistically addressed when exiting the body through the margins. The margins, those seeping bodily orifices, are "dangerous" as they cannot be contained, and put the rigidity of the social system at risk. Taboos and notions of pollutants around these margins then symbolically protect the values of the society.

Douglas' theories are easily applied to LaVey's treatment of feminine fluids in *The Satanic Witch*. LaVey writes in the chapter, "On the Importance of Odors":

As a witch, you should learn some basic principles of enchantment through odors. First of all, DON'T SCRUB AWAY YOUR NATURAL ODORS OF SEDUCTION. It doesn't matter how much brainwashing has been done to make certain bodily odors undesirable. Millions of years have seen to this that such scents will never be reacted to in a negative way.

LaVey is lamenting the tendency for modern women to excessive bathing and cleanliness with chemicals and soaps. He stresses that basic hygiene is certainly necessary, but that one's naturally producing bodily fluids are paramount in attracting mates and seducing partners. As LaVey was born in 1938, he describes how the attitude to bathing shifted from the occasional bath, where people regularly wore the same clothing on consecutive days, even undergarments, to daily bathing and clothes washing. To LaVey, this excessive bathing nullified a woman's powerful natural odiferous aphrodisiac. He details several ways in which women can use their bodily fluids to attract a mate with the sense of smell. Her blood, sweat, and urine are considered potions, when used properly, to appeal to the animalistic nature in us all.

If, according to Douglas, the margins of the body represent a certain vulnerability of social systems, LaVey, then, takes a cue from the subversive nature of the devil himself, and challenges modern conceptions of cleanliness by appealing to a naturalistic and bestial approach to hygiene. LaVey begins with the premise that humans are animals; we are solely carnal, finite beings. As such, our scents function is the same way as that of the animal kingdom; we respond to olfactory cues for mating and survival. He writes:

> This obsession to scrub away dirt (and with it sin) is a by-product of the kind of puritanism and Calvinism that defies all the laws of nature. The Huguenotes even had a hymn equating bodily odors with sin, called: "Everybody Stinks but Jesus." There is no doubt that to many women, a bar of soap has replaced the confessional.

LaVey laments what he deems as Christian holdovers of denouncing bodily fluids as a sign of our flawed materiality, which translates into undue cleansing rituals; we unconsciously wish to denounce our animal natures by washing away its very odiferous essence. Douglas notes that Christian ritual purification is on the decline, "With every century we become heirs to a longer and more vigorous anti-ritualistic tradition." Yet LaVey would claim that modern excessive cleansing is a relic from historical Christian practices. We no longer bathe for theological purposes, but the practice of excessive hygiene remains, without an official spiritual intent.

LaVey focuses on female bodies as he advocates the deliberate inversion of religio-historical feminine sexual repression. Douglas contends that a woman's body is often considered a symbol for the vulnerable conventions of her social group. A woman that violates the conventions is considered to be dangerous, not necessarily for herself, but society's morals; what a woman does to her body represents the culture as a whole. According to Douglas, the special nature of the corporal feminine represents the culture at large: "Female bodies are correctly seen as, literally, the entry by which the pure content may be adulterated." In order to preserve a pure content, the body must be cleansed. LaVey considered this type of repulsion of bodily odors via its fluids as a disconnect with biological realities; realities in conflict with humankind's ostensible divine nature.

LaVey claims that, like many an "old witches' charm," blood is a powerful component for a magical potent seduction. He writes: "Unless the human animal is to be considered the only exception in nature, you are theoretically appealing, rather than offending, during your period." This follows from the premise than humans are responding to olfactory cues for one of their most basic biological drives: reproduction. Like all animals, the female is most alluring when in heat. He writes:

> Some of you may have noticed that men seem to swarm around you most when you have your period. Undoubtedly, such a situation has proved disturbing to many of you, as you feel it an inopportune time to really get involved, especially where sex is concerned. . .the changes that take place in your system at this time are such that the normal sexual odor is highly intensified and, because of this, carries further.

According to LaVey, the scent of a menstruating woman, then, communicates her fertility (if not at the moment of menstruation, then during ovulation), and thus her sexual desirability, at unconscious levels. LaVey suggests that the period-produced scent "potentially has tremendous drawing power perfume-wise but at a time when you can't gracefully do anything about it". To overcome this, he suggests retaining some menstrual blood in a portion of a sanitary napkin or tampon, and keeping it in a small pouch or amulet to be worn around a witch's neck. He stresses that "*any* odor, if strong enough, becomes unpleasant," and the use of menstrual blood as olfactory tool of seduction should be subtle, but recognizable. LaVey claims that men will react to it, whether they know what is contained in the pouch or not, as olfactory cues are the basis of all attraction. He writes:

> If the odor that attracts us in the form of a perfume or cologne, it is usually made from the sexual odors and mating scents given off by beavers (castoreum), cats (civit), whales (ambergris), muskrats (Musc Zibata), deers and goats (musk) and numerous plants and flowers whose odors, we mustn't forget, are intended by nature to attract for the purpose of survival and pollination.

On their own these scents are too potent to be pleasing, says LaVey. It is only when they are cut with a diluting substance or minimized that they are effectively appealing. LaVey argues the same for menstrual blood.

LaVey's use of menstrual blood violates contemporary western taboos, inherited from a Victorian era. Menstruation was considered a harmful pollutant to female bodies and their environment, or as a symptom of the female body being an imperfect male. Today, menstrual blood is always to be disposed of privately, virtually unmentioned in polite conversation, and certainly not worn around one's neck. Recall Douglas' notion of dirt being "matter out of place"; LaVey considers menstrual blood not only as inoffensive in and of itself—and therefore not contagion nor taboo—but actually a potent and effective means to subvert the very taboo it represents. Put another way, if menstrual blood is taboo because it emits from female bodies, and female bodies conventionally suppress their sexual desires, then LaVey subverts and exploits this idea by using menstrual blood for the very thing that stems from its taboo: sexual attraction. He is subverting the social system from within using a pre-existing social framework: blood as a means to attract, not repel. The menses of a human woman, as just another animal, is a (biological) tool to be used for (magical) manipulation, sexual or otherwise.

During LaVey's initial founding of the Church of Satan in 1966 and subsequent writing of *The Satanic Witch* in 1970, cosmetic manufacturers in Europe and North America began producing so-called "feminine hygiene products." These products were chemicals applied to the vulva or inserted into the vagina in order to ostensibly improve her vaginal odor. LaVey lambasted all use of such products. He even wrote a poem condemning astringent soaps and extolling the virtues of naturally sweaty female thighs and sexual secretions in a later publication:

> That I might be so fortunate
> That I might yield to speculate
> What I might do to violate

The sanctity of crotch revealed;
Stained and sodden,
So tantalizingly concealed
Within those naked, sweaty inner thighs.

Feminist discourse, then and now, began to echo LaVey's concern over the popular devaluation of natural feminine scents—especially as it pertains to feminine "hygiene" douches. Elana Levine writes that companies peddling these vaginal deodorants "promised to make women's bodies cleaner, fresher, more appealing, and more socially acceptable". Her article begins with a telling 1970s advertising slogan: "Having a female body doesn't make you feminine". In 1968, American manufacturers of this new range of "gyno-products" gained approval from the National Association of Broadcasters review board to air television adverts. Marketed as "hygienic" they were, in fact, medically dangerous. By the early 1970s, women lodged complaints with the Food and Drug Administration that these products cause "genital burning, irritation, and infection". The medical community also supported the discontinued use of these "cosmetics"; their classification as cosmetic, not pharmaceutical, meant that the products did not have to withstand the same rigorous testing before being sold to consumers. Feminist objections became increasingly louder about the products, declaring them unsafe and exploitative of women's anxiety over her natural vaginal secretions. Women were "'the victim of an ancient taboo, a primal flaw in her sex,' because they portrayed her as obsessed with cleanliness yet perpetually unclean herself".

If Douglas notes that culturally-specific notions of dirt represent culturally-specific notions of immorality, then presenting women's bodies as requiring a cleansing echoes the puritanical ideal of feminine chastity and purity; female bodies are impure both morally and materially, and must be cleansed. The female body becomes a microcosm of social structure. If this microcosm (the female body) is seeping at its vulnerable margins (the female body's orifices), the leakage must be addressed and contained to maintain order. A repulsion with bodily fluids is then a repulsion for social disorder, and a denigration and cleansing of those fluids is a means to uphold social stability.

What is most interesting to note, is that the marketing of feminine hygiene products in the 1970s was geared towards them being associated with sex, not purity. "Some saw the product as a gift to women, a gift of sexual pleasure after years of frigidity". They were sold as reputed aids to sexual freedom, the avenue by which to liberate after rigid Victorian attitudes towards sex. The feminist backlash then highlighted a similar concern as that of LaVey; by stating that a feminine "cleansing" is necessary for sex to be enjoyable, the underlying implication remains that "sex is still dirty, smelly, messy, and unsightly (qualities that bespoke what many saw as its sinful nature), and these unpleasant qualities were located in the female body". The female body was seen as more "naturally" self-polluting, her vaginal odor a real problem, and the products were thus a solution to the preexisting problem. Feminist rhetoric highlights that the male body, by contrast, required no hygienic adjustment, and the purported unpleasantries of sex were not its responsibility.

LaVey had no such concerns over gender politics—at least, not in the same way, and not with the same social interests—but he did agree that any association with sex as dirty or polluting was a morality-based artifice. While feminism declared sex to be natural and healthy, and therefore not "dirty," for LaVey, the contention that sex was messy and smelly was actually a compliment to sexual activities, and an idea that should be embraced without imposing morals; sexual fluids and their scents were a reality of sex, not to be touted as either good or bad polarities. He comments: "It is inconceivable to think that human beings could be the only creatures without appealing sexual odors, yet odors that originate in the sexual parts are considered anathema by a large majority of them" For example, he states that the sight and scent of feminine soiled undergarments is an appeal, not a repeal, for most heterosexual men. He notes that, "Urine is another odor which has only been erotically by-passed by the human animal and there are more men who are stimulated by the smell of urine than will ever admit". LaVey extolled the scent of feminine genitals mixed with urine and sweat, and stated that folds in the flesh of the upper thighs were designed to retain these aromas. "Heed the fact that the most common article of clothing that is employed as a fetishistic substitute are panties, and the ritual accompanying the acquisition of same invariably consists of the sniffing of the crotch, performed in an epicurian fashion".

Again in a later publication, LaVey wrote about the erotic fetish of women peeing in their underwear: "elective incontinence. . .is sexual excitement derived from wetting oneself, and is practiced almost exclusively by women. . .Panty pissing is a fetish which gives pleasure to the viewer but, more importantly, to the perpetrator". He notes that the embarrassment of urinating in one's undergarments, and allowing a suitor to view it, is part of subverting an activity normally deemed for solitude, and improper for sexual excitement; the scent is alluring, and the act is taboo, which both enhance the titillating nature of the experience for perpetrator and audience. Granted, urophilia is likely a fetish particular to LaVey, and not all-pervasive throughout heterosexual men. Notwithstanding this, his notion of scent in urine as an appeal is based on his premise that humans are animals, and thus we react to similar sexual stimuli as four-legged creatures.

Despite the tenuous accord of feminism and LaVey in regards to a theoretical female sexual empowerment, the means by which to exhibit that empowerment differ. LaVey lamented the de-emphasis on feminine aesthetics from the feminist movement. As his many references to stockings, heels, skirts, and lipstick in his writings can attest, he bemoans the tendency of feminists in his day to sweepingly denounce affectations of feminine gender as oppressive or misogynistic. He writes: "I believe that woman is the dominant sex, with or without feminist validation".

Hugh B. Urban disputes LaVey's notion of female sexual empowerment, instead claiming that LaVey's ideas in *The Satanic Witch* and other texts are an "at once classic expression of the rhetoric of sexual liberation and also quite blatant statement of male chauvinism". Because LaVey reinforced notions of a ritualized male-dominant/female-receptive dichotomy, his position is counter to feminist ideologies. I agree that LaVey did indeed, as Urban states, reinforce a patriarchal system: "The witch is not only to *become* a sexual object and focus of the male gaze, she is even to *internalize* that male gaze. Subject herself to it in her imagination, and thereby use it to her own advantage". However, I dispute Urban's claim in part because it ignores the whole of LaVey's worldview; LaVey does indeed reinforce gender polarities, but sanctions individuals to choose which gender they decide to channel. In *The Satanic Rituals* he notes that a group ritual with solely homophiles could potentially have more magical impact than a mixed-gender ceremony, but that the altar of flesh (which is typically a female) would be a male that nevertheless *represents* the receptive qualities. LaVey explains that his ritual scripts are suggestive, not prescriptive, when it comes to gender roles for priests and celebrants:

> Whenever reference in this book is made to a priest, the role may also be taken by a woman who can serve in the capacity of priestess. It must be clarified, however, that the essence of Satanism—its dualistic principle—necessarily imposes an active/passive dichotomy upon the respective roles of celebrant and altar. If a woman serves as a celebrant, then for all intents and purposes she represents the masculine principle in the rite. The pervasive theme of active/passive (Yin/Yang) in human relations cannot be stifled, despite attempts to create matriarchal, patriarchal, or unisexual societies. There will always be those who "might as well be men" or "might as well be women," depending upon their endocrinological, emotional and/or behavioral predilections. It is far sounder, from a magical standpoint, for an ego-driven or forceful woman to conduct a ritual, rather than a shy, introspective man. It might prove awkward, however, to cast a passive man in the role of Earth-Mother—as the altar—unless his appearance conveyed the image of a woman. . . It must be stressed that both male and female principles must be present, even if the same sex portrays both.

For LaVey, being a subject or object is not solely the purview of women versus men or a question of genitalia, but entirely within the realm of individual choice, depending on their preference and sexual orientation. He notes polarity is inherent in sexual attraction, as duality is inherent to magic; tension creates dynamic magical experiences. What he despised most was androgyny.

LaVey was not overly concerned with being an advocate of any political agenda, which would include our modern-day notions of LGBTQ concerns and rights. Yet he was, from the onset, clearly accepting that all forms of (legal) sexual expression were natural and normal. LaVey's tendency towards hetero-normative framing and nomenclature are reflective of his time and place, as well as (primarily) his own sexual preference; he appears to take as a given that his audience can and will adapt his ideas to their particular needs. His chosen terms and language are devoid of our current-day's extreme sensitivity to gendered terminology and inclusivism. This is especially problematic within academia, wherein we are encouraged to use value-free and neutral terms. But to LaVey, neutrality itself is an issue—he lambasts androgyny and uni-sexuality exactly because it is not polarized and dynamic. His prime contention with feminism is that it wished to erase the gender divide, and render everyone unisex. This reduces sexual tensions, as LaVey celebrated the differences. He lamented androgyny as a political act, but not asexuality as a natural choice. For LaVey, promoting a particular sexuality to prove a social agenda is reactionary, not in keeping with one's personal nature, and therefore undesirable. Erasing gender differences violates LaVey's notion of lesser magic as presentation and appearance are an essential aspect of manipulation. As he states, good looks are not necessary, but "Looks Means Everything".

LaVey's stance on feminism is perhaps a direct result of the initial births of the Church of Satan and feminism; they both emerge out of the American counter-culture movements of the socially turbulent 1960s. LaVey and liberal feminism are part of this context, reflecting the larger counterculture statements of a changing society. As such, they are presented as an indication towards a decrease of the hegemonic, traditional American society; they are both challenging the status quo, but taking different positions in their revolution. When second-wave feminism first emerges in the 1960s, it rejected all aspects of what it deemed as sexist popular culture, including enhancing (and flaunting) feminine beauty. This puts early second-wave feminism in direct opposition to LaVey's notion of female sexual empowerment. LaVey's negative response to feminism, while certainly not all-pervasive throughout the satanic milieu, can still be stated to be a relatively common sentiment within the Church of Satan, even today. Lap notes that LaVey is, "not only critical against Christian norms; he also criticizes the new sexual morals proposed by the counterculture". This includes the feminism of his era.

5

Sex

Janet Gyatso

Janet Gyatso is a scholar who has written on gender and sexuality in Buddhism. This excerpt, taken from a chapter entitled "Sex" in Critical Terms for the Study of Buddhism, *discusses the amazing complexities of what constitutes sexual transgression in Buddhist monastic law. It raises a number of intriguing questions about how bodies, either dead or alive, can and cannot enter into sexual relations with each other, and the role of desire and consent in the process. What is especially striking about this reading is the incredible variety of sexual choices and practices that are under discussion, especially if one considers that these regulatory texts are addressed to individuals who are not supposed to engage in sexual activity of any sort. This speaks quite forcefully to the ubiquity of sexual desire and the difficulty of limiting the erotic interactions and choices of human bodies. There are interesting parallels with the Sedgwick text.*

There are several easy observations we can make right away. First of all, sex is given striking prominence as the premier downfall (*pārājika*) that ends a monk's or nun's career. Sex is one of four such principal transgressions, the other three being theft, murder, and boasting of superhuman perfections. Rather shockingly, sex is listed first, before theft and even murder. If the order has any significance, and I would argue that it does, then we can venture that sex is the most serious monastic transgression. This is also to presume that murder (which surely must be considered a more serious offense) would rarely be a problem among Buddhist renunciants. So we see in the monastic code that sex, thievery, and murder are placed in the exact reverse order from their position in the more general Buddhist list of the three bodily demeritorious deeds. That discrepancy already prefigures a key point: monastic law operates on different principles than does karmic law. This essay also proposes more specifically that sex was considered the most difficult bodily transgression from which to refrain; for that very reason it was listed first, as the emblematic site of disciplinary regulation.

One is struck by the sheer amount of discussion of sex in comparison with classic Christian monastic manuals such as those by Saint Benedict or Bernard of Clairvaux, which barely allude to sexual transgression at all. While it would be unfounded to conclude that the plenitude of vinaya attention to sexual regulation means that the Buddhist monastic milieu harbored exceptionally voracious sexual appetites, one is tempted to conclude that anyway. At the very least, the many lusty people and acts depicted in *Suttavibhaṅga* bear witness to a very active sexual imagination. We find monks having sex with fresh corpses, rotting corpses, dolls, dildos, and a plethora of live partners crossing sex, gender, and species lines in every imaginable way. Monks rub against women and hermaphrodites and men and animals, copping a feel; women spot a monk sleeping under a tree and run up to sit on him and rape him; people force a monk to have sex with a woman, pushing their sexual organs together; a woman on the road invites a monk to touch her so as to bring him to orgasm; monks advise devoted laywomen that the best gift to the saṅgha is the gift of sex; prominent laywomen make the same disingenuous proposition to monks.

It is certainly not impossible that some of the rules were formulated in response to things people actually did. But we still have to ask why the law book gives so many illustrations of each kind of transgression. We can't help but imagine the monkish reader, who wrinkles his nose in disgust-cum-fascination at his ridiculous colleague who encouraged a female patron to offer her body for sex as a supreme act of *dāna* (generosity) to the saṅgha, only to turn away, spitting in disgust at her odor, just as he was about to mount her. For it would be easy enough to prohibit such a dubious kind of offering without the story of her—and his—humiliation. What is more, he is not punished for any of the particular details that the story provides, such as being on the verge of doing it, or for sorely hurting her feelings, both of which would justify telling the story for some edifying reason other than our suspicion that, at least in this case, it is here largely for its gratuitous amusement.

Probably, the catalogue of sexual misfires in the early vinaya edified both the prudish and the prurient, perhaps even in the same reader simultaneously. What is certain in any event is that the catalogue sends the message that there are many ways to read the rule and to try get around it, and that these dodges will not work. This in fact must be the bottom line of the presentation: the multitude of examples is to give the impression that the rule book is comprehensive, or to put it another way, that there are no ways to get around the rule. All possible misreadings and tricks have been anticipated by the elders, and none of them will succeed.

If it was obvious that sex for monastics is wrong, its strict definition was nonetheless elusive. Indeed, all that can be managed as the Buddha's most basic definition of *sex* in this section is simply "that which is not the dhamma (*asaadhamma*)." His other glosses, here, such as "village dhamma" (*gammadhamma*) or "vile dhamma" (*vasaladhamma*), don't help much either. Perhaps that is why those with less than sterling character are depicted as seeking to exploit the imprecision, in order to find sexual satisfaction without breaking the rule. A woman suggests to a monk that they could have sex whereby he will move, but she won't (alas, the text shows, that results in his downfall anyway). Again, a woman suggests that she will move while he won't (this, too, will merit a downfall). Or she suggests that ejaculating outside her body will make the act not quite sex (no, that won't do either).

Sex is just that which will bring a monk to defeat. After telling the first few stories, the *pārājika* section tries to pin down what that entails. Sexual intercourse occurs whenever the male organ enters the female organ. To make that even more definitive, a minute specification is formulated: if the male member enters the female genitals for the length of the fruit of the sesame plant, sex has occurred. Any such intercourse will disqualify the monk from being a son of the Sakyans; he can no longer be part of the community.

But we can already see that it wasn't so easy to articulate an ironclad definition after all. First the passage has to include animals in the list of partners. Then the next passage adds more specifications. There are actually three kinds of females: humans, nonhumans, and animals. Nonhumans include various kinds of spirits and ghosts. Not only that, but intercourse with partners other than females also turns out to be sex. The rule book actually comes up with four kinds of partners/sexes/genders: woman (*itthi*), hermaphrodite (*ubhatovyañjanaka*), *paṇḍaka* (which often means someone with minimal or deteriorated genitals), and male (*purisa*). And hermaphrodites, *paṇḍaka*s, and males, too, can be human, nonhuman, or animal.

And not only that. Sex with females can happen not only in one but in any of three orifices—vaginal, anal, and oral—all of which presumably are subject to the one-sesame law. This also is true for hermaphrodites. And just to be complete, it is finally specified that sex with *paṇḍaka*s and males can happen in two orifices, anal and oral. And this is true also for nonhuman *paṇḍaka*s and animal *paṇḍaka*s. And nonhuman males and male animals, in case that wasn't already clear.

Appearances of legalistic precision notwithstanding, the principle of what constitutes a sexual downfall is still not fully nailed down. For one thing, it turns out there is yet another forbidden orifice for the monk's organ: the mouth of the monk himself (there was once a monk with a very supple back who could manage such a feat). And then another: an acrobatic monk who could penetrate his own anus. Putting his organ into those two places also constitutes defeats. But what about other kinds of masturbation? At *Sanghādisesa* 1.1, masturbation performed with the hand is actually recognized to have health benefits, such as clearing up the complexion and filling out a frail frame. Nonetheless, it is a serious sexual transgression.

Actually, masturbation with the hand only institutes a formal sentencing by the saṅgha; it does not make for a full defeat. The Buddha still lectures the masturbating monk Seyyasaka in terms similar to those with which he lectured Sudinna—didn't he realize that the entire purpose of the dharma was for the sake of stilling passion, and so on? So why the difference in punishment? Why is masturbation with one's mouth worse than with the hand? Isn't sexual pleasure subject to passion and attachment no matter what device was used to cause it? Or is there an important distinction that has to do with the device itself? The only specific problem mentioned about masturbation by hand is that the same hand might also be used to accept offerings from the faithful. Is it that using one's own mouth or anus is somehow a more abhorrent transgression?

The more we work through the *pārājika* section, the less clear what really distinguishes the orifices that make for downfall sex. For example, ejaculating into a sore in the vicinity of the sexual organ on a corpse after inserting and then withdrawing his penis from the sexual organ itself will also constitute downfall. (So will the opposite sequence. The case shows that ejaculation is not what counts as sex; rather, it is the entrance into the [dead] woman's organ.) So will intercourse with a relatively fresh corpse. And so will intercourse with the mouth of a decapitated head. These cases are governed by the three-orifice rule, but then other cases show that this rule has still not been pinned down precisely. For one, if his organ enters the mouth of a decapitated head without touching it, it is a lesser transgression: only a "wrong-doing". So this a further specification: his organ has to touch the mouth, not just enter it. Moreover, there even are kinds of vaginas with which intercourse doesn't make for downfall sex: sexual intercourse with a woman whose body is almost fully decomposed counts only as a "grave offense." If his organ enters the genitals of the collected bones of a woman who had died and her bones scattered, it is only a wrongdoing. The same is true of inserting his organ into the genitals of a plaster image or a doll. These latter examples concern his penetration of one of the forbidden orifices, but some yet-to-be-discerned distinction prevents them from creating a downfall. So what is the logic that distinguishes downfall vaginas from other ones, as well as from the other kinds of envelopes that merit lesser punishment, like the masturbating hand—or, in a commentary, even the eye, or nose, or ear, or armpit? Or is there a logic at all?

Before deciding that, first consider another set of anomalies, this time regarding the proscribed sexual partner. The rule says that sex with animals, hermaphrodites, *paṇḍakas*, and males makes for a downfall as much as with women. (And as we just saw, the same is true for sex with oneself.) But in the lesser offenses, partner parity disappears. A sexual overture toward a woman earns a heavier punishment than toward any other kind of partner. Rubbing a woman with sex in mind is worse—incurring a sentencing by the saṅgha—than rubbing the body of a *paṇḍaka*, which incurs a lesser offense; or a man or an animal, which merits a lesser offense still. The same is true of mere physical contact.

Another set of rules legislates that touching a sleeping woman will require sentencing by the saṅgha, while touching a dead woman merits a grave offense, and a female animal or a wooden doll only a wrongdoing. Here the distinction seems to have to do with how close the prospective partner is to a live human woman. The human woman is also considered the most threatening when a monk sits with someone; the ruling is that this may only be deemed suspicious if that someone is a human female, not a female animal or spirit.

We find, then, suggestions that the human female is considered the gold standard for sex: the most likely partner for a monk, and the one with whom the monk's behavior is most closely regulated. This hint of preference might in turn explain the distinction between kinds of orifices: perhaps it has to do with how similar the orifice is to the vagina of a woman. On this theory, sex with fleshly orifices in living creatures such as men, *paṇḍakas*, and animals would be more like the vagina than is a hand, or a detached vagina among a pile of bones or an opening on an inanimate image, even if figured as a vagina.

Later commentarial tradition in Chinese translation suggests that the reason that the female organ is the most restricted is because it is what gives the most pleasure. But pleasure as such does not figure in the root law book, the *Suttavibhaṅga*. Perhaps this reticence reflects a recognition that pleasure makes for a most ambiguous basis of legal definition: surely both masturbation and full intercourse involve pleasure, the relative degree of which would be hard to measure. It is much more plausible that what really made sex with a woman worse than any other kind was its practical upshot: marriage, children, the householder's life; in short, saṃsāra, or what the Buddha calls "village *dhamma.*" Maybe that, in the end, is why sex with a woman's vagina is worse than putting your organ into the mouth of a black snake, for it lands you in hell on earth.

It is left to address, then, why sex with men, neuters, and other barren partners was also forbidden. Given the evidence in the *Suttavibhaṅga* of so much sex with partners of indeterminate or ambiguous sexual identity, not to mention species-crossing sex, it may not have been obvious how to define the legal distinction between human women and other partners. Particularly questionable might have been the childbearing capabilities of the hermaphrodite. The variety of contemporary textual passages concerning spontaneous sex change suggests that sexual identity was considered unstable in any case. So even if women were the gold standard, many other kinds of partners had to be ruled out as well, perhaps not only to be legally exhaustive, but also to be safe.

The theory that woman as fertile mate (with her particular kind of sexual organ) is the paradigmatic and most proscribed kind of partner already sheds a fair amount of light on the Pāli vinaya's sense of sex. It is certainly pertinent to the puzzlingly strict censure of Sudinna's act. Recall, the story goes out of its way to show that there was not a hint of erotic desire on his part. Rather, when the Buddha rebukes him for not being able to lead the Brahma life, it would seem that what he is guilty of is behavioral only. He did violate the Brahma life—but only in deed. But our theory that it is the human woman partner who makes sex so bad for a monk reminds us that even the mere deed with such a partner has enormous implications: it would produce a child, it would draw him back into the householder's life. No matter, then, that Sudinna's wife and child ended up renouncing the world and becoming *arahants*. It still is incumbent upon Sudinna, who in his earlier days had been particularly struck by the impossibility of leading the holy life as a householder, to confront the brute fact that *he performed householder activity*—no matter what the mitigating circumstances, and no matter what his particular intention or subjective state.

This fundamentally behavioral nature of the rule is one of the key grounds upon which monastic law may be distinguished from karmic law, which in most formulations takes mental attitude into account, even for bodily acts. If it can be argued that karma is a kind of "natural law," the same cannot be said of monastic law, for it is rather a legalistic construct. This also means that monastic law is not about spiritual attainment or states of enlightenment; it will be far more convincing if, as below, we argue instead that monastic law serves to define a community. The reason that monks must not have sex with women is because of what that act produces, which in turn will destroy the monastic community. This also explains why the rule disregards desire and attachment.

This is not to say that there is no accounting for desire whatsoever in the *Suttavibhaṅga*'s rules on sex. But most of the times that it comes up, desire serves merely to distinguish what otherwise would be innocent and worthy of a lesser, or even no, offense. This explains, I think, the occasional specification that a monk have the idea of sex (*sevanacitta*) in mind when he commits culpable intercourse. Especially some of the lesser offenses, which are ambiguous as to whether they are sexual or not, will be determined on the grounds of whether being inflamed (*sāratta*) has a role in the act. Otherwise, shaking a bridge upon which a woman stands, or giving her a blow on the shoulder, or pulling on a cord of which a woman holds the other end, or raising his foot, could well be innocent. There are a few occasions when inflammation does figure in the definition of certain heavier sexual offenses, such as when he has sex with the wooden doll. But mentioning this subjective dimension of the act seems to be gratuitous and redundant, since it is not highlighted and the act itself is already so odd that it would be obvious that he did it with passion; otherwise he surely wouldn't do it at all.

Clearly for the *Suttavibhaṅga* itself, the central factor in deciding which sexual activity constitutes downfall is far more about consent and deliberateness than desire or pleasure. Consent is especially germane when sex is initiated by others. It is a recurring refrain: Did a monk consent (*sādiyati*) when a woman sat down on him and had sex with him? If not, no offense. Did he consent when a woman came up to a monk (while paying homage to him) and took his organ in her mouth? Since he didn't, no offense. Other exceptions are also noted on occasion, such as a case where one monk accosts another monk who is sleeping: if the latter is ignorant of the rules, or if he is insane, disturbed, afflicted with pain, or a beginner, he is not held responsible for his part in the sex act. These specifications add sanity, attention, deliberateness, and most of all, knowledge of the rules to what consensual sex means for the early law book. And they reinforce my point above: monastic law is not natural law. Indeed, Sudinna is not shown to have been expelled from the *saṅgha* for his act. Even though he had a sense on his own that it was wrong and regretted it afterward, he is not culpable legally, since the law had not been articulated at the time that he committed the deed.

One of the only cases where the *Suttavibhaṅga* does indict desire (*rāga*) as a deciding factor in whether sex is downfall sex serves rather to raise a different, more interesting question. The Buddha exonerates a monk who has literally been raped by a woman sitting down on him. Clearly responding, I think, to the puzzle of how a man can be made to have sex against his will, the Buddha explains that there are five ways that males can get aroused, only one of which is through desire. The others include a waft of wind, the bite of an insect on top of his penis, and two more which are hard to construe. What's important is that the Buddha explicitly adjudicates that the monk's erection did not result from desire. In this the Buddha distinguishes desire from the bodily responsiveness of the male organ coming into contact with a mechanically stimulating touch.

Action, body, and physical reality

The Buddha's treatment of the rape of a male suggests a category of something like "the body acting on its own," that is, without any consent and without conscious decision to act. Another case of autogenous bodily action, it would seem, would be an involuntary nocturnal emission due to a dream, which is immune from any punishment whatsoever. This suggests that for the *Suttavibhaṅga,* when the body acts on its own, as an automaton, the person is not responsible.

But does this make sense? Is the body really acting totally involuntarily when there is a nocturnal emission, particularly if it is related to an erotic dream? The idea here seems to be that in such a case, an entirely mental affair (the dream) produces a bodily action, but without deliberate intention or bodily mobilization. The dream does, of course, express sexual desire and even an intention to have an emission *within* the dream. Indeed, in stating that "intentional emission of semen except during a dream is an offence," the law book suggests that nocturnal emission is in fact associated with intention (*sañcetanika*), which would refer to the desire that motivated the dream, as well as to a basic awareness (*sañjanata*) of what one is doing, which several of the *Suttavibhaṅga* rules specify in order to exonerate entirely inadvertent actions. But what I am suggesting is that nocturnal ejaculation is immune from punishment because it lacks a very particular kind of intention: intention directed toward a bodily act in the world of physical reality. It is only this that becomes culpable here. Such a reasoning once again distinguishes monastic law from issues of virtue as such. We can recall the famous argument in early Buddhist polemics that he who has a nocturnal emission is not an arhat; there the presumption seems to be that nocturnal emissions are signs of desire and attachment. Monastic law, in contrast, is not concerned with the state of desire or enlightenment of its subjects, only how to determine if they have broken a law. It is just that which is at stake in determining the nuances of intention and bodily action.

One thing that is clear in *Suttavibhaṅga* is that a solely mental act of sex is not an offense. A monk is shown having sex with his former wife in a dream, presumably with passion, but since no actual physical acts occur, the dream deserves no penalty at all.

In short, we have now seen not only that bodily action on its own (for instance, automatic erection) has no penalty; mental activity on its own (dream sex) doesn't either. There has to be some combination: there must be some bodily action for sex to be vinaya-culpable sex, but this action must also be accompanied by something else. What that something else is, is construed variously in the *Suttavibhaṅga*; often it is consent, as already seen, but we can recognize other factors as well. Notably, however, such factors that serve to tip an act into legal culpability can be distinguished whose presence became the classic litmus test to determine karmic responsibility, or one of the defilements (*kilesa*), which also in some passages are what make for karmic liability. In contrast, for monastic law the deciding factor somehow has one foot outside the realm of the strictly mental, and over the edge into bodily action. Consent is a good example: it not only betrays a mental attitude or "intention"; it also marks a crossing of the line into actual realization, sort of like a "speech act," albeit not necessarily spoken. Such a category is not thematized per se in the *Suttavibhaṅga,* but I would argue that a lot of the discussion of sexual violation is exactly about trying to determine what functions as such a bridge.

One telling case provides several options for what makes an action culpable. It concerns a monk who rubs someone else sexually. Here three elements are distinguished: wishing for sex, making effort with the body, and making contact. If all three are present, he incurs a meeting of the saṅgha (the contact that occurs in this case never rises to the level of intercourse). If he has the wish and makes exertion, that is, he tries, but he doesn't make contact, then it's just a wrongdoing. And if he has the wish and makes contact but has made no exertion (in other words, he inadvertently touches someone whom he desires) there is no offense whatever. Thus making a move, exerting effort, is the worst, or the most important, factor of all. Making contact is the second worst: if he tries but it doesn't come to pass, it is still an offense, but a lesser one. This means that whether he makes effort is not the only factor to be considered—it is also an issue if it actually happens or not. But if there is only desire, and no effort to make anything happen, then even if something does happen, there is no offense at all.

The case, then, highlights the inception of mobilization—deliberately setting the body into motion. Such effort would seem to be poised even further along the line from the mental into the bodily than is consent. But while there was a need to protect from punishment the body that moves without such deliberate mobilization and entirely automatically, the *Suttavibhaṅga* was concerned that this clemency could be exploited, for again, what does it really mean for the body to act on its own? Another case, about a pact between a monk and a woman who tried to avoid the appearance of mobilization, illustrates the problem. A woman suggested that she do all the work: she would make the effort, while he would not move. She moved, and his body responded; intercourse happened; the judgment is a full downfall. Here it wasn't mobilizing his body, "making effort," that got him in trouble, but rather what he allowed another body to do: make sex happen. So here the *Suttavibhaṅga* leans instead again on the factor of consent.

That both consent and deliberate bodily mobilization are hard to observe or measure must explain why the rule book frequently reverts to the bottom line or whether something actually happened—whether contact was made, a hole penetrated. We have already noticed in the case of Sudinna how this obsession with the physical act as such brings into high relief the disregard of subjective states such as desire or attachment in the *Suttavibhaṅga*. This disregard is made clearer yet in the case of a monk who was unable to feel anything in sex because of impaired faculties. He was nonetheless guilty of a downfall. A transgression took place, in actual reality—whether he enjoyed it, or even felt it, or not. And yet the law book's circumscription of sex could not turn entirely on a conception of sex as pure action either. At the extreme, sex that is completely objective and devoid of mental correlate must be free of blame—otherwise, given the ever-present possibility for automatic movement, there could be no definitive law. One could only erect inert, physical barriers, and even those would not stave off involuntary arousals and emissions. Most important, an entirely objectivist law cannot serve as a site for personal cultivation and discipline. Thus the law book must continue to struggle with determining the presence of consent—and the critical moment when the monk actually starts to make something happen.

6

The Ultimate Man

John Powers

*J*ohn Powers is a scholar of Tibetan Buddhism, a form of Buddhism found in Tibet,
Mongolia, and parts of the Himalayan region, among other places. The importance
of a religious teaching lineage is emphasized, as is most familiar to Westerners
through the person and example of the Dalai Lama. This reading is taken from A Bull
of a Man: Images of Masculinity, Sex, and the Body in Indian Buddhism. *It offers
a fresh perspective on the body of the Buddha as both a religious and a gendered
figure. The bodies of significant religious figures are most often seen as being
somehow "beyond" gender, but this is not the case here. The Buddha's divine body
is understood as the most perfect exemplar of religious manhood. More broadly, this
text also raises important questions about how the "masculinity" of certain religious
figures should be read and understood and how sexuality and gender always color
our perception of these figures.*

*Masculinities come into existence at particular times and places and are
always subject to change. Masculinities are, in a word, historical.*
—R. W. CONNELL, *MASCULINITIES*

In contemporary Western popular culture, the Buddha is commonly portrayed as an
androgynous, asexual character, often in a seated meditation posture and wearing
a beatific smile. Many (incorrectly) associate the Buddha with Hotei, a corpulent,
jolly figure of Chinese Buddhism traditionally viewed as a manifestation of the future
buddha Maitreya. Buddhist monks, such as the Dalai Lama, have also become images
of normative Buddhism, which is assumed to valorize celibacy and is often portrayed as
rejecting gender categories (at least in theory). In Indian Buddhist literature, however,
a very different version of the Buddha and his monastic followers appears: the Buddha

is described as the paragon of masculinity, the "ultimate man" (puruṣottama), and is referred to by a range of epithets that extol his manly qualities, his extraordinarily beautiful body, his superhuman virility and physical strength, his skill in martial arts, and the effect he has on women who see him. Many Buddhist monks are depicted as young, handsome, and virile, and the greatest challenge to their religious devotion is lustful women propositioning them for sex. This is even true of elderly monks, who also fend off unwanted advances.

The androgynous, asexual Buddha is not only found in contemporary popular culture, however. To date, most studies of the Buddha by both Western and Asian scholars have tended to emphasize the philosophical implications of those teachings attributed to him, events reported in various biographies, historical questions, or philological problems in Buddhist texts. There are many discussions of gender in relation to Buddhism, but most of these focus on Buddhist attitudes toward women or portrayals of women in Buddhist literature. While researching this project, I found two articles that examine Buddhist responses to homosexuality and many studies of Buddhism from feminist perspectives, but as far as I am aware, no one has surveyed Indian Buddhist literature, art, or iconography in terms of how they present normative masculinity. This is a remarkable oversight, since Buddhist literature was overwhelmingly written by, for, and about men, and Buddhist canonical texts (as well as extracanonical works, art, and other sources) abound with discourses and images of masculinity. Moreover, the pervasiveness of such discourses, the ways in which they are highlighted in many Indian Buddhist works, and the sheer inventiveness of Buddhist authors in developing the figure of the Buddha as the paradigm of masculinity indicate that they considered this paradigm to be of great importance.

Why, then, have contemporary interpreters of Buddhism generally overlooked these discourses? Why has the supremely masculine Buddha depicted in the Pāli canon and other Indic literature been eclipsed by the androgynous figure of modern imagination and the ascetic meditation master and philosopher of scholars? Part of the reason probably lies in the backgrounds of contemporary interpreters of Buddhism and the blind spots that every culture bequeaths to its inhabitants. The field of masculinity studies is a recent phenomenon, and many academic disciplines have only just begun to explore discourses relating to manhood. Feminist scholars who assert that religious traditions are overwhelmingly male-dominated and that most scholarship by definition focuses on men are no doubt correct, but studies of masculinity discourses are still relatively rare in religious studies.

In addition, most modern scholars of Buddhism were born and raised in societies in which Judeo-Christian traditions predominate, and even those who are not overtly religious have been influenced by them. The great founders of the Judeo-Christian-Islamic traditions—Abraham, Jesus, and Muhammad—are not, as far as I am aware, portrayed as paragons of masculinity, as exceptionally beautiful, as endowed with superhuman strength, or as masters of martial arts, and so people raised in cultures in which the Judeo-Christian-Islamic traditions predominate do not expect religious figures to be characterized in these ways. Since undertaking this project, I have been struck by the pervasiveness of ultramasculine images in Indian Buddhist texts—texts that in some cases I had read many times without even noticing these tropes. Once I began looking, however, they seemed to leap from the pages and confront me with a completely new version of the Buddha, one who personified the ideals of the Indian warrior class (kṣatriya), who caused women to faint because of his physical beauty, and who converted people to his teachings through the perceptual impact of his extraordinary physique.

In the "Discourse to Cankī," for example, the Buddha is described as "handsome, good looking, graceful, possessing supreme beauty of complexion, with sublime beauty and sublime presence, remarkable to behold." In the "Discourse to Soṇadaṇḍa," a group of brahmans comes to visit him. One of them, a young man named Angaka, is described as "handsome, good-looking, pleasant to look at, of supremely fair complexion, in form and complexion like the god Brahmā, of excellent appearance," but the brahman who gives this description hastens to add that the Buddha is even more handsome. Similar passages abound in Indian Buddhist literature. The transcendent physical beauty of the Buddha is a core trope of every text I have seen that discusses his life and teaching career.

If one compares the way the Buddha is portrayed in Indian literature with descriptions of Abraham, Jesus, and Muhammad, a number of striking differences appear. Abraham and Muhammad were chosen as prophets by God, but their exalted status was not a recognition of their spiritual attainments over many lifetimes, as with the Buddha; rather, Abraham and Muhammad were chosen because they were chosen. God designates some as his messengers and then provides them with missions, but a buddha becomes a buddha by consciously pursuing a path leading to liberation and cultivating a multitude of good qualities over countless incarnations in a personal discovery of truth.

Jesus is believed by Christians to be both God and man, but as a man he is generally conceived of as physically ordinary. If he had superhuman strength or was better able to endure pain than other men, the religious import of the Passion would be seriously undermined. His unremarkable body and common physique are points of emphasis by most Christian churches, who have condemned as heresy various attempts to portray him as nonphysical or as possessing a body that is superior to that of other men. His very ordinariness allowed him to hide from the devil, who was unable to recognize him precisely because he did not stand out. Thus Nicephorus the Patriarch asserts that

> Christ, having truly taken on a body like ours, is circumscribed by His humanity. Nor is it an illusion that this incorporeal being is circumscribed in space, He who, having no beginning but having subjected Himself to a temporal one, is circumscribed in time. By condescending to become corporeally part of humanity, incomprehensible divinity also accepts enclosure within the boundaries of comprehension.

Jesus's salvation mission required that he incarnate in a body like that of other men— that, like them, he would be sustained by food and water, would suffer when injured, and would die if crucified. In his study of representations of Christ in Renaissance art, Leo Steinberg refers to thousands of pictures that depict Jesus's genitals or highlight a bulge in his groin beneath diaphanous clothing to demonstrate that Jesus was truly a man like other men and connects this idea with sermons from the time that emphasized that Jesus was not different physically from the rest of male humanity. Referring to artistic works that highlight Jesus' anatomical masculinity, Steinberg remarks:

> So much of it proclaims over and over that godhood has vested itself in the infirmity of the flesh, so as to raise that flesh to the prerogatives of immortality. It celebrates the restoral which the divine power brought off by coming to share man's humanity. . . . Every right-thinking Christian, whether Latin or Greek, artist or otherwise, confessed that the pivotal moment in the history of the race was God's alliance with the human condition.

The Buddha's mission, however, is aided by his extraordinary physical endowments. In the Indian context, most indigenous religious traditions (including Buddhism) assume that every being is reborn over and over again in a beginningless cycle (saṃsāra) and that every life situation is conditioned by volitional actions of past lives. Those who are well favored, wealthy, good-looking, and long-lived are experiencing the ripening of their past karma, while those who are ugly, misshapen, poor, and sickly similarly are reaping what they have sown. The *Legend of Miserly Nanda* asserts that "the form of a man, possessing the pleasant beauty of a bunch of flowers, which attracts . . . the eyes of men and women, unwavering in energy and strength and perfect in its proportions, is the reward of virtue." And conversely, in the "Connected Discourses with the Kosalas," the Buddha describes various types of unfortunate humans and the endowments they have at birth: those of low social status, who are born in families of outcastes (caṇḍāla), bamboo workers, hunters, cartwrights, and flower scavengers, and those who are "ugly, unsightly, deformed, chronically ill, have deficient vision or maimed hands, are lame or paralyzed." Such people have trouble gaining food, drink, and clothing. Out of force of habit, they engage in misconduct of body, speech, and mind and so will be reborn in a bad destiny, even hell. This is characterized as "moving from darkness to darkness."

During any given lifetime, it is always possible to reverse course, to make decisions and perform actions that will result in different future destinies, but habits of conditioning make this difficult, and most beings tend to follow established patterns. The great value of a buddha for others lies in the fact that he has broken free from negative habituation and found a path to liberation. He then teaches others, and those who are wise and whose past training has made them receptive may follow his example and attain release from cyclic existence.

As a being seeking liberation engages in actions that produce positive karmas, one of the many rewards is improved physical condition. As a fruition of karma, the bodhisattva (a person working toward buddhahood) is born with a better body and greater resources, as well as improved intelligence, wealth, and beauty. Moreover, in the Indian context, a great teacher must have such endowments; in the Buddha's time, a person who was ugly, poor, crippled, or stupid would have had great difficulty convincing people that he or she was a fully awakened master, because people claiming mastery of the religious path were expected to prove their bona fides with their physiques and other endowments. Thus Buddhaghosa (fl. early fifth century; the greatest commentator of the Theravāda tradition) asserts that the physical body of a buddha impresses worldly people, and because of this he is fit to be relied upon by laypeople.

This notion is not confined to the canonical literature of elite monks; it is also found in non-Buddhist texts and in a range of other venues, such as an inscription from cave 22 in Ajaṇṭā: "This is the meritorious gift of the Śākyan monk . . . a follower of the Great Vehicle (Mahāyāna) made for the purpose of attaining supreme knowledge of all beings. Those who cause an image of the Conqueror (Jina, i.e., Buddha) to be made become endowed with good looks, good luck, and good qualities, acquire resplendent brightness in perfect aspects and insight, and become pleasing to the eye." Nor is this notion of the association between physical beauty and morality confined to India. Roy Porter cites a range of discourses from the Enlightenment that link moral excellence with physical beauty and robustness and that depict blemishes or unattractive features as external proof of the sordidness of the inner beings of the people afflicted with them: "beauty of figure and countenance were expressive of goodness of soul, whereas an ugly face, or a deformed body, bespoke the knave. . . . [P]urity, nobility, virtue and health were all distinguished by beauty; ugliness was the mark of Cain."

There is no way to know what the Buddha actually looked like or whether he was in fact a wealthy and handsome prince as reported in Indian sources, but the Buddha of Indian religious construction must be such a fortunate person. It is important to note that we are not dealing with the historical Buddha, and this study is not concerned with questions of when he might have lived or what, if any, valid historical details might be gleaned from traditional accounts of his life. The only Buddha accessible to modern commentators is Buddha the literary character, who was created by his monastic followers. This process probably began during his lifetime and continued for centuries after his passing. Various accounts of his life were constructed and embellished, a range of extraordinary qualities were attributed to him, and legends developed as a result. Even the teachings credited to him cannot with any confidence be assigned to the historical figure referred to as "Buddha." The discourses contained in Buddhist canons were redacted and edited by his followers over the course of centuries—according to tradition beginning with the "first council" at Rājagṛha in which five hundred *arhats* (monks who had eliminated mental afflictions and were assured of attaining nirvana at the end of their lives) gathered to recount from memory what they had heard the Buddha say during his forty-year ministry—and there is no good reason to believe that any of these texts represent his actual words. On the other hand, some parts of the canon may well hearken back to the Buddha's life and preaching, but in our present stare of understanding of his times, any such attributions are most probably speculative.

Despite these qualifications, we do have a vast literature along with a wealth of art and iconography, epigraphic material, and some historical records that provide a great deal of information regarding prevailing attitudes during the centuries when Buddhism existed in India. Much of the literature concerned with the Buddha emphasizes his physique as well as his spiritual attainments. In Pāli texts, the Buddha is said to be distinguished by two types of power: wisdom power *(ñāna-bala)* and body power *(kāya-bala)*. Most academic studies to date have focused on wisdom power, but it is abundantly clear from the tone of Indian canonical descriptions that the authors who created the Buddha character considered body power to be equally important. In addition, there are numerous tropes intended to establish the manliness of the Buddha's male monastic followers and a substantial amount of information regarding monastic sexuality and how the monastic body was conceived, along with discussions of health, diet, and hygiene, which have also largely been overlooked by contemporary scholars. My goal in the following chapters will be to highlight discourses relating to masculinity, sex, the body, and male sociality as described in Buddhist literature and art, not in order to condemn or extol them or to recommend how they should be judged by contemporary readers, but rather to describe and analyze how they are presented in their cultural context, a context in which they apparently were generally considered to be normative and "true."

The Buddha is commonly referred to in Indian Buddhist literature as a "great man" (Pāli: *mahāpurisa;* Sanskrit [Skt.]: *mahāpuruṣa*), and the notion that his body displayed the thirty-two characteristics typifying a great man forms a key aspect of this concept. The Buddha is also said to have perfected the qualities of moral behavior and to have cultivated wisdom surpassing that of other humans (and even of gods), but the Indian writers who constructed his mythos linked physical and mental accomplishments. In the "Connected Discourse on the Foundations of Mindfulness," the Buddha tells Śāriputra,

> It is on account of the liberation of the mind that I call a man "great man." Without that liberation there is no great man. And how is one thus liberated? With regard to his body, feelings, mind, and sensations, he is always master of them by way of insight that is keen, self-possessed, and mindful, and so he overcomes both the dejection and the craving that are commonly found in the world.

In the *Gradual Discourses,* the Buddha defines such a person as one who has concern for the welfare of the great mass of people, who has mastered thought and can enter into the four trance states beyond thought, and who is free from lust and ignorance. In these passages, mental and moral qualities are emphasized, but their attainment is also linked to physical perfection and ideal modes of comportment.

The lists of physical characteristics vary in detail and number, but there is a standard list of thirty-two that is found in a number of texts. Vasubandhu (ca. late fourth century CE) states that each characteristic is produced by cultivation of one hundred merits, and Buddhaghosa similarly asserts that each characteristic "is born from its corresponding action." The Everything Exists school (Sarvāstivāda) also taught that each of the characteristics relates to one hundred acts of merit, and that these acts of merit correspond to one hundred thoughts. A bodhisattva initially has fifty pure thoughts, which provide the basis for attainment of the state of a great man. Thus the first fifty thoughts initiate the process, and the second fifty complete the karmas needed to manifest a particular characteristic. The Everything Exists school also believed that acquisition of the thirty-two traits occurs at the very end of a buddha's training period and represents the culmination of his eons of religious practice.

Discussions of these attributes are found throughout Indian Buddhist literature, including a number of discourses in the Pāli canon, in scholastic works, and in Mahāyāna discourses *(sūtra)* and philosophical treatises *(śāstra)*. Some commentators appear to recognize the unusualness of the features ascribed to the Buddha's body and provide some interesting explanations of how these features should be conceived and why they are desirable and admirable. The *Extensive Sport,* for example, links the Buddha's sheathed penis with the practice of celibacy and his generosity in past lives and views this physical attribute as confirmation of his perfection of these disciplines. The *Great Matter* portrays it as an essential feature of buddhas and states that hosts of buddhas have appeared in the past and that all possessed "penises enclosed in a sheath like a royal stallion." Buddhaghosa explains that the penis retracts when not needed and so is not a dangling, disproportionate appendage like those of other men. He compares the Buddha's penis to those of elephants or bulls and says that the sheath looks like the pericarp of a golden lotus. Similarly, the *Flower Array Discourse* states that the Buddha's "testicles are well-hidden within a sheath, sunk deeply and fully covered, just like those of a thoroughbred elephant or a thoroughbred stallion." Even though this is presented as the perfection of a man's private parts, the text claims that no one—woman, man, boy, girl, elderly person, middle-aged person, or even the lustful or potentially lustful—could possibly conceive thoughts of sexual desire when viewing the Buddha's genitalia because his past practice of celibacy has produced a body so transcendent that people cannot imagine having sexual intercourse with him (the "out of my league" syndrome). As we will see, however, in other texts women who see the Buddha are overcome with desire, while others swoon when in his presence.

Although in Pāli and Sanskrit texts composed prior to the tantras the Buddha is always represented as completely celibate following his attainment of buddhahood, he sometimes employs his penis for other purposes. In the *Discourse of the Ocean-Like Meditation of Buddha Remembrance,* for example, he uses it to convert heretics. His aid is requested in three instances: (1) to defeat the daughters of Māra; (2) to combat prostitutes in Śrāvastī who had become enormously wealthy and were corrupting the youth of the city; and (3) to convert a group of naked Jain ascetics. He and his disciples reportedly performed various miracles, including transforming Māra's daughters into hags and inflicting various torments on them, and the Buddha and his disciples also conquered the prostitutes and rescued the city. The culmination of their efforts is a scene in which the Buddha converts skeptical Jains: he creates a mountain like Mount Sumeru surrounded by water and lays on his back next to it. He begins to emit golden rays of light, and his penis emerges from its sheath, winds around the mountain seven times, and then extends upward to the heaven of Brahmā. Alexander Soper comments that the text declares that "the Buddha was not a eunuch and so naturally exempt from sexual temptation. He possessed, rather, a male member that was normally kept retracted, like a horse's; but that for purposes of demonstration, to quell disbelief, could be marvelously expanded."

Like the retractable penis, the Buddha's enormous tongue is also linked with past practices. According to the *Extensive Sport,* he acquired this outsized tongue by abandoning wrong speech; by praising hearers *(śrāvaka),* solitary realizers *(pratyeka-buddha),* and buddhas; by requesting that they teach sūtras; and by reciting these sūtras himself. Buddhaghosa asserts that "other tongues are either fat, thin, short, or hard. The great man's tongue is soft, long, and wide and also has a pleasing color. Because it is soft, he can extend the tongue and touch and stroke both ears with it. Because it is long, he can touch and stroke both nostrils; because it is wide, he can cover his own forehead."

The *Discourse Resolving the Meaning* describes the Buddha's tongue as measuring a hand in length and breadth and states that it is tender like a lotus leaf. When it comes from his mouth, his tongue can cover his entire face. The idea that a long, supple tongue is a desirable physical feature in men is also found in the classical medical text *Caraka's Medical Compendium,* which states that ideally the tongue should be long, wide, smooth, slender, and a healthy pink color.

According to Buddhaghosa, because the Buddha's tongue is long, wide, and supple, he is able to deliver his words quickly. Unlike other men, he does not have to move his mouth very much when he speaks, and his soft and mobile tongue allowed him to teach the entire higher doctrine *(abhidharma;* a vast collection of scholastic discourses that is one of the "three baskets" of the Pāli canon) to his mother in only three months while he visited her in the Heaven of the Thirty-Three (*Trāyastriṃśa*).

When the Buddha extends his tongue, his audiences conclude that he must be an awakened being. This feature is offered as proof of his attainments to the brahman Brahmāyu, "a master of the three Vedas" and an expert in the lore of the physical characteristics of a great man, who visits the Buddha in order to ascertain whether he is all his followers claim. Brahmāyu verifies thirty of the characteristics and asks, "Upon your body, Gotama, is what is normally concealed by a cloth hidden by a sheath, greatest of men? Though named by a word of the feminine gender, is your tongue really a manly *(narassika)* one." Is your tongue also large? . . . Please stick it out a bit and cure our doubts." In response, the Buddha extends his tongue, inserts the tip into each ear hole, and covers his forehead with it. He then performs an act of supernatural power that enables the audience to view his sheathed penis. Brahmāyu and the other people in the assembly are reportedly highly impressed and conclude that he is indeed a great man, as his followers claim.

Another of the oddities of the Buddha's physiognomy, the cranial lump or *uṣṇīṣa,* has generated controversy among both Buddhist commentators and Western scholars. It is commonly depicted iconographically as a protuberance on top of his head, covered by tight curls of hair. According to the *Extensive Sport,* this lump is indistinct, and no one can clearly see its edges. When Siddhārtha was taken to a schoolroom as a youth, the teacher exclaimed: "Although I can see his face, the crown of his head is so exalted it seems to disappear!" Buddhaghosa describes the protuberance as a mass of flesh covering the forehead and extending to the base of the ears, resembling a royal turban that symbolizes sovereign power. Buddhaghosa also asserts that this feature can refer to the fact that the Buddha's head is perfectly rounded like a water bubble.

Alex Wayman also notes that this feature is sometimes conceived of as turban shaped, while others consider it to be a mass of hair piled on top of the Buddha's head. The Chinese pilgrims Faxian and Xuanzang claimed to have seen the bone relic of the Buddha's *uṣṇīṣa* in a monastery in Haḍḍa in modern-day Afghanistan. Faxian described it as a bone four inches in diameter and shaped like a wasp's nest or an arched hand. Xuanzang said it was twelve inches in diameter. In depictions of the Buddha in India, it is often a round lump on top of his skull covered with hair curls, and in Southeast Asia flames are often depicted coming out of this lump, representing stories in the Pāli canon in which rays of light emanate from the Buddha's head.

The Buddha's head is also distinguished by the *ūrṇā,* a coil of white hair in the middle of his forehead. According to Buddhaghosa, this coil is as long as half his arm when extended. It always remains twisted toward the right and pointed outward, and "it shines like a silver bubble on a golden slab and radiates light with brightness comparable to that of the Osadhī star." The Buddha also issues light rays from the *ūrṇā,* particularly when he is about to preach a new sermon.

The *ūrṇā* and *uṣṇīṣa* are often found in images of the Buddha, along with a few of the other thirty-two physical characteristics. Another common feature of Buddha statues, particularly ones that depict him in a reclining position, is perfectly flat feet marked with a spoked wheel design. According to Buddhaghosa, "The soles of the Buddha's feet are fully fleshed and perfectly flat like golden sandals. When he walks they do not move like the feet of ordinary men; rather, the whole underside of the foot touches the ground at the same time and leaves it at the same time. Nor does the end of the foot touch the ground before the other parts; rather, the entire sole touches the ground at the same time." Caraka also considers this to be an attribute of the ideal masculine type, who has a stable gait in which the entire surface of the soles presses against the earth.

This feature is often linked to the Buddha's dignified comportment and steady gait, which is compared to that of a mighty elephant. Like an elephant, the Buddha turns his entire body when he changes direction and does not swivel his hips or bend at the waist. A related trope compares his straight torso to that of the god Brahmā. Buddhaghosa states that "the Buddha has a straight body like that of Brahmā. He does not stoop or lean backwards, as if catching at the stars, nor does he have a crooked spine, but towers up symmetrically like a golden tower gate in a city of the gods." He is also depicted in some sources as taller than his contemporaries, and a number of texts assert that he had a six-foot halo that emanated from his entire body *(byāmappabhā)* and inspired faith in people.

7

Miẓvot *Built into the Body:*

Tkhines *for* Niddah, Pregnancy, and Childbirth

Chava Weissler

*C*hava Weissler is a scholar of Modern Judaism. Her chapter "Mizvot Built into the Body: Tkhines for Niddah, Pregnancy, and Childbirth" compares two genres of Ashkenazic literature written in the sixteenth and seventeenth centuries. The Ashkenazy are medieval Jews originally living in the Rhineland valley and France, who relocated during the Crusades and settled in Central and Eastern Europe. Defined by their rich culture, Ashkenaic Jews composed literature in their distinctive language, Yiddish (a hybrid of Hebrew and Medieval German). In her analysis, Weissler shows how the ethical teachings of musar literature, which was written by male religious authorities, present alternative understandings of women's bodies, menstruation, and childbirth from what she finds in the tkhines, devotional prayers written for (and in some cases by) women. As such, Weissler raises important questions about the internal diversity of communities as it relates to issues of childbirth and women's bodies.

Introduction

One of the important insights of feminist theory is the alterity, the otherness, of women. Men are the rule, women the exception. Thus, when we ask about the significance of the body in Judaism, we are in the first instance thinking about the significance of the *male* body. The female body, like the female person, is the exception. What, then, does the *female* body signify in Judaism? Perhaps the first additional question should be, to whom? While women as well as men are socialized to see men as the norm, it still may make a difference, in understanding the meaning of the body, whether one is embodied as male or female. This chapter explores the connections between women's bodies and the "women's commandments," especially *niddah,* in two genres of popular religious literature in Yiddish. Ethical literature, written by men, treats women, especially women's reproductive processes, in mythic terms, while devotional literature, which has some female authors, treats women's bodies more concretely.

Recovering women's voices, on this or any other topic, is a difficult process. Traditional Jewish texts are written in Hebrew or Aramaic, by men for a male audience. As a rule, only men mastered Hebrew, the sacred tongue, and the language of scholarly communication. In the late medieval and early modern period, some women in Central and Eastern Europe learned to read Yiddish, the vernacular of Ashkenazic Jewry. But even in popular religious literature in Yiddish, most of the voices are male, albeit often addressed to a female audience. This chapter draws upon an important work from the Yiddish *musar,* or ethical literature, a guide to the observance of the women's commandments, *Ayn shoen froen bukhlein* [A Pretty Little Book for Women], also known as *Sefer mitsvas ha-noshim* [The Book of Women's Commandments], by R. Benjamin Aaron Solnik, first published in 1577. It also makes reference to the *Brantshpigl* [The Burning Mirror], a guide to the upright life addressed to women, by Moses Henoch Altshuler, first published in 1596. Material in these works will be compared to *tkhines,* prayers for private devotion recited by women in Yiddish, published in Western and Central Europe in the seventeenth and eighteenth centuries. While many *tkhines* were written by women, most of the texts to be discussed are anonymous, and I suspect that some of them may have been written by men.

Both the *tkhines* and the ethical works consider the relationship of women's bodies, the biblical story of Eve, and the three "women's commandments," religious acts associated with women since the time of the Mishnah *(ḥallah, niddah,* and *hadlaqah).* And both kinds of texts pay special attention to menstruation as symbolic of the relationship of later women to Eve's punishment. Nonetheless, we shall see a marked difference in attitude toward and significance attributed to women's bodies and bodily processes between the two genres.

Women's bodies and the women's *miẓvot*

There is a well-known rabbinic trope that makes a correspondence between human anatomy and God's commandments. According to this traditional physiology, human beings have 248 limbs and 365 organs, corresponding to the numbers of positive and negative commandments, respectively, and adding up to 613, the traditional number of commandments in the Torah. However, this only describes *male* human beings; women, with a different anatomy, have a different number of limbs. A long *tkhine* to be recited "every day," found at the beginning of *Tkhines,* discusses the implication of this difference:

> . . . Strengthen my bones so that I can stand before you and serve your awesome Name with my whole heart, with all my limbs that you have created within me, two hundred and fifty two. You have given and commanded your children Israel to perform two hundred and forty-eight *miẓvot* (commandments), the same number as men have limbs. And you have promised them that if they keep and do these commandments, you will give them the light that is hidden for the righteous men and women in the next world. And you have given us women four extra limbs, and you have also given us four *miẓvot:* kindling lights to honor the holy Sabbath, and to purify ourselves of our impurity, and to separate *hallah* from the dough of our baking, and that we are obligated to serve our husbands. You have also placed in my body three hundred and sixty five organs—the same number as the negative commandments that you have given to your children Israel . . . (*Tkhines* 1648, no. 1)

Thus, the three women's commandments, which are here bound up with subservience to the husband, are built into women's bodies. Truly, in this case, anatomy is destiny.

The significance of the women's *miẓvot*

There is an obvious connection between the three women's commandments and aspects of women's traditional activities: separating *hallah* and kindling Sabbath lights can stand for domesticity, while the observance of menstrual avoidances structures sexuality and reproduction. However, texts going back to the rabbinic period add another level of meaning. They make both the three women's *miẓvot* and women's post-Edenic physiology emblematic of and punishment for Eve's sin. In Midrash Tanhuma, beginning of parashat Noah, we read:

> . . . And why were women commanded these three commandments? The Holy One, be blessed, said, Adam was the beginning of my creation, and was commanded concerning the Tree of Knowledge. And it is written with regard to Eve, When the woman saw, etc. [that the tree was good for eating and a delight to the eyes, and that the tree was desirable as a source of wisdom, she took of its fruit and ate.] She also gave some to her husband, and he ate [Gen. 3:6]. Thus she caused his death and shed his blood. And it is written in the Torah, "Whoever sheds the blood of man [Adam], by man shall his blood be shed [Gen. 9:6]." So she sheds her blood, and keeps her period of separation [*niddatah*], in order to atone for the blood of Adam that she shed. Whence comes the *miẓvah* of *hallah?* She polluted the *hallah* of the world, as Rabbi Yose b. Dusmeka said: Just as the woman slaps

her dough with water and afterwards takes ḥallah [magbahat hallatah], so did the Holy One, be blessed, with regard to Adam, as it was written, "And a mist came forth from the ground and watered [the whole surface of the earth]" [Gen. 2:6], and then afterwards, "The Lord God formed Adam from the dust of the earth" [Gen. 2:7]. Whence comes the kindling of the lights? She extinguished Adam's light, as it is written, "The light of the Lord is the soul of man [Adam]" [Proverbs 20:27], therefore she must observe the kindling of the light.

Thus, the women's commandments are seen as punishment and atonement for Eve's sin, which is understood, here, as the causing of Adam's death. Menstruation, in this text and others, is seen as part of God's punishment of Eve.

In *Sefer mitsvas ha-noshim*, R. Benjamin Aaron Solnik picks up this midrashic motif and lovingly develops it. He begins by retelling the tale of Eve's sin in the Garden of Eden.

> . . . After Eve ate of the apple, and knew she must die, she wanted her husband to eat of it as well. She said, If I have to die, you have to die with me. And she gave it to him so that he would also have to eat of the apple. Adam, poor thing, at first didn't want to eat of the apple. So she took a tree branch in her hand and beat him until he also ate of the apple. As the verse says, She gave me of the tree, and I ate [Gen. 3:12: *Hi natnah li min ha-eẓ va-okhel*]. She gave [it] to me with the tree, and I ate. And because that foolish Adam let his wife beat him, God, blessed be his name, cursed him, for he should not have let a woman beat him, but he should have beaten her . . . for God made the man to rule over the woman . . . (Solnik 1602:3b–4a)

Thus Eve's sin includes insubordination to Adam—even though the biblical text declares that Adam will rule over Eve only *after* they have eaten the fruit, as part of Eve's punishment (Gen. 3:16). But according to the *Sefer mitsvas ha-noshim*, Eve's sin is even worse than that:

> . . . Therefore the woman must also . . . suffer torment and misfortune. And therefore she must have her period every month, and must fast once or twice [a month], so that she will always remember her sin and remain in a constant state of repentance. Just as a murderer continuously does, who must all his days fast once or twice a month, so that he will think about repentance, and regret his sin, so must the woman do as well. Every month she immerses herself in the ritual bath, so that she will remember her sins, and be pious. . . . Therefore, it is fitting for her to recite the prayers for a repentant sinner . . . (Solnik 1602:4a)

Thus, women's very bodies give evidence against them as murderers once a month; the implication also seems to be that because of Eve's sin, all women are "naturally" more sinful than men, and need, therefore, the monthly reminder of their sins that the observance of *niddah* provides. This periodic penitence will ensure the woman's piety, says the author, even after she reaches the age of forty, and, presumably, menopause. "Therefore, dear daughter," this chapter concludes, "God has commanded you these three commandments. If you keep them and do them properly, he will forgive you your sins in this world and the next" (Solnik 1602:4a).

What should give us pause here is the picture of woman as murderer. Solnik seems to like this comparison, and, again, following the midrashic sources, develops it further with reference to the other two commandments as well:

> Women were commanded to kindle the lights, and they are obligated to observe this commandments, because they extinguished the light of the world [no longer just Adam's light], and darkened it . . . And because of her sin, because she ate from the apple, all of us must die. Since she has extinguished the light of our life, she must kindle the lights. (Solnik 1602:4a–4b)

After giving a variety of interpretations for the requirement that the two candles be lit, the author returns to this theme:

> . . . Therefore women must kindle the lights, for they have extinguished our light. And for that reason they must also suffer the pain of menstruation, because they shed our blood. Therefore they have the suffering of menstruation and must immerse themselves. For the immersion is like the repentance of a penitent sinner who was a murderer. And so it is with *ḥallah*, too. For she has spoiled things for us, we who are called **"Israel was holy to the Lord, the first fruits of his harvest"** [Jer. 2:3]; this means in Yiddish: Hallow, Israel, to God, the firstling of his fruit. Therefore she must "take *ḥallah.*" For she is commanded, **"As the first yield of your baking, you shall set aside a loaf [*ḥallah*] as a gift"** [Num. 15:20]; this means in Yiddish, the first part of your dough shall you separate as *ḥallah*. Therefore the woman must keep the three commandments. (Solnik 1602:4b)

What is fascinating here, even beyond the punitive theory the author develops of the women's commandments, is his complete collapse of all women into Eve. For him they are all the same, and the sixteenth-century women he addresses must repent continuously for Eve's "murder" of Adam. Of course, the text of Genesis does indicate that the punishments of both Adam and Eve will apply to future generations, and the midrashic sources also conflate Eve and later women. However, Solnik goes beyond his sources in two ways. First, he repeatedly uses the term "murderer" avoided by the more delicate language of the rabbinic sources. Second, he implicitly describes all women as the murderers of all men, not just of Adam: "They have extinguished *our* light . . . They have shed *our* blood . . ." (emphasis mine). Near the end of the final chapter of the section on *niddah*, which makes up the lion's share of the book, Solnik remarks, ". . . Women, with their apple eating, brought death to the world, and with their piety, which means behaving as set out above, they can bring about the end of death. . . . Thus has the Lord God spoken; may it come to pass speedily and in our days, . . . amen" (Solnik 1602:39b).

The view of the *tkhines*

While Solnik builds on well-known themes in rabbinic literature, and while these themes are also echoed, if less elaborately, in the *Brantshpigl's* discussion of the women's commandments, they do not appear in the *tkhines* for the women's commandments. I have yet to discover a *tkhine* that links the three women's *miẓvot* to Eve's sin. The biblical figure more likely to appear in *tkhines* for these *miẓvot* is Hannah (the mother of the biblical prophet Samuel), whose name is an acronym of *hallah, niddah,* and *hadlaqah.* According to talmudic exegesis (B. Berakhot 31b), Hannah repeated the phrase "your handmaid" three times in her prayer for a son in order to remind God that she had never transgressed any of the three women's *miẓvot.* As God answered her prayer, Hannah's observance was rewarded with a son, a theme explicitly played out in some *tkhine* texts. Thus, in the *tkhines,* the observance of the women's *miẓvot* is connected with fertility, rather than with penance.

In general, *tkhines* for the women's *miẓvot* stress the rewards for observance and the positive religious significance of the acts. (Some of the specific motifs are also found in the *musar* literature.) The reward most frequently mentioned is pious, scholarly offspring. The light of the Sabbath candles symbolizes the light of Torah and Sabbath peace and joy, while the taking of *hallah* is likened to God's creation of humanity, *without* mention of how Eve spoiled that first human loaf (cf. Exodus Rabba 30:13). Both taking *hallah* and the kindling of Sabbath lights recall Temple rituals: the *hallah* is in memory of the system of priestly tithes, while the kindling of the lights is compared to the action of the High Priest kindling the candelabrum in the sanctuary:

> . . . We must kindle lights for the holy day, to brighten it and to rejoice on it; therewith may we be worthy of the light and the joy of eternal life . . . Lord of the world, I have done all my work in the six days, and will now rest, as you have commanded, and will kindle two lights, according to the requirement of our holy Torah, as interpreted by our sages, to honor you and the holy Sabbath . . . And may the lights be, in your eyes, like the lights that the priest kindled in the Temple. And let our light not be extinguished, and let your light shine upon us. Deliver our souls into the light of paradise together with other righteous men and women . . . (*Seder tkhines* 1650:5b)

Only a small number of *tkhines* for *niddah,* pregnancy, and childbirth raise the topic of Eve's sin. Most *tkhines* for *niddah* are primarily concerned with the themes of purity and impurity, while most *tkhines* for childbirth plead that mother and child may come through the birth alive and unharmed. However, rather than assuming with the *Sefer mitsvas ha-noshim* that all women are complicit in Eve's sin and must suffer for it, those few *tkhines* that mention Eve portray the relationship between Eve's sin and later women's suffering in menstruation and childbirth as problematic. Further, Eve's sin is never described as murder, but rather, disobedience to God.

Three *tkhines* that mention this motif are found in the *Seder tkhines u-vakoshes*, first published around 1750, although at least one of them is considerably earlier. All of these texts raise the question of the relationship between women's present suffering and Eve's sin. It occurs to them to ask the question—even if they also convey the view that God's punishment of women is just. Thus, for example, a *tkhine* to be said during childbirth begins:

> Almighty God, righteous judge, with truth and with justice have you punished as women from the creation of human beings, that we women must bear our children with pain. It is within your power, whomever you punish is punished, and whomever you show mercy is shown mercy, and no one can contradict you. Who would say to you, What are you doing? (*Seder tkhines u-vakoshes* 1762, no. 100)

There *is* question here, even if the *tkhine* asserts that it is improper to ask it. Further, God's "justice," the text implies, is partly a matter of brute power.

A *tkhine* to be said when the woman inspects herself to make certain the flow of blood has ceased, which she must do for seven days before purifying herself by ritual immersion, again articulates and then swallows a question:

> God and my King, you are merciful. Who can tell or know your justice or your judgment? They are as deep as brooks of water and the depths of springs. You punished Eve, our ancient Mother, because she persuaded her husband to trespass against your commandment, and he ate from the tree that was forbidden them. You spoke with anger that in sadness she would give birth. So we women must suffer each time, and have our regular periods, with heavy hearts. Thus, I have had my period with a heavy heart, and with sadness, and I thank your holy Name and your judgment, and I have received it with great love . . . as a punishment . . . (*Seder tkhines u-vakoshes* 1762, no. 91)

This prayer seems chiefly designed to reconcile the women who recited it with both the discomfort of their menstrual cycles and an interpretation of this discomfort as a just punishment. By portraying God's justice as inscrutable, the *tkhine* does recognize, indirectly, that perhaps women's situation might seem unjust, but goes on to squelch this thought by having the reciter thank God for her periodic punishment.

Only one text—significantly, the one that seems to be the oldest, and which gives some indication that it emerged from women's oral tradition—actually dissociates the woman from Eve's sin. This is the prayer for biting off the end of the *etrog* on

Hoshana Rabba, a practice thought to ensure an easy childbirth. Although it was later incorporated into *Seder tkhines u-vakoshes* and several other *tkhine* collections, it appears first in the *Tsenerene,* known as the "women's Bible," an enormously popular homiletical work. Since the *Tsenerene* was first published around 1600, this *tkhine* is contemporaneous with the *musar* literature quoted earlier.

The way the *Tsenerene* introduces this prayer makes it sound like a record of women's practice. The context is a discussion of what kind of tree the Tree of Knowledge in the Garden of Eden was:

> Some sages say that it was a citron tree. Therefore, the custom is that women take the *etrog* and bite off the end on Hoshana Rabba [the seventh day of Sukkot], and give money to charity, since charity saves from death (Prov. 6:2), and they pray to God to be protected from the sufferings of bearing the children they are carrying, that they may give birth easily. Had Eve not eaten from the Tree of Knowledge, each woman would give birth as easily as a hen lays an egg, without pain. The woman should pray and should say:
>
> Lord of the world, because Eve ate of the apple, all of us women must suffer such great pangs as to die. Had I been there, I would not have had any enjoyment from [the fruit]. Just so, now I have not wanted to render the *etrog* unfit during the whole seven days when it was used for a *miẓvah*. But now, on Hoshana Rabba, the *miẓvah* is no longer applicable, but I am [still] not in a hurry to eat it. And just as little enjoyment as I get from the stem of the *etrog* would I have gotten from the apple that you forbade (Jacob ben Isaac of Yanov 1702/3:4b).

The implication, not quite explicitly spelled out, is that since the woman would not have committed Eve's sin, she should not suffer Eve's punishment.

To a greater or lesser degree, all of these *tkhines* distance the woman reciting them from Eve and her sin, at the very least by raising the question of their relationship. Further, while reference to Eve's sin does occur in these texts, it is not presented as the justification for the observance of *niddah* (let alone the other women's *miẓvot*). Eve's sin explains why women menstruate and why childbirth is painful. But the observance of *niddah* itself is not described as a continuous penance for Eve's murder of Adam, or even for Eve's disobedience to God's command. Rather, the texts use quite different images, and express quite different views of the meaning and consequences of the observance of *niddah.* The *tkhine* before ritual immersion, for example, uses a vocabulary of purity and cleansing, and articulates the connection of the woman reciting it to other pious Jewish women:

> . . . God, my Lord, may it be your will that my cleanness, and washing, and immersion, be accounted before you like all the purity of all the pious women of Israel who purify themselves and immerse themselves at the proper time . . . (*Tkhines* 1648, no. 14; *Seder tkhines u-vakoshes* 1762, no. 92)

The *tkhine* to be said after immersion is concerned primarily with hopes for pious offspring, whether male or female (*Seder tkhines u-vakoshes* 1762, no. 93). In both these cases, the meaning of the observance of *niddah* for the woman is pictured quite differently from the *Sefer mitsvas ha-noshim*. Further, and this deserves greater attention than I can give it here, the very language describing women's physiological states differs between the two genres. The *tkhines* consistently use a vocabulary of purity or cleanliness, and impurity. Both the *Sefer mitsvas ha-noshim* and the *Brantshpigl*, by contrast, prefer a different terminology. Borrowing from the language of cuisine, they describe the woman as either *kosher* or *treyf*.

Tkhines, musar, and women's alterity

What can we conclude from the differences between the *musar* literature and the *tkhines* on the subject of the women's *miẓvot* and women's bodies? Before dealing with the differences, it is important to point out one similarity. Both genres find it necessary to inquire as to the meaning of women's bodies and bodily processes; both genres take men as the norm, and women's bodies as that which needs explaining.

But here the similarities end. For the *musar* works, women are less individualized—they form a kind of cosmic class—and more anomalous. Eve, a disobedient and sinful woman, is fully paradigmatic for all women, whose post-Edenic bodies testify monthly to their sinful natures. Indeed, the *Brantshpigl* makes a direct physiological connection, asserting that the blood of menstruation and childbirth originate in the impure venom that the serpent deposited in Eve. This text also states that men find the sight of menstrual blood revolting and that women should therefore keep bloodstained chemises and sheets hidden from their husbands.

For the *tkhines,* by contrast, the view of women's bodies might appropriately be termed less mythical, more rooted in actual physical realities. The question most urgently addressed by the *tkhines* is that of suffering: the physical discomfort, pain, and danger women experience in menstruation and childbirth. The authors of the *tkhines* want to know why women suffer, not why they bleed, and the blood itself does not inspire them with disgust. Further, since the theology implied in the *tkhine* literature in general asserts that people suffer for their own sins, these texts do find the idea that all women suffer because of Eve's sin problematic.

Can we account for the differences between these two genres by the different genders of the authors? The issue is complex, especially since, if we are to be precise about these anonymous *tkhines,* we need to speak of the gender only of the authorial voice. Yet it does seem that men speaking as men, and women (or men) speaking as women, express different attitudes toward, and have different questions about, women's bodies. Let me be clear here: This is not a matter of individual male malice or prejudice toward women. As other parts of the *Brantshpigl* make abundantly clear, Altshuler rather liked women and keenly appreciated their social importance.

Solnik, as a *poseq,* an adjudicator of Jewish law, was quite concerned to extend as much opportunity for religious expression to women as he thought he could justify halakhically. And both men, quite unusually, went to the trouble of writing books for women in Yiddish. Rather, the differences between the two genres are evidence of the multivocality of gender constructions in Ashkenazic culture. And these differences might be phrased as two contrasting questions. The authors of the *tkhines* want to understand how God's justice can require women's suffering. But the authors of the two *musar* works want to know why women are the way they are, whence the archetypal nature of the irreducibly Other springs.

8

Gendering the Ungendered Body:

Hermaphrodites in Medieval Islamic Law

Paula Sanders

Paula Sanders studies the history and culture of medieval Islam. This excerpt, from a chapter entitled "Gendering the Ungendered Body: Hermaphrodites in Medieval Islamic Law," considers how medieval Islamic jurists (experts in Islamic law) interpreted the morphology of ambiguously sexed bodies that did not easily conform to a two-sex binary model. By the twelfth century, Islamic legal debate was a complex endeavor, defined by different schools of thought. Apart from the Qur'an (the holy book revealed to the prophet Muhammad), jurists utilized sources such as the hadith (record of the sayings and traditions of the prophet) as well as consensus of earlier judicial arguments in their decision-making. Sanders shows how jurists' discussions of hermaphrodites aimed to socialize them in ways that would secure the hierarchal familial structures of medieval Muslim society. Her analysis indicates that "intersexed bodies" are defined and viewed differently across time and place, and further, it showcases the social and relational character of sex and gender distinctions.

No aspect of life in medieval Islamic societies was free from considerations of sex. The boundary between male and female was drawn firmly and was deeply embedded both in views of the cosmos and in social structures. The most visible expression of this boundary, the social segregation of men and women, was only a particularly concrete demonstration of the notion that male and female were opposites, and that an ordered human society depended on maintaining boundaries that had been ordained by God.

Men and women not related by blood or marriage lived in separate, but intersecting, spheres. Interaction between them was understood to be both necessary and inevitable, but it was permissible and desirable only under carefully controlled and rigidly prescribed circumstances. The most desirable of these circumstances is expressed by the institution of *nikah,* often narrowly translated as "marriage." Nikah and *zina* (unlawful intercourse) constitute the two fundamental categories of possible interaction between unrelated men and women in the social world. These categories rest upon the existence of the male-female boundary, and therefore even zina, in some sense, affirms that boundary while threatening others.

Violation of those permitted relationships promised not only social disruption, but disorder on a much larger (and perhaps unseen) scale. Those disruptions could be caused not only by actual violations of taboos, but even by the suggestion that such violations had occurred. The false accusation of adultery (*qadhf,* often translated simply as "slander"), for example, is one of only five crimes for which the Quran prescribes punishment. The broad Quranic concepts concerning licit and illicit relationships, as well as modesty, pertain equally to men and to women, but they were interpreted primarily in terms of the dangers that women's disruptive sexuality present to an ordered society.

Men and women were socialized into this world of relations, which assumed that men and women must interact, that they must interact in prescribed ways, and that interaction in other ways threatened the social order and had to be guarded against at all costs. The question of one's maleness or femaleness was a crucial factor in determining what kinds of protection against social disorder needed to be employed. Although men and women presumably bore equal responsibility for such illicit relations, that responsibility was construed in terms of certain assumptions about the natures of men and women. Men were considered susceptible to seduction and the actors, whereas women were considered to be both seductresses (that is, tempting men to act in certain destructive ways) and the recipients of the men's acts.

Furthermore, the relations and dangerous possibilities rested on assumptions about the responsibilities of men to prescribe behaviors and set limits for women, who were considered to be their inferiors. If the spheres of men and women intersected, they were also established in a dear hierarchy that placed men above women. Although women were considered to be the equals of men before God, this spiritual egalitarianism did not imply a similar egalitarianism in the social world. This was the social context in which the Quranic verses stating that "men are a degree above women" and that "men are the managers of the affairs of women" were to be understood.

Women were presumed to be the major site of social disorder (*fitna*) by medieval jurists and commentators as well as in popular literature. But even the notion of the potentially dangerous sexuality of women, of the ever-present threat of fitna, was relational. Although the danger was located among women, it was not their being that represented disorder, but the possibilities of their illicit relationships with men.

Under these circumstances, a person who fit neither of the available categories presented a serious dilemma in a society where the boundary between male and female was drawn so clearly and was so impenetrable. In this respect, medieval Islam differed from medieval and early modern European societies, where the boundary between male and female was more permeable and where the troubling possibility of the mixing of sexes did exist.

Not all boundaries in medieval Islamic societies were as impermeable as that between male and female. There were other, equally fundamental boundaries in Islamic societies that also involved hierarchies: Muslim and non-Muslim, free and slave. But these boundaries could be crossed. One's fundamental category could be changed by conversion or manumission. The sexual boundary was different, since it could not be crossed legitimately simply by an act of will.

What did medieval Muslims do when confronted with a person whose sex was unknown? In societies that took for granted that everyone was either male or female, what place if any was there for the hermaphrodite, who seemed to fit neither category? For occasionally children were born or individuals encountered who did not fall into these two categories, whose anomalies in sexual physiology made it impossible to determine whether the person was male or female.

The biological process of sex determination, according to medieval Muslim natural philosophers and physicians, required the domination or precedence of the semen of one parent over the other. Whereas it was assumed that women were created from man (that is, from Adam's rib) and inferior in most respects, they were considered biologically equal in human reproduction. Both male and female shared equally the power of generation, because both were believed to contribute semen to the reproduction of the child. Semen was regarded as a complex substance that came from all parts of the body, which explained why children resembled their parents. The child would have the sex of the parent whose semen dominated. Ibn al-Qayyim al-Jauziyya attributed this domination to conditions of heat or cold in the womb, as well as to the relative strength or weakness of the semen contributed by each parent.

This theory of generation as advanced in medical texts intersected with Quranic doctrines of creation. There was a deep coherence between Quran, commentary, and scientific literature on this subject. In particular, the preference for the Hippocratic-Galenic over the Aristotelian tradition seems to have been due largely to its consistency with the classical Islamic understanding of the Quranic doctrine of creation. Similarly, the medical assumption that there were two sexes was consistent with the interpretation of the Quranic verse "we have created of everything a pair" (51:49), which was dearly understood by the commentators to refer to male and female.

The insistence on the two sexes of male and female and the articulation of this assumption in the theory of generation found its way even into lexicography. The medieval lexicon Lisan al-'Arab's discussion of the term dhakar (meaning, among other things, "male" and "penis") states: "If the [seminal] fluid of the man dominates the [seminal] fluid of the woman, they will produce a male child. If the [seminal] fluid of the male precedes the [seminal] fluid of the female, she will bear a male child, if God wills." If the semen of neither parent dominated, the child would be a hermaphrodite. Although the jurists were confident that every person had a true sex—known at least, or perhaps only, to God—discovering what that sex was remained a human dilemma subject to the limitations of human knowledge. The first concern of the jurists was to assign sex to such a person, usually an infant born with ambiguous genitalia.

One jurist stated simply, "If the child has a vulva (*farj*) and a penis (*dhakar*) then it is a hermaphrodite (*khuntha*)." Other lawyers and medieval lexicographers defined the khuntha as one who has "what is proper to both men and to women," "what is proper to both the male and the female," or "neither what is proper to the male or to the female." This last condition, according to al-Sarakhsi, was the gravest form of dubiousness (*ishtibah*); he was describing a child who was neither male nor female, excreting from its navel (*surratuhu*).

Al-Sarakhsi told his readers further that "the two characteristics [having what is male and female] are not combined in one person, because they are dissimilar by way of being contradictory." Nowhere in these texts is there even the slightest suggestion that a khuntha is both a man and a woman. Human beings had to be either male or female; sometimes they seemed to be neither, but they could not be both. The difficulty lay in establishing a place for the hermaphrodite until its primary set of organs could be determined, that is, the set of organs that had legal value and to which sex would be attributed.

The basic rule in establishing the sex of the child was *al-hukm li'l-mabal* (the judgment is attributed to the urinary orifice). This principle can be traced to pre-Islamic Arabian custom. It was also established in hadith that "the inheritance is awarded to the urinary orifice" (*al-mirath li'l-mabal*), that is, the sex of the child was determined by the mabal.

If the distinction could be made on this basis at birth, the sex of the child was determined and the additional organs accorded the status of "defect" (*'aib*). In other words, the presence of the extra organs was recognized as an objective reality, but these extra organs were assigned no legal value. Once relegated to the status of 'aib, or defect, they could be removed surgically.

If, however, the child urinated from both of the orifices, then the one from which the urine proceeded first was primary. If it urinated from both simultaneously, some said that primacy would be awarded to the organ from which the greater quantity of urine proceeded. Abu Ja'far al-Tusi, the Shi'i jurist, added another criterion: "If the onset of urination from [the mabals] is simultaneous, then [the sex of the child] is considered on the basis of the one that urinates last."

Other alternatives were offered: "Some say to count the ribs, and if they are equal in number then it is a woman; if they are unequal, it is a man. And some say to consider it on the basis of the inclination of its nature." This is the only instance where anything other than strictly biological measures were suggested to determine the sex of a khuntha; it does not reflect the conventional juridical wisdom on such matters.

If the sex of the child could not be determined by these conventional methods, it remained in a state of dubiousness (ishtibah) or ambiguity (*ishkal*) until the onset of puberty. Puberty (*bulugh, idrak*) in Islam is determined by the appearance of signs (*'alamat*) that indicate sexual maturity. For a man, these are intercourse using the penis, the appearance of facial hair, and nocturnal emissions; for a woman, they are the growth of the breasts, the onset of menstruation, vaginal intercourse, conception, and lactation.

For a khuntha, the appearance of any one of these signs would nullify the dubiousness or ambiguity. Such a sign determined both sex and the attainment of sexual majority. Furthermore, the hermaphrodite was not disabled by the ambiguity surrounding its sex in reporting the appearance of these signs. Its claims of puberty were accepted just like those of a normal child, because no one else could know about it. In this sense, the hermaphrodite benefited from the general ambiguity surrounding childhood. Since children are not considered to be sexual beings in Islam, the rules of-modesty or other precautions aimed at preventing illicit sex between adults do not apply to them. Their sex is known, but they are not part of the social-sexual world of adults. They are, in a word, unsocialized.

Khuntha mushkil was the technical legal term for a hermaphrodite who had passed the age at which puberty normally occurs without manifesting any of its signs. Its sex could not be determined. The mushkil label was a difficult one to contest, once applied, because of the same legal principle of precedence that allowed the jurists to insist on the permanence of sex once it had been assigned. In that case, after the determination of male sex based on a nocturnal emission, the appearance of such contradictory evidence as the growth of breasts had no legal consequence. By the same reasoning, the admission that one was unable to determine sex prevented the hermaphrodite from asserting later that it had reached puberty. Now jurists had to contend with the tension between their desire to determine the sex of every human being with certainty, and the caution that was demanded in attributing sex.

Although Islamic jurists could not establish the true sex of the khuntha mushkil, they nonetheless had to incorporate it into the adult social world in which everyone was either male or female. They had to assign the khuntha mushkil to one of these categories in order to either prescribe or proscribe, because the rules for men and women were different.

This process, as opposed to establishing true sex, I would call *gendering*. I have invoked this most modern of terms with the full awareness that it is anachronistic. But feminist scholarship has created new meanings for what was once simply a grammatical term. Gender goes beyond biological definitions of sex (although these are also cultural constructions). It is embedded in the social understanding of what constitutes maleness or femaleness, as well as the social implications and consequences of being male or female. I use the word *gendering* to describe the strategies by which medieval Muslim jurists constructed the khuntha mushkil—an unsexed, ungendered, and therefore unsocialized being—as a social person in terms of traditional categories of sex.

In doing this, they changed their focus from the true sex of the individual to the prescriptions for whole categories (male and female). This process, in turn, reaffirmed those categories and maintained the boundary between male and female while retaining the emphasis on male and female in relation to one another. This strategy was possible not because new categories were invented, but by virtue of the structure of Islamic law itself. If sex was not arranged on a continuum for medieval Muslims, the moral universe encoded in Islamic law was. There were only two poles for sex: male and female. But all behavior fell somewhere on a scale of religious qualifications that included five categories: obligatory, recommended, neutral, reprehensible, and forbidden. Under certain circumstances, reprehensible behavior might be preferred when the alternative was committing a forbidden act. In determining which course of action to take, jurists employed another fundamental principle of law: precaution (*ihtiyat*), denoting the choice of a course of action that is founded on certainty rather than uncertainty.

The possibilities of the khuntha being a man or a woman had to be considered with respect to every variation that is tied to sex. Decisions were often based on procedural rules not directly related to sex. Depending on the situation, jurists might be informed by a different hierarchy of concerns in negotiating the gender of the hermaphrodite. The negotiation of gender was not invariably difficult or complicated. Gendering seems to have been least problematic when it involved segregation and where spatial relations dearly reflected sexual hierarchy. In these circumstances, the simple arrangement of male above female could be exploited to grant the hermaphrodite an intermediary position.

These concerns informed the discussions of where the hermaphrodite should stand in prayer (*salat*). Prayer is a daily obligation. Numerous occurrences can invalidate a person's prayer, in which case the prayer must be repeated, just as missed prayer must be made up at another time. Men and women may pray in the same room, but the rows of men must always precede the rows of women. This is a dear case of segregation and the spatial expression of male supremacy. Where should the khuntha mushkil stand in prayer? In Friday prayer, between the rows of men and the rows of women:

> It should stand behind the men and in front of the women as a precaution, because if it is a man standing among the rows of women, his own prayer is invalid; and if it is a woman standing among the rows of men, then the prayers of those men on her right, her left, and behind her will be invalid. An adolescent is, in this, like a mature adult. But if the khuntha is in the rows of men, in front of the women, we are certain of the validity of its [own] prayer. If it stands among the women, however, we prefer that it repeat the prayers, because the obligatory nature of prayer for [a man] is well-established, while the non-fulfillment of this duty is doubtful.

This is a perfect example of the way the boundary and the hierarchy were preserved: the validity of the hermaphrodite's own prayer and of those of the other congregants was assured by its segregation, and by standing between the rows of men and women, it neither threatened the superior status of men nor was it threatened with an inferior position. Should it turn out to be a man, he would simply constitute the last row of men; should it turn out to be a woman, she would be the first row of women.

There were other fundamental concerns. Numerous problems in gendering hermaphrodites revolved around the issue of modesty. Many prescriptions for dress, demeanor, and segregation are based on this concept of modesty, called in Arabic *sitr al-'aura,* literally, "covering [one's] nakedness." The exhortation to preserve modesty applies equally to men and women in Islam, but the various law schools have diverging definitions of what constitutes the 'aura for men and women, and they usually emphasize women's responsibility. When the concerns of jurists were centered on sitr al-'aura, the hermaphrodite was almost always gendered as female.

Even insisting that modesty be a priority did not preclude complications in negotiating gender in every situation. The requirements for dress for men and women making the pilgrimage (*hajj*) are, according to some schools of law, contradictory and raise the specter of committing two equally forbidden acts. In the case of a khuntha past adolescence, some Hanafi jurists were confounded, because "a man in *ihram* [a state of ritual purity marked by putting on special clothes at the beginning of the pilgrimage] may not wear seamed clothing, while a woman in ihram is obliged to wear seamed clothing and is prohibited from going without a waistband and cloak." Had the risk involved a choice between committing a reprehensible act or a forbidden one, the judgment might well have been different. Al-Sarakhsi admitted that he did not know the answer because each possibility is equally forbidden. The hierarchy of human activities manifest in the scale of religious qualifications helps negotiate gender only when the two possibilities are not equally forbidden.

But some jurists resolved the problem by returning to the issue of modesty. They suggested that the khuntha dress as a woman because this is closer to the sitr, and her status in a state of ihram is founded on sitr, just as it is at other times. Moreover, al-Shaibani maintained, a man can wear seamed clothing during his ihram when there are extenuating circumstances (*'udhr,* lit. "excuse"), and "dubiousness of the matter of its sex is one of the gravest [extenuating] circumstances."

Protecting against violations of the prescriptions for modesty could create difficulties even in trying to determine the true sex of the khuntha mushkil. Jurists could invoke another boundary to mitigate the complicated circumstances, of slavery. The legal position of the female slave as the sexual property of her master permitted the negotiation of gender without the risk of violating the rules of modesty.

It is reprehensible [*makruh*] for a man or a woman to inspect [the khuntha] until he reaches puberty and the matter of his sex is cleared up, because the adolescent is in the position of the pubescent with respect to the obligation of sitr al-'aura. A person of one sex looking at a person of the opposite sex is not permitted. . . . Whether a man or a woman examines him, there is [still] the suspicion of looking at [the nakedness] of a person of the opposite sex (*nazr khilaf al-jins*). Instead, a slave girl who is knowledgeable in these matters is bought for him from his own money to examine him, so that he owns her by means of actual purchase. If the khuntha is a woman, then the person looking is a member of the same sex (*nazr al-jins ila al-jins*) and if it is a man, then it is a slave [*mamluka*] looking at her master.

That the determination of sex should have been in the hands of someone who, in every other respect, was a disprivileged person is remarkable. Slaves, for example, could not give testimony in an Islamic court. In spite of its legal implications and importance, the determination of true sex apparently took place outside the formal structures both of law and of medicine. Physicians do not seem to have been participants in this process. Because it was permissible for a slave to look at her master, a khuntha was circumcised by a slave girl purchased for him either from his own funds or, if he was indigent, from the funds of the public treasury.

The notion that the sex of the khuntha was a social concern was reinforced by the commitment of funds from the *bait al-mal* (public treasury) to buy the slave girl. The funds of the treasury were to be used for the public good, and what could be more in the interests of the public good than the knowledge of whether someone was male or female? The establishment of sex was not only important to determine the legal status of the khuntha, but also had implications for the position of others within the community. Even a single individual whose sex was not known threatened the social order. The sex of one person was inevitably tied to the status of others.

Whereas conditional gendering worked to preserve social order in many instances, establishing the true sex of the khuntha mushkil was the only remedy under other circumstances. This, as we have seen, was often impossible. If the sex of the khuntha could not be determined, some matters, including the status of other people, simply had to be held in abeyance.

This concern about the social implications of sex is nowhere clearer than in the reasoning displayed in a discussion of the legal validity of the marriage of a khuntha. The validity of the marriage of a khuntha whose father had married it to a man or a woman could not be determined until its true sex was discovered. This was not, as we might think, because of concerns about inheritance, incest taboos, or modesty. It was because, as al-Sarakhsi states, the male entered marriage as a *malik* (owner), whereas the female became *mamluka* (owned) by virtue of marriage. This short statement communicates powerfully not only the necessity of knowing who is male or female, but what it means socially to be male or female. "If it manifests [at puberty] the signs ['alamat] of men and its father had previously married it to a woman, then [that] nikah is regarded as being valid from the time the father contracted it, because it has become dear that his action coincided with the actual status of the khuntha . . . but if the father had married it to a man and it then manifested the signs of male puberty, then it has become clear that the action did not coincide with the khuntha's actual status, and the nikah is null."

What does al-Sarakhsi mean when he talks about the action coinciding with the actual status of the khuntha? That "actual status" is not merely the biological fact of one individual's sex, but the more important categorical fact that all men enter marriage as possessors and all women as possessions. The difficulty thus rests not only in the apparent sexual contradiction and impossibility of two men marrying each another, but also in the related social fact that two people cannot both enter a marriage as owners.

One must enter as the malik (owner), one as the mamluka (owned). And this means that one must be male and one female.

With marriage, an institution founded on the fundamentally sexual relationship between men and women, the separate concerns that the jurists dealt with came together. Questions of sexual hierarchy, as we have just seen, of the protection of the male domain, modesty, and incest taboos, all converged. Sometimes, as with a question of modesty, the relationship established by marriage between husband and wife permitted the jurists to negotiate gender without risking violation of any taboo. Although the marriage of a khuntha to a woman, for example, could not be regarded as valid as long as the sex of the khuntha was unknown, it was still considered to be *mustaqim,* meaning that it did not involve anything forbidden. The jurists reasoned that if the khuntha turned out to be a woman, this meant only that two members of the same sex had seen one another and that the marriage itself was merely a blunder. If it turned out to be a man, this constituted the gaze of a woman upon her husband, and there was no prohibition against that.

The jurists were more concerned, however, that a marriage might violate the incest taboos. The prohibition of affinity could be established by a man kissing an adolescent girl, for example, in which case her mother and sisters would be forbidden to him in marriage. The rule extended to hermaphrodites, and the jurists were careful not to allow the possibility of contracting a marriage that might violate these taboos. "If a man kisses [the hermaphrodite] with lust, then he may not marry the khuntha's mother until the status of its sex has been determined. Because if it is female, his kissing her after [she] reaches adolescence establishes the prohibition of their becoming related by marriage, and the mother would be forbidden to him. This is the prevailing opinion, because it is preferable to forgo nikah with a woman who is permitted to him than to engage in nikah with a woman who is forbidden to him."

Yet the continual attempts to normalize the khuntha also intersected with a conservative thrust within Islamic law that attempts to preserve marriages. If a khuntha married a woman and failed to have intercourse with her, the same rules applied as would to an impotent man—that is, no action could be taken to dissolve the marriage until a period of one year had passed. This delay was intended as a waiting period to see whether the impediment to intercourse was temporary or permanent.

What is striking about the laws concerning marriage of the hermaphrodite is the complete absence of the anxiety about homosexuality that pervades the European texts on hermaphroditism. Where early modern Europeans agonized over the dangers of homosexual activity in a union involving a hermaphrodite, medieval Muslims had other concerns: incest taboos and modesty. Although homosexuality is disapproved in Islam, it does not seem to have been a part of the hierarchy of concerns informing the negotiation of gender in law.

If medieval Muslim jurists had an overriding anxiety, it was not any of the particular concerns—incest taboos, modesty, segregation, or even hierarchy—that organized their negotiation of gender, but maintaining the gendered integrity of their world as a whole. Their received view of the world was as a place with only two sexes, male and female. In this, medieval Muslims were closer to modern Americans than, say, to the ancient Greeks. Their interpretation of the khuntha mushkil was embedded in this bipolar view of the world. A person with ambiguous genitalia or with no apparent sex might have been a biological reality, but it had no gender and, therefore, no point of entry into the social world: it was unsocialized.

In this world where everyone had to be gendered, a person without gender could not be socialized. Such a person could not participate in ritual, in itself a profoundly communal and social activity, until it had been artificially gendered. Hermaphrodites were usually gendered in the world of ritual as female.

Sex and gender were social matters with implications for whole groups—especially because of the complex familial and household networks that characterized medieval Islamic societies. The presence of one ungendered person, as we have seen, could compel an entire network to hold in abeyance questions of marriage, inheritance, and relation to one another. Even the efforts by the jurists to normalize the hermaphrodite in order to permit the continued formation of marital ties, for example, could not be entirely successful. Ultimately, the interpretation of those relationships was suspended until the sex of the hermaphrodite was known. In this world, the ungendered person was not only unsocialized, but could desocialize everyone else by compelling them to suspend the normal formation of social and familial ties.

9

"Mildred, Is It Fun to Be a Cripple?" The Culture of Suffering in Mid-Twentieth Century American Catholicism

Robert A. Orsi

*R*obert A. Orsi is an eminent scholar of American Roman Catholic cultural history. His books include The Madonna of 115th Street and Thank You, St. Jude. *This engaging excerpt, taken from* Between Heaven and Earth: The Religious Worlds People Make and the Scholars Who Study Them, *touches upon the mid-twentieth-century Catholic culture of pain, and the intersections of suffering and the erotic in terms of the life experience of his Uncle Sal, who had cerebral palsy. Orsi also provides an historical overview of how this Catholic conception of pain and suffering impacted the bodies of believers. More generally, Orsi's work is especially compelling because of the ways he is able to uncover what he calls "the corporalization of the sacred," the notion that religion imprints the invisible on tangible bodies, thereby rendering the sacred more real and present. In the case of gender and sexuality, such a process is quite obvious.*

A shut-in should let people know he is the same as other people and not from another planet.

SAL CAVALLARO, "A SHUT-IN'S DAY"

To be a handicap does not mean that you are sick or mentally retarded. A handicap can have a full, healthy, happy life, just like their fellow human beings. There is no need for them to be put or live in the back room.

SAL CAVALLARO, "WHO IS HANDICAPPED[?]"

On the first saturday of every month in the 1960s my uncle Sally, who has cerebral palsy, used to go to a different parish in New York City or its suburbs for Mass and devotions in honor of Our Lady of Fatima and then afterwards to a Communion breakfast sponsored by that month's host church. These special outings for "shutins" and "cripples" were organized by the Blue Army of Mary, an association of men and women dedicated to spreading the messages of apocalyptic anti-Communism and personal repentance delivered by Mary at Fatima in 1917. My uncle would be waiting for my father and me in the hallway of his mother's apartment, dressed in a jacket and tie and smoking cigarettes in a long, imitation tortoiseshell holder that my grandmother fitted between the knotted fingers of his left hand. He smoked by holding his forearm stiff on the green leatherette armrest of his wheelchair, then bending his torso forward and bringing his legs up until his lips reached the burning cigarette. He was always afraid that my father wouldn't show up, and as his anxiety mounted, my uncle clenched again and again over his cigarettes so that by the time we got there—always early—the foyer was dense with smoke.

We laid Sally down on his back on the front seat of the car. My grandmother, in an uncharacteristic moment of hope and trust, had taken my uncle as a boy to a mysterious doctor on the Lower East Side who said he could make him walk. Instead, he had locked Sally's legs at the knees, sticking straight out in front of him, fusing him into a ninety-degree angle, and then had vanished. Sally reached back, hooked his right wrist into the steering wheel, and pulled himself in while we pushed. When he was in the car up to his legs, my father leaned in over him and drew him up. He angled my uncle's stiff limbs under the dashboard and wedged them in.

My father went around the car and dropped in the other side. He looked over at his brother-in-law, the two of them sweating and panting. "Okay?" he asked. My uncle nodded back.

We drove to a designated meeting place, usually another church's parking lot, where members of the Blue Army, wearing sky-blue armbands printed with an image of the Virgin of Fatima and the legend "Legion of Mary," helped us pull my uncle out of the car. Other cripples were arriving. The members of the Blue Army knew who wanted to sit next to each other, and they wheeled my uncle's friends over to him, locking them in place beside him. He greeted them solemnly, not saying very much. From here a big yellow school bus would take the cripples out to the church; we'd follow in the car. My uncle was anxious to get going.

The wheelers teased him in loud voices whenever they brought a woman over. "Here's your girlfriend!" they shouted. "I saw her talking to So-and-So yesterday! Aren't you jealous?! You're gonna lose this beautiful girl! Come on, Sal, wake up." They pounded my uncle on the back. "Don't you know a good thing when you got it?" Their voices and gestures were exaggerated, as if they were speaking to someone who couldn't understand their language.

The women rolled their heads back and laughed with bright, moaning sounds, while their mothers fussed at their open mouths with little embroidered handkerchiefs, dabbing at saliva. "Calm down, calm down," they admonished their daughters, "don't get so excited."

My uncle laughed too, but he always looked over at me and shook his head.

There was a statue of San Rocco on a side altar of the Franciscan church of my childhood. The saint's body was covered with open, purple sores; tending to the bodies of plague victims, he had been infected himself. A small dog licked the open sores on his hands. The Franciscans told us that Saint Francis kissed a leper's sores. Once he drank the water he had just used to bathe a leper.

One woman, a regular of the First Saturday outings, came on a stretcher covered with clean sheets in pale, pastel colors; her body was immobile. She twisted her eyes up and looked out at us through a mirror fixed to the side of the stretcher, while her mother tugged at her dress to make sure it stayed down around her thin ankles.

These were special people, God's children, chosen by him for a special destiny. Innocent victims, cheerful sufferers, God's most beloved—this was the litany of the handicapped on these First Saturdays. Finding themselves in front of an unusual congregation, priests were moved to say from the pulpit at mass that the prayers of cripples were more powerful than anyone else's because God listened most attentively to these, his special children. Nuns circulated among the cripples, touching their limbs kindly and reverently, telling them how blessed they were, and how wonderful. To be standing these mornings in a parking lot or church basement was to be on ground made holy by the presence of beds and wheelchairs and twisted bodies.

At breakfast, the mothers of the cripples hovered over them. They held plastic straws, bent in the middle like my uncle, while their children drank coffee or juice; they cut Danishes into bite-sized pieces; they cleaned up spills. Volunteers from the parish and members of the Blue Army brought out plates of eggs and sausage.

"You have such a big appetite this morning!"

"Can you eat all that? God bless you!"

"If I ate like you I'd be even fatter than I am!"

But why had God done this to his most beloved children? What kind of love was this? What kind of God?

When he was done with his coffee, my uncle cupped himself around his cigarette.

Physical distress of all sorts, from conditions like cerebral palsy to the unexpected agonies of accidents and illness, was understood by American Catholics in the middle years of the last century as an individual's main opportunity for spiritual growth. Pain purged and disciplined the ego, stripping it of pride and self-love; it disclosed the emptiness of the world. Without it, human beings remained pagans; in physical distress, they might find their way back to the Church, and to sanctity. "Suffering makes saints," one hospital chaplain told his congregation of sick people, "of many who in health were indifferent to the practices of their holy religion." Pain was a ladder to heaven. The saints were unhappy unless they were in physical distress of some sort.

Catholic nurses were encouraged to watch for opportunities on their rounds to help lapsed Catholics renew their faith and even to convert non-Catholics in the promising circumstances of physical distress.

Pain was always the thoughtful prescription of the Divine Physician. The cancer afflicting Thomas Dooley, the handsome young doctor and missionary to Southeast Asia in the 1950s who completely captured American Catholic hearts, was celebrated in Catholic popular culture as a grace, a mark of divine favor. Dooley himself wrote, "God has been good to me. He has given me the most hideous, painful cancer at an extremely young age." So central was pain to the American Catholic ethos that devotional writers sometimes went as far as to equate it with life itself—"The good days are a respite," declared a laywoman writing in a devotional magazine in 1950, "granted to us so that we can endure the bad days."

Catholics thrilled to describe the body in pain. Devotional prose was generally overwrought, but on this subject it exceeded itself. There was an excess of a certain kind of sensuous detail in Catholic accounts of pain and suffering, a delicious lingering over and savoring of other people's pain. A dying man is presented in a story in a 1937 issue of the devotional magazine *Ave Maria* as having "lain [for twenty-one years] on the broad of his back, suffering from arthritis . . . his hands and fingers so distorted that he could not raise them more than an inch . . . his teeth set . . . so physically handicapped that in summer he could not brush away a fly or mosquito from his face because of his condition." It was never enough in this aesthetic to say simply "cancer," stark as that word is. Instead, it had to be the "cancer that is all pain." Wounds always "throbbed," suffering was always "untold," pain invariably took its victims to the very limits of endurance.

The body-in-pain was thrilling. Flushed, feverish, and beautiful—"The sick room is rather a unique beauty shop," one priest mused, where "pain has worked more wonders than cosmetics"—it awaited its lover. A woman visiting a Catholic hospital in 1929 came upon a little Protestant girl who was dying and reported:

> He has set His mark upon her. Somehow you guess; those frail little shoulders are shaped for a cross, those eyes are amber chalices deep enough for pain, that grave little courteous heart is big enough to hold Him! He will yet be her tremendous lover, drawing her gently into His white embrace, bestowing on her the sparkling, priceless pledge of His love—suffering.

Pain had the character of a sacrament, offering the sufferer a uniquely immediate and intimate experience of Jesus' presence. Walking amid the "couches of pain" laid out for the sunset service at Lourdes, an American visitor suddenly sensed that "he is here now. . . . Almost I can hear him speak,—almost I can reach out and touch his garment." Another writer reported that she knew "a very holy nun who is herself one of God's chosen ones" (meaning that she is afflicted with the most severe pain), "and one day she said something to me that I have never forgotten. She said, 'Sometimes God's hand seems to rest so heavily upon our shoulder, and we try to squirm away, and we cry, Oh, let me be! And then we begin to realize how tender as well as how heavy is His hand, and we want it there.'"

This was a darkly erotic aesthetic of pain, one expression of the wider romanticism of American Catholicism in this period. But for all this culture's fascination with physical distress, the sensual pleasure it took in feverish descriptions of suffering, it was also deeply resentful and suspicious of sick persons. A nasty edge of retribution and revenge is evident in these accounts. In one priest's typical cautionary tale of pain, "a young woman of Dallas, Texas, a scandal to her friends for having given up her faith because it interfered with her sinful life, was severely burned in an explosion. Before her death, through the grace of God, she returned to the Church." According to a nursing sister, writing in the leading American Catholic journal for hospital professionals, *Hospital Progress,* in 1952: "Physical disability wears off the veneer of sophistication and forces the acceptance of reality. It is difficult for a patient imprisoned for weeks in a traction apparatus to live in a state of illusion." Pain gives people their comeuppance. It serves as chastisement and judgment.

The Catholic tradition was ambivalent about the moral status of the sick. Despite constant injunctions to the contrary, a persistent identification was made between sickness and sin—not only sin in general or Original Sin, but the specific sinfulness of the person in pain—and the suspicion of all physical suffering as merited was never completely absent from devotional culture. "You may complain and moan about a single toothache," Father Boniface Buckley chided the readers of *Sign* in 1945, but be "woefully forgetful of the fact that this particular pain may be due in justice for some sin of that very day." God always has a reason for sending pain. Theology's restraint is evident here in Father Buckley's use of the conditional. More commonly, devotional writers threw such cautions to the winds in order to score some moral points with pain. Learn to take your pain the way a man takes his hangover, another priest scolded, and admit that "you asked for it."

The association between physical sickness and moral corruption was reinforced throughout American Catholic popular literature by the persistent use of metaphors of illness to describe threats to the social fabric and sources of political and moral decay. As the editor of *Ave Maria* put it, aphoristically, in 1932, "Error is due to thought germs," against which only mental and moral hygiene is an effective prophylactic. Another writer even suggested that to visit the sick was to "stand by the bedside of our soul-sick world." The persistent metaphorical use of leprosy to excoriate various moral dangers was so egregious in the Catholic press that missionaries among sufferers of Hansen's disease regularly complained of the effect this usage was having on the people in their care. This was not an unusual rhetorical device, of course, but it achieved its own peculiar, disorienting resonance in Catholic devotionalism, where images of the body-in-pain were used to suggest both the depths of corruption and the highest reaches of spiritual glory. In the case of the leper, the two discrepant usages converged: the leper was at once physically—and morally—scrofulous and (potentially) sacred.

As American Catholics interpreted an ancient tradition in their contemporary circumstances, the idea that sickness was punishment for something the sufferer had done took deeper hold. The more sentimental view of sickness as the training ground for saintliness was commonly reserved for people with genetic or birth trauma conditions, such as Sal and his friends. Their suffering, at least, could not be attributed to any moral failure since they were born this way. The innocence of people born with disabilities made them central to the elaboration of the gothic romance of suffering; because they were "innocent," unalloyed spiritual pleasure could be taken in the brokenness of their bodies. There was a cult of the "shut-in" among American Catholics in the middle years of the twentieth century, a fascination with "cripples" and a desire to be in some relation to them, which was thought to carry spiritual advantages. In the summer of 1939, *Catholic Women's World,* one of the most modern and upbeat of the Catholic magazines, set up a pen-pal system so that readers going away on vacation could write to shut-ins about their trips. The project was so popular that "many readers have written to us requesting that we put them in touch not only with one, but as many as three or four shut-ins." There were a number of organizations dedicated to harnessing the spiritual power of shut-ins and putting it to work for the rest of the church, such as the Catholic Union of the Sick in America (CUSA), which formed small cells of isolated handicapped persons who communicated through a round-robin letter and whose assignment was to direct their petitions, more powerful by virtue of their pain, toward some specific social good. The spiritual pleasure taken by the volunteers on the First Saturdays in their proximity to the handicapped was a reflection of this cult as well.

But the mistrust of the sick, the suspicion that their physical distress was the manifestation of a moral failing, lurked just below the surface of even the fantasy of the holy cripple. The eleventh-century "cripple" Hermann, who composed the Marian hymn "Salve Regina," is described in one article as having been "pleasant, friendly, always laughing, never criticizing, so that everybody *loved* him." Concluding, "What a record for a cripple!" the author implies that just the opposite could have been expected from a man like this. The subtext here is that if Hermann had not been so delightful, he would not have deserved love—there was nothing unconditional about this culture's affection for cripples.

Apart from these "fortunate unfortunates," a favorite Catholic term for people with disabilities, however ambivalently construed, sick people were guilty people, and, not surprisingly, they behaved as such. Sick people were generally depicted as malingering, whining, selfish, overly preoccupied with their own problems, indolent, maladjusted, and self-destructive. They exaggerated the extent of their distress. They were quick to yield to despair and loneliness. Wake up to the fact that life is a vale of tears, one priest scolded the ill, and get rid of your "Pollyanna attitude," by which he meant stop hoping for relief. Above all, the sick could not be trusted. Without the astringent of religion, for example, lepers—even beloved lepers—would be "spiteful, cynical, and debauched," according to one visitor to Molokai, and this was maintained as generally true of all sick people. As late as 1965, a Dominican priest writing in *Ave Maria* derided a sick person as a "spoiled child" and warned against "the tendency to remain in our suffering, to exaggerate the injustice, to pout."

But what exactly constituted complaint? Were devotional teachers warning in these passages against the sometimes dark and self-defeating human impulse to protest the will of God or to rebel against the facts of life?

One Saturday the bus didn't come. Something had happened somewhere along its route. The hot summer's morning dragged on; the sidewalk around Sal's chair was littered with cigarette butts; and the garbled messages—there'd been a crash, no, it was just a flat tire, he'll be here any minute, he's upstate—from the people in charge of the outing, meant to be reassuring, just made the confusion and anxiety worse.

A man I didn't recognize, not one of the Blue Army regulars, strolled over to the back of Sal's chair and gripped its rubber handles as if he were going to push my uncle off someplace. He winked at me and my father. Maybe Sal knew him from someplace. "So, Sal," he boomed at the back of my uncle's head, sounding pleased with his own cheerfulness, "looks like you're gonna have to spend the night in this parking lot, hunh?"

My uncle gave an angry wave of dismissal, but the man behind him, comfortably resting his weight on his chair, went on. "Hey, Sal, you hear what I said? You're gonna have to spend the night out here in the parking lot! I hope you got your blankets! Maybe we can get the girls over there to sing you a lullaby."

My uncle rocked himself from side to side in his seat, as if he wanted to dislodge the man's grip on his chair and move him out from behind his back. Bored with the game, the man let go. "Jesus, I hope we get the hell out of here soon," he said to my father, and walked away.

Sal smacked the brakes off his chair with his hard, calloused hands and began to spin himself around in circles. My father tried to calm him down. "Sally," he said, "the bus'll be here any minute, I know it. It's probably just a flat tire. Come on, don't get like this, you're gonna make yourself sick." But my uncle went on spinning. "Ahhhhhh," he roared, "ahhhhhh."

Everyone teased the cripples, joked with them, and needled them almost all the time. This may have been what the man behind Sally's chair was doing, but I don't think so. He was sweaty and angry. Maybe he was only there that morning because of his wife's devotion to Our Lady of Fatima; maybe he hated cripples and the stories they told about the human body, of all that could and did go wrong with it. He had bent forward, over the back of Sally's head and stared down at his bald crown and coarse gray hair. Maybe he hated the way the cripples drooled when they sucked up their coffee and juice on these Saturday mornings or the mess they made of Communion breakfast.

My uncle began to push himself along the parking lot's chain-link fence, hitting the wheels of his chair with hard shoves. When he got to the end of the fence, where it connected with the church, he spun himself around and began pounding his way back.

Maybe the man found it hard to sustain the idea that Sal and his friends were holier than he was, closer to heaven, when they sprayed him with saliva and bits of egg.

My uncle wheeled around again and started back along the fence.

"This is the only guy I know," my father said to me, "who can pace in a wheelchair."

Someone came over and demanded that Sal stop. "Control yourself! These things happen, Sal," she yelled at him, bending to lock his chair in place, but my uncle pushed her hand away and kept moving.

The morning wore on, and the fortunate unfortunates, disappointed and upset, got on everybody's nerves.

"Complaint" meant any sound that the sick might make, any use of their voices, whether it was to ask for a glass of water in the middle of the night, to question a doctor's decisions, to express a spiritual doubt, or to request that their bodies be shifted in bed. Hospitalized sick people who complained of physical discomfort were referred to in the *Voice of Saint Jude,* a periodical published at the Chicago shrine of the patron saint of hopeless causes, as "c.t.m.p.'s" ("cantankerous, tempestuous, maladjusted patients".) There was only one officially sanctioned way to suffer even the most excruciating distress: with bright, upbeat, uncomplaining, submissive endurance. A woman dying horribly of an unspecified cancer was commended by *Ave Maria* for having written "cheerful, newsy notes" home from the hospital, with "only casual references to her illness." In the spirit of a fashion editor, one devotional writer counseled the chronically ill to "learn to wear [your] sickness becomingly. It can be done. It has been done. Put a blue ribbon bow on your bedjacket and smile." Visitors were instructed to urge their sick friends and kin to make the best use of their time; the sick should be happily busy and productive even in the most extreme pain. "Only two percent of the various types of pain are permanent and continual," wrote Mary O'Connor in an *Ave Maria* article for the sick in 1951. She was onto their games. She knew they were likely to "wallow in the muck of self-pity or sympathy": "If the sieges of pain let up a little now and then, take up an interesting hobby and throw yourself into it with all you've got. You'll be delighted to find that your pain is lessening as a result." Her own experience was exemplary in this regard: since the onset of her pain a decade earlier, she had written over two thousand poems, articles, and stories.

If such pitiless badgering failed to arouse the sick, against their sinful inclinations, to saintliness, there was always the scourge of the suffering of Jesus and Mary: no matter how severe your suffering, the sick were told, Jesus' and Mary's were worse, and *they* never complained. What is a migraine compared to the crown of thorns.? Who could ever suffer a loss like Mary's? Jesus' suffering served the same purpose as Mary's virtue in devotional culture: to diminish the integrity and meaning of ordinary persons' difficulties and experiences. Indeed, there was a hierarchy of scorn for sick people: just as Jesus' suffering outweighed all human pain, so truly awful pain was used to diminish anything less, and all physical distress was greater than any psychological trouble, in a pyramid of suffering with Jesus, all bloody, and Mary, modestly sorrowing, at its top. Leprosy, in particular, functioned in this ethos as a means of denying other forms of physical distress, which partially accounts for its ubiquity. The message to sick people was: someone else is always suffering more than you are—look at the lepers!—and besides, Jesus suffered most of all, so be quiet!

In this way, the priests, nuns, and laypeople writing for the many devotional magazines and diocesan newspapers that made up the popular literary culture of American Catholicism waged a campaign against men and women in physical or emotional distress. The saint offered as patron to the sick in this century was Gemma Galgani, who used violence against herself when she was ill, adding self-inflicted pain to the distress of disease so that she might "subdue even the faintest suggestion of rebellion on the part of the flesh against the spirit", and if sick people would not subdue their own flesh as Saint Gemma had done hers, if they could not bedeck their own pain in ribbons, it would be done for them. (I will return to Saint Gemma Galgani in chapter 4.) The language used against people in pain was harsh and cruel, devoid of compassion or understanding, and dismissive of their experience. As one priest demanded, if a child spends "seven or nine years" in an iron lung, "what of it?" There was only scorn, never sympathy, for the sick who failed to become saintly through pain. Bending the idioms and images of popular religion against them so that even the suffering of Christ emerged as a reproach, devotional writers crafted a rhetoric of mortification and denial for the sick. This was particularly cruel since they were doing so in the language and venues of popular devotionalism, to which sick people customarily turned for spiritual and emotional comfort.

The consequence of this rhetoric was that pain itself—the awful, frightening reality of something going wrong in the body—disappeared. It was hidden behind the insistence that the sick be cheerful, productive, orderly; it was masked by the condescending assurances offered to the shut-in handicapped, offered by those who were not, that it was better to be a cripple; it was occluded by the shimmering, overheated prose, the excited fascination with physical torment, and the scorn and contempt for the sick. There is not nearly as much suffering in the world as people complain of, chided a writer in the pages of *Ave Maria*—two years after the end of the First World War. I enjoyed my week with the lepers of Molokai," a traveler exclaimed as if he had not been sojourning among people he had just described as looking "more like corpses than human beings." Chronic illness brought families together in special joy and intimacy, according to these writers. Even Jesus' pain could be denied: lest they find in his Passion an expression of the reality of their own experience, the sick were occasionally reminded that, since he had been conceived without Original Sin, Jesus himself was never sick—the risk of Docetism apparently less troubling than that of compassion. It was in this spirit that William P. McCahill, executive secretary of the President's Committee on National Employ the Physically Handicapped Week, could report with approval a child's question to a handicapped person, "Mildred, is it fun to be a cripple?" Yes, it is! McCahill assured his readers.

Physical distress that had been thus purged of its everyday messiness, of the limits it imposed on the body, and of the dreariness of its persistence could be transmuted into its opposite. "Pain" became a "harvest" ripe for the gathering, a spiritual "powerhouse" that could light the church, a vein of gold to be mined, minted, and spent. "It isn't suffering that's the tragedy," one of CUSA's mottoes proclaims, "only wasted suffering." In a 1953 meditation that mixed several of these transformative metaphors, Florence Waters urged the readers of *Ave Maria* to "travel the length and breadth of the country and add them up—the cardiacs, and arthritics, the cerebral palsied, the paraplegics, the amputees, the blind, the congenitally malformed, and the victims of countless other ills that tie human bodies to beds, wheelchairs, crutches, to one room or one house." What does all this add up to?—"A vast storehouse of spiritual power." In "stark, unadorned pain, mental and physical," Waters concluded, there is "a subtle but true coin that may be exchanged for spiritual goods for ourselves."

So pain was alienable: coined from the bodies of the (untrustworthy) sick, it could be taken away and applied to the welfare of the healthy in a redistributive economy of distress. God apparently sent pain to some people so that others might be edified, making the bodies of the sick conduits of communications and benefits from heaven to earth. But, again, actual sick people, the real persons suffering from specific illnesses in precise ways, got lost in this process.

Since all pain was God-sent and good, and since it was never in any case as bitter as weak, whining sick people made it out to be, there was no need to account for its place in the universe, to respond to the spiritual and intellectual distress it might have occasioned. Protestants required this, perhaps, but not Catholics, who knew that God sent pain always for a purpose; and priests, who might have been expected to sympathize most compassionately with the spiritual and physical dilemmas of the sick, were said to be always cheerful in the presence of suffering because, unlike their counterparts in other faiths, they knew that the problem of pain had been "solved." In any case, as American devotional writers reminded the sick, comprehensible suffering was not real suffering. Catholics were said to prefer to suffer humbly and submissively, in recognition of their own guilt, rather than attempting to lessen the sting of it through understanding. Only spoiled children required such reassurance.

The crew of Italian, Irish, Puerto Rican, and West Indian janitors, kitchen workers, handymen, and gardeners who hid out from their supervisors in the boiler room of the House of the Holy Comforter (a residence on the Grand Concourse in the Bronx to which my uncle moved in the mid-1960s) had a lot to say about the sexuality of the cripples in the rooms above them. A soft-voiced Italian American man named Aldo usually started these conversations. "Hey, I was up there the other night, they had them in the showers—Jesus Christ, have you ever seen Jimmy's dick? It's like this . . ." He opened his hands about a foot wide. "They all got big dicks," someone else affirmed knowledgeably, and then the men would speculate about whether or not having such huge organs was another consequence of their being cripples, as if nature compensated there for the ravages elsewhere. Aldo was always kind and extremely attentive to the men with cerebral palsy who lived at the "home," stopping on his rounds through the floors to talk with them, bringing them things to eat from the kitchen between meals, but in the boiler room he returned again and again to the subject of cripples and sex. I was shocked, when I went to work at the House of the

Holy Comforter in the summer after my first year of college, to encounter this other Aldo, so different from the one I knew upstairs, and he didn't spare me his fantasies of my uncle's sex life.

Often Aldo, less frequently one of the other men, sat next to Sally on the long back porch of the home and commented on the women walking past them along the garden walkways below. Leaning into Sally, he'd murmur, "Look at that one, Sal. What would you like to do with her?" He made a cupping motion with his hands. "Just one night, hah, Sally, what we couldn't do. Jesus, Mary, and Saint Anthony." My uncle seemed comfortable and happy during these conversations, apparently delighted with Aldo's company and enjoying their salacious bond, although I'm not sure of this.

The men in the boiler room claimed that in the early hours of the morning, the cripples crawled out of bed and wheeled themselves into the shadows for blow jobs from the few women with cerebral palsy living at the home. This was absolutely impossible, of course, if only for practical reasons: none of the residents could get out of their criblike beds by themselves, and there were no deep shadows' in the well-lit building and no times when there were not nurses and orderlies everywhere. But none of the men in the boiler room, who were cynical and skeptical about everything else, ever questioned Aldo's tales of the cripples' nocturnal sexual carnival.

10

Discussion Questions

1 Why is it that we cannot assume "the body" means the same thing in different historical and religious contexts? Explain your answer by using examples of how the human body is understood and dealt with in the readings.

2 From a religious perspective, what does it mean to say that certain individuals or groups of persons are "reduced to their bodies?" Why has that been so often the case? What might be the implications of this?

3 Are some bodies more problematic than others for religion? Describe some of the alternative ways that religious communities have classified bodies. How might these classifications shape the thought and practice of these communities with respect to sexuality and gender?

4 Can the ways in which a religious tradition understands the body or bodies of its holy or sacred figures (gods, goddesses, saintly people, etc.) have a bearing on how they view human bodies more generally? Give examples from different traditions.

5 Can the human body really be distinguished from sexuality and gender? Answer this question in light of some of the readings which address religious attitudes toward, and representations of, women's bodies.

6 Many religious traditions emphasize the importance of disciplining or controlling the body as ways of attaining a state of enlightenment or salvation, especially with regard to sexual desire or practices. Why is that? How might this be viewed in our contemporary world, and why?

7 The introduction to this section claims that religious institutions generally have an ambivalent attitude when it comes to the human body. Discuss this by providing a variety of examples from both the readings and your own knowledge and experience.

8 How does your own religious tradition, or religious traditions with which you might be familiar, view the human body as a means of sexual or erotic expression? Compare and contrast this with some other religious or spiritual perspectives.

9   Why is it that the bodies of LGBTIQ persons are seen as particularly
    problematic or a source of tension and even repulsion in a number of religious
    traditions? Might they be the same reasons why these religious traditions so
    often problematize women's bodies?

10 Discuss some of the intersections between and among sexuality, gender,
    race, ethnicity, and religion. Are their perspectives on the body coherent or
    discordant, and why?

PART TWO

Desires

1

Introduction

In the church of Santa Maria della Vittoria in Rome, there is a famous white marble statue by the Italian Baroque sculptor Bernini. Called *The Ecstasy of Saint Teresa*, it shows the great Spanish Catholic mystic, Teresa of Avila (1515–82), experiencing one of her mystical visions. It depicts an episode from her life where she recounts that her heart was pierced by a golden spear held by a young angel, and the pain was so great that she moaned with exquisite pleasure. What is particularly striking about this sculpture is the look on Teresa's face. It is that of a woman in the throes of orgasmic pleasure. Her head is thrown back, her eyes are semi-closed, and her mouth is slightly open as though she were moaning. Few works of art represent so well the thin line that exists between erotic and religious desire. Nor are any as beautiful.

This section on "Desires" examines the intersections of religion, the erotic, and pleasure. Some religious traditions have occasionally had a highly problematic or ambivalent rapport with human sexual desire, often decrying it as dirty, sinful, or corrupt. Such stigmatization has had particularly devastating effects on marginalized individuals and sexual communities, often resulting in discrimination or persecution. Discussions around religion and sexuality have therefore tended to shy away from some of the more seemingly explicit or controversial aspects of human sexual diversity and practices, or they tend to define some desires and pleasures as especially suspect or questionable, while others are not because they are deemed "normal." On the other hand, and equally significant, many religious devotees, believers, and participants have understood human erotic desire as the best and most worthwhile path to an experience of the sacred or the holy, and they have used the language of human eroticism to describe such an experience. This is common among the great mystics of the world's religious traditions. Human sexual desires and pleasures are therefore neither suspect nor problematic, but rather highly diversified and multifaceted. This section of the reader not only considers how religious people conceptualize desire and pleasure differently; it also includes readings that move deliberately beyond a narrow and limiting heteronormative paradigm of human eroticism. The varieties of ways in which human beings understand desire and pleasure, and the words they use to link that with their experience of the sacred or the holy, are limited, in fact, only by the shortfalls of our own imaginations.

As much as human bodies can quite often be a source of problematic ambivalence for some religious traditions, human desires can be equally if not more challenging. There are many reasons for this. We all have desires of some sort, and these can be quite varied. At times, our desires appear mainstream, while at others they might be seen as "deviant" or even "aberrant." Our desires can be quite secret, or they can be shared rather publicly within a particular sexual community. The sources of our desires are often hidden and mysterious, or they can, in fact, be known and defiantly accepted. In a way, one could also say that human desire is limitless. It is constrained only by our imaginations and, more broadly, by cultural norms and expectations. It is precisely because our desires are so abundant, multifaceted, and infinite that many religious institutions, when faced with them, reveal themselves to be so cautious, fearful, or vigilant. They foster concerns about the appropriateness of human desire in religious contexts, and they try to circumscribe carefully both its parameters and its forms of expression.

Yet desire is not solely or exclusively a question of the erotic and the sexual; religions themselves elicit and nurture desire from their adherents. If one speaks of a loving God, that is a statement of desire. If one performs sacrifices or rituals in order to honor or worship a deity, those are ways of manifesting desire. If one seeks to attain union with the infinite or with some sacred being, that is an expression of desire. In fact, humans can only relate to the holy or the sacred through the language and imagery of desire, especially erotic desire, because that is the most intimate way that we have of experiencing oneness and completion with another. Desire is definitely not foreign to religion; rather, it stands at its very heart. St. Teresa of Avila and other mystics had to use the language of human erotic longing to express most authentically and most fully their experience of mystical union with the source of their ultimate desire.

In religious terms, some forms of desire, as with bodies, might be considered more illicit, dangerous, or perilous than others. Once again, desire that is considered nonnormative in terms of its focus or its object can come under suspicion, and this is particularly true as regards same-sex desire. Religions have adopted a broad spectrum of positions and attitudes with respect to same-sex desire. Many Christian traditions, as with Islam and certain forms of Judaism, abhor and condemn same-sex behavior, while others are more accepting of sexual diversity. Many other traditions tend to favor a less problematic perspective. Some religions run the gamut from full acceptance to complete condemnation. Same-sex desire—how far it should be accepted, celebrated, promoted, or legally protected—has become a major cultural and religious flashpoint in many parts of the world. Some Christian churches, such as Anglicanism, are facing major cleavages over the issue. Nonheterosexual expressions of erotic desire, of whatever form and variety, still continue to elicit strong and passionate reactions from religions.

The readings for this section offer an unusually rich collection of texts about desire and religion. The reading by Paul Gordon Schalow examines expressions of male same-sex desire in Japanese Buddhism. The selection from David Biale looks at Judaism and the ways it has sought to regulate desire and sexual practices within heterosexual marriage. The question can be asked whether some of the norms and observances discussed would remain equally relevant within the context of a same-sex marriage. Eve Sedgwick reminds us quite eloquently how remarkably diverse and unpredictable human beings can be in the expressions of their desires. The passage from Michael Foucault's groundbreaking work on human sexuality—dealing with sex as discourse and the Christian rite of confession—brings to the fore an important question about the ways in which our desires are so often ways of positioning ourselves within relations of power. It also points unmistakably to the role of religious discourse and religious ritual, most certainly in the West, in the construction, elaboration, and maintenance of varieties and types of erotic desire and their expressions in sexual identities. Amy Hollywood, in her text on medieval beguines, provides a telling analysis of the ways in which these religious women were able to express their spiritual desires in "queer" ways, transcending the normative heterosexual paradigms of their time. Finally, the readings by Mark Jordan, Zeb Tortorici, and Michael Warner, all Christian in focus, deal respectively with queer desire, masturbatory religious passions, and Pentecostal gay desire. All three offer insights into the wonderfully complex and nuanced ways that erotic desire can inflect religious desire and vice-versa. These texts remind us that the line between these two forms of desire is a very porous and permeable one.

If one listens carefully to the ways in which religious practitioners speak about their faith or their beliefs, one will routinely be struck by the language used. Quite often, romantic imagery or expressions will be used; in some cases, erotic metaphors are chosen. This is most certainly not because humans choose poorly or haphazardly when it comes to talking about their religious or spiritual experiences. Rather, it points to the noteworthy fact that our bodies and the desires which inhabit them are instrumental in our apprehension of the sacred. This should not shock, unsettle, or frighten us or the religious institutions of which we may be a part. Rather, it should "gladden our hearts," as the saying goes, reminding us that our desires, longings, and cravings, of whatever hue or temperament they may be, are all we bring to our encounter with the ineffable.

2

Introduction:

Axiomatic

Eve Kosofsky Sedgwick

*E*ve Kosofsky Sedgwick (1950–2009) was a scholar, literary critic, and poet whose work on sexual identity helped to establish queer studies. This excerpt is taken from her foundational book, Epistemology of the Closet. Sedgwick reads nineteenth- and twentieth-century writers (including Melville, Wilde, Proust) to show that sexual identity, constructed as a binary of male homo/heterosexual difference, perniciously dominates modern ideas of what it means to be a person. The excerpt recounts one of Sedgwick's presuppositions in the book: people are different. In highlighting this claim, she exposes the limits of homo/heterosexual definition for our sexual and erotic lives.

Axiom 1: People are different from each other

It is astonishing how few respectable conceptual tools we have for dealing with this self-evident fact. A tiny number of inconceivably coarse axes of categorization have been painstakingly inscribed in current critical and political thought: gender, race, class, nationality, sexual orientation are pretty much the available distinctions. They, with the associated demonstrations of the mechanisms by which they are constructed and reproduced, are indispensable, and they may indeed override all or some other forms of difference and similarity. But the sister or brother, the best friend, the classmate, the parent, the child, the lover, the ex-: our families, loves, and enmities alike, not to mention the strange relations of our work, play, and activism, prove that even people who share all or most of our own positionings along these crude axes may still be different enough from us, and from each other, to seem like all but different species.

Everybody has learned this, I assume, and probably everybody who survives at all has reasonably rich, unsystematic resources of nonce taxonomy for mapping out the possibilities, dangers, and stimulations of their human social landscape. It is probably people with the experience of oppression or subordination who have most *need* to know it; and I take the precious, devalued arts of gossip, immemorially associated in European thought with servants, with effeminate and gay men, with all women, to have to do not even so much with the transmission of necessary news as with the refinement of necessary skills for making, testing, and using unrationalized and provisional hypotheses about what *kinds of people* there are to be found in one's world. The writing of a Proust or a James would be exemplary here: projects precisely of *nonce* taxonomy, of the making and unmaking and *re*making and redissolution of hundreds of old and new categorical imaginings concerning all the kinds it may take to make up a world.

I don't assume that all gay men or all women are very skilled at the nonce-taxonomic work represented by gossip, but it does make sense to suppose that our distinctive needs are peculiarly disserved by its devaluation. For some people, the sustained, foregrounded pressure of loss in the AIDS years may be making such needs clearer: as one anticipates or tries to deal with the absence of people one loves, it seems absurdly impoverishing to surrender to theoretical trivialization or to "the sentimental" one's descriptive requirements that the piercing bouquet of a given friend's particularity be done some justice. What is more dramatic is that—in spite of every promise to the contrary—every single theoretically or politically interesting project of postwar thought has finally had the effect of delegitimating our space for asking or thinking in detail about the multiple, unstable ways in which people may be like or different from each other. This project is not rendered otiose by any demonstration of how fully people may differ also from themselves. Deconstruction, founded as a very science of *différ(e/a)nce,* has both so fetishized the idea of difference and so vaporized its possible embodiments that its most thoroughgoing practitioners are the last people to whom one would now look for help in thinking about particular differences. The same thing seems likely to prove true of theorists of postmodernism. Psychoanalytic theory, if only through the almost astrologically lush plurality of its overlapping taxonomies of physical zones, developmental stages, representational mechanisms, and levels of consciousness, seemed to promise to introduce a certain becoming amplitude into discussions of what different people are like—only to turn, in its streamlined trajectory across so many institutional boundaries, into the sveltest of metatheoretical disciplines, sleeked down to such elegant operational entities as *the* mother, *the* father, *the* preoedipal, *the* oedipal, *the* other or Other. Within the less theorized institutional confines of intrapsychoanalytic discourse, meanwhile, a narrowly and severely normative, difference-eradicating ethical program has long sheltered under developmental narratives and a metaphorics of health and pathology. In more familiar ways, Marxist, feminist, postcolonial, and other engagé critical projects have deepened understandings of a few crucial axes of difference, perhaps necessarily at the expense of more ephemeral or less global impulses of differential grouping.

In each of these inquiries, so much has been gained by the different ways we have learned to deconstruct the category of *the individual* that it is easy for us now to read, say, Proust as the most expert operator of our modern technologies for dismantling taxonomies of the person. For the emergence and persistence of the vitalizing worldly taxonomic energies on which Proust also depends, however, we have no theoretical support to offer. And these defalcations in our indispensable antihumanist discourses have apparently ceded the potentially forceful ground of profound, complex variation to humanist liberal "tolerance" or repressively trivializing celebration at best, to reactionary suppression at worst.

This is among other things a way of saying that there is a large family of things *we know* and need to know about ourselves and each other with which we have, as far as I can see, so far created for ourselves almost no theoretical room to deal. The shifting interfacial resistance of "literature itself" to "theory" may mark, along with its other denotations, the surface tension of this reservoir of unrationalized nonce-taxonomic energies; but, while distinctively representational, these energies are in no sense peculiarly literary.

In the particular area of sexuality, for instance, I assume that most of us know the following things that can differentiate even people of identical gender, race, nationality, class, and "sexual orientation"—each one of which, however, if taken seriously as pure *difference,* retains the unaccounted-for potential to disrupt many forms of the available thinking about sexuality.

- Even identical genital acts mean very different things to different people.

- To some people, the nimbus of "the sexual" seems scarcely to extend beyond the boundaries of discrete genital acts; to others, it enfolds them loosely or floats virtually free of them.

- Sexuality makes up a large share of the self-perceived identity of some people, a small share of others'.

- Some people spend a lot of time thinking about sex, others little.

- Some people like to have a lot of sex, others little or none.

- Many people have their richest mental/emotional involvement with sexual acts that they don't do, or even don't *want* to do.

- For some people, it is important that sex be embedded in contexts resonant with meaning, narrative, and connectedness with other aspects of their life; for other people, it is important that they not be; to others it doesn't occur that they might be.

- For some people, the preference for a certain sexual object, act, role, zone, or scenario is so immemorial and durable that it can only be experienced as innate; for others, it appears to come late or to feel aleatory or discretionary.

- For some people, the possibility of bad sex is aversive enough that their lives are strongly marked by its avoidance; for others, it isn't.

- For some people, sexuality provides a needed space of heightened discovery and cognitive hyperstimulation. For others, sexuality provides a needed space of routinized habituation and cognitive hiatus.

- Some people like spontaneous sexual scenes, others like highly scripted ones, others like spontaneous-sounding ones that are nonetheless totally predictable.

- Some people's sexual orientation is intensely marked by autoerotic pleasures and histories—sometimes more so than by any aspect of alloerotic object choice. For others the autoerotic possibility seems secondary or fragile, if it exists at all.

- Some people, homo-, hetero-, and bisexual, experience their sexuality as deeply embedded in a matrix of gender meanings and gender differentials. Others of each sexuality do not.

The list of individual differences could easily be extended. That many of them could differentiate one from another period of the same person's life as well as one person's totality from another's, or that many of them record differentia that can circulate from one person to another, does not, I believe, lessen their authority to demarcate; they demarcate at more than one site and on more than one scale. The impact of such a list may seem to depend radically on a trust in the self-perception, self-knowledge, or self-report of individuals, in an area that is if anything notoriously resistant to the claims of common sense and introspection: where would the whole, astonishing and metamorphic Western romance tradition (I include psychoanalysis) be if people's sexual desire, of all things, were even momentarily assumed to be transparent to themselves? Yet I am even more impressed by the leap of presumptuousness necessary to dismiss such a list of differences than by the leap of faith necessary to entertain it. To alienate conclusively, *definitionally,* from anyone on any theoretical ground the authority to describe and name their own sexual desire is a terribly consequential seizure. In this century, in which sexuality has been made expressive of the essence of both identity and knowledge, it may represent the most intimate violence possible. It is also an act replete with the most disempowering mundane institutional effects and potentials. It is, of course, central to the modern history of homophobic oppression.

The safer proceeding would seem to be to give as much credence as one finds it conceivable to give to self-reports of sexual difference—weighting one's credence, when it is necessary to weight it at all, in favor of the less normative and therefore riskier, costlier self-reports. To follow this proceeding is to enclose protectively large areas of, not mere agnosticism, but more active potential pluralism on the heavily contested maps of sexual definition. If, for instance, many people who self-identify as gay experience the gender of sexual object-choice, or some other proto-form of individual gay identity, as the most immutable and immemorial component of individual being, I can see no grounds for either subordinating this perception to or privileging it over that of other self-identified gay people whose experience of identity or object-choice has seemed to themselves to come relatively late or even to be discretionary. In so homophobic a culture, anyone's dangerous decision to self-identify as gay ought to command at least that entailment of *bona fides* and propriodescriptive authority. While there are certainly rhetorical and political grounds on which it may make sense to choose at a given moment between articulating, for instance, essentialist and constructivist (or minoritizing and universalizing) accounts of gay identity, there are, with equal certainty, rhetorical and political grounds for underwriting continuously the legitimacy of both accounts. And beyond these, there are crucial reasons of respect. I have felt that for this study to work most incisively would require framing its questions in such a way as to perform the least possible delegitimation of felt and reported differences and to impose the lightest possible burden of platonic definitional stress. Repeatedly to ask how certain categorizations work, what enactments they are performing and what relations they are creating, rather than what they essentially *mean,* has been my principal strategy.

3

Scientia Sexualis

Michel Foucault

*M*ichel Foucault (1926–84) was a French philosopher whose work on sexuality has proven foundational in the field of gender and sexuality studies. This classic text, taken from the introductory first volume of The History of Sexuality, posits two broad ways of producing "the truth" about human sexuality, one more typical of Western cultures and societies and the other characterizing non-Western contexts. More specifically, the passage discusses the critical role of the Christian ritual of confession and penance in creating a discourse around sexual desire and identity in the West. As was discussed in the introduction to this reader, Foucault's work posits a non-essentialist understanding of human gender and sexuality, arguing rather for a more nuanced constructivist view. But what Foucault also reminds us is that religion, through the elaboration of forms of power staged as types of discourse, can play a significantly critical role in how people express their sexuality.

Historically, there have been two great procedures for producing the truth of sex.

On the one hand, the societies—and they are numerous: China, Japan, India, Rome, the Arabo-Moslem societies—which endowed themselves with an *ars erotica*. In the erotic art, truth is drawn from pleasure itself, understood as a practice and accumulated as experience; pleasure is not considered in relation to an absolute law of the permitted and the forbidden, nor by reference to a criterion of utility, but first and foremost in relation to itself; it is experienced as pleasure, evaluated in terms of its intensity, its specific quality, its duration, its reverberations in the body and the soul. Moreover, this knowledge must be deflected back into the sexual practice itself, in order to shape it as though from within and amplify its effects. In this way, there is formed a knowledge that must remain secret, not because of an element of infamy that might attach to its object, but because of the need to hold it in the greatest reserve, since, according to tradition, it would lose its effectiveness and its virtue by being divulged. Consequently, the relationship to the master who holds the secrets is of paramount importance; only he, working alone, can transmit this art in an esoteric manner and as the culmination of an initiation in which he guides the disciple's progress with unfailing skill and severity. The effects of this masterful art, which are considerably more generous than the spareness of its prescriptions would lead one to imagine, are said to transfigure the one fortunate enough to receive its privileges: an absolute mastery of the body, a singular bliss, obliviousness to time and limits, the elixir of life, the exile of death and its threats.

On the face of it at least, our civilization possesses no *ars erotica*. In return, it is undoubtedly the only civilization to practice a *scientia sexualis;* or rather, the only civilization to have developed over the centuries procedures for telling the truth of sex which are geared to a form of knowledge-power strictly opposed to the art of initiations and the masterful secret: I have in mind the confession.

Since the Middle Ages at least, Western societies have established the confession as one of the main rituals we rely on for the production of truth: the codification of the sacrament of penance by the Lateran Council in 1215, with the resulting development of confessional techniques, the declining importance of accusatory procedures in criminal justice, the abandonment of tests of guilt (sworn statements, duels, judgments of God) and the development of methods of interrogation and inquest, the increased participation of the royal administration in the prosecution of infractions, at the expense of proceedings leading to private settlements, the setting up of tribunals of Inquisition: all this helped to give the confession a central role in the order of civil and religious powers. The evolution of the word *avowal* and of the legal function it designated is itself emblematic of this development: from being a guarantee of the status, identity, and value granted to one person by another, it came to signify someone's acknowledgment of his own actions and thoughts. For a long time, the individual was vouched for by the reference of others and the demonstration of his ties to the commonweal (family, allegiance, protection); then he was authenticated by the discourse of truth he was able or obliged to pronounce concerning himself. The truthful confession was inscribed at the heart of the procedures of individualization by power.

In any case, next to the testing rituals, next to the testimony of witnesses, and the learned methods of observation and demonstration, the confession became one of the West's most highly valued techniques for producing truth. We have since become a singularly confessing society. The confession has spread its effects far and wide. It plays a part in justice, medicine, education, family relationships, and love relations, in the most ordinary affairs of everyday life, and in the most solemn rites; one confesses one's crimes, one's sins, one's thoughts and desires, one's illnesses and troubles; one goes about telling, with the greatest precision, whatever is most difficult to tell. One confesses in public and in private, to one's parents, one's educators, one's doctor, to those one loves; one admits to oneself, in pleasure and in pain, things it would be impossible to tell to anyone else, the things people write books about. One confesses—or is forced to confess. When it is not spontaneous or dictated by some internal imperative, the confession is wrung from a person by violence or threat; it is driven from its hiding place in the soul, or extracted from the body. Since the Middle Ages, torture has accompanied it like a shadow, and supported it when it could go no further: the dark twins. The most defenseless tenderness and the bloodiest of powers have a similar need of confession. Western man has become a confessing animal.

Whence a metamorphosis in literature: we have passed from a pleasure to be recounted and heard, centering on the heroic or marvelous narration of "trials" of bravery or sainthood, to a literature ordered according to the infinite task of extracting from the depths of oneself, in between the words, a truth which the very form of the confession holds out like a shimmering mirage. Whence too this new way of philosophizing: seeking the fundamental relation to the true, not simply in oneself—in some forgotten knowledge, or in a certain primal trace—but in the self-examination that yields, through a multitude of fleeting impressions, the basic certainties of consciousness. The obligation to confess is now relayed through so many different points, is so deeply ingrained in us, that we no longer perceive it as the effect of a power that constrains us; on the contrary, it seems to us that truth, lodged in our most secret nature, "demands" only to surface; that if it fails to do so, this is because a constraint holds it in place, the violence of a power weighs it down, and it can finally be articulated only at the price of a kind of liberation. Confession frees, but power reduces one to silence; truth does not belong to the order of power, but shares an original affinity with freedom: traditional themes in philosophy, which a "political history of truth" would have to overturn by showing that truth is not by nature free—nor error servile—but that its production is thoroughly imbued with relations of power. The confession is an example of this.

One has to be completely taken in by this internal ruse of confession in order to attribute a fundamental role to censorship, to taboos regarding speaking and thinking; one has to have an inverted image of power in order to believe that all these voices which have spoken so long in our civilization—repeating the formidable injunction to tell what one is and what one does, what one recollects and what one has forgotten, what one is thinking and what one thinks he is not thinking—are speaking to us of freedom. An immense labor to which the West has submitted generations in order to produce—while other forms of work ensured the accumulation of capital—men's subjection: their constitution as subjects in both senses of the word. Imagine how exorbitant must have seemed the order given to all Christians at the beginning of the thirteenth century, to kneel at least once a year and confess to all their transgressions, without omitting a single one. And think of that obscure partisan, seven centuries later, who had come to rejoin the Serbian resistance deep in the mountains; his superiors asked him to write his life story; and when he brought them a few miserable pages, scribbled in the night, they did not look at them but only said to him, "Start over, and tell the truth." Should those much-discussed language taboos make us forget this millennial yoke of confession?

From the Christian penance to the present day, sex was a privileged theme of confession. A thing that was hidden, we are told. But what if, on the contrary, it was what, in a quite particular way, one confessed? Suppose the obligation to conceal it was but another aspect of the duty to admit to it (concealing it all the more and with greater care as the confession of it was more important, requiring a stricter ritual and promising more decisive effects)? What if sex in our society, on a scale of several centuries, was something that was placed within an unrelenting system of confession? The transformation of sex into discourse, which I spoke of earlier, the dissemination and reinforcement of heterogeneous sexualities, are perhaps two elements of the same deployment: they are linked together with the help of the central element of a confession that compels individuals to articulate their sexual peculiarity—no matter how extreme. In Greece, truth and sex were linked, in the form of pedagogy, by the transmission of a precious knowledge from one body to another; sex served as a medium for initiations into learning. For us, it is in the confession that truth and sex are joined, through the obligatory and exhaustive expression of an individual secret. But this time it is truth that serves as a medium for sex and its manifestations.

The confession is a ritual of discourse in which the speaking subject is also the subject of the statement; it is also a ritual that unfolds within a power relationship, for one does not confess without the presence (or virtual presence) of a partner who is not simply the interlocutor but the authority who requires the confession, prescribes and appreciates it, and intervenes in order to judge, punish, forgive, console, and reconcile; a ritual in which the truth is corroborated by the obstacles and resistances it has had to surmount in order to be formulated; and finally, a ritual in which the expression alone, independently of its external consequences, produces intrinsic modifications in the person who articulates it: it exonerates, redeems, and purifies him; it unburdens him of his wrongs, liberates him, and promises him salvation. For centuries, the truth of sex was, at least for the most part, caught up in this discursive form. Moreover, this form was not the same as that of education (sexual education confined itself to general principles and rules of prudence); nor was it that of initiation (which remained essentially a silent practice, which the act of sexual enlightenment or deflowering merely rendered laughable or violent). As we have seen, it is a form that is far removed from the one governing the "erotic art." By virtue of the power structure immanent in it, the confessional discourse cannot come from above, as in the *ars erotica*, through the sovereign will of a master, but rather from below, as an obligatory act of speech which, under some imperious compulsion, breaks the bonds of discretion or forgetfulness. What secrecy it presupposes is not owing to the high price of what it has to say and the small number of those who are worthy of its benefits, but to its obscure familiarity and its general baseness. Its veracity is not guaranteed by the lofty authority of the magistery, nor by the tradition it transmits, but by the bond, the basic intimacy in discourse, between the one who speaks and what he is speaking about. On the other hand, the agency of domination does not reside in the one who speaks (for it is he who is constrained), but in the one who listens and says nothing; not in the one who knows and answers, but in the one who questions and is not supposed to know. And this discourse of truth finally takes effect, not in the one who receives it, but in the one from whom it is wrested. With these confessed truths, we are a long way from the learned initiations into pleasure, with their technique and their mystery. On the other hand, we belong to a society which has ordered sex's difficult knowledge, not according to the transmission of secrets, but around the slow surfacing of confidential statements.

The confession was, and still remains, the general standard governing the production of the true discourse on sex. It has undergone a considerable transformation, however. For a long time, it remained firmly entrenched in the practice of penance. But with the rise of Protestantism, the Counter Reformation, eighteenth-century pedagogy, and nineteenth-century medicine, it gradually lost its ritualistic and exclusive localization; it spread; it has been employed in a whole series of relationships: children and parents, students and educators, patients and psychiatrists, delinquents and experts. The motivations and effects it is expected to produce have varied, as have the forms it has taken: interrogations, consultations, autobiographical narratives, letters; they have been recorded, transcribed, assembled into dossiers, published, and commented on. But more important, the confession lends itself, if not to other domains, at least to new ways of exploring the existing ones. It is no longer a question simply of saying what was done—the sexual act—and how it was done; but of reconstructing, in and around the act, the thoughts that recapitulated it, the obsessions that accompanied it, the images, desires, modulations, and quality of the pleasure that animated it. For the first time no doubt, a society has taken upon itself to solicit and hear the imparting of individual pleasures.

A dissemination, then, of procedures of confession, a multiple localization of their constraint, a widening of their domain: a great archive of the pleasures of sex was gradually constituted. For a long time this archive dematerialized as it was formed. It regularly disappeared without a trace (thus suiting the purposes of the Christian pastoral) until medicine, psychiatry, and pedagogy began to solidify it: Campe, Salzmann, and especially Kaan, Krafft-Ebing, Tardieu, Molle, and Havelock Ellis carefully assembled this whole pitiful, lyrical outpouring from the sexual mosaic. Western societies thus began to keep an indefinite record of these people's pleasures. They made up a herbal of them and established a system of classification. They described their everyday deficiencies as well as their oddities or exasperations. This was an important time. It is easy to make light of these nineteenth-century psychiatrists, who made a point of apologizing for the horrors they were about to let speak, evoking "immoral behavior" or "aberrations of the genetic senses," but I am more inclined to applaud their seriousness: they had a feeling for momentous events. It was a time when the most singular pleasures were called upon to pronounce a discourse of truth concerning themselves, a discourse which had to model itself after that which spoke, not of sin and salvation, but of bodies and life processes—the discourse of science. It was enough to make one's voice tremble, for an improbable thing was then taking shape: a confessional science, a science which relied on a many-sided extortion, and took for its object what was unmentionable but admitted to nonetheless. The scientific discourse was scandalized, or in any case repelled, when it had to take charge of this whole discourse from below. It was also faced with a theoretical and methodological paradox: the long discussions concerning the possibility of constituting a science of the subject, the validity of introspection, lived experience as evidence, or the presence of consciousness to itself were responses to this problem that is inherent in the functioning of truth in our society: can one articulate the production of truth according to the old juridico-religious model of confession, and the extortion of confidential evidence according to the rules of scientific discourse? Those who believe that sex was more rigorously elided in the nineteenth century than ever before, through a formidable mechanism of blockage and a deficiency of discourse, can say what they please. There was no deficiency, but rather an excess, a redoubling, too much rather than not enough discourse, in any case an interference between two modes of production of truth: procedures of confession, and scientific discursivity.

And instead of adding up the errors, naïvetés, and moral-isms that plagued the nineteenth-century discourse of truth concerning sex, we would do better to locate the procedures by which that will to knowledge regarding sex, which characterizes the modern Occident, caused the rituals of confession to function within the norms of scientific regularity: how did this immense and traditional extortion of the sexual confession come to be constituted in scientific terms?

1   *Through a clinical codification of the inducement to speak.* Combining confession with examination, the personal history with the deployment of a set of decipherable signs and symptoms; the interrogation, the exacting questionnaire, and hypnosis, with the recollection of memories and free association: all were ways of reinscribing the procedure of confession in a field of scientifically acceptable observations.

2   *Through the postulate of a general and diffuse causality.* Having to tell everything, being able to pose questions about everything, found their justification in the principle that endowed sex with an inexhaustible and polymorphous causal power. The most discrete event in one's sexual behavior—whether an accident or a deviation, a deficit or an excess—was deemed capable of entailing the most varied consequences throughout one's existence; there was scarcely a malady or physical disturbance to which the nineteenth century did not impute at least some degree of sexual etiology. From the bad habits of children to the phthises of adults, the apoplexies of old people, nervous maladies, and the degenerations of the race, the medicine of that era wove an entire network of sexual causality to explain them. This may well appear fantastic to us, but the principle of sex as a "cause of any and everything" was the theoretical underside of a confession that had to be thorough, meticulous, and constant, and at the same time operate within a scientific type of practice. The limitless dangers that sex carried with it justified the exhaustive character of the inquisition to which it was subjected.

3   *Through the principle of a latency intrinsic to sexuality.* If it was necessary to extract the truth of sex through the technique of confession, this was not simply because it was difficult to tell, or stricken by the taboos of decency, but

because the ways of sex were obscure; it was elusive by nature; its energy and its mechanisms escaped observation, and its causal power was partly clandestine. By integrating it into the beginnings of a scientific discourse, the nineteenth century altered the scope of the confession; it tended no longer to be concerned solely with what the subject wished to hide, but with what was hidden from himself, being incapable of coming to light except gradually and through the labor of a confession in which the questioner and the questioned each had a part to play. The principle of a latency essential to sexuality made it possible to link the forcing of a difficult confession to a scientific practice. It had to be exacted, by force, since it involved something that tried to stay hidden.

4   *Through the method of interpretation.* If one had to confess, this was not merely because the person to whom one confessed had the power to forgive, console, and direct, but because the work of producing the truth was obliged to pass through this relationship if it was to be scientifically validated. The truth did not reside solely in the subject who, by confessing, would reveal it wholly formed. It was constituted in two stages: present but incomplete, blind to itself, in the one who spoke, it could only reach completion in the one who assimilated and recorded it. It was the latter's function to verify this obscure truth: the revelation of confession had to be coupled with the decipherment of what it said. The one who listened was not simply the forgiving master, the judge who condemned or acquitted; he was the master of truth. His was a hermeneutic function. With regard to the confession, his power was not only to demand it before it was made, or decide what was to follow after it, but also to constitute a discourse of truth on the basis of its decipherment. By no longer making the confession a test, but rather a sign, and by making sexuality something to be interpreted, the nineteenth century gave itself the possibility of causing the procedures of confession to operate within the regular formation of a scientific discourse.

5   *Through the medicalization of the effects of confession.* The obtaining of the confession and its effects were recodified as therapeutic operations. Which meant first of all that the sexual domain was no longer accounted for simply by the notions of error or sin, excess or transgression, but was placed under the rule of the normal and the pathological (which, for that matter, were the transposition of the former categories); a characteristic sexual morbidity was defined for the first time; sex appeared as an extremely unstable pathological field: a surface of repercussion for other ailments, but also the focus of a specific nosography, that of instincts, tendencies, images, pleasure, and conduct. This implied furthermore that sex would derive its meaning and its necessity from medical interventions: it would be required by the doctor, necessary for diagnosis, and effective by nature in the cure. Spoken in time, to the proper party, and by the person who was both the bearer of it and the one responsible for it, the truth healed.

Let us consider things in broad historical perspective: breaking with the traditions of the *ars erotica,* our society has equipped itself with a *scientia sexualis.* To be more precise, it has pursued the task of producing true discourses concerning sex, and this by adapting—not without difficulty—the ancient procedure of confession to the rules of scientific discourse. Paradoxically, the *scientia sexualis* that emerged in the nineteenth century kept as its nucleus the singular ritual of obligatory and exhaustive confession, which in the Christian West was the first technique for producing the truth of sex. Beginning in the sixteenth century, this rite gradually detached itself from the sacrament of penance, and via the guidance of souls and the direction of conscience—the *ars artium*—emigrated toward pedagogy, relationships between adults and children, family relations, medicine, and psychiatry. In any case, nearly one hundred and fifty years have gone into the making of a complex machinery for producing true discourses on sex: a deployment that spans a wide segment of history in that it connects the ancient injunction of confession to clinical listening methods. It is this deployment that enables something called "sexuality" to embody the truth of sex and its pleasures.

"Sexuality": the correlative of that slowly developed discursive practice which constitutes the *scientia sexualis.* The essential features of this sexuality are not the expression of a representation that is more or less distorted by ideology, or of a misunderstanding caused by taboos; they correspond to the functional requirements of a discourse that must produce its truth. Situated at the point of intersection of a technique of confession and a scientific discursivity, where certain major mechanisms had to be found for adapting them to one another (the listening technique, the postulate of causality, the principle of latency, the rule of interpretation, the imperative of medicalization), sexuality was defined as being "by nature": a domain susceptible to pathological processes, and hence one calling for therapeutic or normalizing interventions; a field of meanings to decipher; the site of processes concealed by specific mechanisms; a focus of indefinite causal relations; and an obscure speech *(parole)* that had to be ferreted out and listened to. The "economy" of discourses—their intrinsic technology, the necessities of their operation, the tactics they employ, the effects of power which underlie them and which they transmit—this, and not a system of representations, is what determines the essential features of what they have to say. The history of sexuality—that is, the history of what functioned in the nineteenth century as a specific field of truth—must first be written from the viewpoint of a history of discourses.

Let us put forward a general working hypothesis. The society that emerged in the nineteenth century—bourgeois, capitalist, or industrial society, call it what you will—did not confront sex with a fundamental refusal of recognition. On the contrary, it put into operation an entire machinery for producing true discourses concerning it. Not only did it speak of sex and compel everyone to do so; it also set out to formulate the uniform truth of sex. As if it suspected sex of harboring a fundamental secret. As if it needed this production of truth. As if it was essential that sex be inscribed not only in an economy of pleasure but in an ordered system of knowledge. Thus sex gradually became an object of great suspicion; the general and disquieting meaning that pervades our conduct and our existence, in spite of ourselves; the point of weakness where evil portents reach through to us; the fragment of darkness that we each carry within us: a general signification, a universal secret, an omnipresent cause, a fear that never ends. And so, in this "question" of sex (in both senses: as interrogation and problematization, and as the need for confession and integration into a field of rationality), two processes emerge, the one always conditioning the other: we demand that sex speak the truth (but, since it is the secret and is oblivious to its own nature, we reserve for ourselves the function of telling the truth of its truth, revealed and deciphered at last), and we demand that it tell us our truth, or rather, the deeply buried truth of that truth about ourselves which we think we possess in our immediate consciousness. We tell it its truth by deciphering what it tells us about that truth; it tells us our own by delivering up that part of it that escaped us. From this interplay there has evolved, over several centuries, a knowledge of the subject; a knowledge not so much of his form, but of that which divides him, determines him perhaps, but above all causes him to be ignorant of himself. As unlikely as this may seem, it should not surprise us when we think of the long history of the Christian and juridical confession, of the shifts and transformations this form of knowledge-power, so important in the West, has undergone: the project of a science of the subject has gravitated, in ever narrowing circles, around the question of sex. Causality in the subject, the unconscious of the subject, the truth of the subject in the other who knows, the knowledge he holds unbeknown to him, all this found an opportunity to deploy itself in the discourse of sex. Not, however, by reason of some natural property inherent in sex itself, but by virtue of the tactics of power immanent in this discourse.

4

Law and Desire in the Talmud

David Biale

David Biale is a scholar of Jewish history. This passage is taken from his classic text, Eros and the Jews. It offers a succinct overview of a number of heteronormative sexual practices that the early rabbis (teachers of Jewish law) would have been concerned with regulating, specifically in terms of their procreative potential. In many religious traditions, procreation is generally seen and understood as the legitimate and proper end of sexual activity, and this is often based in long-standing scriptural injunctions. Procreative sexual acts are considered "natural," while non-procreative sexuality, especially of the same-sex variety, is cast as "unnatural" or essentially suspect. More generally, this text raises the significant question of the appropriate place of pleasure and desire in the sexual relationship, but always from a heteronormative perspective. The question can be asked how this same paradigm might apply to a same-sex relationship.

In biblical culture, sexual relations within marriage did not attract attention, as long as they were carried on within legal bounds. For the rabbis, however, sex had become a problem to be discussed, investigated, and possibly controlled. If for the Bible, sex was always an issue of bodily practices and their cultic implications, for the rabbis, the problem was not the body as such, but desire, the psychic state of the passions, that might overpower the body. Where biblical culture had taken desire for granted, rabbinic culture made desire itself the subject of much discussion, both as something necessary for the existence of the world and as a potentially destructive, evil force. The challenge confronting the rabbis was to channel this desire so that it might equally serve the ends of Torah study and procreation, the twin values that animated rabbinic culture. At the heart of this discourse was a profoundly ambivalent attitude toward sexuality as such, an ambivalence not found in the biblical sources.

In the Bible, procreation was a blessing to be sought; there was no hint that it must be required. The Bible recounts the trials of people who wish to have children, but cannot; rabbinic law turned this concern into a divine commandment. Several explanations have been proposed for this surprising piece of legislation. For one, it paralleled the Roman law requiring men to marry and have children; as in Rome, the Jews of Palestine, especially after the devastating Bar Kokhba rebellion of the second century c.e., had a desperate need to increase their population. According to this understanding, the rabbinic commandment to procreate was a piece of population policy modeled on Roman law. Others have argued that the rabbis were attempting to give divine status to an activity that was otherwise considered "natural"; by applying this commandment only to Jewish men, they distinguished themselves from women, Gentiles, and animals.

Unlike the Bible, rabbinic literature devoted considerable attention to actual sexual practices between husband and wife. Most of this wealth of material is designed to hide sexual behavior in a cloak of modesty and moderation, yet the law itself allows any sexual practice, as long as it is procreative. As the following text on the menstrual prohibitions suggests, the legal authorities seem to have recognized the limitations on their enforcement powers in the face of patriarchal prerogatives:

> When one's wife menstruates, she is alone with him at home. If he wishes to, he has intercourse with her; if he does not wish, he does not have intercourse with her. Does anyone see him or does anyone know so that they might say anything to him? He fears only [God] who has commanded [the laws] concerning menstruation.

Although the law allows any procreative sexual activity, rabbinic texts nevertheless take up the question of practices under the guise of medical advice. The Babylonian Talmud recounts a debate between Rabbi Johanan ben Dahabai and the legislative majority:

> R. Johanan b. Dahabai said: . . people are born lame because they [that is, their parents] overturned their table [that is, had intercourse in a nonmissionary position]; dumb, because they kiss "that place"; deaf, because they converse during intercourse; blind, because they look at "that place."

Johanan's eugenic warnings, though not intended as law, are part of rabbinic medical lore, similar to the statement: "If a man has sexual intercourse standing, he will be liable to convulsions; if sitting, to spasms; if she is above and he below, he will be subject to diarrhea." The majority rejects Johanan ben Dahabai's position as binding law and invokes against him (a thoroughly minor rabbinical figure) a series of such major mishnaic figures as Judah the Prince and Rabbi Eliezer to demonstrate that "a man may do whatever he pleases with his wife."

The question of sexual practices thus aroused a good deal of controversy. Johanan ben Dahabai claims to have his genetic information straight from the "ministering angels" (*malakhei ha-sharet*), a claim that a later rabbi tries to neutralize by identifying these angels with the rabbis themselves. But in the process of rejecting the legal status of this medical knowledge, the text makes it available to its readers. Did these readers consider it as a warning to be heeded, even though the practices were legally permitted, or as a covert rabbinic *Kama Sutra?* The text brings two cases of women who complain to Judah the Prince that they "set a table" for their husbands, who then "overturned them." Evidently such practices were not theoretical! The response of Judah is instructive: "My daughter, the Torah has permitted you to him and I, what can I do for you?" In his reluctance to intervene, Judah confirms that the law does not restrict the sexual privileges of men, but by symbolically throwing up his hands, he also implicitly criticizes such practices.

These tensions are repeated in another text brought in the Talmud together with this one. The story concerns Imma Shalom, wife of the first-century rabbi Eliezer, and sister of the patriarch Rabban Gamliel; she is said to have had beautiful children because her husband had intercourse with her as fast as possible and by removing only a minimum of clothing. The Talmud brings the story to refute Johanan ben Dahabai: it suggests that even though Eliezer conversed with his wife during intercourse, they still had beautiful children. Nevertheless, Eliezer's other ascetic practices actually support Johanan ben Dahabai. Thus, once again, even as it attempts to establish that the law allows any sexual practice, the Talmud betrays its deep ambivalence about sexual pleasure.

To promote modesty, most rabbinical opinion held that intercourse should take place only at night or in the dark: "Israel is chaste because they do not have intercourse during the day. Rava said: if the house is dark it is permitted, and Rava said and some say Rav Papa, a scholar can darken the house with his cloak [tallit] and then it is permitted." No living creature is supposed to witness the act, and especially holy men such as Abaye are said to have chased away even flies. But another opinion held that one might have intercourse during the day, since otherwise the husband, overcome by sleep, might perform perfunctorily and end up despising his wife.

Opinion was also divided on the question of whether sexual relations should take place clothed or naked. The second-century Rabbi Simon bar Yohai denounced those who engage in sexual intercourse naked. The story of Imma Shalom suggests that she remained clothed during intercourse. Both of these accounts refer to first- or second-century Palestinian rabbis. By contrast, two later Babylonian rabbis, Joseph and Huna, reject such practices as "the manner of the Persians": sexual relations must take place without clothes and a man who requires his wife to wear clothes must divorce her and pay her (marriage contract) [ketubah]. Although medieval Jewish law adopted this lenient position, it would appear that those who lived in Palestine inclined toward remaining clothed while in the conjugal bed.

Roman culture provides the explanation for the greater modesty of the Palestinian rabbis. Not only did the new moral code that became accepted by the early second century dictate chastity until marriage, but the sexual taboos between man and wife clearly resemble rabbinic prescriptions: lovemaking was to take place at night or in a darkened room, and women were to keep their clothes on. Thus, wall paintings in Pompeii reveal that even servants and prostitutes wore brassieres while making love.

Despite the influence of Roman practices on early rabbinic Judaism, the Palestinian rabbis were so hostile to Rome that they rarely had anything positive to say about Roman sexual customs. Some sources from Palestine do, however, speak admiringly of the Persians (or Medes) as paragons of sexual virtue. The first-century patriarch, Rabban Gamliel, is said to have remarked: "There are three things for which I love the Persians: they are modest in their eating, modest in the toilet, and modest in another matter [*davar aher*]," the latter a clear reference to sexual behavior. In a number of other midrashim, the chastity of the "sons of the East" is contrasted with the immoral life of the Canaanites, probably a veiled reference to the Romans. Indeed, some of the sexual practices of the Sassanian Persians bore similarities to those of the rabbis, especially in such prohibitions as sex with a menstruant.

The sexual act therefore required both moderation and modesty. Restraint breeds restraint: "Man has a small member—if he starves it, it is satisfied, but if he satisfies it, it remains starved." It was this saying, which the Talmud refers to as a "law" (halakhah), that King David is said to have forgotten in his lust for Bathsheba. In addition, rigorous, even excessive application of the biblical purity laws might promote moderation. According to a Palestinian tradition, such extra purifications ensured, in a much-quoted phrase during the Middle Ages, that "scholars would not hang around their wives like roosters. . . . Whoever is strict with himself in this regard will have his days and years prolonged. For those who believed that sexual moderation and self-control were signs of holiness, biblical rituals of purification became autodidactic devices.

Naturally enough, the actual behavior of members of the rabbinic elite did not always measure up to the strict norms suggested by their teachings, as in the following amusing story:

Rav Kahana lay under the bed of Rav who was carousing and speaking frivolously with his wife of sexual matters; afterward, [Rav] had intercourse with her. Rav Kahana said to Rav: "You appear to me to be like a hungry man who has never had sex before, for you act with frivolity in your lust." He [Rav] said to Kahana: "Are you here? Get out! It is improper for you to lie under my bed!" [Kahana] said to him: "This is a matter of Torah and I must study.

Whose side does this text take, the teacher's or his pupils'? Does Kahana's shock at Rav's behavior suggest that Rav behaved wrongly? Or if this is, indeed, a "matter of Torah," perhaps the prudish Kahana has learned something new about proper behavior.

The story is embedded in a larger text that relates accounts of disciples who conceal themselves in toilets in order to learn from their teachers how one performs this similarly private function. These other stories follow the same structure: the disciple is caught but protests that "this is a matter of Torah and I must study." Unless this line is intended as a parody of overzealous discipleship, it would seem to support the notion that even the most private acts are part of Torah learning and that privacy, which is otherwise sacrosanct, may be violated in order to observe them. At the same time, by placing sexual behavior in the same category as defecation, the text covertly undermines any affirmation of Rav's unbridled sexuality. These contradictions cannot be resolved; indeed, I would argue, they reveal the ambivalences in rabbinic culture toward both sexual practices and the degree to which they might be controlled.

Although the central purpose of sexual relations for the rabbis was to fulfill the commandment of procreation, they recognized a separate, legitimate realm of sexual pleasure. These laws, called *onah,* guarantee every married woman the right to regular sexual relations, though the frequency depends in part on the husband's occupation. As opposed to at least one Jewish sectarian text, sex on the Sabbath was not only permitted but, in fact, required of scholars. The laws of *onah,* moreover, pertain regardless of procreation: the woman has the right to sexual satisfaction even if she is pregnant or menopausal, that is, incapable of conceiving. Not only is there a *commandment* to engage in sexual relations independent of procreation, but the purpose of such relations is explicitly to give pleasure.

Pleasure and procreation may not have been totally separated from each other in rabbinic thought, however. Ancient medicine held that both male and female sexual pleasure is essential to conception. The very physical mechanics of the sexual act seemed to physicians like Galen necessary to produce the mixtures of fluids necessary for reproduction. While the rabbis do not appear to have discussed male orgasm, they seem to have believed, based on Galen's two-seed, theory that women released some kind of seed during orgasm. Since female pleasure was evidently necessary for conception, the commandment of *onah* was implicitly linked to procreation, even though the two were formally distinct.

Onah applies only to women; men do not have similar rights, as they do in the Paul's marital debt. This asymmetry is connected to the sharp distinction the rabbis drew between the sexuality of men and women: "A man's sexual impulse is out in the open: his erection stands out and he embarrasses himself in front of his fellows. A woman's sexual impulse is within and no one can recognize her [arousal]." Nevertheless, "a woman's passion is greater than that of a man." Women were thus considered to be highly sexual but incapable of asking for sexual satisfaction. Men must attend to these needs to ensure a peaceful household: "It is a man's duty to pay his wife a 'visit' before a journey, for it is said 'and you shall know that your tent is in peace'" (Job 5:24). Women who take the sexual initiative are so rare that if they do solicit their husbands to perform the marital obligation, they will "have children the like of whom did not exist even in the generation of Moses!" This text seems to suggest that women who act against female nature are praiseworthy: rabbinic culture, like its biblical predecessor, cannot be labeled unequivocally patriarchal.

The laws of *onah* clearly had the effect of protecting and advancing women's sexual rights, although the motivation behind the law may have had more to do with the temptation of total abstinence that existed in rabbinic culture than with a protofeminist agenda. It is noteworthy that the law of *onah* first appears in the Mishnah right after a dispute between Hillel and Shammai about the permissible length of time a man may take a vow of celibacy without his wife's permission. While it is always difficult to infer social reality from law, it may be that by mandating regular sexual relations the

Palestinian mishnaic schools were trying to control a problem of scholars absenting themselves to study for excessive periods.

This suspicion is strengthened in the Babylonian *Gemara*, the commentary by the Bablyonian rabbis on the Mishnah. A series of stories suggest that the Babylonian rabbis absented themselves from home in order to study for much longer periods of time than did their Palestinian colleagues. These stories show that the Babylonians not only attempted to modify the strict mishnaic limitations on vows of abstinence but that there was enormous conflict in their culture over the question. According to one account, Rav Rehumi failed to return home because he was so engrossed in his studies; his wife cried bitter tears and he then died. The famous story of how Rabbi Akiva's wife, Rachel, gives him permission to go to study for decades was evidently intended to refute the criticism of Rav Rehumi's practice and to legitimate long periods of marital abstinence. If these stories had their roots in an actual social problem, then there must have been an enormous sense that marital duties conflicted with study of Torah. The laws of *onah* were designed to resolve the conflict, but they clearly did not provide a definitive solution.

Rabbinic law imposed both positive and negative temporal controls on sex. If *onah* dictated when men must have sexual relations with their wives, *niddah*, the prohibition on sex with a menstruating woman, prescribed the period of abstinence. Instead of the biblical period of five to seven days of impurity that ended with the end of the woman's flow, the rabbis imposed a twelve-to-fourteen-day separation, in effect, abstinence for half of every month. The rabbis derived their law of menstruation from the biblical law pertaining to *nonmenstrual* bleeding: it is only the latter, which is the result of illness, that requires a week of cleanness after the bleeding has ceased. The result of this legal innovation was to enforce extensive periods of sexual abstinence on married couples.

Modern observers have repeatedly noted that the extension of the menstrual taboo to nearly two weeks means that resumption of sexual activity coincides with the greatest moment of fertility: the laws of *niddah* seem almost tailor-made to promote procreation. Some rabbis may have been aware of the Fertility consequences of *niddah*. Rabbi Johanan is quoted to the effect that a woman becomes pregnant "close to [her] immersion," that is, immediately after the end of the full rabbinic period of menstrual abstention. Following certain strands of ancient medicine, the rabbis held that menstrual blood is necessary for conception:

> A woman's womb is full of standing blood and from there it flows out in menstruation. And at God's will, a drop of whiteness goes and drops into her and instantly, the fetus is created. This is likened to a bowl of milk: if you put rennet in it, it curdles and stands; if not, it remains liquid.

Menstruation was considered a time when this blood is not in its proper place and is therefore not available for conception, a view reflected in the Bible, but without the physiological explanation. Like *onah,* which also seemed on the face of it unrelated to procreation, the laws of *niddah* turn out to have a hidden connection to this cardinal rabbinic precept.

Given these implicit connections between pleasure and procreation, the rabbis' attitude toward nonprocreative sex was ambiguous. On the one hand, they permitted a wide variety of sexual practices designed purely for pleasure and they mandated marital sex even when a woman was unable to conceive. On the other hand, they were opposed to sexual acts such as coitus interruptus that could never be procreative, even with a fertile woman; coitus interruptus was considered the crime of Er and Onan in Genesis 38. Other types of nonprocreative intercourse, such as anal and oral intercourse, were more problematic. The law frowned upon, but did not technically forbid, nonvaginal intercourse, which it labeled "unnatural" (*she-lo ke-darkha*), possibly because it assumed that Jews did not engage in such practices.

One nonprocreative practice that the rabbis condemned without reservation was masturbation, typically designated *hashhatat zera* (destruction of seed) or *shikhvat zera le-vatalah* (emission of wasted seed). According to biblical law, masturbation, like any other seminal emission, would presumably have created ritual impurity, but no more so than normal sexual intercourse. The rabbis turned masturbation into a heinous crime. The Mishnah states the earliest form of the law by contrasting women who examine themselves to determine if they are menstruating with men who masturbate: "Every hand that makes frequent examination is praiseworthy in the case of women, but in the case of men, it should be cut off." This statement is followed by a series of equally extreme pronouncements in the *Gemara*. Rabbi Johanan is quoted as saying: "Whoever emits semen nonprocreatively deserves capital punishment." Similarly, the biblical verse "your hands are filled with blood" is taken to refer to those who "fornicate [that is, masturbate] with their hands." Rabbi Eliezer adds: "Whoever holds his penis while he urinates is as though he brought a flood to the world." Although urination does not seem a particularly erotic activity, Eliezer was concerned about the consequences of a man becoming accustomed to touching his penis. He may also have associated urine with semen based on a midrash that one of the primary causes of the Flood in Genesis was "wasting of seed."

It is perhaps no coincidence that the laws against masturbation appear in the tractate Niddah of the Talmud. This association between masturbation and menstruation may explain the statement "he who deliberately causes himself an erection shall be in *niddui*" (usually translated "excommunicated" or "ostracized"). Figuratively speaking, he will be like one who has sex with a *niddah*. He, like a *niddah,* is beyond the sexual pale because his sexual fluids are neither retained in his body nor deposited in the body of his procreative partner. But the difference between a menstruating woman and a masturbating man is crucial: the woman cannot control her menstruation, for it is a function of her biology, but a man *can* avoid masturbation.

In this distinction lies the fundamental rabbinic ethic that accepted the sexuality of women as a biological fact but required that men "conquer their desire" (*yetzer*). As women are condemned to be prisoners of their own biology, incapable of willed sexual restraint, there is no point in teaching them the law. In a circular way, this assumption naturally reinforced the male orientation of the whole legal discussion of sexuality: since only men can learn to control their sexuality, the texts are also directed exclusively toward men.

Also at stake in the condemnation of masturbation, in addition to its being deliberately nonprocreative, is that it is the ultimate solipsistic act, the "solitary vice." The rabbis did not reject male sexual pleasure, but they did not believe that it was a legitimate end in itself. According to one midrash, the generation of the Flood took two wives, one for sexual pleasure and one for procreation. This division was a sign of the utter depravity of antediluvian man, who could not subordinate his sexuality to larger social goals, whether procreation, marital harmony, or national survival. The rabbis thus shared with Hellenistic culture the attention to the needs and passions of the individual, but they also agreed with prevailing opinion in late antiquity that sexuality could not remain a private matter.

5

Tongues Untied:

Memoirs of a Pentecostal Boyhood

Michael Warner

Michael Warner is an academic and a queer literary critic and social theorist, and the author of The Trouble with Normal. *This brief text, taken from an edited collection entitled* Que(e)rying Religion: A Critical Anthology, *provides an insightful personal perspective on the intersections between the Pentecostal experience of being ravaged in the Spirit and that of ecstatic same-sex desire. Pentecostalism is a unique form of conservative Protestant charismatic Christianity which has its modern origins in the nineteenth century, and which focuses on worship centered on the Holy Spirit and the gift of glossolalia or speaking in tongues. The reading offers a novel view of the broader intersections between religion and sexuality, and especially of how religious ecstasy and gay desire can be framed and experienced in overlapping ways from a cultural perspective, even though Warner also argues that religion and sexuality are actually quite distinctive.*

I was a teenage Pentecostalist. Because that is so very far from what I am now—roughly, a queer atheist intellectual—people often think I should have an explanation, a story. Was I sick? Had I been drinking? How did I get here from there? For years I've had a simple answer: "It was another life." If you had spent adolescence passing out tracts in a shopping mall, you might have the same attitude. My memory gives me pictures of someone speaking in tongues and being "slain in the spirit" (a Pentecostalist style of trance: you fall backward while other people catch you). But recognizing myself in these pictures takes effort, as though the memories themselves are in a language I don't understand, or as though I had briefly passed out.

Once, when I said, "It was another life," someone told me, "That's a very American thing to say." And it's true; a certain carelessness about starting over is very much in the national taste. On average, we afford ourselves a great deal of incoherence. Americans care about the freedom not only to have a self, but to discard one or two. We tend to distrust any job—peasant, messiah, or queen, for example—that requires people grown specially for the purpose. We like some variety on the résumé (though not necessarily a degree from Oral Roberts University, as in my case). We like people who take you aside, very privately, and whisper, "I'm Batman." In fact there's an impressive consistency on this point in the national mythology, from Rip Van Winkle to Clark Kent and Samantha on *Bewitched.*

Still, even allowing for the traditional naiveté and bad faith that is my birthright as a citizen of this, the last of history's empires, I have never been able to understand people with consistent lives—people who, for example, grow up in a liberal Catholic household and *stay* that way; or who in junior high school are already laying down a record on which to run for president one day. Imagine having no discarded personalities, no vestigial selves, no visible ruptures with yourself, no gulf of self-forgetfulness, nothing that requires explanation, no alien version of yourself that requires humor and accommodation. What kind of life is that?

For us who once were found and now are lost—and we are legion—our other lives pose some curious problems. Is there no relation at all between our once and present selves, or only a negative one? Is there some buried continuity, or some powerful vestige? In my case it would be hard to imagine a more complete revolution of personality. From the religious vantage of my childhood and adolescence, I am one of Satan's agents. From my current vantage, that former self was exotically superstitious. But I distrust both of these views of myself as the other. What if I were to stop saying "It was another life"? What if that life and this one are not so clearly opposed?

Of course, my life in the bosom of Jesus influenced me; but what interests me more is the way religion supplied me with experiences and ideas that I'm still trying to match. Watching Katherine Kuhlman do faith healing, for example, didn't just influence my aesthetic sense for performance and eloquence; it was a kind of performance that no one in theater could duplicate. Religion does things that secular culture can only approximate.

Curiously enough, considering that fundamentalism is almost universally regarded as the stronghold and dungeon-keep of American anti-intellectualism, religious culture gave me a passionate intellectual life of which universities are only a pale ivory shadow. My grandfather had been a Southern Baptist preacher in North Carolina mountain towns like Hickory and Flat Rock, but my family migrated through various Protestant sects, including Seventh-Day Adventists, winding up in the independent Pentecostalist congregations known as "charismatic." We lived, in other words, in the heart of splinter-mad American sectarianism. In that world, the subdenomination you belong to is bound for heaven; the one down the road is bound for hell. You need arguments to show why. And in that profoundly hermeneutic culture, your arguments have to be *readings:* ways of showing how the church down the road misreads a key text. Where I come from, people lose sleep over the meaning of certain Greek and Hebrew words.

The whole doctrine of Pentecostalism rests on the interpretation of one brief and difficult passage in the book of Acts. The apostles have been sitting around with nothing to do: "And there appeared unto them cloven tongues like as of fire, and it sat upon each of them. And they were all filled with the Holy Ghost, and began to speak with other tongues, as the Spirit gave them utterance." In the late 19th century, certain Americans decided you not only could but should do the same thing. In 1901, for example, Agnes Ozman of Topeka, Kansas, asserted that after being filled with the Holy Ghost she spoke and wrote Chinese for three days. (The Paraclete's literary tastes seem to have changed; nowadays people who speak in tongues favor a cross between Hebrew and baby talk.)

Pentecostalism interprets this verse as a model to be followed mainly because of another verse that comes a little later, in which Peter tells passersby to be baptized and "receive the gift of the Holy Ghost." My mother, my brother, and I, like other Pentecostalists, accepted an interpretation in which "the gift" means not the Holy Ghost himself (i.e., "receive the Holy Ghost as a gift"), but the glossolalia given by him/it (i.e., "receive incomprehensible speech from the Holy Ghost as a gift"). We were known as "charismatics" because of this interpretation of the word *gift* (charisma); on the basis of this one interpretation my family was essentially forced out of our Baptist church. But only after a lot of talk about the texts and their interpretation. Throughout my childhood and adolescence, I remember being surrounded by textual arguments in which the stakes were not just life and death, but eternal life and death.

When I was 15 or so, my family moved to Tidewater, Virginia, in part to be closer to the great revival led by the then obscure Pat Robertson. There, we went to special Bible study sessions for charismatics, held in the basement of a Lutheran church on nights when the room wasn't need by Alcoholics Anonymous. (The Lutherans were the only Protestants in town who cared so little about theology that their scorn for us was only social rather than cosmic. For just this reason, of course, we regarded the Lutherans with limitless contempt, while in their basement we studied the grounds of their damnation.) The leader of these Bible study groups was a brilliant and somewhat unsettled man who by day worked as an engineer for International Harvester and by night set up as the Moses Maimonides of the greater Tidewater area. He had flip charts that would have impressed Ross Perot. He also had a radical argument: God could not possibly be omniscient. The Old Testament, he said, clearly showed God acting in stories, stories that, like the concept of free will itself, made no sense unless God doesn't know the future. If God does know the future, including your own decisions, then narrative time is illusory and only in farce can you be held responsible for your decisions. (Like most modern fundamentalists, he was deeply committed to a contract ideal of justice.)

Every Wednesday night without fail, as this man wound himself through an internal deconstruction of the entire Calvinist tradition, in a fastidiously Protestant return to a more anthropomorphic God, foam dried and flecked on his lips. For our petit-bourgeois family it was unbearable to watch, but we kept coming back. I remember feeling the tension in my mother's body next to me, all her perception concentrated on the desire to hand him the Kleenex which, as usual, she had thoughtfully brought along.

Being a literary critic is nice, I have to say, but for lip-whitening, vein-popping thrills it doesn't compete. Not even in the headier regions of Theory can we approximate that saturation of life by argument. In the car on the way home, we would talk it over. Was he right? If so, what were the consequences? Mother, I recall, distrusted an argument that seemed to demote God to the level of the angels; she thought Christianity without an omniscient God was too Manichaean, just God and Satan going at it. She also complained that if God were not omniscient, prophecy would make no sense. She scored big with this objection, I remember; at the time, we kept ourselves up to date on Pat Robertson's calculations about the imminent Rapture. I, however, cottoned onto the heretical engineer's arguments with all the vengeful pleasure of an adolescent. God's own limits were in sight: this was satisfaction in its own right, as was the thought of holding all mankind responsible in some way.

Later, when I read Nietzsche on the ressentiment at the heart of Christianity—the smell of cruelty and aggression in Christian benevolence—I recognized what that pleasure had been about. In my experience, ressentiment wasn't just directed against Power. It was directed against everything: the dominant cadres of society, of course, parents, school, authority in general; but also God, the material world, and one's own self. Just as the intellectual culture of religion has an intensity that secular versions lack, so also Protestant culture has an intricate and expressive language of power and abjection that in secular life has to be supplied in relatively impoverished ways. The world has not the least phenomenon that cannot, in Christian culture, be invested both with world-historical power and with total abjection. You are a soldier of the Lord, born among angels, contemplated from the beginning of time and destined to live forever. But you are also the unregenerate shit of the world. Your dinner-table conversation is the medium of grace for yourself and everyone around you; it also discloses continually your fallen worthlessness. Elevation and abasement surround you, in every flicker of your half-conscious thoughts. And the two always go together.

People often say, as though it's a big discovery, that Christians have a finely honed sadomasochistic sensibility. But this doesn't come close to appreciating religion's expressive language for power and abjection. The secular equivalents, such as Foucauldian analysis, have nothing like the same condensation. I realize this every time I read Jonathan Edwards:

The sun does not willingly shine upon you to give you light to serve sin and Satan; the earth does not willingly yield her increase to satisfy your lusts; nor is it willingly a stage for your wickedness to be acted upon; the air does not willingly serve you for breath to maintain the flame of life in your vitals. . . . And the world would spew you out, were it not for the sovereign hand of Him who hath subjected it in hope. . . . The sovereign pleasure of God, for the present, stays His rough wind; otherwise it would come with fury, and your destruction would come like a whirlwind, and you would be like the chaff of the summer threshing floor.

You almost expect the next paragraph to be a manifesto for ecofundamentalism. Not even the final paragraphs of *The Order of Things* contain a more thorough distrust of everything in the human order. American religion has lost much of that antihumanism, even in the fundamentalist sects that rail against the "religion" of secular humanism, but they retain the imagination of abjection. And the abjection can be exquisite:

The bow of God's wrath is bent, and the arrow made ready on the string, and justice bends the arrow at your heart, and strains the bow, and it is nothing but the mere pleasure of God, and that of an angry God, without any promise or obligation, at all, that keeps the arrow one moment from being made drunk with your blood.

In the film version the role of *you* will be played by a trembling and shirtless Keanu Reeves. Stuff like this can displace almost any amount of affect because of the strobe light alternation of pleasure and obliteration: "it is nothing but His mere pleasure that keeps you from being this moment swallowed up in everlasting destruction." *Nothing but pleasure,* indeed. When I read this my blood heats up. I can hardly keep from reading it aloud. (Maybe that comes from hanging out with Oral Roberts.) The displacement and vicarious satisfaction provided in consumer culture is, by contrast, low-budget monochrome.

About the same time that we were going to hear the holy prophet of International Harvester, my mother made a new church friend, Frankie. Frankie was very butch. She was sweet to me, but visibly seething toward most of the world. Her sidekick Peggy, however, was the devoted servant of everybody, making endless presents of macramé before finally opening her own macramé store in a strip mall. Frankie, Peggy, and my mother belonged to a circle of women who held Bible studies in one another's living rooms (furnished in Ethan Allen early American, most of them), swapped recipes, came to each other in trouble, and prostrated themselves in the power of the Holy Spirit together.

I remember watching the way they wept together, their implicit deference to Frankie, their constant solicitation of one another's sufferings. Most of them worked. All were unhappy in the family dramas to which they nevertheless held absolute commitments. None of them liked her lot in life. They would pray in tongues while vacuuming the shag carpet. When the bills could be paid, it was because Jesus provided the money. In church, weeping in the intense but unfathomable love of Jesus, they repeated certain gestures: head slowly shaking no, eyes closed above damp cheeks, arms stretched out in invisible crosses, the temporarily forgotten Kleenex clenched in the hand. (Because Pentecostalists exalt weeping and catarrh so much, I still associate the smell of tissue with church.)

At the time I remember thinking that this social-devotional style, in which I was often a half-noticed participant, had a special meaning for these women. Not that it was a mere displacement or substitute for an articulate feminism; my mother and her friends felt, I'm sure, that Jesus spoke to them on more levels, and deeper ones, than did the feminism they had encountered. But certainly the redemption of Jesus compensated sufferings that were already framed by women's narrative. Think about the consequences of having fundamental parts of your life—gender, especially— filtered through fundamentalism's expressive language of power and abjection. In their descriptions of the love of Jesus—undeserved, devastating benignity—one heard always the articulation of a thorough resentment of the world and themselves, but also of hitherto unimaginable pleasures, and of an ideal which was also an implicit reproach against their social world. It was not lost on me that we migrated to more extreme versions of Protestant fundamentalism as my mother saw more and more clearly her dissatisfaction with the normal life to which she was nevertheless devoted. Even now, her sons have left home, three husbands have been reluctantly divorced, her friends have parted ways, and she's had to go back to teaching school—but Jesus still pays the bills.

C. S. Lewis once complained that English pictures of Jesus always made him look like an adolescent girl; I think this was and is part of the appeal, for me, for my mother's friends, *and* for Lewis, whose desire for a butch deity said more about his own queeny tastes than about the Jesus we continue to reinvent. As Harold Bloom has pointed out in his recent book *The American Religion,* many American Protestants, particularly Southern Baptists, have essentially reduced the trinity to Jesus. "He walks with me, and he talks with me, and he tells me I am His own," as we always sang. During this hymn, I would look around to make sure no one noticed that these words were coming, rather too pleasurably, from my mouth.

Jesus was my first boyfriend. He loved me, personally, and he told me I was his own. This was very thrilling, especially when he was portrayed by Jeffrey Hunter. Anglo-American Christian culture has developed a rich and kinky iconography of Jesus, the perma-boy who loves us, the demiurge in a dress. Here, for example, is Emerson's Divinity School Address of 1838: "Jesus Christ belonged to the true race of prophets. He saw with open eye the mystery of the soul. Drawn by its severe harmony, ravished with its beauty, he lived in it, and had his being there. . . . He said, in this jubilee of sublime emotion, 'I am divine.'" Well, it's fun to exclaim, "I am divine," and Emerson's point is that we all should. But he does some extra fantasy work in this picture of Jesus the happily ravished, Jesus the perpetual jubilee of sublime affect. Jesus, it seems, is coming all the time. This wouldn't make him good for much *except* being a fantasy boyfriend. With spikes in him.

Since the early days of Methodism, of course, it has been commonplace to see enthusiastic religion as sexual excess. In a characteristically modern way, writers such as Lacan and Bataille have regarded all religion as an unrecognized form of sexuality. Bloom, in *The American Religion,* writes that "there is no way to disentangle the sexual drive from Pentecostalism." He calls it "sadomasochistic sexuality," "a kind of orgiastic individualism," a "pattern of addiction," "an ecstasy scarcely distinguishable from sexual transport."

There's something to this, but I worry about putting it like that. You can reduce religion to sex only if you don't especially believe in either one. When I learned what orgasm felt like, I can't say that the difference between it and speaking in tongues was "scarcely distinguishable." It seemed like a clear call to me. And the two kinds of ecstasy quickly became, for me at least, an excruciating alternative. God, I felt sure, didn't want me to come. And he always wanted to watch.

The agony involved in choosing between orgasm and religion, as I was forced to do on a nightly basis, is the sort of thing ignored by any account that treats religion as sublimated, displaced, or misrecognized sexuality. At the beginning of *Two Serious Ladies,* the great Jane Bowles novel, one little girl asks another to play a new game, "It's called 'I forgive you for all your sins,'" she says. "Is it fun?" asks the other. "It's not for fun that we play it, but because it's necessary to play it." This, undoubtedly, is just why religion is so queer; it's not for fun that we play it.

What I think critics like Bloom are trying to say, against their own anerotic reductivism, is that religion makes available a language of ecstasy, a horizon of significance within which transgressions against the normal order of the world and the boundaries of self *can be seen as good things*. Pentecostalists don't get slain in the spirit just by rubbing themselves, or by redirecting some libido; they require a whole set of beliefs about the limitations of everyday calculations of self-interest, about the impoverishment of the world that does not willingly yield its increase to satisfy your lusts. In this way ecstatic religions can legitimate self-transgression, providing a meaningful framework for the sublime play of self-realization and self-dissolution. And once again, the secular versions often look like weak imitations. Only the most radical theories of sexual liberation (Marcuse's *Eros and Civilization,* for example) attribute as much moral importance to self-dissolution as fundamentalist religion does. (And nobody believes them any more.) Simple affirmations of desire, by contrast, don't supply a horizon of significance at all.

The bliss of Pentecostalism is, among other things, a radical downward revaluing of the world that despises Pentecostalists. Like all religions, Pentecostalism has a world-canceling moment; but its world-canceling gestures can also be a kind of social affirmation, in this case of a frequently despised minority. I suspect that the world-canceling rhetorics of queer sexuality work in a similar way. If you lick my nipple, the world suddenly seems comparatively insignificant. Ressentiment doubles your pleasure.

Both my moral, Christian self and my queer, atheist one have had to be performed as minority identities. What queers often forget, jeopardized as we are by resurgent fundamentalisms in the United States, is that fundamentalists themselves are not persuaded by "moral majority" or "mainstream values" rhetoric; they too consider themselves an oppressed minority. In their view the dominant culture is one of a worldliness they have rejected, and bucking that trend comes, in some very real ways, with social stigmatization. For instance, as far as I can make out, Jehovah's Witnesses believe in almost nothing *but* their own minority status and the inevitable destruction of the mainstream.

The radical Protestant and quasi-Protestant (i.e., Mormon) sects in this country have helped, willingly or not, to elaborate minoritarian culture. Left political thought has been remarkably blind to this fact. Most of us believe, I think, that we are in favor of all oppressed minorities, and that you can tell an oppressed minority because the people concerned say that's what they are. Who gets to say, and by what standards, that Pentecostalists, or Mormons, are not the oppressed minority they claim to be? This is not a rhetorical question.

One way that fundamentalists have contributed to the culture of minority identities is by developing the performative genres of identity-talk. Sentences like "I'm Batman" or "We're here, we're queer, get used to it" take for granted a context in which people are accorded the power of declaring what they are. In the world of Southern Baptists and charismatics, people practice a genre known as witnessing, in some ways the Ur-form of all modern autobiographical declarations. Witnessing might mean telling a conversion narrative or a miracle narrative in church, but it also might mean declaring yourself in suburban shopping malls. It is the fundamentalist version of coming out, and explained to the budding Pentecostalist in much the same language of necessity, shame and pride, stigma and cultural change.

In writing all of this, of course, I am stuck between witnessing and coming out. One of the most interesting things about the gap between religious and secular culture is that no matter which side you stand on, conversion or deconversion, the direction seems inevitable. Religious people always suppose that people start out secular and have to get religion. People like me don't secularize: we *backslide.* Of course, I have slid back to places I never was or thought of being, and it may be to halt this endless ebb that my mother has recently begun trying out a new paradigm: she's willing to consider me as having a lifestyle. I might prefer backsliding, but the concept of an alternative path marks progress in our relations. Meanwhile, those of us who have gotten over religion find ourselves heir to a potent Enlightenment mythology that regards religion as a primitive remnant, a traditional superstition. This has been the opinion not only of thinkers with very little religious imagination, like Marx and Freud, but even those who have given us our most profound analyses: Nietzsche, Weber, Durkheim, Bataille. (William James is a rare exception.) It's almost impossible to broach the subject of religion without taking the movement of this narrative for granted. To be secular is to be modern. To be more secular is to be more modern. But religion clearly isn't withering away with the spread of modern rationalism and home entertainment centers. In a recent Gallup study 94 per cent of Americans say they believe in God. Better still: 88 per cent believe that God loves them personally. Yet this is the country that has always boasted of *not* having a feudal past, of being the world's most modern nation. It's enough to make you ask: Are we sick? How did we get here from there?

I'm as secular and modern as the next person, but I doubt that these statistics indicate a residue of pre-Enlightenment superstition. And I don't think that my own personal incoherence is entirely of the linear and progressive type. Even to raise the subject of personal incoherence, identity, and rupture is to see that, in a way, the secular imagination and the religious one have already settled out of court. For both the notion of having a rupture with your self *and* the notion of narrated personal coherence are Protestant conventions, heightened in all the American variants of Protestantism. No other culture goes as far as ours in making everything an issue of identity. We've invented an impressive array of religions: Mormons, Southern Baptists, Jehovah's Witnesses, Pentecostalists, the Nation of Islam, Christian Scientists, Seventh-Day Adventists—every last one of them a conversion religion. They offer you a new and perpetual personality, and they tell you your current one was a mistake you made. They tell you to be somebody else. I say: believe them.

6

Sexual Desire, Divine Desire; or, Queering the Beguines

Amy Hollywood

*A*my Hollywood is a scholar of sexuality and Christian studies and also the author of, among other works, Sensible Ecstasy: Mysticism, Sexual Difference, and the Demands of History. *This text is taken from an edited collection entitled* Toward a Theology of Eros: Transfiguring Passion at the Limits of Discipline. *In it, she discusses the writings of a number of medieval beguines and the ways in which they subverted or "queered" traditionally heteronormative readings of certain Christian spiritual writings. The beguines were religious women who lived together in Christian communities without being bound by the traditional vows that nuns would have taken. They purposely removed themselves from male authority and oversight, were self-sufficient, and many beguines were considered mystics. Hollywood reminds us of just how fluid erotic and religious desire can be, and how it can easily subvert heterosexual normativity, even when not seeming to do so.*

What I want to show here is that some late medieval women did use explicitly erotic language to discuss their relationship with Christ and they did so, often, in ways that challenged the prescriptive heterosexuality of the culture in which they lived. The challenge occurs not only through the feminization of Christ's body discussed by Lochrie, but also through an intense, hyperbolic, and often ultimately self-subverting deployment of apparently heterosexual imagery. This excess often involves a displacement of Christ as the center of the religious life and emphasis on a feminized figure of divine love. Among the beguines, semi-religious women who flourished in thirteenth-century northern Europe and are best known for their so-called bridal mysticism (and hence, it would seem, for a resolutely heterosexual, non-queer sexual imaginary) we find accounts of insane love and endless desire in which gender becomes so radically fluid that it is not clear *what* kind of sexuality—within the heterosexual/homosexual dichotomy most readily available to modern readers—is being metaphorically deployed to evoke the relationship between humans and the divine. Rather, as Rambuss argues with regard to early modern male-authored religious poetry, the absence in these texts "of a polarizing system of sexual types tends to open these works in the direction of a greater plasticity of erotic possibilities, possibilities not entirely containable by our own (often only suppositiously coherent) sexual dichotomies." The very inability to contain medieval divine eroticism within modern categories points to its potential queerness.

Religious desire and sexual desire are not the same, as Bennett usefully reminds us. Yet, in the evocative words of Michael Warner, "religion makes available a language of ecstasy, a horizon of significance within which transgressions against the normal order of the world and the boundaries of the self can be seen as good things." Moreover, religious writers often use the language of eroticism to express that ecstasy, excess, and transgression. Perhaps this is because erotic language is able, in ways that devotional language both exploits and intensifies, to engender affective states that push the believer beyond the limitations of his or her own body and desires. At the same time, the intensity of divine desire forces sexual language into new, unheard-of configurations. Hence the emergence in the later Middle Ages of what Lochrie aptly calls the "mystical queer." These religious representations do not reflect, nor even legitimate, particular configurations of human sexual relations—they often indeed seem to involve a movement beyond sexed and gendered bodies, even that of Christ, as the locus of pleasure and desire—but they do denaturalize and destabilize normative conceptions of human sexuality in potentially radical ways.

The centrality of the Song of Songs to medieval Christian devotional literature, images, and practices sets the stage for an intensely erotic and, at least on the surface, heterosexualized understanding of the relationship between the soul and God. Origen (ca. 185–254), the first Christian commentator on the Song of Songs whose work survives, reads the series of erotic poems as an allegory both for the relationship between Christ and the church and for that between Christ and the individual believer. The latter reading provides a central source for twelfth-century mystical exegetes like Bernard of Clairvaux (1090–1153), William of St. Thierry (ca. 1080–1148), and Rupert of Deutz (1077–1120), who increasingly emphasize the intensely erotic nature of the relationship between the lover and the beloved, the bridegroom and the bride, or Christ and the soul. When undertaken by male authors, these allegorical readings often involve a kind of linguistic transvestitism, whereby the male devotee becomes the female soul joined in loving union with the male figure of Christ. When undertaken by women, on the other hand, apparently normalized sexual roles often prevail.

So, for example, in Mechthild of Magdeburg's (ca. 1260–1282/94) *Flowing Light of the Godhead,* an understanding of the soul as the bride of Christ is joined with traditions derived from courtly literature. In Book I, Mechthild describes the soul as a lady, who dresses herself in the virtues so as to be prepared to welcome the prince.

After much waiting, in which the soul watches other holy people dance, "the young man comes and says to her: 'Young lady, my chosen ones have shown off their dancing to you. Just as artfully should you now follow their lead.'" The soul replies:

> I cannot dance, Lord, unless you lead me.
> If you want me to leap with abandon,
> You must intone the song.
> Then I shall leap into love,
> From love into knowledge,
> From knowledge into enjoyment,
> And from enjoyment beyond all human sensations.
> There I want to remain, yet want also to circle higher still.

Their dance is recorded in song: The young man sings, "Through me into you/ And through you from me" while the soul responds, like the alternately joyful and despondent bride of the Song of Songs, "Willingly with you/Woefully from you."

Mechthild makes explicit her preference for erotic over maternal metaphors in her conception of the relationship between the soul and Christ. Weary of the dance, the soul says to the senses that they should leave her so that she might refresh herself. The senses, wanting to stay with the soul, offer a series of refreshments in which they too might take part: "the blood of martyrs," "the counsel of confessors," the bliss of the angels, and finally, the milk of the Virgin enjoyed by the Christ Child. To this, the soul replies, "That is child's love, that one suckle and rock a baby. I am a full-grown bride. I want to go to my Lover." Although there the senses will "go completely blind," the soul asserts that her true identity is found in the nature of God:

> A fish in water does not drown.
> A bird in the air does not plummet.
> Gold in fire does not perish.
> Rather, it gets its purity and its radiant color there.
> God has created all creatures to live according to their nature.
> How, then, am I to resist my nature?
> I must go from all things to God,
> Who is my Father by nature,
> My Brother by his humanity,
> My Bridegroom by love,
> And I his bride from all eternity.

Just as Mechthild will insist that she is God's child by both grace and by nature (see 6.31), so here she claims to be daughter, sister, and bride of Christ, multiplying metaphors (all derived from the Song of Songs) without undermining the eroticism of the dance of love in which the dialogue appears.

Moreover, identification does not preclude, but rather seems to follow from the intensity of desire. After asserting the commonality of her nature with that of the divine,

> the bride of all delights goes to the Fairest of lovers in the secret chamber of the invisible Godhead. There she finds the bed and the abode of love prepared by God in a manner beyond what is human. Our Lord speaks:

> "Stay, Lady Soul."
> "What do you bid me, Lord?"
> "Take off your clothes."
> "Lord, what will happen to me then?"
> "Lady Soul, you are so utterly ennatured in me
> That not the slightest thing can be between you and me. . . ."
> Then a blessed stillness
> That both desire comes over them.
> He surrenders himself to her,
> And she surrenders herself to him.
> What happens to her then—she knows—
> And that is fine with me.
> But this cannot last long.
> When two lovers meet secretly,
> They must often part from one another inseparably.

As long as the soul remains within the body, the lovers can only meet fleetingly. The intensity of her desire and fusion with the divine both demands the use of erotic language and subverts it, for the body cannot sustain the experience of the divine embrace. (Although, as I will show below, Mechthild insists that the body will ultimately be reunited with the soul and share in its final glory.) The suffering to which God's presence and absence gives rise is then itself taken up as crucial to the path of desire for and identification with Christ.

The interplay of suffering and desire is also crucial to the poetry and prose of Hadewijch (fl. 1250) in ways that ultimately disrupt the hetero-normativity of the relationship between the soul and the divine prevalent in Mechthild's work. In a poem on the seven names of love, Hadewijch makes the spectacular claim that love, Hadewijch's favored name for the divine, is hell:

> Hell is the seventh name
> Of this Love wherein I suffer.
> For there is nothing Love does not engulf and damn,
> And no one who falls into her
> And whom she seizes comes out again,
> Because no grace exists there.

As Hell turns everything to ruin,
In Love nothing else is acquired
But disquiet and torture without pity;
Forever to be in unrest,
Forever assault and new persecution;
To be wholly devoured and engulfed
In her unfathomable essence,
To founder unceasingly in heat and cold,
In the deep, insurmountable darkness of Love.

For Hadewijch, the constant "comings and goings" of Love are a source of continual suffering, for the soul is caught between the ecstasy of the divine presence, Love's unrelenting demands for fidelity, and the constant threat of God's absence. Suffering does not preclude erotic desire, but is central to it. As Lochrie argues, "aggression, violence, masochism, and dark despair are as fundamental to the visions of some women mystics as the tropes of marriage and . . . languorous desire." For Lochrie, this kind of excessive, violent desire is "queer in its effects—exceeding and hyperbolizing its own conventionality and fracturing the discourses of mystical love and sex."

Hadewijch, like Mechthild, argues that this suffering love itself becomes a part of the soul's identification with Christ. As she writes in a letter to fellow beguines, "we all indeed wish to be God with God, but God knows there are few of us who want to live as human beings with his Humanity, or want to carry his cross with him, or want to hang on the cross with him and pay humanity's debt to the full." Yet this demand that the soul identify with Christ in his suffering humanity does not preclude a desire for the divine best expressed through the language of eroticism. Again like Mechthild, Hadewijch, particularly in her visions, makes use of imagery derived from the Song of Songs as the basis for her understanding of the union between the soul and Christ. One day while at Matins, she writes, "My heart and my veins and all my limbs trembled and quivered with eager desire and, as often occurred with me, such madness and fear beset my mind that it seemed to me I did not content my Beloved, and that my Beloved did not fulfill my desire, so that dying I must go mad, and going mad I must die." This leads Hadewijch to desire that her humanity "should to the fullest extent be one in fruition" with that of Christ, so that she might then "grow up in order to be God with God."

The vision that follows is the fulfillment of that desire. Looking at the altar, she first sees Christ in the form of a child of three years, holding the eucharistic bread in his right hand and the chalice in his left. The child then becomes a man and administers the sacrament to Hadewijch.

After that he came himself to me, took me entirely in his arms, and pressed me to him; and all my members felt his in full felicity, in accordance with the desire of my heart and my humanity. So that I was outwardly satisfied and transported. Also then, for a short while, I had the strength to bear this; but soon, after a short time, I lost that manly beauty outwardly in the sight of his form. I saw him completely come to naught and so fade and all at once dissolve that I could no longer recognize or perceive him outside me, and I could no longer distinguish him within me. Then it was to me as if we were one without difference. . . . After that I remained in a passing away in my Beloved, so that I wholly melted away in him and nothing any longer remained to me of myself.

Full union with Christ, expressed here through intensely erotic language, leads to a fusion and identification with profound theological implications. Although heterosexual in its imagistic operation, moreover, the melting away of the soul into the divine radically undermines any stable distinction between male and female and, more importantly for Hadewijch, between human and divine. The incarnation, in which God becomes human, is the basis for humanity's full identification with the divine.

Yet Hadewijch's work also undermines the association of masculinity with the divine and of femininity with the human, particularly in her stanzaic poems, in which the divine is represented as Love (*minne*, which is feminine), the unattainable female object of desire, and the soul as a knight-errant in quest of his Lady. Love cannot be clearly identified with Christ, the Holy Spirit, God the Father, or the Trinity; Hadewijch continually shifts and overlaps various divine referents. These poems again stress the cruelty of Love and the anguish to which her demand for desirous fidelity reduces the knight.

Sometimes kind, sometimes hateful,
Sometimes far, sometimes to hand.
To him who endures this with loyalty of love
That is jubilation;
How love kills
And embraces
In a single action

Those who are "Knight-errants in Love" live in an endless oscillation between darkness and light, the divine presence and her absence. The knightly soul is suspended between activity, "laying siege" to Love in desire and fidelity ("the brave," one poem advises, "should strike before Love does") and recognition that his "best success" lies in the suffering he undergoes when "shot by Love's arrow." Even as Hadewijch stresses the gap between the (feminine) divine and the (masculine) soul, then, she both undermines rigid gender distinctions and lays the groundwork for the eventual union of the soul and the divine through the soul's "mad love" and suffering desire—a union that occurs through Christ but is often poetically imagined without reference to his human body.

In the dialogues that make up Marguerite Porete's (d. 1310) *The Mirror of Simple Souls,* Porete similarly employs the feminine figure of Love as the most prominent representation of the divine. She goes even further than Hadewijch, moreover, in suggesting that while Christ and Christ's body play a crucial role in the path of the soul to union with love, ultimately the role of the body and of Christ will be surpassed. Instead, the female soul engages in a loving dialogue both with Lady Love and with the feminine Trinity, giving the text an intensely homoerotic valence absent in Mechthild's heterosexual account of the love between the soul and Christ and Hadewijch's transvestitism, in which the female soul becomes male in order to pursue Lady Love. Porete's Love and Soul provide a representation of those souls who have become so free of all created things, including will and desire, that they are indistinguishable from the divine.

I have argued elsewhere that Porete's pursuit of annihilation is a result of her desire to escape the intense suffering engendered by endless desire and "mad love." Absolute union with the divine occurs through the sacrifice of desire by desire. Yet the resulting loss of distinction between the soul and the divine also radically subverts, even erases, gender distinctions, a move both dependent on and subversive of the text's homoeroticism. (Porete uses the femininity of the Soul and Love to elicit pronominal ambiguities in which the gap between them is erased.) Porete's work, with its distrust of spiritual delights, ecstasies, and visions, stands in a critical relationship to that of her beguine predecessors. This is evident in her relationship to the imagery of erotic love. For Porete, like Hadewijch, Love is the primary name of the divine and she at times makes use of language and imagery derived from the Song of Songs, yet always in ways that undermine the initial gendered dichotomy between lover and beloved. This subversion seems dependent, as it is in Hadewijch, on a displacement of Christ's body.

The process can be seen most starkly in a crucial scene toward the end of the *Mirror* in which a now masculine God challenges the soul concerning the strength of her fidelity. Nicholas Watson argues that the series of hypothetical scenes recounted by the soul "are eccentric versions of the love-tests found in the tale of patient Griselda." Just as Griselda is honored for patiently submitting to the various tests of her fidelity posed by her distrustful husband, so the soul imagines a series of tests posed by God. She asks herself:

> as if He Himself were asking me, how I would fare if I knew that he could be better pleased that I should love another better than Him. At this my sense failed me, and I knew not how to answer, nor what to will, nor what to deny; but I responded that I would ponder it.
>
> And then He asked me how I would fare if it could be that He could love another better than me. And at this my sense failed me, and I know not what to answer, or will, or deny.
>
> Yet again, He asked me what I would do and how I would fare if it could be that He would will that someone other love me better than He. And again my sense failed, and I knew not what to respond, no more than before, but still I said that I would ponder it.

Using the imaginative meditative practices recommended within contemporary devotional treatises as a means of participating in and identifying with Christ's passion, Porete here enacts a Trial of Love reminiscent of those within secular courtly literature.

The trial leads to the death of the will and of desire (that same desire more often elicited and exploited through such meditative practices). In acquiescing to demands that go against her desire to love and be loved by God alone, the soul "martyrs" both her will and her love, thereby annihilating all creatureliness and, paradoxically, attaining a union without distinction with the divine. In Watson's evocative words, Porete "out-griselded Griselda," taking the test of submission to such extremes that subservience becomes the means by which the soul forces God to merge with her. Porete takes the cultural stereotype of the patient bride, who will submit to anything in fidelity to her bridegroom, and converts it into an account of how the Soul's fall into nothingness is itself the apprehension of her full share in the divine being. Like Mechthild, who insists that the soul is God's child by nature, thereby challenging late medieval versions of the doctrine of grace, Porete stresses throughout the *Mirror* the ways in which the soul, by emphasizing and embracing her sinfulness, abjection, and humility, can become one with God. Most crucially, as Watson argues, Porete shows the soul achieving "mystical annihilation of her own volition, *by telling herself stories.*" This particular story both depends on and subverts the hierarchically ordered gender expectations of late medieval culture.

Porete's use of erotic and gendered language is, like that of her fellow beguines Mechthild and, particularly, Hadewijch, remarkably complex. As the example offered here suggests, however, unlike Mechthild and Hadewijch—or perhaps better, more starkly than they—Porete posits the goal of the soul as the eradication of any distinction between herself and the divine. Porete evokes this union without distinction through the unsaying or apophasis of gender and the displacement of Christ's body as the center of religious devotion. With the overcoming of gender comes also the annihilation of desire and radical detachment from the body. (Perhaps the starkest evidence of this detachment from the body lies in the fact that Porete never mentions the doctrine of bodily resurrection.) With the annihilation of gender, will, and desire, also comes an end to the painful and ecstatic eroticism that runs throughout the texts of Mechthild and Hadewijch.

Porete's subversion of gender difference (grounded, needless to say, in her desire to overcome the gap between the soul and the divine) leaves no room for the vagaries of desire expressed in the closing dialogue of Mechthild's *Flowing Light*. There we hear the words of a body and soul who refuse, finally, to renounce their ambivalent and multivalent desires:

This is how the tormented body speaks to the lonely soul: "When shall you soar with the feathers of your yearning to the blissful heights to Jesus, your eternal Love? Thank him there for me, lady, that, feeble and unworthy though I am, he nevertheless wanted to be mine when he came into this land of exile and took our humanity on himself; and ask him to keep me innocent in his favor until I attain a holy end, when you, dearest Soul, turn away from me."

The soul: "Ah, dearest prison in which I have been bound, I thank you especially for being obedient to me. Though I was often unhappy because of you, you nevertheless came to my aid. On the last day all your troubles will be taken from you."

Then we shall no longer complain.
Then everything that God has done with us
Will suit us just fine,
If you will only stand fast
And keep hold of sweet hope.

This promise depends on the body's self-denial, for "the less the body preserves itself, the fairer its works shine before God and before people of good will." It is precisely the intense suffering of this desire and the self-denial to which it leads that give rise to Porete's attempt to save the soul and body through the martyrdom of the will.

Porete's utopian vision involves an effacement of differences—between God and soul, uncreated and created (including the body, will, and desire), and male and female—that, paradoxically, both queers hetero-normative desire and sacrifices the bodies and desires from which, in their multiplicity, contemporary queer theory and practice emerge. There is clearly no straight road from medieval mystical writings to contemporary practices and politics. In the writings of the beguines, desire is both a resource, an opportunity, and a problem—a problem to which Mechthild, Hadewijch, and Marguerite respond in very different ways. The divergence between them shows that although we cannot simply identify these women's accounts of religious experience with human sexual practices, what they write about their relationship to the divine originates in and remains tied to their experiences of themselves as embodied and desirous human beings. And even the most apparently heteronormative texts queer sexuality in that the object of this desire is not another human being, but (a) divine (Godman). The ecstasies of religion and those of sexuality are metaphorically linked at least in part because of their shared bodiliness, intensity, and tendency toward excess, an excess that, in the case of Marguerite Porete, leads to the subversion of the very grounds from which it emerges.

7

Kūkai and the Tradition of Male Love in Japanese Buddhism

Paul Gordon Schalow

*P*aul Gordon Schalow is a scholar of Japanese literature. This reading is taken from a
groundbreaking edited volume entitled Buddhism, Sexuality, and Gender. It offers
an uncommon and uncompromising look at the tradition of male same-sex desire
in Japanese Samurai culture, specifically that between men and boys. It recounts
the legend of how this sort of erotic practice was introduced as a type of spiritual
teaching. Though this is a highly problematic issue in the contemporary West, this
text reminds us that desire has been inflected in a wide variety of ways throughout
human history, and that one must be cautious about making general ahistorical
moral statements about sexual behavior. Very often, such age-differentiated sexual
relationships, as was the case in ancient Greece, were framed in pedagogical terms
as being necessary to the proper intellectual and social development of youth.

Apopular legend in Japan stated that male homosexual love (*nanshoku*) was
introduced to Japan from China in the ninth century by Kūkai (774–835), founder
of the True Word (*Shingon*) sect of esoteric Buddhism. This legend cannot be taken as
fact, of course. The introduction of a uniquely "priestly" mode of male homosexual
practice may have been accomplished in the eighth and ninth centuries during Kūkai's
lifetime, but it is safe to conclude that Kūkai played no more role in its introduction
than to serve as a focus for attribution of the phenomenon. The legend's significance
lies, rather, in the purpose it served in the lives of Buddhist believers and in how it
was given new meaning for secular society in the seventeenth century. To clarify the
scope of the legend, this chapter will look at three texts in which the legend appears:
Kōbō daishi ikkan no sho (1598, *Kōbō Daishi's Book*); *Iwatsutsuji* (1667, *Rock Azaleas*)
by Kitamura Kigin; and *Nanshoku ōkagami* (1687, *The Great Mirror of Male Love*) by

Ihara Saikaku. These texts will show that the Kūkai legend affirmed same-sex relations between men and boys in seventeenth century Japan, both in the spiritual world of temples and monasteries and in the secular world of samurai and merchants.

The Kūkai Legend

Kūkai transmitted the Buddhist esoteric tradition to Japan in 806 after his return from China, where he studied for almost two years under the Chinese master Hui-kuo (764–805). It was customary in True Word Buddhism for the mysteries of the faith to be transmitted orally from master to pupil, rather than in book form, and this meant that the relationship between master and disciple was of greatest importance. By the time Kūkai founded the True Word temple complex on Mt. Kōya in 816, his remarkable spiritual powers had already attracted a large number of disciples and made him the subject of legend even before his death there in 835.

During his lifetime, Kūkai made great contributions to the life and culture of Heian Japan through major civil engineering projects, his mastery and teaching of Chinese scholarship, and his original writings on Buddhist doctrine. In recognition of his contributions and the continued spiritual hold he exerted on Japanese believers, the imperial court conferred on him the posthumous title of Kōbō Daishi ("Great Teacher Transmitting the Dharma") in 921. In the centuries after Kūkai's death, the name Kōbō Daishi became associated with several important cultural, social, and historical developments that occurred during his lifetime and in which he may have played a role. In aggregate, the legends constituted a religious construct called Kōbō Daishi worship. Among the legends in that religious invention was one that he introduced male homosexual love to Japan. It is not known when this legend first developed, but a poem in Chinese by Ikkyū (1394–1481) is the first evidence we have of it. "Monju, the holy one, first opened this path; Kōbō of Kongō then revived it. Without male and female, its pleasures are like an endless circle; men shout with pleasure when they attain entrance." Far from detracting from his reputation as the object of Kōbō Daishi worship, this legend, like others, enhanced Kūkai's stature and apparently was thought of as compatible with his other spiritual and secular accomplishments.

Kōbō Daishi's Book

One of the earliest surviving manuscripts—dated 1598—to state a connection between Kūkai and male love is *Kōbō Daishi's Book*. The use of Kūkai's posthumous name in the title indicates that the connection was already well established, and that *Kōbō Daishi* is used largely as a byword for male love. The preface of the brief work describes how a layman goes into seclusion to pray to Kōbō Daishi for instruction in "the mysteries of loving boys in Japan" (*nihon shudō no gokui*). On the seventeenth day of the man's austerities, Kōbō Daishi appears and agrees to present him with a one-volume book explaining the love of boys, the basics of which "even monkeys in the hills and fields can comprehend." The text speaks of the "mysteries" of loving boys, implying a connection with the esoteric mysteries of True Word Buddhism. The fact that the preface identifies the book as personally transmitted by Kōbō Daishi substantiates the primary importance of the relationship between master and pupil in True Word Buddhism and, in a sense, legitimizes the book's contents.

Kōbō Daishi's Book, divided into three sections, claims to reveal secret teachings regarding the love of boys. The first section describes hand positions used by young acolytes to communicate their feelings to priests; the second section advises priests on how to evaluate an acolyte's emotions by observing him closely; and the final section describes methods of anal intercourse. The categories—hand positions, observations and penetration—bear a close resemblance to the four classes of Indian *tantras* associated with looking, touching, embrace, and penetration.

Part One

Part One decodes ten hand signals. The concern with positions of the hands and their meaning mimics, and possibly parodies, the holy hand positions (*mudrā*) that were an integral part of True Word teaching and religious practice. Priests and acolytes communicated their sexual feelings in the esoteric idiom of hand positions.

1   If an acolyte clenches his fingers—from the index finger to the little finger—it means "You are the only one I love."

2   If an acolyte clenches both hands completely except for one thumb, it means "I acknowledge your love and will make myself yours to do with as you please."

3   If an acolyte touches the index and middle finger to his thumb, it means he wants to see you.

4   If an acolyte flips the tassel of his fan, it is an invitation to visit.

5   If an acolyte forms a circle with the index finger and thumb on both hands, it means "Tonight." If he uses the middle finger, it means "Tomorrow night." And if he uses the ring finger, it means "Some other time."

6   If an acolyte touches the middle finger and ring finger to his thumb on both hands, it is an invitation to come visit.

7   If an acolyte touches the ring finger and little finger to his thumb, it means he wants to tell you something but cannot because people are watching; he'll try again the next night.

8   If something will prevent his coming as promised, he will touch the ring finger to his thumb on both hands.

9   If an acolyte touches the index and little fingers to his thumb, it means he will come again tomorrow night.

10   If an acolyte tugs at your sleeve, it means he definitely wants you to visit.

Part Two

Part Two instructs priests on seven ways to observe an acolyte so they can tell whether he is ready for lovemaking; and, if he is not, how to arouse him and make him ready. Several of the instructions are accompanied by twenty-one syllable Japanese poems (*waka*) that illustrate the lesson. The most important quality a priest looks for in an acolyte is *nasake,* an empathetic sensitivity to love. When a boy possesses this sensitivity, seduction is hardly necessary; without it, the task of seduction is difficult, at best.

1   After an acolyte has spoken, observe him carefully. The acolyte who speaks quietly is sensitive to love. To such a boy, show your sincerity by being somewhat shy. Make your interest in him dear by leaning against his lap. When you remove his robes, calm him by explaining exactly what you will be doing.

> White snow on a mountain peak
> turns to pure water on the rocks
> and finally flows down.

As this poem illustrates, snow on even the highest mountain peak is destined to melt and flow downward. Likewise, no matter how lacking in sensitivity to the mysteries of love an acolyte may be, he can be made yours if you approach him right.

2   An acolyte may be very beautiful but insensitive to love. Such a boy must be dealt with aggressively. Stroke his penis, massage his chest, and then gradually move your hand to the area of his ass. By then he'll be ready for you to strip off his robe and seduce him without a word.

> I gaze up at the distant top of a cedar tree;
> the wind blows strong,
> and even the cedar bends.

The poem illustrates that even a proud heart will yield if the effort is strong enough.

3   It is best to deal gently, not aggressively, with a gentle-hearted acolyte. Quietly put him at ease, and then penetrate him.

> I gaze up at the quiet moon at Isobé
> and my heart, too, grows calm.

4   If an acolyte practices martial arts, be sure to praise his swordsmanship. Then tell him some warrior tales. Things will proceed naturally from there.

> Before snow accumulates,
> it is shaken off the branches;
> in a windy pine, snow breaks no limbs.

As this poem illustrates, if snow is shaken off a pine before it has a chance to build up, it will not accumulate to the breaking point. Likewise, an acolyte's resistance should not be allowed to accumulate but be met as it comes; this is the only way to success.

5   If an acolyte is known to like birds, talk about birds—even if you hate them—as if you shared his interest. To an acolyte who likes to study, talk about his studies. After he opens up, you can do what you will with him.

6   The greatest pleasure is to proceed without resistance with an acolyte who possesses a great sensitivity to love.

7   If an acolyte is too shy to show himself to you, delay by plucking the hairs of your nose and then try again.

Part Three

Part Three concerns final consummation of the seduction in the form of anal intercourse with the acolyte. Seven positions are described in the idiom of tantric meditation postures; the sexual positions are given names evocative of those used in Buddhist texts to describe postures for meditation.

1   There is a method called *skylark rising*. The ass is raised in the air like a skylark rising in the sky. Insertion is painless.

2   Always keep "cut plums" on hand in case you want to attempt insertion without saliva.

3   There is a method call *turned-up soles*. Place the acolyte's legs on your shoulders and penetrate him from the front.

4   There is a method called *reverse drop*. Insertion is from above the turtle's tail, and should be accomplished gradually.

5   There is a method called *summer moat*. Press the boy's ass to the moat of your belly as you enter. The method is painless, even for a young acolyte.

6   There is a method called *dry insertion*. Moisten only slightly with saliva, then penetrate. The method causes severe pain.

7   The method for initiation is called *tearing the hole*. In this method, a man with a large penis penetrates in one thrust without lubrication. The method causes severe pain.

Conclusion

In the conclusion, the author attributes the teachings in *Kōbō Daishi's Book* to Kūkai himself, conveyed to him as a reward for his religious devotion. That attribution is the central legitimizing fact of the book. The postscript to the main manuscript consists of three popular beliefs about boy love that have parallels in beliefs about women: that women with small mouths were amorous, and that facial features gave clues to the shape of a woman's genitals.

I received this book of secret teachings from the founder of boy love in Japan, Kōbō Daishi, under the condition that I not show it to anyone. Signed Mitsuo Sadatomo, a hermit in Satsuma Fief.

1   An acolyte with a tiny mouth is best. They say that those with large mouths do not have tight asses.

2   It is best if the ass is slightly reddish in color. A dull ass may contain feces.

3   One look at a boy's face will tell you what his ass looks like.

I have taken the liberty of adding the above three lines. Submitted with humble respect by Mitsuo Sadatomo, in the third year of Keichō [1598], third month, a felicitous day.

Kōbō Daishi's Book bears the date 1598, well before the Genroku era (1688–1703) when books on sexuality were tinged with irony. Although not meant to be read ironically, the book nevertheless foreshadows the more modern Genroku approach to sex in the playfulness that comes through in certain passages. One such passage appears in the book's introduction: "The love of boys began in olden times when Kōbō Daishi made a vow of love with Wen Zhou. Sentient Being (*shujō*) refers to a man and boy who fall in love with each other, become fast friends, and make a vow of brotherly love; the phenomenon is recorded in many books. Because Kōbō Daishi began the practice of this way of love, it has been preserved all these years and continues to the present day in both Japan and abroad."

Sentient Beings (*shujō*) is a proper Buddhist term referring to all living things, but here it is defined as the love of boys (*shudō*). The confusion of the two terms may have been meant to elicit a laugh from the book's readers. If that is the case, what necessitated this linguistic inventiveness? The use of religious language and symbols in *Kōbō Daishi's Book* may represent not just religious heterodoxy but a challenge directed at a society defined by Confucian ethical constructs that discouraged sexual activity as socially disruptive in all but its most conventional forms.

Rock Azaleas

Rock Azaleas was the first collection of homoerotic poetry and prose in Japan, compiled in 1667 by Kitamura Kigin (1624–1705), scholar and adviser to the ruling Tokugawa shoguns. Most of the poems in the collection are addressed by priests to their acolyte lovers. The title comes from the opening poem, thought to be the first homoerotic poem in Japan, which appeared originally as an anonymous love poem in the tenth-century imperial anthology, *Kokinshū*.

> My stony silence
> recalls the rock azaleas
> of Mt. Tokiwa:
> you cannot know of my love—
> but how I long to meet you!

Kigin attributes this anonymous poem to Shinga Sōzu, one of Kūkai's ten major disciples who carried on the True Word tradition after Kūkai's death. Kigin's attribution is based on a fourteenth century commentary by Kitabatake Chikafusa (1293–1354), *Kokinshū-chū*, containing oral traditions about *Kokinshū* from the Nijō and Fujiwara court families and other sources. It is generally recognized that many anonymous poems in Japan's imperial anthologies were listed as such to conceal the identity of the poet. It therefore is a remote possibility that Kigin's attribution is based on knowledge of the true circumstances of the poem's composition. Far more likely, however, is the possibility that the poem's connection with Shinga Sōzu was a later invention.

Preface

Kigin's preface to *Rock Azaleas* is of great interest for the insight it provides into the way the connection between Buddhism and male love was conceptualized by at least one seventeenth century scholar.

> To take pleasure in a beautiful woman has been in the nature of men's hearts since the age of male and female gods, but for a man to take pleasure in the beauty of

another man goes against nature. Nevertheless, as relations between the sexes were forbidden by the Buddha, priests of the law—being made of neither stone nor wood—had no recourse but to practice the love of boys as an outlet for their feelings. Just as the waters that plummet and flow below the pass at Tsukubané form the deep pools of the Mino River, so this form of love proved to be deeper than the love between men and women. It afflicts the heart of aristocrat and warrior alike. Even the mountain dwellers who cut brushwood have learned of its pleasures. This form of love is rarely celebrated in Japanese poetry, however. Perhaps the first poem to do so was the one in *Kokinshū* by Kūkai's disciple, Shinga. This poem made the nature of male love apparent to the world, like a tassel of the pampas grass waving in the wind, so that even the uninitiated learned of its existence.

For our purposes, the most interesting point made in the preface is the connection between the supposed origins of male homosexuality in Japan and the Buddha's injunction forbidding priests to have sexual relations with women. It gives evidence of a generous view of human sexual need in the Japanese religious tradition, that "need"— in the unnatural situation where relations with the opposite sex are forbidden— supersedes the "natural" legitimacy of male and female relations. Whether physical necessity is enough to explain why priests became enamored of boys is an issue that will be discussed in the following section, where Saikaku's stories suggest that more is involved in the love of boys rather than just deprivation. By the seventeenth century, men may have entered the Buddhist priesthood because they were predisposed to the love of boys, the complete reverse of Kigin's vision.

The Great Mirror of Male Love

Ihara Saikaku (1624–1693) was known for most of his life as a poet of comic linked verse *(haikai)*, but in the last ten years of his life he turned to prose and became Japan's first commercial writer. His works are now ranked among the classics of Japanese literature. In 1687, he published a book called *The Great Mirror of Male Love,* a collection of forty short stories idealizing romantic relations between men and boys in samurai and merchant class circles. The introductory chapter of the book recounts the history of male love in Japan. Because Saikaku's purpose was to entertain his readership, he was inventive in his account. At one point he makes reference to the Kūkai legend: "Kōbō Daishi did not preach the profound pleasures of this love outside the monasteries because he feared the extinction of humankind. No doubt he foresaw the popularity of boy love in these last days of the law."

Saikaku took the legend of Kūkai and made it relevant outside the Buddhist tradition by claiming that Kūkai originally suppressed knowledge of male love except in Japan's monasteries and temples because the time was not yet ripe for universal dissemination of its secrets; he foresaw that male love would gain followers and be better suited to the "last days of the law" (*mappō*), the period of degeneration and decline heralding the end of the world, when the impending extinction of humankind made sexual procreation a moot issue. What more fitting form of sexuality for a doomed age—Saikaku seems to suggest—than nonprocreative love between men and boys? Saikaku's readership must have enjoyed the bold humor of this claim.

The Great Mirror of Male Love contains several detailed depictions of Buddhist priests and monks involved in homosexual relations with boys. The second story in the collection, "The ABCs of Boy Love" (1.2), is the story of Daikichi and Shinnosuké, two boys who "were always side by side, inseparable as two trees grafted together or a pair of one-winged birds. When the boys later reached their peak of youthful beauty, men and women, clergy and layman alike were all smitten with the handsome youths. The two were the cause of a thousand sorrows, a hundred illnesses, and untold deaths from lovesickness." The narrative continues with a brief but fascinating passage about the effect of their beauty on a certain Buddhist monk.

At about this time, there lived in the far reaches of Shishigatani a Buddhist ascetic who was over eighty years old. They say that from the moment he chanced to see these two splendid boys, his concentration on future salvation failed him and the good deeds he had accumulated in previous incarnations went to naught. News of the priest's feelings reached the boys. Not sure which of them the old gentleman had his heart set on, both went to his crude abode for a visit. Predictably, he found it impossible to dispense with either cherry blossoms or fall foliage. Thus, he satisfied with both of them the love he had harbored from spring through autumn.

The next day, both boys paid another visit to the priest, for there was something they had neglected to tell him, but he was nowhere to be found. They discovered only a poem, dated the previous day, tied to a forked branch of bamboo:

Here are travel weeds
Tear-stained like my faithless heart
Torn between the two;
I shall cut my earthly ties
And hide myself away in bamboo leaves.

Of what was this old priest ashamed? Long ago, the priest Shinga Sōjō wrote:

Memories of love revive,
Like rock azaleas bursting into bloom
On Mt. Tokiwa;
My stony silence only shows
How desperately I want you!

The boys took the bamboo branch and had a skilled artisan make it into a pair of flutes.

The juxtaposition of these two poems and the implication of guilt suggests an interpretation of their meaning. The first poem represents the parting words of an old monk who consummated his love for the boys, whereas the second poem is by a priest who denied himself even the expression of his love in words. There is deliberate ambiguity in the line "torn between the two" in the first poem; does it refer to the choice between two boys, or the choice between earthly and spiritual concerns? The poem states that the conflict has caused the monk to vow to sever his ties with the world—a vow first made when he originally took the tonsure—and live in seclusion. It implies that he was ashamed by his failure to concentrate on spiritual concerns. But that failure ultimately led to the renewal of his vow and represents a triumph of sorts. The positive outcome is typical of the literary tradition of Acolyte Tales *(chigo monogatari)* dating from the Muromachi period (1392–1568). The old ascetic's faithless heart in the first poem contrasts dramatically with the other priest's faithfulness to his vows in the second poem. Shinga's heart—if the poem is indeed by Shinga Sōjō—burns in silence, unconsummated but guiltless. Ironically, unspoken passion may be the greater sin of the two, for unresolved lust is among the most powerful earthly ties in Buddhism. By sinning, the old priest achieves a spiritual renewal that eludes the second poet. Perhaps that is why Saikaku asks, "Of what was this old priest ashamed?"

In "The Sword That Survived Love's Flames" (3.3), Saikaku's narrative tells the story of two traveling companions on their way to worship at Mt. Kōya, Kūkai's seat of spiritual power. Along the way, they observe the following:

[A] priest who looked as if he might be in charge of one of Mt. Kōya's temples came by with a young cowherd from one of the temple-owned farm villages. He had obviously tried to disguise the boy as a temple acolyte, but dirt was plainly visible behind the boy's ears. His hair was properly bound up, but it looked reddish and dry. The sleeves of his plain, light-blue hemp robe were far too short; it seemed to be an adult's round-sleeved robe slit under the arms to make him look boyish. He sported a pair of long swords, no doubt consigned to the temple by a parishioner in mourning. The sword guards were too big for the small hilts. The boy slouched under their unaccustomed weight as he walked along in the priest's tow. The men watched them pass, impressed with the priest's ingenuity.

The humor in this passage derives from the priest's not entirely successful attempt to disguise a farmboy as an acolyte so that he can smuggle the boy into his temple quarters. The majority of temple acolytes would have been of samurai or aristocratic birth, making it difficult for a farmboy to resemble them. His hair lacked the luster of a samurai boy's well-groomed and oiled hair; he was unaccustomed to the weight of a sword, something samurai always carried; and as he already was too old to wear the open-vented sleeves of an adolescent boy, slits had to be cut in the sleeves of his own adult robe so he would look like a younger man. Saikaku was writing primarily for an urban merchant-class audience, who would have enjoyed making fun of the Buddhist clergy. The humor is directed not at the priest's taste for boys, which Saikaku's readers shared, but at the duplicity involved in smuggling a young man into the temple for sexual purposes. Saikaku's concern is not to moralize, but to draw attention to the hypocrisy in much of human behavior, and he does so to great effect.

Saikaku reserves his most scathing depiction of hypocrisy in the clergy for the latter half of *The Great Mirror of Male Love,* where he deals with boy prostitution in the kabuki theater. Although merchant-class men can properly engage kabuki actors for prostitution without breaking any vows, priests who do so are branded as wayward for their failure to abandon sexual pleasures. In "A Huge Winecup Overflowing with Love" (6.1), Saikaku opens the narrative with biting sarcasm.

> They say that Buddhist priests are "scraps of wood" purged of all feeling, but there is no occupation more pleasant in the world. They can hold parties in their temples whenever they please, their only duties to intone the *sūtras* of their sects and don robes when meeting parishioners. Rather than waste the offerings of the faithful on things without meaning, they use the money to buy the love of young actors, entertainment well suited to the priest's lot.
>
> Even when entertaining boys in their rooms, they never once forget the gravity of their vows and adhere religiously to their vegetarian diet of stewed dumplings and mushrooms, chilled chestnuts with silvervine pickled in miso, and clear soup of sweet seaweed and salted plums. With these delicacies they extend their drinking bouts through the long nights. (How they can drink!) Such sincere devotion to their vows is highly commendable. Just because they do not suffer Buddha's immediate divine punishment does not mean chief priests can go ahead and enjoy the meat of fish and fowl. After all, if priests could indulge in fish and women to their hearts' content, it would be foolish for a man not to take the tonsure!

The preceding passage sets a humorous tone in a story about a boy actor, Itō Kodayū. Condemnation of priests for humorous effect is not uncommon in Saikaku's narratives. In an earlier narrative, Saikaku went so far as to blame priests of the wealthy Rinzai sect for inflating the price of boy prostitutes. "Tears in a Paper Shop" (5.1) begins with a brief history of boy prostitution in the kabuki theater, the major features of which are historically accurate, though his comments about priests are difficult to verify.

> [O]ne year wealthy priests assembled in the capital from all over the country to commemorate the 350th anniversary of the death of Zen Master Kanzan, first rector of Myōshin-ji. After the religious services were over, they went sightseeing at the pleasure quarter on the dry riverbed. They fell in love with the handsome youths there, the likes of which they had never seen in the countryside, and began buying them up indiscriminately without a thought for their priestly duties. Any boy with forelocks who had eyes and a nose on his face was guaranteed to be busy all day.
>
> Since that time, boy actors have continued to sell themselves in two shifts, daytime and nighttime. The fee for a boy who was appearing onstage rose to one

piece of silver. The priests did not care about the cost, since they had only a short time to amuse themselves in the capital. But their extravagance continues to cause untold hardship for the pleasure-seekers of our day.

Saikaku's narrator expresses resentment of the priests for making boy actors too expensive for local men to afford as prostitutes, a perspective that would have appealed to Saikaku's merchant-class readers. The Rinzai sect, of which Kanzan Egen (d.1359) was a major spiritual leader, was known as a wealthy one, so its priests could have afforded actor's fees more easily than most. Priests from less well-to-do sects often went to extreme lengths to pay for their nights of love. Saikaku records some of their methods in "Love's Flame Kindled by a Flint Seller" (5.3).

At his appointments, Sennojō entertained with a slight flush of wine on his cheeks, pale red like maple leaves in autumn. One look could drive a man mad with desire. Wayward priests from Takao, Nanzen-ji, and Tōfuku-ji, not to mention myriad other temples, sometimes sold entire collections of calligraphy passed down for generations in their temples, whereas others cut down and sold whole forests of trees and bamboo under temple jurisdiction, all for the sake of acquiring the love of this boy. Afterwards they were invariably thrown out of their temples with nothing but an umbrella to hide their shame.

If there were those, as the preceding passage suggests, who were driven from Buddhist orders for the sake of boy love, there also were those who joined Buddhist orders for the same reason. One such example appears in "Bamboo Clappers Strike the Hateful Number" (7.4). In the story , a group of young actors and their patrons are on an excursion to pick mushrooms in Fushimi, outside the capital of Kyoto. They come upon an isolated hut in the hills and look inside. It is the home of a recluse monk.

Inside, the walls were papered at the base with letters from actors. Their signatures had been torn off and discarded. Curious, the boys looked more closely and discovered that each letter concerned matters of love. Each was written in a different hand, the parting messages of kabuki boy actors. The monk who lived there must once have been a man of some means, they thought. He apparently belonged to the Shingon sect, for when they opened the Buddhist altar they found a figure of Kōbō Daishi adorned with chrysanthemums and bush clover, and next to it a picture of a lovely young actor, the object no doubt of this monk's fervent devotion.

When they questioned him, the monk told them about his past. As they suspected, he was devoted body and soul to the way of boy love.

"I was unhappy with my strict father and decided to seclude myself in this mountain hermitage. More than two years have passed, but I have not been able to forget about boy love even in my dreams." The tears of grief he wept were enough to fade the black dye of his priestly robes. Those who heard it were filled with pity for him.

This passage indicates the strong hold that the legend of Kūkai must have had on the imaginations of both Saikaku and his readers. It suggests that there was a strong positive association between Buddhist tradition, particularly in the True Word sect, and male love. The association of True Word Buddhism with male love stemmed in part from its condemnation of sexual relations with women, in part because of its emphasis on the personal transmission of secret teachings from master to pupil, something that apparently led to strong emotional bonds between priests and their acolytes. Finally, because of the strong Confucian orthodoxy that discouraged overly personal visions of self and society, it was perhaps natural that the esoteric religious tradition and its founder in Japan, Kūkai, be rediscovered and, in a sense, reinvented in the seventeenth century as a social heterodoxy legitimizing the sexuality of men in the urban merchant class. Only further study clarifying the complex blend of social, religious, and sexual issues at play in the Kūkai legend will allow us to answer why this component of the Japanese Buddhist tradition of male love had such an impact on secular life and literature in the seventeenth century.

8

The Passions of St. Pelagius

Mark D. Jordan

*M*ark D. Jordan is a theologian and scholar of gay religious history who has been influential in the development of a distinctively queer religious scholarship. He is the author of, among other works, The Silence of Sodom: Homosexuality in Modern Catholicism *and* Recruiting Young Love: How Christians Talk about Homosexuality. *This excerpt, taken from the first chapter of* The Invention of Sodomy in Christian Theology, *offers a richly nuanced "queer" analysis of the life and death of the young martyr St. Pelagius as seen through the eyes of two medieval male and female monastic authors. It raises questions about how religious desire is framed and written about, and thereby appropriated for particular cultural and literary purposes, and how it might intersect with sexuality, especially same-sex desire in a Christian context. The reading also considers issues of racialized colonial discourse, particularly with respect to Islam.*

With time, the martyr Pelagius would become younger, more eloquent, more desirable. In 925 or 926, when he was martyred, he was thirteen years old, precociously pious, and a prisoner in Cordoba with other Christians. According to the testimony of his fellow prisoners, his beauty was such that the caliph, 'Abd al-Rahmân III, desired to add him to his household as another sexual attendant. Pelagius refused to succumb to the king's desire, as he refused to renounce Christianity. And so, the witnesses say, he was first tortured and then dismembered.

In reading some medieval variations on this story, I do not mean to be cynical about whatever was suffered in fact by the boy behind it. Who can be cynical about torture, for whatever reason, or about the savageries of religions? But I do mean to examine what cynicism there is already in medieval tellings of the story of Pelagius. The appalling events, whatever they were, became early on the vehicle for increasingly overbearing lessons, both patriotic and religious. From the first, there is no disentangling the "facts" of Pelagius's suffering from the polemical uses of it. Nor is it possible to disentangle the retellings of the passions of Pelagius from the ambivalent relations of Iberian Christianity to the same-sex love it thought was preached and practiced by Islam.

The dating and the interrelation of the earliest texts about Pelagius are not known, though it seems clear that three different kinds of texts were written within fifty years of his death. The first presents itself as a narrative of his passion based on eyewitness accounts. It was written in Iberia before 967 by an otherwise unknown priest, Raguel. The second text is a metrical life of Pelagius by the Saxon canoness Hrotswitha. It may also belong to 960s. The third text is a Mozarabic liturgy, an office of St. Pelagius from León, written perhaps in or after 967 to mark the arrival of the saint's relics—or perhaps thirty years earlier to memorialize his wonders. I am less interested in the precise dating of the works than in the ways their genres transmute the underlying account and deflect its dangers.

The first genre for the telling of Pelagius's death is a narrative constructed from the testimony of eyewitnesses. The narrative does not pretend to be transcribed testimony. It is a well-crafted story of a martyrdom, beginning with an invocation of divine aid and ending with a claim on Pelagius as patron of the local church. In between there are deft quotations of Scripture, moral applications, and classical allusions. The author is a priest, Raguel, who is identified in one manuscript as the "teacher of this passion." Raguel is not without his teacherly pretensions. He begins with self-conscious reflections on beginning. He proceeds often through antitheses, which he uses in series to amplify or punctuate the basic narrative. Questions about the scope of Raguel's literary learning will soon become important, but his polished and polemical purposes in telling the story stand forth no matter how one decides them. Raguel is eloquent in order to condemn the religion, the morals, and the savagery of the young saint's Islamic captors.

Pelagius himself was not captured by them. He was given as a substitute for a clerical relative, the bishop Hermoygius. Hermoygius had been taken prisoner after the rout of Christian forces at Valdejunquera in the summer of 920. He was at risk of death because of the hardships of imprisonment. So he arranged for his ten-year-old cousin to take his place, hoping all the while, our chronicler notes, that other captives would be sent in place of his young surrogate. Once in prison, Pelagius lived an exemplary life under divine guidance. He was able to overcome even those temptations that had afflicted him in the world. Principal among his virtues was chastity. He kept his body whole. He "purified the vessel" to prepare it as a fitting chamber in which to rejoice as the spouse (*sponsus*) of Jesus, to delight in the bloody embrace of martyrdom as marriage.

Jesus, teaching him inwardly, began to transform Pelagius outwardly. Raguel cannot find words enough for description. The boy's appearance "praised" the teacher within. He was "signally decorated" by the signs of his destination in paradise. His face took on a "lovelier beauty." Indeed, word of this attractiveness reached the Muslim "king," who is not here named by Raguel. (The name is given only in a colophon.) The king sends for Pelagius to be brought to him at a banquet. Pelagius is dressed in royal robes and led into the hall, the attendants whispering that he is fortunate to have his beauty carry him so far. The king offers the boy much to renounce Christ and affirm Mohammed: wealth, opulent clothing, precious ornaments, life in the court. There is even the offer of the companionship of any of the court's young men (*tiruncult*), with whom Pelagius can do what he will. The king further promises to free from jail a number of other Christians, including Pelagius's relatives.

All of this Pelagius refuses with a string of contrasts between the passing of temporal things and the eternity of Christ. Ignoring the refusal, the king reaches out to touch Pelagius *joculariter*. The adverb is odd. It could mean something like "humorously," but that meaning hardly fits here. In Ovid, who may well be on Raguel's mind, the root verb, *joco*, is used as a metaphor for copulation. So *tangere joculariter* may mean at least "to touch sexually" and perhaps even "to fondle" in the quite sexual sense. How else can one explain Pelagius's reaction? He strikes the king and spits out a contemptuous question: "Do you think me like one of yours, an effeminate (*effeminatum*)?"

Raguel's Pelagius may mean "effeminate" in the general sense that connects any form of sexual self-indulgence with womanliness. This would seem to go along with the martyr's choice of Paul as model. But Pelagius may also have in mind the more specific sense that *effeminatum* has in one passage of the Vulgate. There, in a condemnation of the reign of Roboam, the "effeminate" are those who commit "all the abominations of the gentiles, which God destroyed before the face of the sons of Israel." The reference would seem to be both to the destruction of Sodom and to the sexual abominations condemned in Leviticus. So the "effeminate" would seem to be those who "lie with a man as with a woman." Certainly Pelagius's next response emphasizes the sexual character of the king's touch. The martyr rips off the fine gown in which he has been dressed and he stands forth, naked, like a "strong athlete in the palaestra."

The king does not immediately command Pelagius's destruction. He imagines rather that the boy might be changed by the "pimping persuasions" of the court's young men. It is only when these prove unsuccessful, when the king feels his own desires spurned, that the anger rises in him. He orders Pelagius to be seized with iron tongs and twisted about, until he should either renounce Christ or die. Pelagius does neither. So the king demands at last that the boy be cut to pieces with swords and thrown into the river. Raguel describes the dismemberment graphically. What is more, he likens the frenzy of Pelagius's executioners to the mad rites of the Bacchae: "they were turned into Bacchae (*debacchati sunt*) through the mad desires" unleashed in the hacking, so much so that one would have thought that they were sacrificing the boy rather than executing him. Throughout these torments the voice of Pelagius is heard calling out for God's help. The "athlete's" voice is stilled only after he is called to the martyr's crown by the Lord.

The reference to the Bacchae and the emphasis on the unstilled voice are striking, especially in a passage so rich in the customary images of Christian martyrdom. The verb *debacchor* is rare. Not just the allusion, but the archaizing word used to make it put the reader in mind of poetic learning, of expertise in pagan mythography. Poetic associations seem to be confirmed by what happens in Raguel's narration to the saint's speaking body. The martyr who would not be silent is to be cut apart and then drowned.

So it is. His limbs come to rest on one shore, his severed heard on another. Any reader of Latin poetry will hear in these events echoes of the death of Orpheus. Orpheus too was cut apart by a tribe of Bacchae, who seized tools from terrified farmers in order to kill him. The voice that had charmed animals with its singing fell silent under the blades. Yet once thrown into the river, Orpheus somehow still sang, borne down towards the sea. Only this miracle is lacking in Pelagius to make the likeness complete.

Is the dismemberment of Pelagius meant by Raguel to call to mind the death of Orpheus? Certainly parts of the Orpheus myth had been allegorized for Christian purposes long before Raguel began to write. The allegory is presented in Boethius's *Consolation,* for example, and then appropriated by a number of his readers in both vernacular and Latin forms. But the part of the myth that matters to the passion of Pelagius is not the already allegorized loss of Eurydice. It is rather Orpheus's dismembering because of his refusal to have sexual relations with women after Eurydice's second death. Indeed, Ovid begins his narration of the dismembering by noting that Orpheus taught Thracian men the love of boys. The connection between Orpheus and same-sex love would be registered by later commentators, as it would pass into the vernacular traditions. Now Ovid's *Metamorphoses* was known in Spain as Raguel wrote. It may be that he means to Christianize this other part of the Orpheus myth by inverting it: Pelagius becomes the Christian Orpheus because he is dismembered not just for his purity, but for his explicit rejection of same-sex desire.

One could hear other mythic resonances. The martyrdom of Pelagius inverts or reclaims the well-known tale of Zeus and Ganymede. If Zeus kidnapped the Phrygian boy to be his cupbearer, the Muslim king wants to abduct Pelagius from Christianity for service in his hall. The change of condition from the hillsides near Troy to Olympus is no greater than the change from the dark prison to the resplendent court. But Pelagius is in fact called for service at the table of a higher king. His beauty is the visible sign of his having been chosen for the service of Christ, to whom he will be both *sponsus* and *famulus,* both spouse and household intimate. Christ already intends that he should stand beside the heavenly throne in the chorus of virgins. Pelagius, spurning the crown of the Muslim tyrant, receives the long-promised crown from the hands of Jesus. And his spirit "migrates" to heaven—as if carried by eagle's wings. Of course, and to interrupt the series of echoes, it is always difficult to judge how far these literary associations can be assigned to Raguel. I want to assign them only in the most specific case. Raguel does mean to call up Ovid on Orpheus, though he may not have any clear notion of how he will manage the Ovidian allusions once they are called to mind.

Even if the relation to Ovid were denied, it could not be denied that Raguel suggests complications in the story that he cannot quite control. There is, for example, Pelagius's familiarity with practices of same-sex desire. However the king wished to touch him, no single touch could communicate all that is contained in Pelagius's contemptuous question, "Do you think me like one of yours, an effeminate?" Pelagius already knows that there are "effeminates" and that they serve for certain kinds of sexual uses. He not only recognizes the king's gesture as sexual, he recognizes the sexual script from which it comes. How does he know this? From the clichés of anti-Islamic polemic preached in Christian communities? He does call the king "dog," one of many animal epithets familiar from anti-Islamic tracts. Or does Pelagius know the king's sexual customs from prison whispers, from the sight of prisoners taken out overnight? Or from the bragging promises of servants? However he knows, Pelagius comes into the presence of the king forewarned that he is a likely object of male sexual desire.

So the martyr's next gesture of rejection is the more striking. Pelagius strips off the costly robes with which he has been decorated. He thus repudiates "effeminacy." He also exposes the body that is the object of desire. Instead of concealing what the king wants, he presents it aggressively. Raguel assimilates this to the tradition of Christian martyrology by likening Pelagius to an athlete, naked in the palaestra. In context the gesture taunts the king. Pelagius the martyr is quite plainly Pelagius the ephebe, the type of young male beauty. He rips off his own clothes, as an eager lover might, just to show the king what he cannot have. The sight of that body may be one reason the king is slow to anger, preferring persuasion instead. Only when persuasion fails does the royal desire, excited by Pelagius's display, turn ferocious. Even then, the king hopes that the pain of the iron forceps may bring Pelagius to denounce Christ and so recover his body from pain for pleasure.

Pelagius knows the customs of same-sex desire, and he plays with that desire itself when he strips before the king in order to spurn him. He spurns the king as well in what he says. When Pelagius proclaims that he "cherishes Christ," when he chooses to the or to suffer "for Christ," when he invokes no one other than "the Lord Jesus Christ," he is speaking the name of his true love in the face of a rival. For the king, the choice facing Pelagius seems to be between pleasure and pain, between his own gracious self and a fictive god. For Pelagius, the choice seems to lie between ephemeral and permanent pleasure, between an earthly and a heavenly king, between an imperfect lover and a perfect one. The story of the martyrdom is, through Pelagius's eyes, the story of a passionate triangle in which all the parties are male. He does not deny same-sex love so much as he vindicates it by choosing Christ as his lover.

Pelagius vindicates it tacitly. It is remarkable that Raguel nowhere gives a special name to the sin that the king wishes to practice on the body of the young martyr. He does not even describe the king's motives except to note that what he heard of Pelagius "pleased" him. The ensuing events are placed under other, more general categories of sin. The Moors want to "cover over his form with the torrents of vices." Certainly there is no detailed description of the acts the king might have wanted to perform with the boy, much less any sense that the king is peculiar in wanting them. If the vices are meant to disgust Raguel's readers, they are also presumed to be familiar to them.

They are familiar not only or principally as acts, but as a cluster of habits. Extravagance, pride in power, and sexual perversion go together for Raguel as they do in late Roman notions of *luxuria,* in patristic commentary on the story of Sodom, and in early medieval categorizations of sin. To say this again: Erotic disorder is caught up in a system of causes with opulence, which is itself viewed as feminizing, and with arrogance, which is the root of all spiritual disorder. Raguel knows this from many sources. He also knows that the vice of same-sex copulation has been implicated in darker causalities—that it has been linked to bestial cruelty, to the loss of humanity. In Prudentius, for example, Luxury is characterized more by violent rage than by softness. Raguel's polemical use of Pelagius's suffering against Islam, his appropriation of Pelagius for the cause of Christian Iberia, is perfectly compatible with a simultaneous use of the story to reinforce the nascent theological project of moral categorization. Within this categorization, sexual sins will come to have a more and more prominent place. Indeed, the sins of same-sex copulation will soon become a favored synecdoche for sin itself.

But not without introducing various instabilities. Raguel's apparently ingenuous testimony to the sufferings of the young boy is polemical and ideological. It is also unstable, so far as it must presume that same-sex desire is familiar, domestic, imaginable. After all, God shows favor to Pelagius by making him desirable, not repulsive. Pelagius is beautiful, not ugly. The boy's body is the body of the ancient ephebe, and the telling of his triumph necessarily calls to mind a string of earlier tales in which ephebes have been loved by gods—and onlooking poets. The passion of Pelagius as retold by Raguel passes down a number of difficult problems alongside its obvious lessons.

The explicit lessons are, on Raguel's telling, eminently scriptural. The *Passion* echoes scriptural language throughout, as it recalls the oldest lives of the Christian martyrs. Beneath these obvious lessons lie others, especially the lessons of Christian struggles against the Muslim regimes. The final request that Raguel makes of the boy-saint is a request for patronage. The martyr who rejected earthly allurements in favor of Christ's promises should accept the offerings of the local church, the church that struggles against his murderers. There is now no mention of his beauty, only a reference to his refusal of "pleasures" (*deliciae*) and "enticements" (*blanditiae*) The details of the caliph's proposal are now subsumed in a crusading spirit, reduced only to an outrage that must be avenged. What is to be retained from the story is a sense of Pelagius's patronage in the coming battle to avenge him. Of the problems posed by Ovid or the customs of the Moors or the descriptions of Pelagius's own desire, the listener is to retain only the motive of pious warfare.

The story of Pelagius did not remain confined within Iberia. It traveled, quickly and far, by unknown means. If the means are unknown, the genres for recording and disseminating the story were anciently familiar to Christians. The story could spread so quickly because it fit—or was made to fit—into one of the oldest of Christian literary forms. The events of Cordoba were not only news, they were confirmation that the God of the ancient martyrs continued to work miracles down to the present day. The passion of Pelagius is incorporated into the writings of the canoness Hrotswitha of Ganderheim in Saxony with just these motives. Much has been written about Hrotswitha, much of it admiring. Rightly so, since her works show eloquence and erudition. Certainly she stands, as an author, above the level reached by Raguel. But my aim here is not to praise Hrotswitha's authorship. It is to notice what changes she makes in rewriting the desires that Pelagius provoked.

Hrotswitha writes her verse passion of Pelagius, as she writes her plays, according to elaborate symmetries. Some of these are thematic, others are formal or ornamental.

Her versification of the martyrdom of Pelagius stands out within these patterns for its newness. It is the only hagiographical text to record recent events. The second nearest story is no more recent than the eighth century. Moreover, Hrotswitha's title underscores the story's newness: "The Passion of St. Pelagius, Most Precious Martyr, Who Was Crowned with Martyrdom in Cordoba in Our Own Day (*nostris temporibus*)." Pelagius is particularly present to Hrotswitha because he is so recent. Indeed, her knowledge of him comes not from antecedent texts, but from hearing stories. One of her tasks is to bring these tales under the control of the established textual patterns.

Hrotswitha begins to do so in the very first lines. She deploys a literary formula to call on the young saint. Raguel had invoked Pelagius at the end of his narrative as patron of local churches. The invocation was public and corporate. Hrotswitha begins her verse legend with a personal call to the boy-saint. This noble knight of the King who reigns through the ages is to look down on her, his handmaid, who attends to him in mind and heart. He is to grant her the ability to write of his marvels and his triumph. What Pelagius grants is a poem in several parts, much more suited for non-Iberian audiences than Raguel's terse recital. The poem's first part sets the stage by describing the long-standing idolatry and luxury of the Muslims in Cordoba, a city "inclined to delicacies." The next section narrates the reign of "Abdrahemen," a man "stained by the excess (*luxus*) of the flesh," and his successful war against the Christian armies. It ends with the capture of Christian leaders and the Muslim ruler's treacherous dickering over the terms of their release. The poem's third part introduces Pelagius, who is distinguished at once by his bodily beauty. Indeed, Hrotswitha mentions his beauty before going on to talk of his prudence and goodness, and she ends the introductory description by noting the he had attained "the first flowers of the age of adolescence."

Differences from Raguel's account have already appeared, and not merely in the richness of the artifices employed. In Hrotswitha's telling, for example, Pelagius volunteers for imprisonment in place of his father, a Christian nobleman. There is a direct speech in which the boy pleads with his father to be sent as a substitute, using the argument that his body can better withstand the sufferings to be inflicted. The reader notes both Pelagius's filial piety and his physical attributes. What is more, the reader gets to hear the boy's extraordinary eloquence. Both eloquence and beauty bring Pelagius to the attention of some courtiers once he has been imprisoned. For Hrotswitha, the courtiers are mostly blameless in their dealings with the boy. They wish to free him from the harshness of the prison. Unfortunately they decide to appeal to their king's taste for special pleasures. The courtiers know that he has been "corrupted by Sodomitic vices." He wants "to love" beautiful youths "ardently" and join with them in "particular friendship." Surely the king would want to see the outstanding form (*praenitida forma*) of Pelagius—to enjoy his honeyed speech, to have his shining body (*corpus candidulus*) for service in the great hall.

Where Raguel allowed the motive vice to remain nameless and to hang over the whole court as a general condemnation, Hrotswitha names it with the requisite

Christian term and confines it to a single, sinning soul. It is the king, and only the king, who has been corrupted by "Sodomitic vices." If Cordoba as a whole was rather too prone to sins of the flesh, 'Abd al-Rahmân was egregiously corrupt, "worse than his parents, smirched with the excess of the flesh." By appealing to his allegedly exceptional vice, the Cordoban courtiers do succeed in persuading the king. He orders Pelagius bathed, swathed in purple, and adorned with a gem-encrusted necklace. The ornamented youth is brought before him. Overcome by the beauty, the king begins to burn. He puts his arm around Pelagius's neck and kisses him. Pelagius responds bitingly to this "pagan king" who is, Hrotswitha says again, "marred by the excess of the flesh." No Christian knight who has been washed by baptism will submit himself to barbarian embraces, much less allow his lips to be touched by the filth of demonic kisses. Pelagius urges the king to turn instead to the "stupid men" who will serve him because of a desire for riches. As in Raguel's story, the king is not angered by this first rebuff. He tries to persuade "the ephebe" gently. "O lascivious boy," he begins, and then goes on to make his offer of riches, power, ease. The king then puts his hand firmly against Pelagius's face, lays another arm around his neck, and draws him near for at least one kiss. Pelagius strikes him hard enough to draw blood. It runs down the king's beard and onto his robes. His sorrow turns to rage and he orders Pelagius's torture.

We need not guess at metaphors to know from Hrotswitha what 'Abd al-Rahmân did to Pelagius. Hrotswitha does also employ metaphors of the game or the joke to describe the king's actions. But she tells the reader quite explicitly how the king touched Pelagius and what he tried to do to him. What she assumes, along with Raguel, is that Pelagius can immediately interpret that kiss as a sexual overture. The kiss is not fatherly or brotherly; it does not bear compassion or pardon. It is felt immediately by the youth as the overture to a sexual exchange. Indeed, Pelagius retorts to the king that he ought to save his kisses for his fellow Muslims, with whom he shares the stupidity of idolatry. If Hrotswitha's Pelagius is not so scathing as Raguel's, he is no less well informed about the sexual customs of the Muslim court. So must Hrotswitha's readers be. The "Sodomitic vices" are here condensed into a single kiss, which must be understood as prelude to all of them. The project of moral codification that is suggested in Raguel seems already presupposed in Hrotswitha.

The clarity of the moral code makes it imperative that Hrotswitha be equally clear about her own position as narrator, her own relation to Pelagius. The poem begins as a prayer for the saint's help; it ends with mention of his patronage. The prologue may be considered formulaic and the end is not spoken in Hrotswitha's voice. But it is her voice that describes throughout the beauties of Pelagius's body. How does it keep them at a proper distance? By always juxtaposing them with equally sensual descriptions of his eloquence. Indeed, every character in the poem except one subsumes appreciation for Pelagius's beauty in appreciation for his beautiful speech. Physical beauty is thus etherealized into verbal beauty. The only exception is the caliph himself, who burns with passion on first seeing Pelagius's face. The caliph wants to love the boy's form before ever hearing him speak. This is a mark of the caliph's depravity. The danger of a woman speaking about the body of an adolescent boy is deflected by making mere reaction to a body something ignoble. Hrotswitha can praise his body safely because she praises his divine eloquence more enthusiastically. We see here a recurrent substitution in Christian writing. Christian language takes the full charge of a beauty that it pretends to reject. The beauties of body are condemned in prose of extraordinary beauty.

The poem ends with a longish section on the dispersion and recovery of Pelagius's body. The narrative is considerably more detailed than in Raguel. The recovery of the body is followed by the beginning of a cult of Pelagius. Many persons "of either sex" are moved to sing hymns and offer prayers. After three days, they prepare a fire in which to offer up the body. The fire is to be a proof of Pelagius's sanctity. Those standing by ask God to show his power in preserving the youth's severed head. After more than an hour in the waves of flame, the head remains intact, the eyes still lustrous. The faithful break forth in final hymns to God.

At least two things are striking in this section. The first is that God's power is shown in the miracle of preserving Pelagius's physical beauty. Hrotswitha typically abridges or omits the details of the mutilations of martyrdom. She does so here, with a twist. Where Raguel stresses the mutilation of the boy's body, Hrotswitha exalts its intact beauty. The unburned head of Pelagius is much like a female martyr's hymen. It is the physical evidence of his virginity, his innocence of Sodomitic kisses. At the same time, second, the Christian faithful show themselves more avid fetishists of the physical body even than the lecherous 'Abd al-Rahmân. He did not think to collect the pieces of the body he had so much desired. The Christians do, and they begin to enact a reverence much stronger and more persistent than the king's burning desire. The name for that reverence is cult.

9

Masturbation, Salvation, and Desire:

Connecting Sexuality and Religiosity in Colonial Mexico

Zeb Tortorici

Zeb Tortorici is a scholar of Colonial Latin America, queer and archival studies. His article "Masturbation, Salvation, and Desire: Connecting Sexuality and Religiosity in Colonial Mexico" examines the seventeenth-century Inquisition trial of Agustina Ruiz, a young woman who was reported engaging in masturbation while having erotic visions of sex, touching, fondling, and kissing Jesus, various saints, and the Virgin Mary. The Spanish Inquisition, or the Tribunal of the Holy Office of the Inquisition, ensured and promoted Catholic orthodoxy among all subjects of the Spanish crown. The Inquisition took the form of hearings and court trials (which produced voluminous records) of all baptized Catholics, and could mete out sentences for the guilty of corporeal punishment, and in extreme cases, even death. Ruiz, therefore, was being interrogated to discover whether or not she had committed heresy in her erotic imaginings. In this excerpt, Tortorici examines her trial records to draw out the complex entanglements of sexual and religious desire that they reveal. These entanglements are on display in the fantasy life of Ruiz, and in the questions her inquisitors posed to her, which forced Ruiz to recount her fantasies in lurid detail.

On 23 January 1621 a Spanish priest and commissary of the Mexican Holy Office of the Inquisition in Querétaro, Fray Manuel de Santo Thomas, came forth to denounce the twenty-year-old Agustina Ruiz, who had, according to him, never completed the confession that she had begun with him on the eve of Pascua de Reyes (Feast of the Three Kings) a few weeks earlier. He told the Inquisition that Ruiz had begun to confess her sins to him in the church of the Carmelite convent of Santa Theresa, asking for mercy and forgiveness, and then declared that since the age of eleven she had carnally sinned with herself nearly every day by repeatedly committing the act of pollution (polución)—masturbation. Most unsettling to the priest, however, was not the act of masturbation itself but rather the vivid, obscene, and sacrilegious descriptions that went alongside her masturbatory fantasies. According to the priest's denunciation, Ruiz confessed that she had spoken dishonest words with San Nicolas de Tolentino, San Diego, and even Jesus Christ and the Virgin Mary and that they had carnally communicated with her in a variety of sexual positions: "They join themselves with her [Ruiz] in different ways, with her underneath them, and from the side, and her on top of them, and also with her lying face down while they conjoin themselves with her through both of her dishonest parts [ambas partes deshonestas]," meaning both vaginally and anally. Given that the primary aim of the Holy Office of the Mexican Inquisition—established in 1569 by royal decree of Phillip II of Spain and founded in 1571—was to extirpate heresy, it is no surprise that the Mexican Inquisition would take a strong interest in Ruiz, who was eventually sentenced to spend three years in a Mexico City convent.

What most perturbed this priest and local judge of the Inquisition was Ruiz's declaration that at times when she attended mass and saw the Eucharist being raised, she would see Jesus Christ with his genitals exposed, feel sexually excited—experiencing "carnal alteration" (alteración carnal)—because of this sight, and would sin with herself right there in the church: a heretical profanation of the sacraments. She also alluded to having sinned in a similar manner with the image of the Virgin Mary in mind. This is merely the beginning of a unique and richly detailed Inquisition case in which the issues of female sexuality and religiosity merge through the experiences of one young woman charged with a variety of heretical sins relating to her visions, her actions, and her body. Any close reading of this case, however, should be placed within a proper historiographical framework. In her influential essay, "Sexuality in Colonial Mexico: A Church Dilemma," Asunción Lavrin examines the gap between the proper types of sexual behavior described in treatises of moral theology and confessional manuals and the quotidian and transgressive behaviors of the population at large. Discussing the large number of criminal and Inquisition cases dealing with sexuality, Lavrin asserts: "These cases were either self-confessions or denunciations of breaches of the ecclesiastical norms, and they represent the reality of daily life for those who failed to practice fully the teaching of the church." Lavrin's discussion of this undeniable disjunction offers valuable insight into colonial Mexican society. Especially interesting, however, is that many whose actions and sexual behaviors did fall short of church teachings often envisioned themselves as good Christians and veritably thought that their actions did little or nothing to challenge church dogma. By situating sexuality and religiosity as not necessarily antagonistic, historians have opened up other ways to think about sexuality and its complex relationship to religion and spiritual devotion.

By turning to desire as a category of historical analysis, historians might better understand the reasons upon which people based their everyday decisions. In terms of historicizing desire, however, desire need not be sexual in nature. Many pious women in colonial Mexico were simultaneously subjects of their own desire and objects of the desires of others. Many women and men, including Agustina Ruiz, fervently desired spiritual salvation alongside an intense love for Jesus, the saints, and the Virgin Mary. They desired other men and women on physical, sexual, emotional, and spiritual planes. Whether or not women had "agency" through their desiring—or even how to define and apply that contemporary concept—is not my concern here. Rather, I aim to explicate how for the women and men of colonial Mexico desire—broadly defined by its everyday sexual, spiritual, corporal, and emotional materializations—was omnipresent. Desire manifested itself through hunger, thirst, lust, and carnality but also through the equally common forms of devotion, rapture, and religiosity. More often than one might expect, the desires in these spiritual arenas functioned symbiotically and constantly influenced the decisions, acts, and beliefs of individuals who were often merely trying to live with conflicting desires, church teachings, and daily pressures, in the late sixteenth century, the placement of divorced women, prostitutes, women involved in marital disputes, and women accused of bigamy, adultery, or concubinage became much more common. In colonial Mexico and Peru, as in Spain, the *recogimiento* was based ultimately on the firmly held belief in female vulnerability and predisposition to sexual deviance and lasciviousness. It comes as no surprise, then, that the young and unwed Agustina Ruiz, like so many other "wayward" women who were forced behind the walls of *recogimientos,* was "deposited" by Cristóbal Felipe in the care of another household. This placement likely served simultaneously to punish, protect, and separate her from the outside world and its sinful influences, to which she had already showed herself to be especially vulnerable.

As stated earlier, Agustina Ruiz was formally denounced to the Inquisition by her confessor in part because she failed to finish her initial confession on the eve of Pascua de Reyes and be absolved of her sins. Because it was already late in the day when Ruiz started her confession and her confessor deemed it necessary to ask her a number of other questions, he asked her to return the next day to continue the confession. Ruiz did return but left the church before her confessor, Fray Manuel de Santo Thomas, could even see her. After many days passed without her return, the priest sent for her at the house of Garibaldi. She entered the confessional, he said that he merely desired the best for her soul, and she replied that she felt somewhat faint because of fasting and would return that same day after she ate something at two o'clock. When she failed to return the priest denounced her to the Inquisition, which quickly took matters into its own hands.

During her first testimony, taken on 6 February 1621, Ruiz, like so many other women and men who were brought before the Holy Office, started out by saying that she had no idea why she was being questioned by the Inquisition. She said that she knew nothing when she was asked if she or anyone close to her had said, done, or committed anything that appeared to be against the Holy Catholic faith or evangelical law of the church. Only when she was asked more specifically about the conversations between her and her confessor a few weeks earlier did she admit to having told him about touching herself and basing had "bad thoughts and bad images" of Jesus, the Virgin, and saints for years. In this first confession she denied ever having told her confessor that she saw Jesus with his genitals exposed during the consecration of the Eucharist, though this is something she later admitted, and she denied that she ever masturbated in the church but instead always did so at home in the comfort of her bed.

It is here that the questions of the inquisitors turned more specifically toward the acts of masturbation and the accompanying fantasies for a more detailed and intimate examination of Agustina Ruiz. They first asked Ruiz if it was true that she had touched herself since the age of eleven. To this she replied quite graphically that "since the age of eleven until six months ago she committed the sin [of pollution] with her hand by touching her dishonest parts and realizing that she was carnally communicating with the saints, Jesus, and the Virgin. These acts took place more or less three times a day for the last nine years. The inquisitors then asked Ruiz if she had ever used any "instruments" (instrumentos) aside from her hand in order to stimulate herself. She denied having ever used anything except her hands and then, in response to other questions posed to her, stated that no one saw her or heard her while in the act of pollution, nor had she told anyone aside from her confessor of her visions and actions. They also asked if the dishonest words that she exchanged with Jesus, Mary, and the saints were words used to name the dishonest parts of the man and the woman and used to describe the physical act of a man and a woman having sex. While Ruiz admitted to all of these accusations, she asserted that she had stopped touching herself six months earlier, though she never mentioned why.

One of the most unique aspects of this case is its explicit reference to female masturbation and corresponding fantasies. In broaching the issue of masturbation among women in colonial Mexico, Lavrin asserts that in theological discourse "masturbation, always described as a masculine problem, deeply concerned the church." While Lavrin's statement is generally true, this case demonstrates that masturbation was not described solely as a masculine problem. More importantly, masturbation mostly did not concern the church on any practical or enforceable level. Even in Europe during the later Middle Ages, when theologians began to more closely associate masturbation with the "sins against nature" of sodomy and bestiality, "it was decidedly the most innocent of the bunch and in fact received far less attention in the succeeding ages than its essential wickedness would lead us to expect." Masturbation played a minor role in the hierarchical drama of sexual sins. One of the few places for the colonial Latin American and early modern European contexts to look for direct references to masturbation are the confessional manuals. The increased importance of the confessional manuals is linked directly to Counter-Reformation

Catholicism after the Council of Trent (1545–63), which sought to reemphasize the central role of the sacraments in the everyday lives of Catholics. Partaking in penance and the act of confessing the insinuations of the flesh—one's thoughts, desires, voluptuous imaginings, and movements of the body—was deemed an important part of salvation.

The 1634 *Confessionario Mayor,* written in Spanish and Nahuatl by Franciscan friar Bartolomé de Alva, is one of many confessional books from early Mexico that deal with the intimate matters that the Catholic hierarchy wished to regulate. It is also merely one of many bilingual manuals for priests to follow when hearing the confessions of the indigenous populations in Mexico. This text is obviously not a guide to what individual women and men were actually doing in private, but it clearly demonstrates the church's concerns with the broad sweep of sexual conduct. Specific topics that are broached include abortion, midwifery, witchcraft, incest, masturbation, sodomy, adultery, rape, bestiality, menstruation, and prostitution. Regarding women, a few of the many concerns of Bartolomé de Alva are recorded through the following questions:

> Here is what the women will be asked. Were you menstruating sometime when your husband or some other man had sexual relations with you? Did you repeatedly feel your body, thinking of a man, and wanting him to sin with you? Did you do it to yourself with your hands, bringing to a conclusion your lust? When your husband was drunk: did he have sex with you where you are a woman, or sometimes did he do the disgusting sin to you [anal sex]? Did you restrain him? Were you responsible for dirty words with which you provoked and excited women? When you cohabited with some woman: did you show and reveal what was bad in front of those who had not yet seen the sin? Did you ever pimp for someone? On account of you, did they know themselves through sin, you yourself provoking a woman for whom you had summoned someone? Did you know the failings of your mother or your father, your children and your relatives, your household dependents, that they were cohabiting, and you did not restrain them? When they were drunk and intoxicated in your home, there committing before you sins unworthy of doing: didn't you restrain them? Did you just look at them?

While in the confessional guides there was a clear preoccupation with he supposedly dangerous and polluting nature of female sexuality, in reality neither criminal courts nor the Holy Office of the Inquisition—unless some potential heresy was involved—worried much about regulating the manifestations of female sexuality, which included masturbation and same-sex sexual activities between women. This rare window into the act of female masturbation and its accompanying desires and fantasies is partly what makes the case of Agustina Ruiz so unique. Inquisitors themselves expressed a great deal of surprise and asserted that they were not accustomed to hearing any woman go into so much intimate detail in her testimonies.

Ultimately, during Ruiz's first declaration inquisitors asked her some twenty one questions about her actions and beliefs surrounding her masturbatory experiences.

While the initial denunciation of Agustina Ruiz by Fray Manuel de Santo Thomas and her own confession corroborate for the most part, at this point in the document there are many still-unanswered questions regarding what Ruiz actually did and what she believed, due in part to the ambiguity and semantic slippage around the words Ruiz used to describe her visions. Throughout her testimonies she continually used the phrase *hacer cuenta,* meaning "to realize" or "to recall," in reference to her recognition of Jesus, Mary, and the saints, In one of many examples, she stated that she "recalled that she was with [i.e., engaged in the carnal act with] the said saints, Christ, and the Virgin" [haciendo q^{ta} que estaba con los dhos santos X° y la Virgen]. Much like Benedetta Carlini, the "lesbian" nun, visionary, and mystic in Renaissance Italy described by Judith C. Brown, Ruiz was "living as a believer in a profoundly religious society, [and] she did not question the reality of the visions." Did Ruiz merely fantasize that Jesus, Mary, and the saints came to her to exchange lewd words, kisses, and embraces? Or did she believe that they had actually appeared to her and had had tangible contact with her? Ruiz used identical language to describe many of the acts that took place between her and the religious figures and often went into such detail that, at certain moments, there was both confusion and ambiguity between physical reality, fantasy, and imagination. What is clear throughout Ruiz's first testimony is the intense level of religiosity and devotion with which she imbued her acts and "visions." Ruiz framed her relationships with the saints, Jesus, and the Virgin in terms of divine sanction and gratitude toward her and confessed that "they showed that they were thankful to her with the words they spoke to her—dishonest and amorous words that corresponded to those used to describe the dishonest parts of men and women." Both amorous and dishonest in nature, the words spoken to Ruiz by her divine visitors signal the intense love and devotion that they had for her and that she had for them.

In her second declaration, taken only shortly after the first, we begin to see some of the intense pressures and fears that Ruiz must have felt once she realized that her case was not going to be taken lightly by the inquisitors. Ruiz strangely and suddenly—especially after going into so much detail with her confessor and in her first declaration to the Inquisition—retracted all of her previous testimony and alleged to be suffering from a certain *mal de corazón,* or "illness of the heart." Given that the ubiquitous *mal de corazón* in the early modern Spanish world could refer to a variety of physical, spiritual, and emotional maladies, including vertigo, swooning, spasms, heart troubles, loss of consciousness, apoplexy, and melancholy, it is difficult to determine exactly what Ruiz suffered. It is unmistakable, however, that Ruiz unsuccessfully tried to convince the inquisitors that due to her malady she did not remember anything that she had said in her first declaration. Inquisitors obviously remained skeptical of her professed *mal de corazón,* and shortly after this second testimony Ruiz, described in some detail as a woman "small in body and skinny, with brown skin, . . . with a small birthmark above her right eyebrow," was taken out of the home of Alonso de Garibaldi and María Meneque and placed in the care of Andrés de Montoro, the head of the textile factory, who put her in a presumably more trustworthy home. There, "in the good company of women," she would not be allowed to leave or to speak with any man unless given permission by the commissary of the Inquisition. To some extent the official treatment of Ruiz and the decisions made about where to place her were influenced by factors such as local gossip that were outside of her immediate testimony. A woman named Ana Nuñez who was interviewed in the course of the trial spoke of Ruiz's "dishonesties" (*deshonestidades*) and referred to an incident she'd heard about from another woman in which Ruiz was seen in public by a number of women allowing an unidentified man to put his hand up her skirt.

It was after this relocation of Ruiz that a third confession was taken from her on 1 April 1621. This confession—subsequently and repeatedly referred to by Ruiz herself as her "true confession"—not only confirmed much of her first confession but went into far greater detail than any previous confession, including that given to the confessor, Fray Manuel de Santo Thomas, mouths earlier. In what is only a small segment of this confession, Ruiz asserted that the saints, Jesus Christ, and the Virgin appeared to her in the following manner.

> They came to her with their dishonest parts physically excited. Each of them explained how they wanted to see her both loved and desired, and for this reason they came down from heaven to earth. As they hugged and kissed her, their passions became inflamed, and they began to exchange dishonest words similar to those a man speaks to his wife in the act of carnal copulation. And with regard to the Virgin who came to her in her bed to hug and kiss her, they would sit with their dishonest parts rubbing against each other. Of all the rest, it was Jesus who gave her the most in terms of dishonest words and acts. For Jesus told her that he had made her so beautiful and gracious, much to his liking, so that she would be his whore [*puta*] and so that he could enjoy himself with her.

It was immediately following this statement that inquisitors found it necessary to explain to her that "it is a Catholic truth that the saints in heaven, Jesus Christ, and the Virgin do not sin, cannot sin, and could not have come down from heaven to earth in order to do and say the things that she [Ruiz] has confessed that they said and did. Instead, it was the devil." According to the logic of the inquisitors, it must have been the devil, who, taking the physical form of Jesus, Mary, and the saints, had tricked Ruiz into believing what she did, for, as Jacqueline Holler tells us, "demonically inspired sexual activity by women, however serious and suggestive of a pact with the devil, would not have surprised a sixteenth-century inquisitor. Immediately after hearing this explanation by the inquisitors, she admitted her guilt and formally acknowledged that all along the devil had tricked her: "Her soul was in a state of error and had offended God, the saints, and the Virgin with the moral turpitude and lewdness . . . and she asks Him [God] for forgiveness." Ruiz then pleaded for mercy from the inquisitors.

Yet throughout her testimony and before accepting the inquisitors' interpretations of her fantasies Ruiz painted a picture of sincere and even singular devotion. A large part of this devotion was clearly Ruiz's relationship with the Virgin Mary. Given her fantasies, visions, and imaginings with the Virgin, in which they hugged, kissed, and rubbed their "dishonest parts" against one another, this case also broaches the topic of same-sex physical and spiritual desire between women. In colonial Latin American archival sources, references to same-sex sexuality between women are, at best, exceedingly rare. For the colonial Latin American historiography, Ligia Bellini's *A coisa obscura: Mulher, sodomia, e Inquisição no Brasil colonial* is the only full-length study of same-sex sexual acts between women. While this study makes a valuable contribution to colonial Latin American historiography, it uses a mere ten Inquisition cases to trace fragments of the lives of twenty-nine women in late-sixteenth-century Brazil who were prosecuted for *sodomia focminarum* (sexual relations between women that included anal or vaginal insertion of objects). Many of these young girls were clearly not cognizant of the gravity of their crimes and often interpreted their own actions as sexual games. While seriously questioning the extent to which any of these sodomy cases can or should be seen as part of a larger history of homosexuality, Bellini concludes that what all these women have in common is that "they put into practice what they desired in certain moments," and because of it they became targets of the Inquisition. Perhaps this was also Ruiz's mistake.

An important component of Ruiz's expression of her devotion is its simultaneous sacralization and vulgarization. When speaking of her fantasized experiences with Jesus in her third confession, she stated that "before having carnal copulation, Jesus would have her and tell her, 'I put you in my soul.' To this she would reply, 'My eyes, your cock [*el carajo*], I [want to] put your cock [*el carajazo*] in me.' And Jesus asked, 'Where will you put it?' And she responded, 'In my pussy [*por cl coño*], which is yours.' Jesus then asked her what he would do to her then. To this she responded, 'Fuck me, you me, you are fucking me [*me hoder, me estas hodiendo*].'" According to Ruiz, Jesus then told her that he was having sex with her because "you are my soul and my life and the one whom I love above all else, besides, you have a tasty and delicious pussy [*un coño sabroso y gostoso*] just for me." The use of the Spanish verb *meter*—to put or place one thing inside of another—is used in reference to Jesus spiritually putting Ruiz in his soul as well as his physically putting his penis into her vagina. For Ruiz, the devotional metaphors of putting herself within the heart and soul of Jesus, and vice versa, transcend the spiritual plane to the physical and the sexual. The pious desire for spiritual salvation manifests itself through Ruiz's belief that it is she who, over anyone else, is the soul, the life, and the beloved of Jesus.

This description of heavenly love alongside intense physical and spiritual joy also raises the issues of bridal mysticism and spiritual union with Jesus so common among the early modern female mystics. Central to the tradition of Christian mysticism are the notion of the exchange of hearts between Jesus and the mystic, the metaphor of marriage with Christ the bridegroom, and the transformation of carnal desire into spiritual desire. We cannot be sure to what extent Agustina Ruiz may or may not have been influenced by widely publicized female mystics like Saint Catherine of Siena (died 1380), Saint Teresa of Ávila (died 1582), or the only recently deceased Peruvian mystic, Saint Rose of Lima (died 1617), but it appears that there are a number of similarities and overlappings, given the highly erotic language used by mystics to describe the ineffable nature of ecstasy and the mystical experience, with the important difference that Ruiz—given her lack of a clerical education and likely scant exposure to the rhetoric of the mystics—used vulgar street language to describe her experiences. Just as Ruiz used the language of penetration to describe the simultaneous physical and spiritual love of Jesus for her, Saint Teresa of Ávila told of how a beautiful angel with his great golden spear "plunged [it] into my heart several times so that it penetrated to my entrails. When he pulled it out, I felt that he took them with it, and left me utterly consumed by the great love of God. The pain was so severe that it made me utter several moans. The sweetness caused by this intense pain is so extreme that one cannot possibly wish it to cease, nor is one's soul content with anything but God." A purely sexual reading of the mystical experience in this context or even a forced implication of the sexual organs would be an "unjustified oversimplification," yet in many mystical experiences it is through the idiom of sexual pleasure that the ineffable nature and ecstasy of intense physical and spiritual union with Jesus is most closely approximated. For Ruiz it was ultimately this desire for spiritual salvation that merged with the desire for physical salvation and that manifested itself through the acts of copulation with Jesus, who was both spiritually and physically in love uniquely with her. Ruiz recognized and knew that some of her actions and visions contravened religious dogma, and still she continually described her interactions with Jesus, the Virgin, and the saints in ways that elucidate the erotic nature of her piety and spirituality. The testimonies offered by Ruiz show not only the conflicts between the sexual, the mystical, and the spiritual but also how often these spheres worked together and reinforced one another.

10

Discussion Questions

1 Why might sexual or erotic desire or pleasure so often be seen as a source of suspicion or even fear in a number of religious traditions? Give examples from the readings.

2 Is there a fundamental variance between religious desire and sexual or erotic desire? What might be some of the differences or similarities? Is there a danger or difficulty in confusing them, or are they rather complementary?

3 Do you agree that "human desire is limitless?" What might such a statement mean in terms of any religious practice or belief? Can or should religions seek to accommodate all types of sexual or erotic desires? Why, or why not?

4 Some of the greatest mystics from the world's religious traditions have used explicitly erotic language to describe their desire for, and experience of, the sacred. What might that tell us about the ubiquity of human desire? Do you consider this to be problematic and even sacrilegious, or rather poetic and insightful? Discuss your reasons.

5 Religions will often teach that human desires must be kept under control for a number of reasons. From the readings, can you provide a counterargument to such a position?

6 "Non-heterosexual expressions of erotic desire, of whatever form and variety, still continue to elicit strong and passionate reactions from religions." Discuss. Provide concrete examples as to why that might be the case.

7 The reading by Eve Kosofsky Sedgwick makes the very strong argument that there is absolutely nothing fixed or determined about human sexuality, and that it is distinguished by its infinite variety and diversity. Could one apply her argument to how religions view certain forms of sexual behavior? Give two or three examples.

8 The reading by Mark Jordan offers an interesting analysis of how religious desire can be constructed from the multiple ways in which individuals write about "the object" of their desire, what might be called a "queer" rhetorical strategy. What struck you the most about this text? Can you provide other examples of such queer religious strategies?

9   The reading by Zeb Tortorici provides an uncommon analysis of the intersections between erotic desire, sexual behavior, and religious passion in a colonial context, and it raises questions about the traumatic sources of religious longing. How did you respond to this text? What might it teach us about "gendered" religious desire?

10 In his text, Michel Foucault has argued that the Catholic rite of confession, by allowing individuals to "speak" their sexual sins, has been instrumental in the creation of sexual knowledge in the West. Do you agree? What might this tell us about the power of religion in molding or influencing human sexuality?

PART THREE

Performances

1

Introduction

In 1931, Mahatma Gandhi traveled to London to bring attention to Indian Independence from British rule. He wore a dhoti (loincloth) and shawl, not a Western-style suit. Gandhi's scantily clad and slight body was something of a scandal in British media; it offended; it suggested starvation and primitiveness; it suggested weakness and effeminacy: it symbolized the otherness of the Orient itself. Gandhi never abandoned this garb because, he noted, to wear it was to wear the clothing of India's poor. It was to bring their cause as well as their struggles to light. Yet to wear it to the British Parliament, in meetings with those under whose power he fell, had even more political poignancy. In the dhoti, Gandhi stood as a subject of his own nation, and not as one subjected to the British imperial order.

Throughout his life Gandhi drew on the symbolism of bodily performance, and he did so (despite criticism) to draw media attention to his cause for Indian sovereignty. From his nonviolent protests to his vegetarianism, fasting, semi-nakedness, and numerous experiments in *brahmacharya* (the cessation of desire), Gandhi engaged in corporeal displays that linked his body to the Indian nation he was helping to build. Gandhi's experiments additionally offered up a complex gender performance (perceived as such not only by a Western audience who found his emaciated, lightly dressed body effeminate, but also to those in his inner circle). While his *brahmacharya* experiments never found him dressing in female clothing, like nineteenth-century Sri Ramakrishna, Gandhi shared with the sage the notion that embodying femininity was a key step in overcoming carnal desire. The young girls who made their way to sharing Gandhi's bed at the end of his life reported that the "Great Soul" was successful in his attempts. Lying with him was like lying with a mother. Others were dubious, convinced of the sexual nature of this nightly ritual, or at least of its shameful character. Gandhi's bodily experiments in *brahmacharya* indicate how one's performance of gender and sexuality can give rise to conflicting interpretations.

This section entitled performances is informed by the work of scholars and activists who have reframed our understanding of how gender and sexuality are understood, positioned, appropriated, and constructed. Discussions of sexuality particularly from the nineteenth century into the present are grounded in male and female difference. The complex intersections between sex/gender and sexuality come into focus when we realize how bodily desires and pleasures get coded as masculine or feminine in our (Western) culture, so that to sexually penetrate another is a "masculine" position, whereas to give pleasure to another is "feminine." Indeed, homophobic discourse in our own time disqualifies gay-identified people by calling on the notion that in their sexual encounters (also their dress, actions, bodily comportment, and tastes) they transgress gender boundaries. The study of sexuality, queer theorists argue, cannot be divorced from the study of gender. Sex and gender, that is man/woman and male/female or masculine/feminine, shore up heterosexuality's normative status by indicating there are but two sorts of people resulting from the fact of two sorts of bodies. The equation sex/gender posits not only fundamental difference between these two sexes/genders but also subordinates woman and female to man and male.

As with sexuality, gender has been seen as something one fundamentally is, some inner disposition revealed on our bodies and through our behaviors. Alternatively, in her groundbreaking study, *Gender Trouble: Feminism and the Subversion of Identity*, Butler treats gender as performative. An excerpt of her argument is included here. According to Butler, gender is a doing, a corporeal style that is repeated and gives the appearance of a stable identity. Moving from the narrow confines of identity politics, work by queer theorists like Butler has sharpened our understandings of human sexual behavior. It has had rich implications as well for reflecting on how gender and sexuality intersect with religious life, practices, and subjectivities. It has helped underscore how rites, rituals, and other embodied religious practices have been used to control, discipline, and police sexual and erotic choices and identities. The notion of performance—that gender is not a given, but rather constructed through performance—in particular has become key in how we understand ourselves and others as sexual and gendered beings, and in how we, and others, relate to the religious.

The readings collected here highlight the performative character of gender and sexuality and religion in various contexts. Carolyn Watson's analysis of Yoruba religion in Cuba shows how over time the potentially gender destabilizing elements of its spiritual practices were domesticated and reformulated in Christian terms, bringing women centrally into the religious community around the values of reproduction and domesticity. Examining Haitian Vodou in North America, Karen McCarthy Brown explores the intimate bonds women practitioners develop with the spirits to make sense of their own lives and struggles for empowerment. Gayatri Reddy offers an intriguing study of a contemporary Indian *hijra* community whose distinctive corporeal style conforms to and disrupts South Indian gender norms. Jakob Hero explores his own transgender experience from the perspectives of Christian theology and bioethics to offer a new way to envision queer subjectivity.

Additionally, three of the pieces included in this section look more closely at the performative aspects of sexuality. Debates over Muslim women's head-covering in France occupy Mayanthi Fernando. The complex intersections of sexuality and religion in French Republicanism, she argues, have dire implications for Muslim women's ability to make their religious subjectivity intelligible in that context. Daniel Lehrman considers the compelling notion that BDSM entails the desire for sanctity, sacrifice, and self-abasement, cultivated and given meaning through ritual life and bodily encounters, and find expression in Judaism as well. Vinay Lal brings us back to Mahatma Gandhi. By way of *brahmacharya*, the Indian revolutionary aimed to eschew the very limits, including those of gender, which constrained his attempts to encounter the Infinite. Gandhi's disavowal of sexual activity was not, suggests Lal, a rejection of the body, but rather a rejection of the constraining forces of carnal desire.

Together these readings point to the entanglements of gender and sexuality in religious contexts. They illuminate the fundamentally malleable nature of gender norms, and the power of bodily performance in giving them expression. They suggest that gender can and has taken manifold forms in religious life. They suggest that meanings we attach to the performance of sexuality and gender are contextual and, further, that they can vary, shift, or change altogether. They remind us that the strict binary of male/female, masculine/feminine, and homo/heterosexual obscures and restricts our understanding of the richly diverse character of religious expression and subjectivity.

2

Gender Trouble:

Feminism and the
Subversion of Identity

Judith Butler

Judith Butler is a philosopher and gender theorist whose work has been paramount in the development of queer studies. Her study, Gender Trouble: Feminism and the Subversion of Identity, *from which the excerpt is drawn, challenges feminist theorists (such as Simone de Beauvoir and Monique Wittig). Butler claims that gender be rethought as a social performance, which does not reflect some prior essence of a person. Gender is a "stylized" set of acts, recited and repeated, giving the impression of a stable identity. Butler's work also suggests that gender's performative character leaves open the possibility that such enactments could expose the arbitrariness of gender norms.*

If the body is not a "being," but a variable boundary, a surface whose permeability is politically regulated, a signifying practice within a cultural field of gender hierarchy and compulsory heterosexuality, then what language is left for understanding this corporeal enactment, gender, that constitutes its "interior" signification on its surface? Sartre would perhaps have called this act "a style of being," Foucault, "a stylistics of existence." And in my earlier reading of Beauvoir, I suggest that gendered bodies are so many "styles of the flesh." These styles all never fully self-styled, for styles have a history, and those histories condition and limit the possibilities. Consider gender, for instance, as *a corporeal style,* an "act," as it were, which is both intentional and performative, where *"performative"* suggests a dramatic and contingent construction of meaning.

Wittig understands gender as the workings of "sex," where "sex" is an obligatory injunction for the body to become a cultural sign, to materialize itself in obedience to a historically delimited possibility, and to do this, not once or twice, but as a sustained and repeated corporeal project. The notion of a "project," however, suggests the originating force of a radical will, and because gender is a project which has cultural survival as its end, the term *strategy* better suggests the situation of duress under which gender performance always and variously occurs. Hence, as a strategy of survival within compulsory systems, gender is a performance with clearly punitive consequences. Discrete genders are part of what "humanizes" individuals within contemporary culture; indeed, we regularly punish those who fail to do their gender right. Because there is neither an "essence" that gender expresses or externalizes nor an objective ideal to which gender aspires, and because gender is not a fact, the various acts of gender create the idea of gender, and without those acts, there would be no gender at all. Gender is, thus, a construction that regularly conceals its genesis; the tacit collective agreement to perform, produce, and sustain discrete and polar genders as cultural fictions is obscured by the credibility of those productions—and the punishments that attend not agreeing to believe in them; the construction "compels" our belief in its necessity and naturalness. The historical possibilities materialized through various corporeal styles are nothing other than those punitively regulated cultural fictions alternately embodied and deflected under duress.

Consider that a sedimentation of gender norms produces the peculiar phenomenon of a "natural sex" or a "real woman" or any number of prevalent and compelling social fictions, and that this is a sedimentation that over time has produced a set of corporeal styles which, in reified form, appear as the natural configuration of bodies into sexes existing in a binary relation to one another. If these styles are enacted, and if they produce the coherent gendered subjects who pose as their originators, what kind of performance might reveal this ostensible "cause" to be an "effect"?

In what senses, then, is gender an act? As in other ritual social dramas, the action of gender requires a performance that is *repeated.* This repetition is at once a reenactment and reexperiencing of a set of meanings already socially established; and it is the mundane and ritualized form of their legitimation. Although there are individual bodies that enact these significations by becoming stylized into gendered modes, this "action" is a public action. There are temporal and collective dimensions to these actions, and their public character is not inconsequential; indeed, the performance is effected with the strategic aim of maintaining gender within its binary frame—an aim that cannot be attributed to a subject, but, rather, must be understood to found and consolidate the subject.

Gender ought not to be construed as a stable identity or locus of agency from which various acts follow; rather, gender is an identity tenuously constituted in time, instituted in an exterior space through a *stylized repetition of acts.* The effect of gender is produced through the stylization of the body and, hence, must be understood as the mundane way in which bodily gestures, movements, and styles of various kinds constitute the illusion of an abiding gendered self. This formulation moves the conception of gender off the ground of a substantial model of identity to one that requires a conception of gender as a constituted *social temporality*. Significantly, if gender is instituted through acts which are internally discontinuous, then the *appearance of substance* is precisely that, a constructed identity, a performative accomplishment which the mundane social audience, including the actors themselves, come to believe and to perform in the mode of belief. Gender is also a norm that can never be fully internalized; "the internal" is a surface signification, and gender norms are finally phantasmatic, impossible to embody. If the ground of gender identity is the stylized repetition of acts through time and not a seemingly seamless identity, then the spatial metaphor of a "ground" will be displaced and revealed as a stylized configuration, indeed, a gendered corporealization of time. The abiding gendered self will then be shown to be structured by repeated acts that seek to approximate the ideal of a substantial ground of identity, but which, in their occasional *dis*continuity, reveal the temporal and contingent groundlessness of this "ground." The possibilities of gender transformation are to be found precisely in the arbitrary relation between such acts, in the possibility of a failure to repeat, a de-formity, or a parodic repetition that exposes the phantasmatic effect of abiding identity as a politically tenuous construction.

If gender attributes, however, are not expressive but performative, then these attributes effectively constitute the identity they are said to express or reveal. The distinction between expression and performativeness is crucial. If gender attributes and acts, the various ways in which a body shows or produces its cultural signification, are performative, then there is no preexisting identity by which an act or attribute might be measured; there would be no true or false, real or distorted acts of gender, and the postulation of a true gender identity would be revealed as a regulatory fiction. That gender reality is created through sustained social performances means that the very notions of an essential sex and a true or abiding masculinity or femininity are also constituted as part of the strategy that conceals gender's performative character and the performative possibilities for proliferating gender configurations outside the restricting frames of masculinist domination and compulsory heterosexuality.

Genders can be neither true nor false, neither real nor apparent, neither original nor derived. As credible bearers of those attributes, however, genders can also be rendered thoroughly and radically *incredible*.

3

Witches, Female Priests and Sacred Manoeuvres:

(De)stabilizing Gender and Sexuality in a Cuban Religion of African Origin

Carolyn E. Watson

*C*arolyn E. Watson is a scholar of Latin American history. This passage is taken from a longer article examining the ways in which women tried to destabilize or reframe gender in a male-dominated Cuban religion of African origin marked by spirit possession and divination. It asks serious questions about how and why patriarchal authority so often remains rigidly in control in such situations, effectively domesticating women's positions and roles in the process. It raises wide-ranging issues having to do with how gender is performed in religious contexts, but also how inherently unstable and fragmentary these gender constructions can ultimately be. What is the cost of such gender tensions and reversals for women? Compare this reading with that from Karen McCarthy Brown, which proposes a significantly different reading of how women can act as ritual leaders within a comparable religious tradition.

Ocha-Ifá arrived in Cuba from West Africa via the nineteenth-century slave trade. Religious praxis was, and continues to be, based on an elaborate series of orally transmitted myths and proverbs that prescribe, prohibit and rationalize behavior and distinct levels of participation in both religious and secular life. A religious complex concerned with solving the problems of the present, Ocha-Ifá entails direct and indirect divination via the *orishas,* or deities linked to the powers of nature, which control human destiny. Indirect divination involves interpreting patterns of pieces of coconut, palm nuts or metal disks as they are tossed onto a mat as the *orisha*'s message. Direct divination occurs through spirit possession of a medium. Only Ocha employs this method of divination, which is often described through the analogy of horse and rider. Originally practiced only by non-whites, by the late twentieth century Ocha-Ifá counted a significant number of white Cubans among its adherents.

In exchange for guiding and protecting humans from danger, the *orishas* demand worship and offerings. Worship may take many forms such as dressing in the colors representing a particular deity, caring for sacred objects, greeting the material representation of the *orisha,* and holding drumming ceremonies. Offerings, however, are foods specific to each deity and always involve the sacrifice of an animal and the spilling of its blood, both of which are believed to reinvigorate the *orisha* and its power.

Gender played a central role in organizing and defining praxis throughout the twentieth century, although research is only beginning to address its significance. Nonetheless, analyses of nineteenth-century Yoruba sociopolitical organization in West Africa have offered some insight into gendered ritual relationships in Cuban praxis. Anthropologist J. Lorand Matory argues that gender was the paradigm of all relationships among eighteenth- and early nineteenth-century Yoruba. Sociologist Oyèrónké Oyèwùmí argues, in contrast, that gender did not exist in the pre-colonial Òyó Empire and that hierarchy and sociopolitical power were based exclusively on seniority. Both of these scholars caution against universalizing analyses of gender and, perhaps more importantly, contend that the Yoruba understood gender as being much more fluid and complex than western, colonizing cultures could comprehend.

It was not uncommon in nineteenth-century Yorubaland for men to assume some roles identified as female, especially as possession priests of certain *orishas,* or for women to assume more masculine roles, such as hunters. This behavior did not provoke social disapproval, but individuals usually cross-dressed, adopting the cultural genitals of the opposite sex in order to perform the gender corresponding to their public activities. In Cuba, cross gender behavior and cross-dressing was punishable by law. Rather than discarding Yoruba gender metaphors for social organization, therefore, practitioners wove them into religious praxis so that the *orisha,* not the medium, contravened certain comportments, thereby subverting Cuban gender identities that were believed to follow naturally from anatomical sex.

Networks of fictive kinship forged through initiation into the religion preserved several aspects of Yoruba social life. The ritually experienced who trained a novice in *orisha* worship became the individual's *padrinos,* or godparents. And while the newly initiated person was considered their *ahijado(a),* or godchild, s/he was also considered the *iyáwò,* or bride, of the *orisha* to whom s/he was initiated. '*Iyáwò*' was recoded to mean 'child' in contemporary Cuba, but its origin reveals the relationship between practitioners and *orishas.* Speculation has led researchers to argue that as the bride, all new initiates were gendered female in relationship to their divine husbands who could have been male or female *orishas* that spiritually penetrated their human 'mounts' during possession. The husband-bride relationship in this argument represents metaphorical copulation.

Following certain elements of Oyèwùmí's argument, however, the concept of *iyáwò* suggests that the husband-bride relationship represented an insider-outsider relationship through which each party exercised certain obligations and responsibilities. Brides, in virilocal marriages, were always outsiders in their husbands' families, but insiders in their own. In Cuba, as the *iyáwò* status lasted only a short period following initiation and incorporation into a religious family, the relationship was more likely to have been constructed around the fictive kin group, and unrelated to copulation. After fulfilling certain initiatory criteria within a defined period of time, an individual became an insider and was no longer referred to as *iyáwò* but as a full member of the religious family, which was organized hierarchically based on number of years initiated in the religion. Status was acquired over time.

Recoding notwithstanding, *orisha* worship both in Africa and Cuba centered on establishing and maintaining control over the material world via the spiritual. Possession by an *orisha*, therefore, put an individual in direct contact with an entity that could advise on personal, social and political matters. Mediums behaved like the *orisha* in possession of their bodies and often conducted themselves in ways that western observers described as sexual. Many *orishas*, for example, were connected to fertility, which was equated with political and social stability, as well as human and agricultural reproduction. Religious festivals generally took place in these symbolic contexts. Oyèwùmí has demonstrated that certain concepts, such as fatherhood, were also symbolically rather than sexually produced. She explains that biological contribution to conception of a child was unnecessary for men to become fathers; rather, marriage to the biological mother of the child and public declarations of paternity established fatherhood and perpetuated the lineage. As in ceremonies designed to stabilize and perpetuate social relations, sex and sexuality, in western conceptualization of the terms, had little to do with procreation or reproduction. The opposite was true in Cuban society, where sexuality was considered sinful and immoral and could only be sanctified through marriage for the purpose of procreation.

In spite of these significant gender differences between the Yoruba and Cubans, colonial authorities in Cuba initially concerned themselves with the potential for rebellion that African religions represented, rather than their sexuality, although Spain periodically manipulated the image of black men raping white women as a means to maintain gender, class and racial divisions to thwart independence movements. Although permitted on Sundays and holidays, colonial authorities limited observance of African traditions to the *cabildos de nación,* small, legally inscribed religious chapters under the supervision of the Catholic Church that restricted membership to Africans of the same ethnicity as a way to maintain ethnic tensions and reduce the likelihood of unified rebellions. The Spanish hoped that, under the tutelage of the Church, Africans would become more Catholic; however, feeble efforts at catechization and the demands of a plantation society limited the impact of the Church. Nonetheless, slaves practiced their religious traditions during the little free time they had, with periodic repression or control from the plantation owners throughout the colonial period.

Towards the end of the nineteenth century, as abolition became inevitable, the Spanish crown attempted to abolish the *cabildos* and replace them with mutual aid societies that would better serve the needs of a society based on free, rather than slave, labor. Many simply renamed their *cabildos* and began to admit other African ethnic groups and their descendants, while maintaining the basic character of a religious entity. In both cases, slaves and free blacks hosting religious celebrations in their homes had to request permission to do so and were kept under surveillance. Non-participants in these festivities repeatedly lodged complaints with authorities concerning noise and large gatherings of people in the street late at night, with varying degrees of success in enforcing the peace. While these grievances served to intensify racial divisions in society by characterizing African cultural practices as raucous and disorganized, they had yet to reorient the focus of aggression to sexual morality. Republican authorities maintained this policy of scrutinizing African religious activities after independence from Spain in 1898, referring to these practices, and a number of popular beliefs and superstitions of European origin, as witchcraft.

Babalawo Victor Betancourt was initiated to Ifá in 1985 after participating in Palo Monte (a Bantu religion) and Ocha for more than thirty years. Through experience, he had realized that women in Ocha-Ifá possessed as much ritual knowledge as men; even concerning rituals in which gender restricted their participation. Furthermore, Betancourt identified domestic slavery and Cuban machismo as responsible for relegating women to the kitchen in the nineteenth century. Their qualification as cooks and cleaners had been absorbed into the religion during the republican period. Betancourt aimed to expand the role of women in Ifá and rewrite the history of the religion in Cuba as one in which gender roles appeared far less circumscribed than they were by the 1990s. He also sought to use symbols and imagery of the past to judge and comment on race in late twentieth-century Cuban society.

Research of his religious heritage led Betancourt to believe that equally capable and respected female diviners of Ifá had arrived in Cuba as slaves. Several women, he argued, such as Ma Monserrat González, Fermina Gómez, Latuán and María Towá, were known for their divination skills and had enjoyed prestige as a result of their extensive knowledge of the *odús* (myths) of Ifá. These women were so influential that *babalawos* heeded their advice. Furthermore, it was a former female Yoruba slave who gave the first ritual power of Ifá to a Cuban *babalawo*. While not all practitioners agree that women arrived in Cuba as initiates to Ifá, the majority recognize the power, influence and reputation of the women Betancourt cited to support Iyáonifá.

After 1959, the Cuban state still expected women to form nuclear families and become mothers, even if they did not marry, but it also expected them to contribute to building socialism, a task that required their labor at all levels of the workforce. The establishment of daycare centers, cafeterias and laundries helped to reduce women's workload, although a continued focus on changing women's behavior made changing men more difficult. Nonetheless, in spite of their under-representation in high levels of government and other sectors, women had made enormous gains by the 1980s, entering all areas of the workforce and even outnumbering men in some of the more traditionally male occupations. This process, however, had required some skillful maneuvering in service of the revolution and, in a similar fashion, Betancourt had to do the same. Overturning pre-revolutionary idealizations of gender roles in the workplace, if not the home, forced at least some practitioners of Ocha-Ifá to reflect on equitable religious praxis.

Betancourt's study of Yoruba texts, both on the history of Ifá in West Africa and the *odús* that contain prohibitions against initiating women revealed that, although several myths criticized the involvement of women in Ifá, only one, Ireté Ogbé, had been employed to justify their exclusion. In this myth the supreme Yoruba deity Olodumaré invests the *orisha* Odú with great powers:

> Upon being called to earth by the *awos* (diviners), Olodúmare gave Odú a bird and told her that it would go anywhere she wanted it to and do anything she wanted it to do. She named it Aragamago, put it in a calabash and said that no one else could look at it. Those who looked at the bird would be blinded. The *awos* consulted Ifá [considered separate from Odú] who recommended that Orúnmila make an offering to the earth so that he could marry Odú. She let Aragamago out of the calabash to eat the offering. Odú then told Orúnmila that she had tremendous powers but did not wish to fight him. She would share her power with him if he obeyed her taboo – his wives could not look upon her face. Additionally, the one initiated to Ifá will not be allowed to suffer.

This myth reveals the origin of Ifá and the source of Orúnmila's power – marriage to Odú. The calabash and the bird appear as symbols of spiritual power and the power of female deities is usually contained in some form of calabash. Birds are potent messengers associated mainly with two *orishas* – Orúnmila, the medium between Odú and the *babalawo,* and Osaín, the deity of herbs and cures. Birds are also routinely passed over the body of an initiate to cleanse it of negative elements or are offered in sacrifice to the *orishas* in exchange for their assistance with a minor problem. The bird in the calabash symbolizes the female power of Odú and its consumption of the offering acceptance of the pact between Odú and Orúnmila. Female power is often viewed as polluting or destabilizing, but thus contained or controlled Odú's potential became available for Orúnmila's use.

Most Cuban *babalawos* have interpreted Odú's taboo against Orúnmila's wives looking upon her face as traditional justification for prohibiting the initiation of women to Ifá. As the interpreters of the oracle, *babalawos* are equated with Orúnmila. Odú communicates via the oracle. Complete ritual fabrication of myths would put both the adherent and the religion at risk; however, alternative meanings of many *odús* have always been present in Cuban praxis, although practitioners identify them as incorrect or corrupted. Rather than challenge conventions, Victor Betancourt reinterpreted the myth as meaning that women could not look at the oracle. Looking at the oracle may or may not be relevant to working with Ifá and this issue will be discussed in the following section. More salient for the moment is Odú's reassurance that those who joined her would not be harmed. And to join Odú, Betancourt determined that women would have to become insiders, or witches.

As in Cuba, witches existed in Yoruba culture. Unlike in Cuba, only women practiced witchcraft and they were generally believed to have control over life and death in a very broad sense. These usually post-menopausal women joined Egbe Gëlèdé, or societies of witches, from which they exercised their power. The term witch, however, is misleading because the Yoruba word for witch, *ajé*, does not imply malevolence. Their actions are more closely related to reproduction, fertility and political stability. The *ajés* can impact these aspects of human life in both positive and negative ways that are not always interpreted as life or death.

In Yorubaland, men dedicated themselves to honoring these powerful women during times of social or political strife in order to appease and control their potentially destructive behavior, convincing them to focus on life-giving activities. They donned women's attire and elaborate wooden masks representing birds or women's faces and entertained the *ajés* by dancing in annual masquerade ceremonies. These ceremonies continued well into the twentieth century among some Yoruba.

Founded in Havana in 1998, the Cuban Egbe Gëlèdé is based on the Gëlèdé from the Yoruba city of Ketú, where the practice originated. Worship centered on the feminine power, Igba Iwa, or Iyamí, known as the beginning and end of all life. In different regions of Nigeria, Iyamí is also known as Iya Nla, who in turn is sometimes identified as the *orisha* Odú, while in other instances Iyamí is identified as Yemoja, the *orisha* of salt water and the mother of all the deities. Cuban members of the Egbe Gëlèdé strive to be good mothers and wives, attend to the upbringing of their children and the family, and to study the lives of little-known or undiscovered women. The Gëlèdé is one way in which women in Ocha-Ifá are attempting to halt and reverse the cultural destruction occasioned by the slave trade. At a time in which the bodies of non-white women are eroticized in tourist brochures and billboards, making claims on motherhood demands an alternative view of women of African descent from Cubans and tourists complicit in the consumption and perpetuation of these stereotypes.

There is no indication that the masquerade currently takes place in Cuba, although certain societies and practices associated with it existed at the turn of the twentieth century or were introduced sometime in the middle of the century. There is, however, a liturgical recognition of the Gëlèdé in Cuba in one of the 256 myths of Ifá. Osa Meji, one of the sixteen major *odús* of Ifá with which all practitioners are familiar, accounts for the Gëlèdé's existence and prescribes certain procedures to follow to avoid running afoul of the *ajés*. In this myth, the creator, Olodumaré, sent three *orishas* to earth:

Obarisa, Ogún and Iya Nla. Oludumaré gave Obarisa *aché* (spiritual power) and war to Ogún, but Iya Nla did not receive anything, so she complained to Olodúmare who responded by giving her the title 'Mother of All' and a calabash with a bird in it. When Olodúmare asked Iya Nla what she would do with her powers she told him that she would use them against her enemies but would give wealth and children to all who appeased her. Moreover, those who joined her could not be harmed.

Once again, the bird contained in a calabash appears as symbolic of the female *orisha's* power. Reproduction and the ability to bestow life are also central elements that serve to organize ritual structure and praxis. Iya Nla is therefore a significant deity for both men and women and as such is highly regarded and respected. Like all *orishas,* however, Iya Nla could be dangerous if underappreciated or challenged. To establish equilibrium between the human and spiritual worlds, Osa Meji also reveals how to appease Iya Nla.

The *orishas,* like human beings, are impulsive, curious and flawed. Out of curiosity, Orúnmila wanted to go to the land of the *ajés,* so he consulted the oracle to determine the best approach:

The Ifá oracle [Odú] advised Orúnmila to sacrifice a wooden image, a baby sash, and metal anklets before going to visit the 'haven of the-wielders-of-bird-power'. Orúnmila did this and returned safely singing: 'I have entered into a covenant with Death, and never will I die. Death, no more. I have entered into a covenant with Sickness, and never will I die. Death, no more'.

In order to go to the land of the *ajé,* Orúnmila had to *be* one of them. He therefore disguised himself as a woman by wearing a mask and a baby sash (for carrying babies, worn only by women). The metal anklets kept him anchored in the material world. This appropriation of female cultural genitals enabled Orúnmila to 'know' the secret of the *ajé* and he used it to 'trick' them. Yet, in becoming an *ajé,* however transitorily, the *ajés* could not harm Orúnmila.

Perhaps more important than establishing the relationship between Odú and Orúnmila, however, these myths repeatedly insist that those who join Odú (Iya Nla, the *ajés*) would not be harmed. Odú would protect the appropriately initiated insiders to the Egbe Gëlèdé . . . and also Ifá.

Protected from the wrath of Odú through prior initiation to the Egbe Gëlèdé, María Cuesta Conde and Nidia Águila de León were the first two Cuban women Victor Betancourt initiated to Ifá in March 2000. Calling the female version of Ifá and the women initiated to it Iyáonifá, Betancourt insisted that he was 'restor[ing] women's legitimate right [to work in Ifá] . . . contribut[ing] to the development of moral ethics in the Ifá tradition [and] purif[ying] the cult through the new incorporation of the feminine gender'. Betancourt merged the once diametrically opposed images of Africa, witchcraft and Ocha-Ifá with women, morality and purity to serve Cubans of African descent. Something had gone awry in Ifá during the twentieth century and, in Betancourt's analysis of the situation, women were the morally superior symbols of purity that would solve the problem.

In justifying and defending Iyáonifá, Victor Betancourt has repeatedly referenced the history of the religion in Cuba and a handful of female possession priestesses universally recognized as powerful and capable diviners of Ocha and as important ritual ancestors who practitioners continue to recognize in *moyubas* (songs) to honor the ancestors. These women, however, were also known as astute, cunning and wily, hardly characteristics associated with morality and purity. Moreover, one of these women was responsible for some of the most significant innovations of the early twentieth century.

In addition to amalgamating the multiple *orisha* traditions into Ocha, Latuán also created the *obá oriaté* (master of ceremonies), a religious specialist who performed all initiation ceremonies and consecrated sacred objects in Ocha. Moreover, in a struggle for dominance of Ocha, Latuán used her position to sanction or condone particular practices. She trained only one disciple, Lorenzo Samá, who in turn trained only two men to succeed him. By the time of Samá's death in 1944, the office of the *obá oriaté* had become an increasingly male domain and, in spite of the prominent role women had played in both the development of the specialty and the training of their successors, they quickly disappeared from the office.

The elimination of women from such a powerful ritual function suggests that creole adherents, unlike their African mentors, accepted and absorbed into their religious practice notions from the Cuban elite concerning the appropriate gender roles for men and women where respectability and status were tied to notions of honor, controlled through marriage, to reinforce and regulate women's subjugation. Although non-whites could never remove the stain of slavery, they employed a variety of techniques to distance themselves from it, including marrying white Cubans to lighten the skin of their offspring and conforming to elite behavioral expectations. Yielding a great deal of power and challenging the alleged natural authority of men was not consistent with the behavior becoming for women in the twentieth century, especially among black Cubans who struggled to minimize differences between themselves and white Cubans, even as they continued to recognize their distinct heritage.

These gendered changes taking place in Ocha also impacted Ifá. While related, Ocha and Ifá had maintained a certain ritual distance in Cuba. Very few *babalawos* had arrived in Cuba as slaves and they in turn trained very few men in the tradition until the mid-twentieth century, a custom that partially explains the popularity of Ocha, and other African-derived religions, among both men and women. While practitioners of Ocha and Ifá participated in the same ceremonies, neither relied on the other to perform rites or initiate new members. *Babalawos* initiated *babalawos* to Ifá and the *obás oriatés* initiated adherents to Ocha. Men consecrated to Ocha, however, could later enter Ifá and at some point during the mid-twentieth century it became common for men to follow their Ocha initiation with initiation to Ifá. This staging of initiations enabled *babalawos* to both observe and participate in Ocha rituals from which they would have been excluded if initiated only to Ifá, thereby compelling closer religious ties between the two traditions. Critics of Ifá argue that the practice gave *babalawos* more control over Ocha while others suggest that the ritual links between the two traditions helped to provide practitioners with a united front when faced with state repression intent on eliminating the cultural expressions of a race it could not accept.

David H. Brown has also suggested that control over Ifá and its originally scarce ritual power began to weaken by mid-century, as the creole *babalawos* trained by Africans passed away. These first generation creole *babalawos* had hand-picked the men who they would eventually initiate into Ifá and forced them to undergo extensive training prior to initiation. Their successors attracted more disciples and relaxed the rules, leading to an overall expansion of Ifá. But one *babalawo* in particular was responsible for the majority of initiations that took place between the 1960s and 1980s. Taking advantage of this mid-century power vacuum, Miguel Febles Padrón began initiating men to Ifá based on their ability to pay for the initiation ceremony. This practice continued until his death in the mid-1980s, although by that time many other *babalawos* had also begun to initiate large numbers of men, mostly to be able to compete with Febles Padrón for spiritual capital. It is no mere coincidence, therefore, that Victor Betancourt often refers to Febles Padrón in defense of his own innovations.

As a result of this expansion of Ifá, it had become the main objective for many men interested in joining a religion of African origin by the 1990s and they began skipping the initial step of joining an Ocha house. The overall impact of these aspirations to Ifá has, however, feminized Ocha. Men who can, prefer to become *babalawos* and those who do not could be suspected of being homosexual. Spirit possession, for example, continues to be a central and desirable part of Ocha religious praxis and is understood as confirmation that initiation to a particular *orisha* was appropriate. Men, however, generally avoid being possessed by female *orishas* for fear of having their masculinity questioned. Being spiritually passive in relation to a male *orisha*, paradoxically, does not imply such speculation. Public performance, rather than private acts, determines an individual's gender in Ocha-Ifá and compels men, much more than women, towards heterosexuality, indicating that adherents ultimately accepted twentieth-century Cuban assumptions of gender as flowing naturally from anatomical sex.

Betancourt unmistakably seeks to use Iyáonifá to restore some of the power women lost over the twentieth century as men usurped their specialties – he has openly stated this in interviews with journalists and scholars, as well as in articles he has written on the subject. What he does not state, yet is implicit in the logic used to justify the participation of women in Ifá, is an observance of the compulsory heterosexuality that the majority of *babalawos* absorbed after decades of repression based on alleged sexual non-conformity, a revolutionary obsession with homosexuality and its association with counter-revolutionary activity. *Babalawos* confronted racist culture by denying male sexual transgression and embracing the longstanding ideal of masculinity that praised men for their virility and effective control of women.

Betancourt does not, however, identify sociopolitical processes, persistent racial stereotypes and what Alejandro de la Fuente calls the 'traumatic process of dealing with racism and discrimination' as the origin of the prohibition against homosexuality.

Rather, he appeals to what he calls the 'natural complementarity' between men and women:

> we know that in order for a human being to be born, two must intervene, in the same way. And the ceremonies can be different, the woman on the bottom and the man on top or the man on the bottom and the woman on top, the man gives and the woman receives. Right here, in the sacred encounter, there are ceremonies and rituals that remind us of how a man and a woman can give birth.

Not only does Betancourt advocate a particular variety of heterosexuality, as Gayle Rubin might argue, he advocates sex for the purpose of procreation, at least metaphorically, in a ritual context. A causal relationship between sex, gender and desire must exist to stabilize ritual practice. This vision restricts entry to Ifá, albeit in a less limited sense than before, and maintains a gender hierarchy in which binary relationships privilege heterosexuality, reinforcing the authority of men in Ifá. In order to illustrate this point, it is useful to examine some of the criticism Betancourt has received from other *babalawos* in Cuba.

Condemnation of Betancourt and his initiation of women to Ifá follows one of two arguments. The first posits that because women cannot become *babalawos* and work with Odú, Betancourt and others like him are deceiving the women, exposing them to certain danger and retaliation from the *orisha* for disobeying her taboo. A number of *babalawos* argue that in Nigeria there exist three categories of women who can work with Ifá: the *apètèhí* (apeterbi), *ìyánífá* and *ìyálówò*. As in Cuba, the *apètèbí* fulfills the limited role of preparing the Ifá room or ritual space for the *babalawo,* but the *ìyánífá* and *ìyálówò* can care for the deity and divine with the divining chain once they reach menopause. Betancourt's error is in allowing pre-menopausal women to come into contact with Odú.

Yet, an examination of the initiation process for the *iyáonifás* in Cuba demonstrates that Betancourt does indeed observe these taboos. Both *babalawos* and *iyáonifás* receive the red parrot feather that is later placed in a calabash during the initiation ceremony. *Babalawos,* however, eventually enter Odú's grove (a sacred exterior space inhabited by the *orisha*) to be 'reborn' through their contact with Odú. *Iyáonifás* must remain outside of Odú's grove and forego the 'rebirth', although their heads are shaved to symbolize their new beginning in Ifá. If entering Odú's grove is as crucial to Ifá praxis as it appears, then women do not enjoy all the benefits of initiation and divination. The grove and contact with Odú serve to privilege men and place them at the top of the religious hierarchy. Women are viewed as potentially, if not actually, destabilizing elements.

The second argument against the *iyáonifás* sustains that Cuban tradition simply does not permit the initiation of women to Ifá and that such initiations would never have occurred under the guidance of older *babalawos* because they followed Cuban traditions. Significantly, these critics cite Cuba, not Africa as the source of gender discrimination in Ocha-Ifá and refer to the *odú* Eyila Shebora to justify their position.

In this myth, Yemayá learned to divine by watching her husband Orúnmila. She then made a living through divination in her husband's absence. Upon discovery of Yemayá's betrayal, Orúnmila consulted Ifá and was told that he could give Yemayá advice or spiritual influence (*cofá*) but he could no longer live with her. As one particularly irate *babalawo* stated in response to Betancourt's initiation of women, 'This is the birth of women not as *babalaos,* nor as priests, but as *apeterbi* of Orula [Orúnmila], slave of Ifá. This notion of women being unable to contain secrets or other ritual information is a particularly Cuban phenomenon, as is the masculine response to chastise women by reducing or eliminating their religious power. Women are seen as interlopers who must be kept in their place.

More than a decade after the initiation of the first *iyáonifás,* it is clear that while they crossed a significant gendered barrier, women have yet to gain acceptance among the men in Ifá. Although they interpret Odú's message, the *iyáonifás* do not participate in the largest Ifá ceremony that augurs the events of the New Year and attracts thousands of *babalawos* from all over the world. Moreover, those seeking the assistance of Ifá in solving their problems continue to prefer the *babalawo* to the *iyáonifás* although a few individuals approach the *iyáonifás* out of curiosity. Nidia Águila de León, however, has confessed that she has yet to be taken seriously by those seeking advice.

4

Mama Lola and the Ezilis:

Themes of Mothering and Loving in Haitian Vodou

Karen McCarthy Brown

The late Karen McCarthy Brown (1942–2015) was an anthropologist and practitioner of Vodou. This syncretistic religious tradition originated in eighteenth-century Haiti, a combination of different African traditions influenced by Catholic devotion to saints as well. Spirits are central to Vodou devotion, and these larger-than-life figures are engaged through trance-possession by a ritual specialist, a priest or priestess (manbo). This excerpt draws from research that was part of her longer study Mama Lola: A Vodou Priestess in Brooklyn. *This critically acclaimed work traces the family history and spiritual practices of Alourdes, a Vodou priestess and healer now residing in America. In it, McCarthy Brown focuses on two female spirits, Ezili Dantor and Ezili Freda, special to Alourdes' ritual life. She demonstrates how these Vodou spirits give meaning to the experiences, the tensions, disappointments, and desires that Haitian women encounter.*

Mama Lola is a Haitian woman in her mid-fifties who lives in Brooklyn, where she works as a Vodou priestess. This essay concerns her relationship with two female *lwa*, Vodou spirits whom she "serves." By means of trance states, these spirits periodically speak and act through her during community ceremonies and private healing sessions. Mama Lola's story will serve as a case study of how the Vodou spirits closely reflect the lives of those who honor them. While women and men routinely and meaningfully serve both male and female spirits in Vodou, I will focus here on only one strand of the complex web of relations between the "living" and the

Vodou spirits, the strand that connects women and female spirits. Specifically I will demonstrate how female spirits, in their iconography and possession-performance, mirror the lives of contemporary Haitian women with remarkable specificity. Some general discussion of Haiti and of Vodou is necessary before moving to the specifics of Mama Lola's story.

The Haitian Ezili's African roots are multiple. Among them is Mammy Water, a powerful mother of the waters whose shrines are found throughout West Africa. Like moving water, Ezili can be sudden, fickle, and violent, but she is also deep, beautiful, moving, creative, nurturing, and powerful. In Haiti Ezili was recognized in images of the Virgin Mary and subsequently conflated with her. The various manifestations of the Virgin pictured in the inexpensive and colorful lithographs available throughout the Catholic world eventually provided receptacles for several different Ezilis as the spirit subdivided in the New World in order to articulate the different directions in which women's power flowed.

Alourdes, like all Vodou priests or priestesses, has a small number of spirits who manifest routinely through her. This spiritual coterie, which differs from person to person, both defines the character of the healer and sets the tone of his or her "temple." Ezili Dantor is Alourdes's major female spirit, and she is conflated with Mater Salvatoris, a black Virgin pictured holding the Christ child. The child that Dantor holds (Haitians usually identify it as a daughter!) is her most important iconographic detail, for Ezili Dantor is above all else the woman who bears children, the mother par excellence.

Haitians say that Ezili Dantor fought fiercely beside her "children" in the slave revolution. She was wounded, they say, and they point to the parallel scars that appear on the right cheek of the Mater Salvatoris image as evidence for this. Details of Ezili Dantor's possession-performance extend the story. Ezili Dantor also lost her tongue during the revolution. Thus Dantor does not speak when she possesses someone. The only sound the spirit can utter is a uniform "de-de-de." In a Vodou ceremony. Dantor's mute "de-de-de" becomes articulate only through her body language and the interpretive efforts of the gathered community. Her appearances are thus reminiscent of a somber game of charades. Ezili Dantor's fighting spirit is reinforced by her identification as a member of the Petro pantheon of Vodou spirits, and as such she is associated with what is hot, fiery, and strong. As a Petro spirit Dantor is handled with care. Fear and caution are always somewhere in the mix of attitudes that people hold toward the various Petro spirits.

Those, such as Alourdes, who serve Ezili Dantor become her children and, like children in the traditional Haitian family, they owe their mother high respect and unfailing loyalty. In return, this spiritual mother, like the ideal human mother, will exhaust her strength and resources to care for her children. It is important to note here that the sacrifice of a mother for her children will never be seen by Haitians in purely sentimental or altruistic terms. For Haitian women, even for those now living in New York, children represent the main hope for an economically viable household and the closest thing there is to a guarantee of care in old age.

The mother-child relationship among Haitians is thus strong, essential, and in a not unrelated way, potentially volatile. In the countryside, children's labor is necessary for family survival. Children begin to work at an early age, and physical punishment is often swift and severe if they are irresponsible or disrespectful. Although in the cities children stay in school longer and begin to contribute to the welfare of the family at a later age, similar attitudes toward childrearing prevail.

In woman-headed households, the bond between mother and daughter is the most charged and the most enduring. Women and their children form three- and sometimes four-generation networks in which gifts and services circulate according to the needs and abilities of each. These tight family relationships create a safety net in a society where hunger is a common experience for the majority of people. The strength of the mother-daughter bond explains why Haitians identify the child in Ezili Dantor's arms as a daughter. And the importance and precariousness of that bond explain Dantor's fighting spirit and fiery temper.

In possession-performance, Ezili Dantor explores the full range of possibilities inherent in the mother-child bond. Should Dantor's "children" betray her or trifle with her dignity, the spirit's anger can be sudden, fierce, and uncompromising. In such situations her characteristic "de-de-de" becomes a powerful rendering of women's mute but devastating rage. A gentle rainfall during the festivities at Saut d'Eau, a mountainous pilgrimage site for Dantor, is readily interpreted as a sign of her presence but so is a sudden deluge resulting in mudslides and traffic accidents. Ezili's African water roots thus flow into the most essential of social bonds, that between mother and child, where they carve out a web of channels through which can flow a mother's rage as well as her love.

Alourdes, like Ezili Dantor, is a proud and hardworking woman who will not tolerate disrespect or indolence in her children. While her anger is never directed at Maggie, who is now an adult and Alourdes' partner in running the household, it can sometimes sweep the smaller children off their feet. I have never seen Alourdes strike a child, but her wrath can be sudden and the punishments meted out severe. Although the suffering is different in kind, there is a good measure of it in both Haiti and New York, and the lessons have carried from one to the other. Once, after Alourdes disciplined her ten-year-old, she turned to me and said: "The world is evil. . . . You got to make them tough!"

Ezili Dantor is not only Alourdes's main female spirit, she is also the spirit who first called Alourdes to her role as priestess. One of the central functions of Vodou in Haiti, and among Haitian emigrants, is that of reinforcing social bonds. Because obligations to the Vodou spirits are inherited within families, Alourdes's decision to take on the heavy responsibility of serving the spirits was also a decision to opt for her extended family (and her Haitian identity) as her main survival strategy.

It was not always clear that this was the decision she would make. Before Alourdes came to the United States, she had shown little interest in her mother's religious practice, even though an appearance by Ezili Dantor at a family ceremony had marked her for the priesthood when she was only five or six years old. By the time Alourdes left Haiti she was in her late twenties and the memory of that message from Dantor had either disappeared or ceased to feel relevant. When Alourdes left Haiti, she felt she was leaving the spirits behind along with a life marked by struggle and suffering. But the spirits sought her out in New York. Messages from Ezili and other spirits came in the form of a debilitating illness that prevented her from working. It was only after she returned to Haiti for initiation into the priesthood and thus acknowledged the spirits' claim on her that Alourdes's life in the U.S. began to run smoothly.

Over the ten years I have known this family, I have watched a similar process at work with her daughter Maggie. Choosing the life of a Vodou priestess in New York is much more difficult for Maggie than it was for her mother. To this day, I have yet to see Maggie move all the way into a trance state. Possession threatens and Maggie struggles mightily; her body falls to the floor as if paralyzed, but she fights off the descending darkness that marks the onset of trance. Afterwards, she is angry and afraid. Yet these feelings finally did not prohibit Maggie from making a commitment to the *manbo's* role. She was initiated to the priesthood in the summer of 1982 in a small temple on the outskirts of Port-au-Prince. Alourdes presided at these rituals. Maggie's commitment to Vodou came after disturbing dreams and a mysterious illness not unlike the one that plagued Alourdes shortly after she came to the United States. The accelerated harassment of the spirits also started around the time when a love affair brought Maggie face to face with the choice of living with someone other than her mother. Within a short period of time, the love affair ended, the illness arrived, and Maggie had a portentous dream in which the spirits threatened to block her life path until she promised to undergo initiation. Now it is widely acknowledged that Maggie is the heir to Alourdes's successful healing practice.

Yet this spiritual bond between Alourdes and Maggie cannot be separated from the social, economic, and emotional forces that hold them together. It is clear that Alourdes and Maggie depend on one another in myriad ways. Without the childcare Alourdes provides, Maggie could not work. Without the check Maggie brings in every week, Alourdes would have only the modest and erratic income she brings in from her healing work. These practical issues were also at stake in Maggie's decision about the Vodou priesthood, for a decision to become a *manbo* was also a decision to cast her lot with her mother. This should not be interpreted to mean that Alourdes uses religion to hold Maggie against her will. The affection between them is genuine and strong. Alourdes and Maggie are each other's best friend and most trusted ally. In Maggie's own words: "We have a beautiful relationship . . . it's more than a twin, it's like a Siamese twin. . . . She is my soul." And in Alourdes's: "If she not near me, I feel something inside me disconnected."

Maggie reports that when she has problems, Ezili Dantor often appears to her in dreams. Once, shortly after her arrival in the United States, Maggie had a waking vision of Dantor. The spirit, clearly recognizable in her gold-edged blue veil, drifted into her bedroom window. Her new classmates were cruelly teasing her, and the twelve-year-old Maggie was in despair. Dantor gave her a maternal backrub and drifted out the window, where the spirit's glow was soon lost in that of a corner street-lamp. These days, when she is in trouble and Dantor does not appear of her own accord, Maggie goes seeking the spirit. "She don't have to talk to me in my dream. Sometime I go inside the altar, just look at her statue . . . she says a few things to me." The image with which Maggie converses is, of course, Mater Salvatoris, the black virgin, holding in her arms her favored girl child, Anaise.

It is not only in her relationship with her daughter that Alourdes finds her life mirrored in the image of Ezili Dantor. Ezili Dantor is also the mother raising children on her own, the woman who will take lovers but will not marry. In many ways, it is this aspect of Dantor's story that most clearly mirrors and maps the lives of Haitian women.

In former days (and still in some rural areas) the patriarchal, multigenerational extended family held sway in Haiti. In these families men could form unions with more than one woman. Each woman had her own household in which she bore and raised the children from that union. The men moved from household to household, often continuing to rely on their mothers as well as their women to feed and lodge them. When the big extended families began to break up under the combined pressures of depleted soil, overpopulation, and corrupt politics, large numbers of rural people moved to the cities.

Generally speaking, Haitian women fared better than men in the shift from rural to urban life. In the cities the family shrank to the size of the individual household unit, an arena in which women had traditionally been in charge. Furthermore, their skill at small-scale commerce, an aptitude passed on through generations of rural market women, allowed them to adapt to life in urban Haiti, where the income of a household must often be patched together from several small and sporadic sources. Urban women sell bread, candy, and herbal teas which they make themselves. They also buy and re-sell food, clothing, and household goods. Often their entire inventory is balanced on their heads or spread on outstretched arms as they roam through the streets seeking customers. When desperate enough, women also sell sex. They jokingly refer to their genitals as their "land." The employment situation in urban Haiti, meager though it is, also favors women. Foreign companies tend to prefer them for the piecework that accounts for a large percentage of the jobs available to the poor urban majority.

By contrast, unemployment among young urban males may well be as high as 80%. Many men in the city circulate among the households of their girlfriends and mothers. In this way they are usually fed, enjoy some intimacy, and get their laundry done. But life is hard and resources scarce. With the land gone, it is no longer so clear that men are essential to the survival of women and children. As a result, relationships between urban men and women have become brittle and often violent. And this is so in spite of a romantic ideology not found in the countryside. Men are caught in a double bind. They are still reared to expect to have power and to exercise authority, and yet they have few resources to do so. Consequently, when their expectations run up against a wall of social impossibility, they often veer off in unproductive directions. The least harmful of these is manifest in a national preoccupation with soccer; the most damaging is the military, the domestic police force of Haiti, which provides the one open road toward upward social mobility for poor young men. Somewhere in the middle of this spectrum lie the drinking and gambling engaged in by large numbers of poor men.

Ezili Dantor's lover is Ogou, a soldier spirit sometimes pictured as a hero, a breathtakingly handsome and dedicated soldier. But just as often Ogou is portrayed as vain and swaggering, untrustworthy and self-destructive. In one of his manifestations Ogou is a drunk. This is the man Ezili Dantor will take into her bed but would never depend on. Their relationship thus takes up and comments on much of the actual life experience of poor urban women.

Ezili Dantor also mirrors many of the specifics of Alourdes's own life. Gran Philo, Alourdes's mother, was the first of her family to live in the city. She worked there as a *manbo*. Although she bore four children, she never formed a long-term union with a man. She lived in Santo Domingo, in the Dominican Republic, for the first years of her adult life. There she had her first two babies. But her lover proved irrational, jealous, and possessive. Since she was working as hard or harder than he, Philo soon decided to leave him. Back in Port-au-Prince, she had two more children, but in neither case did the father participate in the rearing of the children. Alourdes, who is the youngest, did not know who her father was until she was grown. And when she found out, it still took time for him to acknowledge paternity.

In her late teens, Alourdes's fine singing voice won her a coveted position with the Troupe Folklorique, a song and dance group that drew much of its repertoire from Vodou. During that period Alourdes attracted the attention of an older man who had a secure job with the Bureau of Taxation. During their brief marriage Alourdes lived a life that was the dream of most poor Haitian women. She had a house and two servants. She did not have to work. But this husband, like the first man in Philo's life, needed to control her every move. His jealousy was so great that Alourdes was not even allowed to visit her mother without supervision. (The man should have known better than to threaten that vital bond!) Alourdes and her husband fought often and, after less than two years, she left. In the years that followed, there were times when Alourdes had no food and times when she could not pay her modest rent but, with pride like Ezili Dantor's, Alourdes never returned to her husband and never asked him for money. During one especially difficult period Alourdes began to operate as a Marie-Jacques, a prostitute, although not the kind who hawk their wares on the street. Each day she would dress up and go from business to business in downtown Port-au-Prince looking for someone who would ask her for a "date." When the date was over she would take what these men offered (everyone knew the rules), but she never asked for money. Alourdes had three children in Haiti, by three different men. She fed them and provided shelter by juggling several income sources. Her mother helped when she could. So did friends when they heard she was in need. For a while, Alourdes held a job as a tobacco inspector for the government. And she also dressed up and went out looking for dates.

Maggie, like Alourdes, was married once. Her husband drank too much and one evening, he hit her. Once was enough. Maggie packed up her infant son and returned to her mother's house. She never looked back. When Maggie talks about this marriage, now over for nearly a decade, she says he was a good man but alcohol changed him. "When he drink, forget it!" She would not take the chance that he might hit her again or, worse, take his anger and frustration out on their son.

Ezili Dantor is the mother—fierce, proud, hard-working, and independent. As a religious figure, Dantor's honest portrayal of the ambivalent emotions a woman can feel toward her lovers and a mother can feel toward her children stands in striking contrast to the idealized attitude of calm, nurture, and acceptance represented by more standard interpretations of the Holy Mother Mary, a woman for whom rage would be unthinkable. Through her iconography and possession-performances, Ezili Dantor works in subtle ways with the concrete life circumstances of Haitian women such as Alourdes and Maggie. She takes up their lives, clarifies the issues at stake in them, and gives them permission to follow the sanest and most humane paths. Both Alourdes and Maggie refer to Ezili Dantor as "my mother."

Vodou is a religion born of slavery, of wrenching change and deep pain. Its genius can be traced to long experience in using the first (change) to deal with the second (pain). Vodou is a religion in motion, one without canon, creed, or pope. In Vodou the ancient African wisdom is preserved by undergoing constant transformation in response to specific life circumstances. One of the things which keeps Vodou agile is its plethora of spirits. Each person who serves the spirits has his or her own coterie of favorites. And no single spirit within that group can take over and lay down the law for the one who serves. There are always other spirits to consult, other spirit energies to take into account. Along with Ezili Dantor, Alourdes also serves her sister, Ezili Freda.

Ezili Freda is a white spirit from the Rada pantheon, a group characterized by sweetness and even tempers. Where Dantor acts out women's sexuality in its childbearing mode, Freda, the flirt, concerns herself with love and romance. Like the famous Creole mistresses who lent charm and glamour to colonial Haiti, Ezili Freda takes her identity and worth from her relationship with men. Like the mulatto elite in contemporary Haiti who are the heirs of those Creole women, Freda loves fine clothes and jewelry. In her possession-performances, Freda is decked out in satin and lace. She is given powder and perfume, sweet smelling soaps and rich creams. The one possessed by her moves through the gathered community, embracing one and then another and then another. Something in her searches and is never satisfied. Her visits often end in tears and frustration.

Different stories are told about Freda and children. Some say she is barren. Others say she has a child but wishes to hide that fact in order to appear fresher, younger, and more desirable to men. Those who hold the latter view are fond of pointing out the portrait of a young boy that is tucked behind the left elbow of the crowned Virgin in the image of Maria Dolorosa with whom Freda is conflated. In this intimate biographical detail, Freda picks up a fragment from Alourdes's life that hints at larger connections between the two. When Alourdes was married she already had two children by two different men. She wanted a church wedding and a respectable life, so she hid the children from her prospective in-laws. It was only at the wedding itself, when they asked about the little boy and girl seated in the front row, that they found out the woman standing before the altar with their son already had children.

Alourdes does not have her life all sewn up in neat packages. She does not have all the questions answered and all the tensions resolved. Most of the time when she tells the story of her marriage, Alourdes says flatly: "He too jealous. That man crazy!" But on at least one occasion she said: "I was too young. If I was with Antoine now, I never going to leave him!" When Alourdes married Antoine Lovinsky she was a poor teenager living in Port-au-Prince, a city where less than 10% of the people are not alarmingly poor. Women of the elite class nevertheless structure the dreams of poor young women. These are the light-skinned women who marry in white dresses in big Catholic churches and return to homes that have bedroom sets and dining room furniture and servants. These are the women who never have to work. They spend their days resting and visiting with friends and emerge at night on the arms of their men dressed like elegant peacocks and affecting an air of haughty boredom. Although Alourdes's tax collector could not be said to be a member of the elite, he provided her with a facsimile of the dream. It stifled her and confined her, but she has still not entirely let go of the fantasy. She still loves jewelry and clothes and, in her home, manages to create the impression, if not the fact, of wealth by piling together satin furniture, velvet paintings, and endless bric-a-brac.

Alourdes also has times when she is very lonely and she longs for male companionship. She gets tired of living at the edge of poverty and being the one in charge of such a big and ungainly household. She feels the pull of the images of domesticity and nuclear family life that she sees everyday on the television in New York. Twice since I have known her, Alourdes has fallen in love. She is a deeply sensual woman and this comes strongly to the fore during these times. She dresses up, becomes coquettish, and caters to her man. Yet when describing his lovable traits, she always says first: "He help me so much. Every month, he pay the electric bill," and so forth. Once again the practical and the emotional issues cannot be separated. In a way, this is just another version of the poor woman selling her "land." And in another way it is not, for here the finances of love are wound round and round with longing and dreams.

Poor Haitian women, Alourdes included, are a delight to listen to when their ironic wit turns on what we would label as the racism, sexism, and colonial pretense of the upper-class women Freda mirrors. Yet these are the values with power behind them both in Haiti and in New York, and poor women are not immune to the attraction of such a vision. Ezili Freda is thus an image poor Haitian women live toward. She picks up their dreams and gives them shape, but these women are mostly too experienced to think they can live on or in dreams. Alourdes is not atypical. She serves Freda but much less frequently than Dantor. Ezili Dantor is the one for whom she lights a candle every day; she is the one Alourdes turns to when there is real trouble. She is, in Alourdes' words, "my mother." Yet I think it is fair to say that it is the tension between Dantor and Freda that keeps both relevant to the lives of Haitian women.

There is a story about conflict between the two Ezilis. Most people, most of the time, will say that the scars on Ezili Dantor's cheek come from war wounds, but there is an alternative explanation. Sometimes it is said that because Dantor was sleeping with her man, Maria Dolorosa took the sword from her heart and slashed the cheek of her rival.

A flesh and blood woman, living in the real world, cannot make a final choice between Ezili Dantor and Ezili Freda. It is only when reality is spiced with dreams, when survival skills are larded with sensuality and play, that life moves forward. Dreams and play alone lead to endless and fruitless searching. And a whole life geared toward survival becomes brittle and threatened by inner rage. Alourdes lives at the nexus of several spirit energies. Freda and Dantor are only two of them, the two who help her most to see herself clearly as a woman.

To summarize the above discussion: The Vodou spirits are not idealized beings removed from the complexity and particularity of life. On the contrary, the responsive and flexible nature of Vodou allows the spirits to change over space and time in order to mirror people's life circumstances in considerable detail. Vodou spirits are transparent to their African origins and yet they are other than African spirits. Ancient nature connections have been buried deep in their iconographies while social domains have risen to the top, where they have developed in direct response to the history and social circumstances of the Haitian people. The Vodou spirits make sense of the powers that shape and control life by imitating them. They act out both the dangers and the possibilities inherent in problematic life situations. Thus, the moral pull of Vodou comes from clarification. The Vodou spirits do not tell the people what should be; they illustrate what is.

Perhaps Vodou has these qualities because it is a religion of an oppressed people. Whether or not that is true, it seems to be a type of spirituality with some advantages for women. The openness and flexibility of the religion, the multiplicity of its spirits, and the detail in which those spirits mirror the lives of the faithful makes women's lives visible in ways they are not in the so-called great religious traditions. This visibility can give women a way of working realistically and creatively with the forces that define and confine them.

5

(Per)formative Selves:
The Production of Gender

Gayatri Reddy

Gayatri Reddy is an anthropologist and scholar of gender and women's studies. This excerpt comes from her study With Respect to Sex: Negotiating Hijra Identity in South India. A hijra is an Indian man who dresses and adorns to acquire a "feminine" appearance. Some hijras have their penis and testicles excised in honor of the goddess Bahuchara Mata or Bedhraj Mata who grants them the power to confer fertility on newlyweds and infants in repayment. Reddy's study examined one group of hijras in the city of Hyderabad, who settled near the city's water tank (a community nearly wiped out by the HIV/AIDS pandemic in the 1990s). Hijras define themselves as sexual ascetics, yet in modern India they have survived by engaging in prostitution. Reddy's study is sensitive to the intersectional nature of hijra identity, placing it in the multifaceted ethnic, class, and religious landscape of South Indian society, rather than reading hijra simply as a "third gender." In this excerpt, Reddy examines hijras' dress, bodily modification, and gestures as a complex gender performance that confirms and challenges the gender norms of South Indian society.

Practice makes the perfect woman:
Markers and methods of gender enactment

"When I was very young, I used to love going to my uncle's shop. He was a tailor. All the little bits of cloth that were lying around, I used to gather all of them and tie them on my head like I had long braids. Then I would use other bits to make a sort of midi [skirt] and go hide under the bed. My uncle used to have a radio in his shop. He used to love old film songs. I used to sit under the bed and listen to these songs, [flick] my long hair, and feel really happy. The only person who knew [that I used to do this] was my sister, but she didn't tell anyone because I would have been thrashed by my father and brothers if anyone knew."

Kajal, one of the hijra sex workers living under the water tank, related this incident about her childhood to me, her eyes shining at the memory. I had asked her how and when she first knew she was a hijra. In response, she said this to me, following which she narrated the incident above: "From when I was very young, I used to like wearing my sister's clothes, combing her hair, playing with girls—everything that a girl would do. That is how I knew I was a hijra." This theme—the realization of hijra identity by way of sartorial desire and gendered (female) practice—was one that recurred over and over again throughout my fieldwork. In addition to stating that they were "born this way," almost all hijras would add sartorial and performative elements to their (re)constructions of identity. Shakuntala, another hijra sex worker, said almost the same thing: "I knew I was a hijra because I always liked to wear women's clothes, do women's work, and dance and sing." Similarly, Surekha provided a version of the same story: "From birth, I always liked to put *moggus* [designs made on the ground with colored powder, primarily by women], play with girls, dress like them, and help with the cooking and cleaning." In hijra conceptualizations, constructing a feminine appearance and enacting gendered practices were some of the foremost determining criteria of gender and sexuality: to a certain extent, such performative (gendered) attributes defined hijras' sense of self.

This gendered component is evident in their delight at passing as women, an ability that was highly valued in the community and was explicitly articulated by hijras as a positive attribute. For instance, when Munira returned after a month-long trip to Delhi, the first thing she told me was how she was mistaken for a woman on the journey to Delhi a month ago. She was sleeping in the "ladies compartment" along with her cela, Aliya. "I always travel in the ladies compartment. If I cannot get a reservation in the ladies compartment, then I don't go," Munira said with respect to this issue. There were three other women in the compartment, and a small child, the daughter of one of these women. Because Aliya looked "exactly like a man," everyone knew she was a hijra, "but they were not sure about me," Munira said. Soon, it was night and everyone got ready to sleep. Munira had the lower berth. Because they had closed the door to the compartment, Munira kept her window half-open. In the middle of the night, when they had stopped at a station, she felt a movement and woke up with a start. A man had put his hands through the bars of the window and was going to snatch her gold necklace from around her throat. She was too scared to shout, but the woman in the berth across from her saw his hand and started screaming. The man hastily withdrew his hand and ran away. Everyone in the compartment had woken up in the meantime and began to inquire after Munira. "They called me *behenji* [sister] and asked if I was all right. Then they started cursing men and saying that nowadays it was impossible for women to get out of their house and feel safe with these ruffian men everywhere. Obviously, they thought I was a woman," Munira concluded with pride.

While looking like a woman is not a necessary criterion of hijra authenticity. It is valued and contributes significantly to their sense of self and identity. In fact, the physical appearance of a hijra and the degree to which she looked (or did not look) like a woman was a common topic of conversation within the group, often being the subject of their jokes when teasing one another. For instance, Saroja had nicknamed Surekha *kukka sandlu* (dog-breasts) on account of her flat chest, an epithet that was invoked gleefully by all the other hijras whenever they wanted to make fun of Surekha. Despite popping "Sunday-Monday *golis* [pills]"—oral contraceptives that contain estrogen and progesterone—by the dozen, much to her frustration, Surekha's breasts did not grow.

In contrast, Saroja was much respected for her ability to pass. She was the only hijra among the sex workers under the tank who was a *daiamma cibri,* that is, one who had been operated on by a hijra *daiamma* or midwife. This practice—of having a *daiamma* perform the operation—although considered significantly more dangerous to one's life than a "doctor *cibri,"* and perhaps because of it, was more respected than the latter. It was also believed to produce a more feminine and therefore coveted appearance. *Daiamma cibris* have significantly less facial and body hair growth, and their skin is believed to become softer after their operation—"just like a woman's." As Surekha restated, "their bodies become more rounded, more like a woman's body." This construction of femininity—rounded, voluptuous bodies, absence of body hair, smooth, soft skin, and, they would add, long, thick hair that could be braided without any need to attach false hair—is also hijras' ideal of beauty and the goal toward which they all strived.

Erasing "masculinity"

Apart from undergoing the *nirvan* operation and ingesting dozens of Sunday-Monday *golis* among other hormonal substances (see Kulick 1998), hijras also engage in several less harmful practices to erase vestiges of masculinity and enhance their femininity. One of the most common of these is the use of tweezers (*cimte*) to pluck out their facial hair. All hijras are required to tweeze their facial hair. The leaders impose a fine on those who disregard this rule. The reason for this painful practice is that facial hair does not grow back as quickly and coarsely as it would if shaved. Hijras willingly undergo the torturous practice largely because they want to look as much like women as possible. "If someone uses a razor, then we can make out immediately. The face gets all black and the hair grows thicker and more quickly. It looks like a man's face; it does not look good at all," Munira informed me when I asked initially. As a result whenever I went to visit the hijras, I would invariably find at least one of them sitting and plucking out her beard, holding a mirror to her face so she could get at every hair. If possible, hijras would get another to do it for them, lying in her lap while their hair was systematically plucked out with a special pair of tweezers. These tweezers have a large, flat blade, wider than I've ever seen in regular shops in India. I was told that this was a special *cimte* made by hijras for the use of other hijras. It was not available in any store and therefore was a prized possession.

The term *darsan* was used by all kotis to refer both to the beard and to the act of plucking out one's beard. If someone asked where another hijra was, the answer was often "She is doing [her] *darsan.* " Interestingly, this term is one of the most ubiquitous in Hindu religious worship, and refers in that context to the ritual viewing of the god/goddess and the receiving of his/her blessing in return. Lawrence Babb has noted that for Hindus, vision is the cosmologically crucial sense, and being seen is "not just . . . a passive product of sensory data originating in the outer world," but a constant flow of energy emanating from "the inner person, outward through eyes to engage directly with objects seen, and to bring something of these objects back to the seer". In this substantive sense, as Bernard Cohn notes, the concept of *darsan* operates both at the sacred and profane levels: "Indians wish to see and be seen, to be in the sight of, to have the glance of, not only their deities, but persons of power . . . [such as] . . . a movie star or the Prime Minister". In the context of this chapter, perhaps the hijras' act of *darsan*—a performative act of desirous sight/agency—indexes the importance of praxis as well as the significance of the desire to see and be seen in the everyday world as nonmasculine.

Augmenting "femininity"

In contrast to methods of erasure such as the use of the tweezers and the bleaching of their faces, hijras also adopt more additive methods of beautification namely, the use of makeup, jewelry, and the growing of their hair, to approximate a "female" appearance. At least once a week, I was asked by hijras if I knew of any "foreign" medicine that "made people white [fair], like those people in Amrika." One of the essential items for hijras was a tube of Fair and Lovely cream, a moisturizing cream sold widely in Indian markets that they applied liberally on their faces in an attempt to make themselves look "fair and lovely." This desire for whiteness, while it may not have the same racial undertones that it might have in the United States, is nevertheless widespread in India, especially in South India, where people are often darker than in the north. Almost the first comment about a newborn is about the child's coloring. "Oh! Look how dark she is. That is too bad," or "She has nice eyes, even though she is so dark," might be common statements at the birth of a child, particularly a daughter. In this sociocultural context, whiteness or being fair is beautiful, especially for women. Hijras appear to subscribe to this belief too. Not only do many of them use Fair and Lovely cream, but they also apply "phanking" (pancake, or foundation makeup) fairly liberally on their faces to achieve this effect. Every evening, when hijra sex workers under the tank were getting ready for work, they invariably fought over accusations of excessive use of one another's "cream" or "phanking." Dressing up invariably involved whitening one's face to look beautiful. Since I was fairer than most hijras under the tank and supposedly had access to all the "special creams and medicines [that were] 'foreign,'" I was constantly asked to get them miracle cures so all of them could become "whiter" (fairer) and thereby "more beautiful."

In addition to skin color, another gendered aspect of hijras' beauty ideal was the use of jewelry, which accentuated their femininity as well as their hijra identity. In all the time I was in Hyderabad, the only hijras I saw without any jewelry were those who were *munda,* or widowed a stigmatized and temporary condition that hijras attempted to alleviate as soon as possible. Other than a *munda* hijra, all others, however poor, wore at least some jewelry, if only plastic earrings or a fake pearl necklace. Richer hijras, including some of the older hijra sex workers, possessed and often wore solid gold jewelry. Gold was most often the first substantial purchase that hijras made, and most of the hijras I knew in Hyderabad had at least one or two items of gold jewelry.

Another marker of beauty was the length of a hijra's hair. All hijras were required to grow their hair once they joined the community. This rule was obligatory; any infraction brought a fine (*dand*). Although not all hijras followed the rule, especially the younger hijra sex workers who wanted to experiment with different hairstyles, they tried to conceal from the senior nayaks the fact that they had cut their hair primarily by using false hair attachments (*saurams*). Almost all hijras I knew had *saurams* that they braided into their hair. These *saurams* were not cheap, each one costing from two to five hundred rupees, yet almost all the hijras had their own *sauram,* and some of the older ones had two or three each.

Tailored identities: Sartorial markers and gender hierarchies

Perhaps the single most important marker of hijra identity and femininity/beauty, however, is their clothing. As Umberto Eco said more than twenty-five years ago, "[1] speak through my clothes". Although he was alluding more generally to the semiotic potential of all objects. Eco's statement could be referring directly to hijras' emphatic use of clothing style. Hijras are identified by society, and often identify themselves as hijras, through and by their adoption of women's clothing. Such clothing is the single most visible marker of their identity and sets them apart both from heterosexual men and pantis as well as most other kotis.

Hijras are identifiable on the streets by their explicitly gender-ambiguous appearance. Most hijras have a fairly masculine musculature and physique, have deep, baritone voices, and despite their attempts to temper its growth, have at least the basic rudiments of facial hair; for the most part, they are physically distinguishable from women. Further, many hijras adopt an exaggerated feminine hip-swaying walk, grow their hair long, and most important, *all* of them wear saris. This latter attribute is what distinguishes hijras most visibly in public arenas.

Not only does their sartorial style differ from mainstream male attire, it also sets them apart from other kotis in Hyderabad. In fact, the catla (sari) serves as an important axis of koti identity and hierarchy. The only other kotis who also wear saris are jogins, and for this reason, jogins are also believed to "have izzat" according to hijras. Kada-catla kotis, who do not wear saris, are spoken of extremely disparagingly by hijras, who explicitly indicate that sartorial preference/performance accounts for such differences in izzat. "Among regular people, they [kada-catla kotis] might have more izzat because they dress like men and act like them. But among kotis, we have more izzat. We don't try to hide anything. We wear saris openly and throughout the day, unlike these 'king by day, queen by night' people," Munira told me in no uncertain terms. Female attire (saris in this context) serves as a marker of (public) recognition, and for hijras it is the quintessential symbol of izzat. Those who are "out" on this scale of sartorial identity (like hijras) might be more stigmatized by the wider community, but they have greater respect within their community precisely because of their sartorial practices.

Moreover, this symbol of difference apparently distinguishes hijras, in their conceptu-alizations, from zenanas and kada-catla kotis. My questions regarding the differences between themselves and these kotis were invariably answered by pointing to the fact that "those people are kada-catla people. They don't wear saris like us. And they have less izzat." In hijra terms this was the single most important marker of difference among kotis, in addition to the *nirvan* operation and *rit*. Clearly, "clothing matters".

Hormone use and the sculpting of "female" bodies

One of the most commonly expressed desires on the part of hijras I met in Hyderabad was their desire for a *chati* (bosom). Over and over again, I heard hijras wish for this symbol of femininity and attempt to translate this desire into practice. Despite repeated sermons on my part about the deleterious effects of drugs on their bodies, almost all hijras I knew injected or ingested female hormones in order to develop a *chati*.

The most common of these hormonal products are oral contraceptives for women, commonly referred to as "Sunday-Monday *golis*," which are sold across the counter in all pharmacies. The one most commonly used is sold under the brand name Lyndiol, which contains primarily estrogen/progesterone compounds. While the normal dosage for ovulating *women* is one pill a day, hijras would take as many as nine to twelve pills a day, believing in their cumulative effects to produce the "biggest breasts in the shortest time." Hijras would frequently compare their breasts, commenting on their shape, size, and lactating potential. Even though many of them knew that these *"golis* were not good for the body," they continued to take them in alarming dosages. "We want a *chati*, Gayatri. If you want us to stop taking these pills, then tell us what to do to get a *chati*," Sati responded angrily one day, when I told her, somewhat moralistically, that such excessive use of these *golis* was not good for her. Similarly, Surekha said, "So what if it is bad for you? Anyway we all die. But this way we will have a *chati* and look just like women. Look at Lekha and those other hijras anyway. They take at least fifteen *golis* a day, and nothing has happened to them. No illness, no nothing. They sleep well, eat like buffaloes, and have a nice *chati* and everything! She even gets milk from her *chati,* do you know?" she added enviously.

Perhaps more deleterious to their health than this unrestricted use of oral contraceptives is hijras' recent habit of injecting themselves with estrogen and progesterone concentrates, bought illegally from the local pharmacies. Not only were they completely unaware of exactly how these products affected their hormone levels and more generally their bodies, none of them would go to a doctor or nurse either to get a prescription or in order to be injected. Shanti claimed to know how to give an injection, having "watched a doctor many times," and it was to her that hijras under the tank went for their weekly injections. Shanti not only had no training, but she used the same needle for multiple injections, facilitating the transmission of HIV (among other infections). Although hijras had heard that these *golis* and *sudis* (injections) were bad for them, they also knew that these substances produced results. Given their strong desire for a *chati,* they felt this risk was worth taking. The yearning to possess womanly attributes—breasts being one of the most visible and significant of these— was an extremely important motive for such practices.

The other corporeal symbol of femininity for hijras was the vagina, or sipo as they called it in their (Farsi) vocabulary. As some of the hijras told me, they had repeated operations to construct a vagina after their *nirvan* operation. Significantly, only the kandra hijras and only those among them who had had the *nirvan* operation expressed the desire for and subjected themselves to this operation. This procedure does not approximate a transsexual operation, but it does result in the semblance of a vagina, if only just "for show." Munira told me very proudly that her husband. Zahid, thought she had a "real" vagina immediately after her operation. Apparently, hijras ask the doctor who performs the (illegal) *nirvan* operation to stitch up the flap of skin immediately below the urethra to give the appearance of a "woman's body." Vasundara told me she had had as many as three operations because the skin had not been stitched up properly. Although the practice is not essential for constructing hijra authenticity, this corporeal symbol does assume some significance in hijras' mimetic production of female gender.

The mimesis of femininity and parodic gender subversion

Despite all these accoutrements of femininity, hijras and other kotis did not unequivocally think of themselves as women. Whenever I asked a question regarding their gender affiliation, hijras would laugh and say, "We are neither men nor women; we are hijras". As Amir nayak stated categorically, "there are three *jatis* [castes] in this world—men, women, and hijras." Hijras are "born this way," a result of the "different mixing of 'creams' in the mother's womb," as Madhavi believed.

In one of the most widely read treatises on the production of gender in recent years, Judith Butler outlines a genealogical critique, arguing for the understanding of (all) gender as "performance" and, relatedly, for parody as the most effective strategy for subverting the fixed "binary frame" of gender. For Butler, as for Erving Goffman, "Our identities, gendered and otherwise, do not express some authentic inner 'core' self but are the dramatic *effect* (rather than the cause) of our performances." In such a framework, all identities are performative, and conscious parody of such performance is what subverts both the category and lived reality of gender. But who or what decides the parodic nature of a performance? In some of Butler's early work, discourse is viewed as foundational; the body, in many ways, is seen as thoroughly "text." Hence, in a Butlerian reading, determinations of the parodic or subversive nature of a particular act or performance can presumably be "read" from the "textual surface" of the body, without a necessary contextualization of such meanings through history, lived experience, materiality, and cultural or institutional context.

In the case of hijras, for instance, does their gendered performance constitute parodic subversion, or does it merely constitute a resignification of normative gender ideals and practices? Hijras clearly express an overwhelming desire for the accoutrements of femininity. Does this imply that hijras are merely reinscribing given, normative patterns of gender ascription and aspiration? Equally clearly in many contexts, hijras appear to perceive their identities as outside the binary frame of gendered reference. Given hijras' realization of the constructed nature of their (gendered) identities, does this in itself constitute their performance as parody and therefore as potentially subversive? What constitutes resistance in such a scenario? In other words, are hijras primary agents of gender subversion in the Indian cultural context, or are they uncritically reinscribing gendered categories through their desires and practices?

While hijras' sartorial preferences, cosmetic practices, and excessive hormone use seem to favor the latter interpretation, that is, an uncritical reinscription of normative gender ideals, other hijra performances problematize such an easy characterization. Not only do hijras explicitly locate themselves outside the binary frame of reference, they also deploy specific practices that appear to focus attention explicitly on their gender liminality rather than accentuate their femininity. Two such practices are their distinctive hand-clap and the lifting of their saris to expose their genitalia (or lack thereof). These practices serve as performative correctives to an easy understanding of their identity as merely embodying a resignification of existing gender patterns.

"Troubling" performances: Hijra hand-clapping

Scene 1: When I was in the marketplace one day, I saw a group of four hijras who had come to ask for money from the shop owners. On being refused payment by a shop owner, all four hijras began to clap loudly, hurling abusive epithets at the shopkeeper.

Scene 2: "*Arre,* what kind of hijra are you?" Munira asked Gopalamma half-jokingly, clapping her hands together vigorously when the latter informed her that she was going to cut her hair (a transgression of hijra rules) because of lice infestation.

Scene 3: A knife-sharpener had come to the tank at the beckoning of one of the hijras. On being flirted with and teased mercilessly by them, the distinctly uncomfortable man started to slap his thighs like a wrestler and say repeatedly, "I am a man, I am a man." Sati, a hijra who was one of the chief provocateurs, started clapping her hands in response and saying defiantly, "We are hijras, we are hijras. What do you think, *re?*"

Scene 4: A group of zenana kotis was sitting in a circle on the central lawn of the Public Garden. One of the newcomers to their fold turned to his neighbor and asked him if he had a *rit* (kinship marker). The latter, apparently offended, promptly started clapping his hands and said in reply, "What do you think? We have izzat. We are *rit-riwaz* people [people with a kinship custom/tradition]."

In all of the above scenes, the distinctive clapping of hands served as an unambiguous marker of hijra/zenana identity. All four individuals used it self-consciously both to signal their allegiance to these identities and to be marked as such by the audience(s) in question. More than any other gesture or movement, this loud clapping of hands is indelibly associated with hijras. Any parodic imitation of hijras would need to include only this gesture to be recognizable as such.

In scene 4 above, the group of zenanas looked like any group of men sitting on the lawns of the garden until Arif began to clap. Automatically, all those in their immediate vicinity cast them as hijras. As I was walking out of the garden on my way home a short while later, a man who identified himself as a (plain clothes) policeman followed me to the gate and asked me what I was doing with those *hijre-log* (hijra people). Even when hijras could have passed as women, the minute they started clapping their hands they were marked unambiguously as hijras. On one occasion, I had gone to the market with Surekha because I wanted her help in buying a sari. Apparently the salesmen in the two shops we went to thought she was a woman too. We bought the sari and had just stepped out of the shop when two junior hijras from the Sheharwala house walked up to Surekha and extremely belligerently asked her to pass on a threat to Rajeshwari, another hijra in the tank group. There had been a recent flare-up in antagonism between these two groups (the Lashkarwala hijras under the tank and another, smaller group of Sheharwala hijras engaging in sex work close by), with each being accused of sending ruffians to beat the other. Surekha reacted immediately and, clapping her hands loudly, said, "We are not scared of you. What are you going to do?" The shop owner who was standing next to me was extremely surprised and said, "I didn't realize that was a hijra! What are you doing with people like that?" The clapping of hands, more than any other embodied performance, publicly identifies a hijra.

Hijras know that better than anyone else and consciously use this act to mark their identity and negotiate the sentiments at play. In scene 1 above, the hijras wanted to attract attention to themselves *as hijras.* The clapping served to mark them as hijras in this public space, an identity they then levered to their advantage by signaling their difference and disruptive potential, both social/symbolic and physical. They played on their potential for shaming the shop owner to get what they wanted: once they start their performance, the owner usually pays up quickly to get rid of them. Hijras, perhaps even more than others, recognize their marginality as nonprocreative, disfigured people who are "neither men nor women." But rather than acquiesce in this marginalization, they proclaim their status publicly, acknowledging their stigma and playing on it. They draw attention to themselves with their hand-clapping, recognizing its potential both to label them and to threaten the public. While marking them as hijras, the clapping gesture also symbolizes their potential, precisely because of their acknowledged marginality, to shame the public and make them lose their respect. Hence, although it is often a double-edged sword, hijras use this clapping gesture to mark their identity and to deploy this identity to their advantage.

Clapping, however, is not merely a *public* hijra practice; it is used even within the hijra community to symbolize both identity and relative izzat. In scene 2, for instance, Munira's clapping was meant to signal to Gopalamma not only the inappropriateness of her action according to hijra rules, but also Munira's self-proclaimed superiority on account of this transgression: Munira, in contrast to Gopalamma, was a "real hijra" who did not commit such infractions. The hand-clapping served to reinforce this sentiment, signaling its specific use as a hijra marker of identity and authenticity. Similarly, when Arif, the self-identified zenana, clapped in the garden in response to his fellow koti's remark, he was doing so to indicate his greater izzat in this relationship. Although it marks him as a hijra in the public eye, this practice also signifies his allegiance to this community and his voluntary subjection to its rules and regulations. Having a *rit* in a hijra house serves to elevate the status of a koti (at least according to hijras and zenanas), and by clapping like a hijra, Arif is acknowledging his acceptance of this fact and his greater izzat on account of it.

Further, this practice is also utilized as an explicit means of distancing in-group from out-group and signaling solidarity within the community. As Kira Hall (1997) notes, hijras have a special clap—what they refer to as *dedh tali*, or one-and-a-half clap—that signals the onset of a particular discursive performance for the benefit of the public. As she states, "When in the presence of non-hijras, . . . hijras create scripted quarrels amongst themselves to shock and embarrass their eavesdropping bystanders, [with] some hijra communities having a special *tali* [clap] used expressly for signaling the onset of this discursive strategy". Clapping, in other words, explicitly marks the liminality of hijra identity and is explicitly deployed to indicate both solidarity and authenticity within this marked category.

(Dis)embodied exposures, revealing practices

Yet another performance that focuses attention explicitly on hijra sex/gender ambiguity is the practice long associated with the hijra community of lifting their saris to expose their lack of genitalia. This action, more than the hand-clapping, is threatening to the public on account of its potential for shaming them. Hijras' lifting of their saris is embarrassing and even shameful not only because many people find exposing oneself distasteful, but because it is especially so when "there is nothing there"—a fact, however, that makes the act potentially empowering for hijras. The absence of genitalia signals a paradoxical inversion of power in favor of hijras, both by exposing the mutilation of the body and by implicitly incorporating a potential curse, as if to say, "By exposing myself to you, I curse you with such a fate."

To a large extent, hijras are constructed as people without *sarm* (shame). "[Hijras] are shameless. They have no honour. They are answerable to no one," Ved Vatuk contends. By rejecting the centrality of procreation—"the question of progeny" hijras are perceived to be outside the social order. As Kira Hall notes, they are "a people freed from the constraints of decency that regulate the rest of society." Quoting a hijra in Benares, she adds, "Hijras are just hijras, and women are just women. If there's a woman, she'll at least have a little *sarm*. But hijras are just hijras. They have no *sarm*". As Satish Sharma and other anthropologists maintain, it is by virtue of their impotence/sexual dysfunctionality and gender ambiguity that hijras are considered to be outside the social mainstream and thus to have "no *sarm*". Hijras serve as potential repositories of shamelessness, and by exposing that by which they are construed as shameless, they serve as purveyors of this stigma to the public. Given their perception as *besarm* (without shame) and knowing their potential to invoke shame in others, people are afraid of provoking them. As Morris Carstairs states, "[Hijras'] shamelessness [makes] people reluctant to provoke their obscene retaliation in public." Serena Nanda echoes this statement when she notes that "hijras know that their shamelessness makes most people reluctant to provoke them in a public confrontation." Hijras in turn use this knowledge to their advantage, threatening to lift their saris if their demands are not met. Interestingly, hijras also explicitly see their action as one of reclaiming respect or izzat. When I asked Munira the meaning of their practice, she said, "If people give us respect, then we are also respectful. But if they do not show us respect, then we also abuse them verbally and lift our saris. Then they bow their heads in shame and give us respect. It is like that."

In addition, the act of exposing themselves in itself conveys a potential curse to those who are subjected to the sight. There is a strong belief that by exposing their mutilated genitals, hijras can curse those present and render them impotent or infertile. In fact, as Serena Nanda notes, in highly orthodox families hijras were not allowed access to new brides for fear of their potential to contaminate the brides with their infertility. By employing this strategy, hijras embrace this construction of them and use it to gain power.

This act is most often deployed during the explicitly public badhai performances. Almost every such performance ends with hijras haggling with the family of the bride or newborn child over the acceptable payment, and they often threaten to expose themselves if more money is not forthcoming. Even the threat of this action often produces results; to avoid the shameful exposure, the family often gives in to the hijra demands. As one South Indian neighbor of mine told me, "You just cannot get rid of [hijras] easily. They came to my house when my son was born, and, until we gave them what they wanted, they didn't leave. They started shouting obscenities, and they were even ready to lift their saris! So, to preserve our honor, we had to give them what they wanted."

One occasion when I witnessed this act was during the scene described in the previous section with the kandra hijras under the tank and the knife-sharpener. Not only did Sati start clapping her hands when the man did not stop his assertions regarding his masculinity, Shakuntala got up and, without warning, lifted her sari in front of him. Publicly shamed, the knife-sharpener immediately packed his things and literally ran from the tank. In recounting this incident to Munira later, Sati triumphantly told her, "When that *bhadva* [pimp] did not shut up, Shakuntala put her sari [*catla esindi*] on him." This phrase—*catla esindi*—is used expressly for this action in koti terminology. As in this instance, it is used in a self-denigrating way but one that is paradoxically empowering at the same time. While Shakuntala's act of lifting her sari clearly focused attention on her stigmatized hijra identity, this action was simultaneously a statement that mocked male power and the procreative imperative. Much like the *nirvan* operation, this practice focuses attention precisely on the ascetic, non-reproductive gender liminality of hijras—a position that they embrace and use to their advantage.

Both these practices serve as unambiguous markers of muddied gender (as well as critical symbols of abjection and asceticism). Unlike the various accoutrements of femininity described earlier, these gender performances explicitly counter a reading of hijras as *merely* reinscribers of normative femininity. At the very least by focusing attention on themselves as liminal figures both in terms of embodiment and gender ascription, hijras appear as potentially subversive agents, serving self-consciously to cause "gender trouble."

And yet, such an uncritical reading, which disregards their heartfelt desire to pass as women and does not view their embodied desires/practices as signifiers of more than merely muddied *gender* difference, is inadequate to any rigorous analysis of hijras' lives and the investments that are at stake for them. In many ways, these hijra practices and empowering stances encapsulate the limitations of a binary analysis that neither takes into account the imbrication of gender with/within the multiplicity of differences that constitute an individual's life, nor adequately captures what Margaret Trawick describes as the "intentional ambiguity of Indian life".

As figures that simultaneously enact mutually exclusive interpretive frames and encode potentially discrepant presentations of self, hijras display such ambiguity in all its subtle, complex forms. They do not, in any simple way, *merely* subvert or reinscribe gender difference, but actively and intentionally court ambiguity in this regard. As "troubling" agents extraordinaire—for academics perhaps more so than for their own sense of self—hijra instantiations of ambiguity allow us to move beyond the aporia of the structure/agency debate undergirding much sociological and feminist analyses and to capture the fundamental, if elusive, quality of ambiguity—with respect to gender as well as religion, kinship, and class—that constitutes hijras' sense of self and relationship to wider society. Hijras, more than any gender theorists, are aware of this complexity and ambiguity. As Munira once said to me, "We are neither men nor women, but at the same time we are both. Hijras are *adha-bic* [half-in-the-middle] people, and that is why we are both feared and respected at the same time."

6

Toward a Queer Theology of Flourishing:

Transsexual Embodiment, Subjectivity, and Moral Agency

Jakob Hero

*J*akob Hero is a transgender activist and a candidate for ordination in the Universal Fellowship of Metropolitan Community Churches, a denomination whose ministry is geared specifically to LGBTIQ Christians. This excerpt, taken from a two-volume collection entitled Queer Religion, provides a theological reflection on the concept of "flourishing" as a necessary moral paradigm to understanding the transsexual experience. It offers a compelling and eloquent challenge to normative Christian interpretations which are so often based on notions of biologically fixed and unchangeable gender categories. Transsexuality refers to when gender identity is not coherent with one's assigned sex. As the author points out, transsexuals may or may not choose to opt for full biological change of sex. In the long history of sexual diversity, and especially as regards religion, transsexuals have been the targets of virulent and oppressive forms of discrimination.

So God created humankind in his image,
in the image of God he created them;
male and female he created them.
—GEN. 1:27

I entered the first stage of my transition process as a twenty-one-year-old college student, living in Florida, with no access to a transgender community for support or guidance. I sought out a therapist who advertised as a "gender specialist." With total openness and honesty—and a fair amount of naïveté—I told the truth about my experience of gender embodiment, sexuality, and identity. Without other trans people in my life to advise me, I had no idea that telling the truth in therapy was a mistake. The truth was that although I felt extremely uncomfortable living as a woman, I was uncertain where the transition process would take me. I did not know that I was expected to express extreme revulsion at the very thought of the supposedly terrible and shameful body parts that had bestowed on me the legal category of "female." I was not sufficiently repulsed by my own genitalia. My therapist specifically asked me if having a vagina made me want to commit suicide. When I answered honestly that it did not, she frowned and wrote something on her notepad. To this day I will never understand how a therapist can look at a patient—especially someone as young as I was at the time—and find it troubling that this patient does not possess *enough* body hatred. For me, the extremely large breasts I had been carrying around since the age of fourteen, which (whether clothed or unclothed) were the most obvious markers of my femaleness, were far more problematic than what could be found between my legs. I was unaware that I should lie and say that I was already living as a man. My rather high-pitched voice and soft, feminine, facial features made attempting to live as a man prior to hormone treatment nearly impossible.

I also had not known that my access to the process would be denied largely because I admitted to being sexually attracted to men. Even though at the time I had never acted on this attraction, for my therapist the notion that I would not necessarily be a heterosexual man post-transition was especially problematic. This factor, compounded with the reality that my own vagina did not make me want to kill myself, and that I—in the absence of the medical technology to make this possible—was not already living as male, meant that I was denied the "true transsexual" diagnosis. It is difficult to explain how strange this situation is to someone who has not lived through it. How can an outside other determine my own subjective self-identity claim?

Initially I allowed this clinical encounter to shape the way I conceptualized my own gendered self. I believed that I would never be allowed to change my body. I felt violated by this system. I hated that those who had never walked in my shoes could tell me that my own embodiment and performativity were insufficient. *These are my shoes, damn it!* And only I get to name what it means to walk in them. Although at the time, I lacked the language to name it as such, what I was missing was not only the ability to flourish, but also the framework to comprehend what true flourishing would mean. How could I even start to flourish when I did not know how to advocate for myself within the clinical encounter?

It was not until I met other trans people that I learned that there was still hope: I could reach my goals if I simply lied. I learned that lying was a rite of passage into the transsexual world. Armed with the manufactured narrative of a "true transsexual," I, too, could gain access to a more comfortable embodied self. But clearly this was not an unproblematic solution. I have always viewed myself as a person of integrity. Lying about who I am, especially to my therapist, was counter-intuitive. However, I found a new therapist and did exactly that. Within months I started hormone therapy, which produced near immediate masculinizing results (which more or less directly led to finding my first boyfriend and coming to accept my gay male identity). In less than a year I had undergone chest reconstruction surgery and was living unquestioned as male in all areas of my life. I was happy with the outcome but felt there was a price to pay for how I reached it. While I do not feel that my eternal soul was in danger, I do think that these lies came at an enormous cost to my psychosocial well-being.

I hate that this was the route I was forced to take. I must admit that, if I were put in the same situation, I would do it again. Yet, I believe it to have been an impediment to my overall flourishing and human dignity. I gained the freedom of embodiment I sought. I was able to access the biotechnology necessary for me to be recognized as male by others. These things came with incredible benefits, not the least of which was the feeling of amazing freedom. But before I could even begin the medical process, the joy at the idea that I can be any kind of man I wanted to be was already burdened by a lingering question. Had I already become the kind of person who gets what he wants through deception and lying?

The human dignity of transsexuals is highlighted and strengthened when we understand and develop our own subjectivity. We must assert our own validity within self-defining categories of gender embodiment and determine for ourselves what unique combination of medical interventions are necessary to reach an acceptable level of comfort in our bodies. This does not mean that I advocate a hands-off approach in terms of medical treatment for gender conflict. I do not want to divorce transsexuality from the medical paradigm altogether. Like countless others, I benefited greatly from medically transitioning. Had I continued to be denied access to biotechnological intervention, my male identity would never have been fully recognizable to others—or indeed even to myself.

Even in light of the difficulty I had with approval to enter the process, I am not willing to advocate for a system that allows unregulated and immediate access to these types of biotechnology for simply anyone who can afford it financially. The Standards of Care are a manufactured structure, not legally binding, and not actually enforced by any governing body. It is only the patients who suffer under these rules. With no official oversight process, there is no possibility of appeal if one is denied access. In the delicate balance of self-assertion and approval seeking, the transsexual entering the transition process must exercise agency and must also navigate the policies that can be used to deny us access.

I propose that transsexual subjectivity necessitates agency in two primary categories: embodiment and integrity. When the agency of the trans person is not validated by those who function as gatekeepers, we must often choose between obtaining an embodiment that makes us comfortable in our gender expression or the ability to speak freely and accurately about how we see ourselves now and in the future. A doctor or therapist who will only accept the stereotypical "true transsexual" narrative places the trans person in a moral dilemma. Which is more important—obtaining treatment or maintaining integrity? This counters the potential flourishing of transsexuals as moral agents by limiting our ability to transition without sacrificing probity.

Gender is an issue of embodiment for all people. It is the way in which we all, as human persons, live in uniquely sexed bodies and validate the genders of other people—whether trans or cisgendered. Although certainly connected to sexuality, the embodiment of gender is not about sexual attraction to others; it is about one's own lived experience of the individual, inner manifestations of masculinity and femininity.

Without the proper support for embodied identity formation, many transsexuals are forced into a system that claims to validate our subjective assertions of self; but this system inflicts on us specific (and largely unattainable) hegemonic ideals of maleness and femaleness. These ideals are overwhelmingly genitally focused. They emerged from writings on transsexuals by cisgendered doctors whose gaze focused mainly on body parts and lacked holistic viewpoints that considered transsexual experience. This objectification of transsexuals in terms of the genitocentric standards of non-trans bodies strikes at the very core of our embodied selves. And while genitals certainly do matter for sexual identity formation and lived gendered experience, the reality of transsexual lives—particularly the lives of female-to-male transsexuals—is that genital reconstruction is often not a viable option. The various procedures available for transsexual genital surgeries are typically cost prohibitive, and often do not produce the desired outcome for sensation or aesthetics. Yet people link maleness and femaleness to penises and vaginas, and our gender justification is often linked to whether our genitals have been surgically reshaped. A woman with a penis or a man with a vagina is seen as an affront to the ontological nature of humanity itself. In practical reality this can manifest as instant justification for meting out violence against such a "wrong" or incongruent body.

A reality of transsexual subjectivity is that our unique experiences of incongruence between our gendered self-identification and our bodies—particularly genitalia—carry different weight for different individuals. How we embody our full sense of selfhood is clearly a common concern for transsexual identity formation, yet there is no singular "true transsexual" experience of embodiment. Body modification is an important piece of coming into authenticity with our selves, but we each need to come to terms with the possibilities and the limits of biotechnology. It should be pointed out that surgeons themselves are often intentionally vague or willfully dishonest about these limitations. The idea of sexual desire and fulfillment in bodies that would appear incongruent is challenging within the medical purview (and indeed the larger society within which that purview functions). Whether intentionally or as a subconscious response to an internal "ick factor," doctors have produced a narrative for transsexuals that places the importance of external appearances of genitalia above functionality. In conversations with trans people—particularly female-to-male transsexuals—I have encountered very different experiences of genital surgeries than the images presented by the medical community. This is particularly the case with phalloplasty, in which a penis is constructed from tissue taken from elsewhere on the body. Every transman I have spoken to who has undergone phalloplasty complains of significant, if not total, loss of sensation. Problems with urination are also extremely common. Interestingly, despite varying levels of thwarted expectation, many of these men are extremely happy with the post-surgical results.

For many transsexuals the risks associated with genital reconstruction are worth it, for others not. What I believe matters most in terms of transsexual embodiment is not any one specific decision regarding biomedical interventions that any particular trans person makes. What matters is that trans people have the ability to make these decisions within their own subjective identity claims, which must not be reliant on an external outside other. To do this, we need frameworks and support networks that enable us to make informed decisions about our bodies. This requires a break from the philosophy behind the allopathic "fix-what's-broken" model of Western medicine, in which these biotechnological procedures are executed, but not necessarily a break from the procedures themselves. Most important, those on the outside cannot name for us the requisite amount of discomfort we are expected to feel because of our genitals or any other sexual marker. A pre-transition transsexual need not view his or her birth gender as broken embodiment that is in need of fixing. A queer theology of flourishing allows us to utilize biotechnology simply as a tool toward gender recognition. The value of this recognition cannot be overstated, yet it also must not be conflated with the ultimate end of the transsexual as a human person on the path to flourishing. As a tool, biotechnology enables trans people to live into forms of sexual embodiment that go beyond gender performativity; particularly in terms of hormone treatment, these tools are necessary for self-affirmation in gender congruence and in being recognized in one's gender by others.

When Tanis states, "[t]hat we reflect outwardly that which is inwardly true for us is a matter of integrity, he is referring to the freedom to express our genders in dress, in behavior, and through the use of biotechnology. I propose that transsexual authenticity calls for integrity in two overlapping spheres: relationality with others and self-relationality. How we live in our gendered reality reflects integrity. However, one's ability to pass as one's internally understood gender is not the litmus test of integrity. A painful reality of transsexual embodiment is that most of us will never reach a point of total comfort in our gendered bodies. Public acceptance as the men and women we know ourselves to be is unattainable for many of us, no matter how much we change our bodies. Despite the fact that the limits of biotechnology are very real and frustrating, one's integrity can remain intact—even if she is six feet tall and balding or if he has wide hips and cannot grow a decent beard.

In her essay "On Being True to Form," Margaret Mohrmann explains the relationship of identity and integrity. "I have identity because, however much I develop over time, I am still the same created person; I have integrity because the conduct of my life is consistent with the way I was created to live." While this notion of consistency with creation may seem problematic for the transsexual, Mohrmann is actually speaking of the distinction of humans from other aspects of creation—not of the distinction between types of gendered human embodiment. The differences between individual human persons do shape our identities; the human condition is universally a process of unfolding and formation. Static identity is not part of Mohrmann's integrity thesis. She traces the Greek etymology of the words "integrity" and "identity," and explains that, like the Christian notion of the *logos,* these are centered on the intentionality of human creation, which "meant that human beings were created in this way and not that; creation imparted a specific form to humans generally and to each human being in particular." Mohrmann offers a twofold definition of integrity, the first part of which, *integrity as consistency,* speaks to creation. The human being's integrity is displayed "insofar as she is consistently true—physically, mentally, spiritually—both to the intentional design of her divine creation and to the trajectory of her ongoing formation toward God.

The all-too-common interpretation of transsexuality is that the processes of transition fundamentally go against our intended creation. Anti-trans arguments from religious voices in the Abrahamic traditions most often look to the accounts of creation, naming a created binary gendered order as "natural" and the utilization of biotechnology as "unnatural," thus against creation. A queer theological lens allows us to see humanity not as a thing created in the past, but as an ongoing process itself. Integrity is not reliant on a static, lifelong, physical embodiment or the faithful commitment to only one performative script. Furthermore, as both process and queer theologians have taught us, the work of creation is never complete. Creation was not a onetime event that living beings simply experienced as passive recipients. Today, biotechnology presents humanity with myriad medical possibilities. These many medical advances provide evidence of our ability to participate in the ongoing processes of creation.

I propose an agent-centered transsexual subjectivity that allows us to view intentional participation in creation with a fresh understanding, not as *going against,* but as *being called to.* Tanis explains the idea of calling as a helpful way to comprehend transgender identity. He explains that a calling "is a way of being—a calling to awaken to, realize, and manifest who we are. For trans people, our calling is to a way of embodying the self that transcends the limitations [of our embodiment]." The consistency of our integrity as transsexuals does not lie in our ability to fulfill gender expectation that we were born into, but to manifest a consistent integration of identity so that we "physically and literally materialize who we are on the inside and bring it to reflection on the outside."

My own experience of bringing my internal understanding of my gendered self to my external embodied identity has been an exercise in integrity as consistency. God created me to be exactly who I am. My transsexual status is not a mistake of creation; it is a call to a continual process of transformation. As Mohrmann points out, "Creation is not the only way in which human beings are formed. Another, equally vital sense of formation has to do with the developments of the nascent ideal form into that of a mature adult human being."

The consistency of my integrity is not dependent on my loyalty to the lifelong embodiment of the sex assigned to me at my birth. I have been formed in valuable ways from my experiences on both sides of the gender divide.

To form is not merely to cultivate or develop, but to mold, to prepare, to realize. Moreover, it is generally the case that one is formed toward something, some telos, some ideal shape or condition. It is through formation that one is helped to acquire certain dispositions or virtues and thus to become a particular kind of person progressing on the moral journey toward perfection of conduct and of humanness.

My formation as an individual on the moral journey must not be conflated with my formation as an individual who is male. The end toward which I am formed, and as I am indeed continuing to be formed, is not a gendered identity at all, but rather my development of selfhood as a moral agent. Being a man who was born and raised as a girl is an important piece of my formation, but it is not the totality of my calling in this life; just being a man is not the telos of my development.

Mohrmann defines the second aspect of integrity, *integrity as oneness*, as "the 'parts' of a person—body, mind, soul, spirit—[that] comprise, in actuality, one being, a single unity and not a hierarchically ordered conglomerate." Achieving a sense of wholeness of self is essential for transsexuals to embody integrity as oneness. This can be a challenge for those who have spent a lifetime feeling at odds with their own embodiment. Tanis captures this experience and its spiritual implications.

A common conception of transgendered people is that we are "women trapped in men's bodies" or "men trapped in women's bodies." . . . In my opinion, this way of looking at our bodies necessarily sets up dualisms: not only the split between female and male but also the division between body and spirit. In this view, these pairs become essentialist and oppositional and no collaboration can exist between them. In a certain sense, another being which inhabits the body must be liberated from it, rather than coming to a place of unity between body and spirit.

To foster integrity as oneness, trans people must be allowed the necessary agency to make the appropriate choices about our bodies. If we enter the transition process with a self-conception of wholeness, we can transform our bodies out of love for ourselves, not by manifesting a clinically "appropriate" level of self-hatred and shame. Seeking wholeness and self-acceptance throughout the entire transition process is essential for overcoming the conceptual dualisms of selfhood that plague trans people.

It is because of this second aspect of integrity that the experience of lying to our therapists is problematic to the transsexual. As transsexuals, we must take seriously what we choose to do to our bodies surgically and hormonally; in doing so, we would benefit from considering the spiritual and psychological effects, as well as the possible physical ramifications. We must be vigilant to balance the priorities of our physical, spiritual, and emotional needs throughout the whole transition process. When I lied about my embodied experiences, I compromised my sense of wholeness and placed my bodily needs above my ethical beliefs about truth telling. I feel my spirit was compromised. As Mohrmann says, "The oneness of integrity forces us to take entirely seriously things that are done to bodies as well as things that violate minds, precisely because each sort of action is done to persons, who are not body *plus* mind and soul and spirit, but are body/mind/soul/spirit: all one, non-hierarchically integrated."

Let us not forget that while a trans person is going through the process of transition, he or she is also trying to handle all the other aspects of life. As my own therapy debacle was unfolding, I sought out the other source I had for guidance and support: my church. In the years prior to my decision to start the transition process, I was a very active member of a liberal, inclusive, "Open and Affirming" Christian church. The fact that they prided themselves on their acceptance of gays and lesbians, however, I quickly learned, did not mean that this church was equipped (or willing) to support a person in gender transition. On the morning that I came out as transgender to my pastor, I found that the well of compassion had run dry. This story is not unique; many trans people face the loss of their church families—and far more—when they come out. But what happened next is where my story deviates from the norm. I was blessed to find a new church, after being rejected from my church home, which made all the difference. My flourishing did not come from a wholehearted experience of acceptance as soon as I walked into the door of this new and unfamiliar church. In fact, many people there were confused by me and did not accept me right away. But although they may not have initially recognized my gender identity in the ways I would have wanted, they always recognized me as part of God's creation. This church affirmed that I, just like everyone else, am a divine creature. This affirmation came at a time when everything in my life felt unstable. In this church I was shown that I possess a God-given human dignity that nothing and no one can take away from me—not a therapist, not a doctor, not a transphobic pastor, not even the lies I was forced to tell about myself, could erase that divine spark. With the ever-present connection to the presence of God within all of us, this church community invites its (mostly LGBT) members to participate in a lifelong process of discernment and communion with God. A queer theology of flourishing, in which we engage in a co-creative process with God, starts with human dignity.

The dignity of the human person is an important and elusive element of theology and bioethics. But its enigmatic qualities need not detract from its efficacy. Ultimately, agent-centered transsexual subjectivity must be oriented toward the flourishing of the trans person if it is to have any true significance. Dignity plays an important role in identity, highlighting the common good of the human race, and the justification of a moral threshold to establish a minimum level of rights for all human beings. These are some functions of dignity, but they do not serve to define it as a concept.

Human dignity is complex and multifaceted, which is precisely what makes it useful as a concept for bioethics. The medical ethicist Holmes Rolston III defines the multiple manifestations of dignity:

> Our dignity figures in our personal identity, first at basic levels, where dignity is inalienable and common to us all, and further at developmental levels, where dignity can be achieved or lost, recognized or withheld. . . . A person's dignity resides in his or her biologically and socially constructed psychosomatic self with an ideographic proper-named identity.

Historically, human dignity has often been defined in terms of the ability of an individual to think rationally. This is obviously problematic if we are to seek a universalized understanding of dignity that speaks to the reality of all human beings, some of whom live with cognitive disabilities and lack the ability of rational thought. Martha Nussbaum argues that it is not only our rationality, but also our vulnerability and many other aspects of the human condition that define human dignity.

> In general, when we select a political conception of the person we ought to choose one that does not exalt rationality as *the* single good thing and that does not denigrate forms of need and striving that are parts of our animality. . . . There is dignity not only in rationality bur in human need itself and in the varied forms of striving that emerge from human need.

Nussbaum's conception of dignity is rooted in what she names the "capabilities approach." In this, she argues specifically for universally, cross-culturally applied, basic minimal entitlements for all human beings. All persons access dignity through any of a list of *capabilities* that are commonly shared among human beings. The capabilities list emerged from examination into different areas of human existence, asking within each area, what ways of being, living, and acting are "minimally compatible with human dignity"? We are not to define dignity in contrast to or independently of these capabilities, "but in a way intertwined with them and their definition. . . . The guiding notion therefore is not that of dignity itself, as if that could be separated from capabilities [but instead that a life worthy of human dignity] is constituted, at least in part, by having the capabilities on the list."

As we come to an understanding of a basis of dignity, we are faced with the question of whether dignity is something that can, in fact, be lost. Returning to Pellegrino's use of the clinical encounter, we remember the potential loss of dignity within the vulnerable relationship of patient and practitioner. His is not only a hypothesis of loss, but also of self-reflection and understanding through relationality. He argues that relationships of intersubjectivity force human beings to assess our own dignity. "Only in the encounter with others do we gain knowledge of how we value each other and ourselves." Transsexuals are all too familiar with the shame generated in a patient by an encounter with an intolerant physician. Like anyone else who seeks medical care, we must expose our vulnerable selves to the scrutiny of medical professionals, and this often feels like a threat to dignity. Pellegrino explains, "Usually, we must disrobe and expose our body to expert scrutiny with all its imperfections revealed. What we are and who we are is suppressed in the objectification of our person that a scientific appraisal of our physical state might demand." The painful irony of medical transition is that in order to change our bodies we must invite people to view, touch, examine, comment on, and handle the very parts of our bodies that carry the most pain and shame for us.

Even though years have passed since my chest reconstruction surgery, when I think of that experience, I remember being prepped for surgery. I can still feel my surgeon's cold hands as he lifted and moved my breasts, marking with a pen the lines that his scalpel would soon follow. He was the first person in many years to touch, or even see, my naked breasts, and he would be the last person to ever do so. The surgery left me with considerable loss of sensation, and so this uncomfortable memory is the only connection I have to the way my nipples and the skin on my chest felt when handled by another human being. In the room along with my doctor were three nurses and my lover at the time—a man who had never, before that day, seen my chest, free of the tight binder I had used to conceal what was there. I was not even fully naked, and yet I was shamefully naked. The parts of me that had brought me so much pain and discomfort were on display. I became objectified as the bearer of these large breasts, which were sagging and exposed, now atrophied and misshapen by the effects of testosterone and years of binding. Even though everyone in that room affirmed my male identity and my decision to have this surgery, I still found it hard to hold on to my internal sense of dignity in that moment. In retrospect, I recognize that the loss of dignity in this memory is linked to my inability to access my sense of *integrity as oneness*. I had tried to reconcile with my breasts before they were gone. But, in all honesty, instead of saying good-bye, I could really only muster a slight apology that things had not worked out for us. I was terrified, being seen and touched as an object. I was also cold and very hungry. The clinical encounter reminds us that certain aspects of our dignity are fleeting.

Medical ethicist, physician, and Franciscan friar Daniel P. Sulmasy offers three categorizations of dignity that are helpful in understanding dignity as both constant and ephemeral. These categories are: attributed, intrinsic, and inflorescent. Attributed dignity is, "in a sense, created. It constitutes a conventional form of value." Intrinsic dignity is the "worth or value that people have simply because they are human, not by virtue of any social standing, ability to evoke admiration, or any particular set of talents, skills, or powers." In the clinical encounter I just described, my intrinsic dignity was never at stake. My membership in the human race was never questioned. The sense of lost dignity that any human being feels when exposed and naked in front of the clinical gaze of medical professionals threatens attributed dignity; that is what I encountered. Sulmasy's final category, *inflorescent dignity,* brings the most relevant understanding of dignity to the question of flourishing of moral agents—a key concept, we recall, in the notion of agent-centered transsexual subjectivity. Inflorescent dignity refers to individuals who flourish "as human beings—living lives that are consistent with and expressive of the intrinsic dignity of the human."

Returning to Tanis's hypothesis that gender is a calling, we see that ultimately—despite the discomfort and vulnerability of preparing for surgery, and the physical pain that came after—the clinical encounter of my chest surgery affirmed my inflorescent dignity. It allowed me access to the life I knew I was called to live. It also, in a mundane way, connected me to dignity through the reality of a shared sense of human embodiment. Instead of just viewing the clinical encounter as a potential for lost dignity, I would like to offer another view, one in which even the cost to attributed dignity ultimately leads to the overarching goal of flourishing, namely, through the experience of vulnerability.

As Nussbaum points out, vulnerability is one of the key ways that we encounter dignity. The vulnerability I experienced helped to form me as an individual oriented toward connection with God. While transsexual surgery is certainly not a typical path to inflorescent dignity, through living in a space of vulnerability as a human being, facing my fears, and fully accepting what I had to do in order to achieve an authentic embodiment of integrity, my dignity was upheld and affirmed. The experience of lost attributed dignity also aided my growth toward inflorescence, through my own self-relationality and in my spiritual connection to other vulnerable human beings. While my specific circumstances were relatively rare, this clinical encounter connects me to all other people whose own unique medical circumstances have left them scared, cold, exposed, and even hungry as they awaited surgery. Although I could have understood these things in a theoretical way prior to that experience, I could not fully conceptualize them when I was an outsider to this kind of clinical encounter. By extension, the potential loss of attributed dignity can lead to flourishing, when the moral agent allows that vulnerability to transform personal suffering into solidarity with others. Ideally, the trans person who feels cold, terrified, naked, and hungry before surgery can experience flourishing, even in that moment, through connection to the rest of creation—not only to the pain of others receiving medical treatment, but also to broader tragedies of terror, pain, helplessness, and want.

The affirmation of my inflorescent dignity in my transition experience points me toward an understanding of human dignity, but it does not mean that I have achieved my ideal embodied self, or that I am finished in my task of personal formation toward God. The affronts to my attributed dignity throughout my time of gender transition have left psychological scars as real as those physical reminders that stretch across my chest. I have offered this analysis of my own experience, not because it carries any unique moral weight, but rather because it is only the details that separate it from any other narrative of an individual who seeks to flourish. When the transsexual is no longer the object of another's gaze, but embodies the necessary subjectivity for moral agency, he or she is open to the potential for human flourishing. Our pain links us to the suffering of all sentient beings, and perhaps a call to ease that pain, whether or not it resembles our own.

The paths one takes through the processes of transition are often mistakenly seen as salvific. Although it is a secular manifestation, this reflects a familiar theological trope. A broken being, made monstrous in a disgustingly flawed embodiment, is freed from bondage. In this view, who functions as the sanctified savior? The surgeons with their scalpels and the endocrinologists with their prescription pads hold the power to allow or deny access to salvation—the correction of gender incongruence. By shifting from a language of salvation to a language of flourishing we open up new possibilities for the entire field of transsexual health care. But beyond that, a queer theological notion of flourishing allows us to envision all of creation as a continual process of cooperation in God's work. As such, all human persons gain responsibility to one another through solidarity. It thus becomes clear that the issue is not, and never has been, gender embodiment and performativity, but rather a totality of wholeness and transcendence. Queer theology and transsexual bodies can teach all of us something very valuable about flourishing. The natality of queer culture comes not in the reproduction of living beings, but in the continual creation of solidarity and community. The final outcome is never final; the process of flourishing, like the process of creation itself, is always ongoing.

7

Intimacy Surveilled:

Religion, Sex, and Secular Cunning

Mayanthi Fernando

M *ayanthi Fernando is an anthropologist of Islam and scholar of religion and sexuality. The excerpt from her essay entitled "Intimacy Surveilled: Religion, Sex, and Secular Cunning" explores the tensions within French secularism in which the boundaries between public and private are repeatedly transgressed. Fernando highlights how the construction of secular religiosity (that is, religion that operates within the "private" domain) works with normalized views of sexuality to police these boundaries. Yet in order to ensure that public/private distinctions are maintained, both religion and sexuality demand constant surveillance. It is Muslim women who are ultimately caught in this double bind, as a result of the "conspicuous" sign of their religiosity, the veil, and are incited to account for their religious and sexual "normality" in a context in which doing so ultimately fails. Fernando's analysis not only highlights the conflicted position of Muslim women in secular society, it also raises critical questions about secularism's claims to promote religious and secular freedom.*

D rawing on political and legal debates, media representations, and ethnographic fieldwork, this article examines the construction and trespass of the public/private boundary foundational to secularism and, in so doing, analyzes the competing and often contradictory imperatives of secular rule. The secularization of Islam, understood as necessary to Muslim integration in France, requires the constant regulation and surveillance of religious life—including the definition of what "real" Islam entails—in order to verify that Muslims are being properly religious. Similarly, within the dominant narrative of immigrant integration, the future of secular France depends on the sexual regulation and normalization of immigrant-origin populations. Thus, secular government is undergirded by the two competing imperatives of privatization and surveillance: the political, legal, and institutional discourses and practices that attempt to separate private from public have as their effect the contravention of the public/ private distinction that subtends both normative religiosity and normative sexuality, rendering public the ostensibly private spiritual and sexual lives of Muslim women in order to regulate them. These competing imperatives of secular rule produce another set of contradictory demands on the objects of regulation, namely, to hide and to exhibit, to make private and to render public. To show that they are properly religious— that is, secular—Muslim women are compelled to speak about their religious beliefs and practices and to justify various forms of "aberrant" religiosity (wearing a headscarf, praying regularly, fasting at Ramadan). A similar compulsion applies to their sex lives. Given the extent to which normative (hetero)sexuality has been foundational to French secularism, Muslim women have to disclose intimate information about themselves (the beliefs and practices that constitute their sexual lives) in order to demonstrate their sexual normality. Yet in so doing—in bringing their sexual and religious lives into the public sphere and making public that which must be private—they end up rendering themselves as not secular and not French. The simultaneous incitement to exhibit and to hide, and the grim consequences of exhibiting that which must be bidden, constitute the cunning of secular power.

In attending to the nexus of sex and religion in the articulation of secularity in France, this article makes a series of interventions. Talal Asad's work has paved the way for contemporary scholars to study secularism as a particular pattern of political rule that entails the intervention into and transformation of religious and ethical life and therefore to examine what we have come to call "religion" as an effect of secularism. Scholars have now also begun to attend to the ideological and political formation that Joan Scott terms "sexularism," whereby sexual freedom and sexual equality are seen as the defining features of secular citizenship and secular democracy. This latter work extends a broad body of existing literature on sexual normativity and democratic citizenship. Yet, with a few important exceptions, analyses of the regulation of religion (what might be called the religion-secularity nexus) and the normalization of sex (the sex-secularity nexus) have heretofore remained largely separate. As Scott herself observes, "there is a link between religion and sex that needs further exploration". This article does just that, analyzing how the secular state's regulation of religious life is interwoven with its project of sexual normalization in its interpellation of French Muslims. I argue not only that the regulation of sex and of religion are parallel phenomena—with similarly competing imperatives to render private and to surveil, and similarly contradictory incitements to hide and to exhibit—but also that these modes of regulation are imbricated: proper religion and proper sex, I hold, are mutually constituted by secular rule. Moreover, pace Janet R. Jakobsen and Ann Pellegrini, who regard the secular state's regulation of sexuality as a religious project and therefore a contradiction of secularism, and who call for a properly secular state that would fully separate religion from politics, I regard the regulation of sex and religion and the competing imperatives of secular rule as essential to secularism's operation. I am interested precisely in the intractable tensions of secular rule. But I am also interested in how these tensions are deferred onto the subjects of regulation who, summoned to hide and simultaneously to exhibit their sex and religion, become responsible for transgressing the boundary between public and private that secular rule both implements and constantly undermines.

Religion in the halls of government

When Truchelut demanded that Demiati and her mother remove their headscarves in all common areas of the vacation cottage, she stated explicitly that she was acting against the headscarf, not against Islam. Truchelut's statement draws on a widespread secular-republican discourse that seeks to distinguish between Islam and Islamism, between real religion and politicized religion—that is, between religion and politics. Real religion takes place in the private sphere, either within the realm of individual belief or in designated religious spaces like the mosque. Public expressions or practices of Islam outside these private spaces are, as a consequence, turned into forms of religious fundamentalism, an excess of religion that in fact is not religious but rather political. Thus, discussion prior to the passage of the 2004 law banning conspicuous religious signs in public schools sought to fix the meaning of the headscarf as the politicization of (otherwise private) religiosity. "The wearing of the veil is not the manifestation of piety or modesty," proclaimed Alain Juppé, then head of the center-right Union for a Popular Movement, "it is a militant act sustained by a veritable fundamentalist propaganda". Françoise Hostalier, the former secretary of education, was equally certain: "To wear the Islamic veil is not a religious gesture but a political gesture".

The constant designation of the *hijab* as a political rather than religious symbol makes its interdiction under a law banning religious signs somewhat confusing. What I want to highlight, though, is the authoritative act of interpretation involved in that designation and the concomitant determination by secular political and legal authorities of what constitutes real religion. Though *laïcité,* and secularism more generally, are conventionally defined as the separation of church and state, and of religion and politics, a number of scholars argue that secularism demands instead administrative and legal intervention into and regulation of religious life. Agrama, for example, argues that "the [secular] state is always drawing a line between the religious and the secular [by] promoting an abstract notion of 'religion,' defining the spaces it should inhabit, authorizing the sensibilities proper to it, and then working to discipline actual religious traditions so as to conform to this abstract notion to fit into those spaces, and to express those sensibilities". In France, *laïcité* has long entailed the remaking of communal and ethical life, and with regard to Islam in particular, the state has, since the nineteenth-century colonization of Algeria, restructured the Islamic tradition and refashioned Muslim sensibilities (including the definition of what it means to be Muslim) into forms consistent with secular-modern norms.

Rather than separating religion from politics, then, secular government (including the particular French formation of *laïcité*) necessarily involves the intersection of the religious and the political, since it entails the regulation, transformation, and definition of religion (or "real religion") by political and legal authorities. After all, in order to deal with religion—either to regulate it or to protect it—secular authorities must first identify what constitutes religion. As Asad writes, "in order to protect politics from religion [and] in order to determine its acceptable forms within the polity, the state must identify 'religion.' To the extent that this work of identification becomes a matter for the law, the Republic acquires the theological function of defining religious signs and the power of imposing that definition on its subjects." That theological function was enacted by Juppé and Hostalier, who determined that the headscarf was not properly religious— because not private—and was therefore a political act. Theological designations were also made by the 2003 Stasi Commission, which, after proposing the enactment of a law, helpfully defined what constituted a religious sign (*hijabs*, yarmulkes, and large crosses). Hence one of the immanent tensions of secular rule: the political, legal, and institutional discourses and practices that attempt to separate private religion from public politics necessitate the constant trespass of the boundary between religion and politics, and between public and private, that secular government ostensibly seeks to establish. Beyond this initial tension, however, lies a second one: secularization requires the constant surveillance of the private spaces to which religion has been assigned in order to verify that subjects (Muslims in this instance) are, in fact, being properly religious. These, then, are the contradictory imperatives of secular rule: to separate and to surveil, to make private and to regulate. Michel Foucault's influential dictum about repression and/as incitement—how "the 'putting into discourse' of sex, far from undergoing a process of restriction, on the contrary has been subjected to a mechanism of increasing incitement"—applies, it turns out, to the regulation of religion as well. Far from undergoing a process of simple restriction by secular legal and political authority, religion, like sex, has been subjected to a mechanism of increasing incitement.

Indeed, beyond the state's various regulations that seek to make Islam into a real religion and to refashion Muslim sensibilities to accord with secular religiosity, what is remarkable is how much Islam is talked about in the French public sphere. If the hallmark of what has been called the Islamic revival remains the participation of ordinary practitioners untrained in classical Islamic theology and jurisprudence, the same can be said about contemporary *laïcité*. The media and the halls of government have become sites for separating Islam from political Islamism: the headscarf is emphatically declared *not* a Quranic obligation and *not* one of the pillars of Islam, thus neither necessary to being a Muslim nor protected by a fundamental right to religious liberty (Fernando 2010). Concomitantly, since the headscarf is not deemed a legitimate religious practice, anyone wearing it immediately becomes suspect. Varault is not the only one asking "Why do you wear this headscarf?"

The constant posing of that question, and the scrutiny of the motivations, desires, and intentions of veiled women, constitute an incitement to speak about one's religious life, to justify one's practices, and to reveal the inner workings of one's faith. Consider an article by Felwine Sarr in Oumma.com, a generalist Franco-Islamic website. Sarr criticizes the fact that "Muslim women are questioned in an inquisitorial manner about the reasons for their choice [to wear the headscarf]," declaring, "They don't have to justify themselves . . . with regard to the validity of their reasoning. It is complex, belongs to them, and comes from an intimate casuistry." Having affirmed that veiled women do not need to justify themselves, Sarr then spends the next four paragraphs doing just that, laying out in detail the "intimate casuistry"—the relationship between self and body and attendant notions of intimacy—upon which the practice of veiling rests.

Responding to the question "Why do you wear this headscarf?" by explaining one's motivations and revealing one's inner subjective life does not, however, make one any more acceptable or intelligible for a secular-republican public; in fact, it often does the opposite. For most Muslim French women like Demiati, veiling is both an individual choice and a religious duty. Veiling cannot be imposed by others and must be undertaken willingly, according to the dictates of individual conscience, but veiling is also a necessary means by which to embody a particular model of female Muslim piety. Yet the formulation of the headscarf as both a choice and an obligation remains unintelligible to a secular public. On the one hand, justifying the headscarf by emphasizing its status as an obligation makes one a fundamentalist, since secular republicans take that obligation to be incumbent upon all women; on the other hand, by declaring the headscarf a choice, Muslim French women lose the capacity to express the ethical stakes of what it means to veil as a religious duty and as integral to one's subjectivity. Yet framing the headscarf as both a religious duty and a personal decision constitutes a kind of the doublespeak for secular republicans, an insidious attempt to mask a fundamentalist agenda with liberal terms. Incited by secular power to speak of religion, to reveal their inner religious selves, Muslim French women can only reinforce the suspicions that generate this incitement, only confirm their status as anti-secular, fundamentalist subjects.

Neither whore nor doormat

Significantly, a number of self-declared secular Muslim women (*musulmanes laïques*) have become key players in the state's project to reform immigrant sexuality, most notable among them Fadela Amara and Loubna Méliane, the cofounders of Ni Putes Ni Soumises (NPNS; Neither Whores nor Doormats), a group protesting the denigration of immigrant-origin women in the *banlieues* (outer suburbs). Both Amara and Méliane published popular autobiographies about their traumatic personal experiences with Islamic patriarchy, and, speaking as experts on "Islamic fundamentalism" and the suffering of Muslim women, both established a strong presence in media and politics. Much of NPNS's success can be attributed to the way in which its leaders offer themselves, and are eagerly read, as lib-crated, integrated counterpoints to the paradigmatic menace of the veiled woman (*la musulmane roilée*). Somewhat paradoxically, then, a few non-white Muslim women have become spokespersons for the sexual equality and sexual freedom that are thought to define French culture in contrast to the sexual oppression and gender inequality of Islam.

The juxtaposition of the *musulmane laïque* and the *musulmane voilée* and the narrative of successful sexuality as successful integration remain consistent features of discussions about Islam in France. In televised debates about the law banning headscarves in public schools, for instance, secular Muslim women like Amara and Méliane were often seated next to or opposite women in headscarves. On the October 19, 2003, edition of *Ripostes* (aired on France 5), Méliane was placed across from Siham Andalouci, a member of the Collective of French Muslims. Andalouci, a Muslim French activist who was relentlessly attacked as an anti-republican and antisecular fundamentalist by Méliane, wore a cream-colored turtleneck sweater and matching headscarf, with only her face visible. Méliane was dressed in a fashionable blouse that left her shoulders bare and her bra straps visible. Méliane's secularity and integration were demonstrated through her bodily comportment and her embrace of normative hetero-femininity, underscoring the dominant narrative of successful integration through successful sexuality. That the juxtaposition of veiled and unveiled female bodies was staged during an episode of *Ripostes* titled "Is *Laïcité* under Attack?" (and it was clear both that it was and by whom) highlights the way in which sex norms and secular norms have become coextensive.

Méliane's bodily comportment visually echoes the broader rhetoric of publicly secular Muslim women who, in their autobiographies and media appearances, actively embrace the particular coordinates of secular-republican heterosexual norms. For example, in Amara's autobiography, she identifies wearing makeup and certain forms of dress—"short skirts, tight-fitting jeans, low-cut blouses, and short T-shirts"—as necessary for "showing off our femininity" against the backdrop of repressive Muslim patriarchy. Similarly, Méliane once remarked, "It's better to wear a miniskirt and take up one's femininity than to hide it behind a veil in order to avoid the gaze of others". Like other republican neofeminists, Méliane and Amara identify certain sartorial practices as essential to femininity and consequently define femininity as sexual desirability and sexual availability to the male gaze. Méliane and Amara also naturalize this particular mode of femininity, so that taking up one's natural qualities as a woman has a particular sartorial form. And both posit wearing makeup and revealing clothes as acts of sexual liberation and sexual equality. Within this rhetoric of sexual availability as sexual normality, veiling comes to be seen as sexually abnormal and fundamentally repressive.

As the organization's name suggests, the model of heterofemininity embraced by Ni Putes Ni Soumises is produced and reproduced through a sexualized contrast between the sexually normal *musulmane laïque* and her two sexually abnormal counterparts: the veiled doormat (*la soumise*) and the whore (*la pute*). If *la soumise* represents repressed sexuality and a lack of femininity, *la pute* represents an excessive sexuality that breaches the bounds of proper femininity. As Anna Kemp writes, "Prostitutes who claim to have sex for money out of choice are disturbing because they have separated sexuality from desire [while] Muslim women who choose to veil create confusion because they have opted out of a mainstream vision of female sexuality as overtly and publicly alluring". If the sexual abnormality of the unfashionable *soumise* emerges from her refusal to participate in consumerist femininity, the *pute* takes consumerism too far, commodifying her own body. Importantly, as Ruth Mas reminds us, these secular Muslim subjects emerge within the constraints of the dominant norms that precede and condition them. The semantic juxtaposition enacted by NPNS therefore reiterates the broader regulatory regime of which the various laws criminalizing prostitution and veiling are part. In other words, NPNS merely makes explicit a wider secular-republican logic: to be sexually normal, and therefore fully secular, is to be *ni pute, ni soumise*.

That *ni/ni* (neither/nor) structure of secular-republican sexuality repeats itself within the figure of *la soumise* (or *la musulmane voilée*) herself. Scott persuasively argues that within republican ideology, subjectivation is not just dialogic but also fundamentally gendered. To put Scott's point into Althusserian terms, man hails woman into being: "Feminine identity depend[s] on male desire; male desire depend[s] on visual stimulation." Hence the common notion that veiled women "hide [their femininity] behind a veil" and, in so doing, hide the fact that they are women. Sex and gender are collapsed in this interpretation of the veil as hiding "the fact that one is a woman": the quality of being a woman depends on one's femininity, which in turns depends on one's normative (hetero)sexuality. And that normative sexuality requires that a woman be uncovered, that she show off her femininity, that she reveal her sex.

Yet as Scott further observes in her analysis of republican reactions to the headscarf, if there was "something sexually amiss about girls in head-scarves . . . it was as if both too little and too much were being revealed." Scott productively reads the "too much"—not merely the absence of sexuality but its excessive presence— as an uncomfortable reminder of French republicanism's inability to deal fully with the problem that sexual difference poses for the abstract universalism on which republicanism rests. In other words, Muslim recognition of sexual difference via the headscarf reveals the contradictions of French republicanism, hence the discomfort provoked by the veil. I want to take the notion of "too much" in a somewhat different direction, one that points to the ambivalence of secular republican sexuality and to the resulting, and contradictory, demands on Muslim French women to exhibit and to hide simultaneously. On the one hand, mainstream republican feminists now equate gender equality with sexual emancipation and the visibility of the female body. On the other hand, many of these feminists have long criticized sexual exhibitionism for reducing women to their sexed bodies. Gender equality seemingly depends on some kind of visibility, thus public school teachers' consistent demand, before 2004, that veiled students, apparently showing too little of themselves, reveal their necks, earlobes, and hairlines as a "compromise." But girls should not show too much of themselves either, as demonstrated by the 2003 *affaire du string*, when some schools began sending home girls whose thong underwear was visible between their low-cut pants and cropped T-shirts. Pundits bemoaned the over-sexualization of young women and the way in which, as Socialist Party leader Ségolène Royal put it, "the *string* [thong] reduces young girls to a behind" (in Scott 2007, 161). This ambivalent relationship to the sexual visibility of the female body comes together in critiques of the veil. For as much as the veil is thought to hide the fact of one's sexed body, it is equally criticized, sometimes by the same detractors, for unnecessarily sexualizing the body and drawing attention to it.

Let's talk about sex

If successful integration into the republic entails the inhabitation of secular sexuality, it is perhaps unsurprising that the autobiography—the most intimate of nonfiction genres— has emerged as a popular source of information about Muslim French women's lives (see Bellil 2003; Méliane 2003b; Amara 2006). Structured like conversion narratives, these auto-biographies first describe gender and sexual dysfunction within the Arab-Muslim home and community at large before recounting a story of self-realization achieved by breaking away from that dysfunction. The most powerful remains Samira Bellil's *Dans l'enfer des tournantes* (In the hell of gang rapes), in which Bellil narrates her journey from abuse at the hands of her father, to her trauma as the victim of multiple gang rapes by predatory males in the housing projects (*cités*), to her descent into alcohol and drug addiction, to her ultimate recovery. Kemp has pointed out the ways in which Bellil's testimony, which Bellil clearly considered a profoundly personal story, was nonetheless marketed by her publisher as a window into the general sexual savagery of the *banlieues*. According to the publisher, the text "unveils the sexual violence that has been institutionalized and made ordinary in *cités* and in the *banlieues*, where everything is reduced to a relationship of power and domination." The metaphor of unveiling used by the publisher is significant. For as Bellil pulls back the veil on life in the *banlieues*, she does so by offering up her own troubled familial, sexual, and romantic life for public perusal. The structure of that double unveiling underscores the way in which the narrative of secular-republican integration, in which normalized sexuality signals successful integration, requires women like Bellil, Amara, and Méliane to reveal publicly the most intimate details of their private lives in order to be recognized as integrated subjects. If normal sex is private sex, these secular Muslim women must nonetheless prove their normality precisely by bringing their sex lives into the public sphere for monetized consumption by a literary public.

Karima is a woman of Moroccan descent in her late twenties and a longtime interlocutor from my fieldwork. She described to me the deontic and discursive compulsions she experiences in her day-to-day life as a result of putting on the veil almost a decade ago. "When you're a veiled Muslim woman," Karima began, "people want to know you intimately." Because the veil remains so maligned in France, "you do everything to be accepted." Though she now feels less dependent on others' acceptance for her own self-worth, she related how, in the first years of wearing the headscarf, she was constantly smiling and engaging others in order to prove that she was *"sans complexes"* (without hang-ups): "They take away your speech in the media, you speak with abandon in private space to say, 'look, I'm normal!' . . . When I first wore the headscarf, I needed to speak. . . . It's stupid, but I needed to speak, to prove that I was normal." Karima's urge to speak echoes that experienced by Demiati when Maître Varault demanded to know why she wears the headscarf. Although Demiati realized that her inner spirituality was her own private affair, she felt compelled to answer the question, to speak back about herself in a context in which others were speaking about (and for) her and women like her. Demiati felt obliged, as Karima did, to show that underneath her headscarf, she was "normal."

The cunning of secular power helps, then, to defer and displace the fundamental tensions of secularism that emerge from its contradictory imperatives to separate and to regulate, to privatize and to surveil. As I have argued, the public discourses and political practices that attempt to regulate sex and religion have as their effect the contravention of the public/private distinction that underpins normative sexuality and normative religiosity. Secularism constantly trespasses the very boundary it seeks to erect. The burden of that trespass, however, falls elsewhere. Secular power's cunning lies in its double gesture: secular authorities incite Muslim French women to reveal publicly the innermost details of their sexual and religious lives, then take them to task for doing so, for exhibiting in public that which should be private. What I want to highlight, in conclusion, is how that cunning serves to displace the burden of trespass onto Muslim French women, who become responsible for the tensions and contradictions of secular rule. Thus, in a masterful dissimulation of the nature of its rule, it is Muslim French women who are seen to undermine the boundary between public and private, not secular power itself.

8

Release from Bondage:
Sex, Suffering, and Sanctity

Daniel A. Lehrman

*D*aniel A. Lehrman is a rabbi and licensed psychoanalyst. This reading is taken from an edited collection entitled The Sacred Encounter: Jewish Perspectives on Sexuality. It offers a seldom-explored perspective on the question of spirituality and BDSM (Bondage, Discipline, Sado-Masochism), delineated and argued within a uniquely Jewish frame of reference. In talking of "the spiritualization of suffering," something which also intersects with the Robert Orsi text in this reader, the author opens up the possibility of a radically different understanding of religious and sexual performativity. Flagellation refers to a distinctive religious or sexual practice that involves whipping or beating the body with some implement designed to cause temporary pain. As a spiritual practice in a number of religious traditions, it is thought to be a way of disciplining the body and bringing its urges or temptations under control, especially those of a sexual nature.

Not to laugh, not to lament, not to curse, but to understand.

(BARUCH SPINOZA, *THEOLOGICAL-POLITICAL TREATISE* 1:4)

From sex within marriage to premarital sex; from the missionary position to a Kama Sutra variety; from taboos on masturbation to a recognition of it as a natural part of sexual functioning; from intra-racial sex to inter-racial sex; from genital sex to oral and anal sex; from heterosexuality to gay and lesbian, to lesbian, gay, bisexual (LGB), to transgender (LGBT) to queer (LGBTQ), and perhaps now to "intersex," someone whose anatomy is not clearly male or female (LGBTQI)—since the sexual revolution of the 1960s, our culture's openness about the realities of sex has grown both socially and legally, with an uninhibitedness in the public sphere that seems to grow with every year.

What's next? What frontiers of sexuality remain to be brought out of the closet and into the arena of acceptable public discourse, to be depicted in popular movies and sitcoms, discussed on morning television shows, written about in magazines and best sellers, blogged about, tweeted about, joked about?

The series of novels by British author E. L. James called *Fifty Shades of Grey*, first published in 2011, has brought one such frontier of sexuality to mainstream awareness in its path to selling twenty-five million copies in four months alone, discussed in book clubs across the nation and on morning news programs, advertised in metropolitan commuter trains, spawning copycat novels, even giving rise to a new coinage, "mommy porn," and—sure enough—soon to become a major motion picture.

Fifty Shades of Grey centers around a BDSM sexual relationship between the characters Christian and Anastasia. An acronym for bondage/discipline (or sometimes domination), sadism/masochism, BDSM covers a wide range of activity in which partners take on roles of dominant or submissive. Some BDSM practices involve inflicting and suffering physical pain, such as when established rules have been broken, requiring punishment and discipline. Issues of power and authority, vulnerability and helplessness, shame and humiliation, come into play. BDSM encounters are understood by participants, however, to be consensual activity; typically, the partners have agreed on a code word with which the submissive partner has the power at any time to bring any activity to a stop. *Fifty Shades of Grey* contains scenes in which Christian, the dominant, pulls Anastasia's hair "painfully," hits her with his hand, whips her with a riding crop, and binds her in leather cuffs.

It can be disturbing to consider behavior in which one adult controls, dominates, and sometimes inflicts pain on another adult to be consensual behavior, let alone sexually arousing or relationship-enhancing. BDSM occupies a dark space where sex and violence meet, and while it may be seen as a "game," the pain that sometimes occurs is not pretend. It is a game that seems to flirt with the space where brutal crime can take place, where consent and pleasure, if they are possible at all, may understandably be judged perverse—a scandal and an outrage. Indeed, sadomasochism has long been treated as a pathology of interpersonal and sexual relations, associated with early childhood trauma and developmental interference. Sex therapist Esther Perel notes a common assumption even among colleagues (who might be expected to be particularly nonjudgmental of sexual practices) that some pathology must underlie the acting out of dominant and submissive roles. In a discussion of a BDSM relationship at a professional conference she attended, she observed, "the unspoken subtext," despite the fact that women are not always in the submissive role in such relationships, that "such practices are inherently degrading to women, a rebuke to the very idea of gender equality, and antithetical to a good, healthy marriage."

Other psychotherapists and professionals in human sexuality have weighed in differently, called to comment because the phenomenal popularity of James's novels thrusts important questions to the fore. Are all forms of BDSM unhealthy, damaging, perverse, a sickness in need of treatment? Sex therapist Sari Cooper, for instance, avers in *Psychology Today* that BDSM "is not weird, it is not pathological, it is a flavor of erotica, just as chocolate (and vanilla) are flavors of ice cream."

Where sexual practices raise moral issues, Judaism, like many religions, has much to say. So concerned is Judaism with what we should do and what we shouldn't do sexually that the chapter in Torah most extensively enumerating the sexual prohibitions, Leviticus 18, is put front and center as the traditional Torah reading on the afternoon of Yom Kippur. Large sections of the Talmud, moreover, pertain to issues of "family purity," rules regulating sexual relations within marriage. Many resources are available in our textual tradition for evaluating the moral dimensions of sexual practices.

We could pass moral judgment on BDSM right here at the beginning, and it might be a relief, like de-venoming a snake to make it safe to handle. In order to understand something about BDSM more deeply, however, we need to risk handling it without cursing it from the start. In the spirit of Spinoza, we will suspend the urge to declare judgment, not in order to revise our judgment from bad to good, but in order to think about it from a perspective in which good and bad are not the primary categories. In addition—and complicating things still more!—our project here is as much to understand something about Judaism through the lens of BDSM as to understand something about BDSM from the perspective of Judaism. Therefore our inquiry may be put from these two points of view: (1) What is there about BDSM that Judaism can help us to understand? (2) In exploring BDSM from the perspective of Judaism, what aspects of our tradition come to the fore and reveal themselves with particular clarity?

We begin by turning to a contribution by psychiatrist Emmanuel Ghent called "Masochism, Submission, Surrender: Masochism as a Perversion of Surrender," in which Ghent explores some of the meanings of BDSM behavior as he has come to understand them from his intensive work with patients. Ghent uses the word "surrender" to name an experience for which he believes everyone has a wish or longing. Surrender is "a quality of liberation and expansion of the self." It involves "a letting down of defensive barriers." Surrender for Ghent is not about hoisting a white flag; it is not about defeat. What is surrendered is the armor of the ego, the protective layers that maintain a feeling of subjective isolation. He describes it as "a controlled dissolution of self-boundaries," *which is both sought and feared,* and he identifies other features of surrender:

- Its ultimate direction is the discovery of one's sense of wholeness, even one's sense of unity with other living beings.

- It is not a voluntary activity. One can provide facilitative conditions for surrender, but in the event, it just happens; it cannot be made to happen.

- It is an experience of being "in the moment," totally in the present, where past and future recede from consciousness.

- It is accompanied by feelings of acceptance—of self, of others, perhaps of things as they are.

- There is an absence of domination and control.

- It may be accompanied by feelings of dread and death, and/or clarity, relief, even ecstasy.

Ghent's description of surrender sounds notes that are echoed by mystics of many traditions. Dissolving the normal boundaries of the self is a core theme in the teachings of the Chasidic masters, who speak of being "stripped of selfhood," of being "no longer aware of [one's] own self," of "overcoming the bonds of self." A name for this is *bitul* or *bitul yeish,* which means nullifying one's "somethingness" or "selfness," or ego; it is even called "self-annihilation." Says Dov Ber of Mezritch, "You need to think of yourself as nothing. Forget yourself entirely." *D'veikut,* an experience of *clinging* or *cleaving* to God, may similarly be seen as involving a "dissolution of self-boundaries" that Ghent describes. In such mystical states of being, "the ego's will is submerged in the divine will so that one's acts serve God rather than a limited self." This is the path to "ultimate unification" with God, an experience Ghent articulates as "sense of unity with other living beings."

Common as well to the two descriptions, Ghent's and the Jewish mystics', is a transformed awareness of time. In surrender as in *bitul yeish,* there is a feeling of "transcending time" such that "past and future have receded from consciousness." Or we might put it positively and say that the three tenses—past, present, and future—are all at once present, which is the meaning of *YHVH,* the name of God that expresses God's timeless being and that is expressed in our song *Adon Olam: God was, God is, and God will be.* While liberating, the experience of timelessness is also disorienting, so it is no surprise that "fear" and "dread" (Ghent's terms) would accompany it— "awe," in religious language.

Yet this awe exists in a signal combination with joyous release. "It is joyous in spirit," says Ghent. There is "limitless joy and incomparable delight" among those who stand in the light of God, says a Chasidic master. Celebration and merriment are hallmarks of the Chasidic way of life, and *hitlahavut* is a name for its most impassioned form—a "burning enthusiasm" reached in intensest prayer. The word itself combines the awe and fear with the joy of it, stemming from a Hebrew root for "flame," our earthly portion of the life-supporting, dangerous sun. Or to change the elemental image, a fitting metaphor for this multiform experience of timelessness/dread/awe/joy might be diving into the ocean, into both the freedom and the overwhelm of boundlessness, into a disorienting but enlivening loss of a dependable here-and-now. *Terra firma* is gone, and with it both security and limitations.

Now what does this kind of spiritual experience, described by both Ghent and the Jewish mystics, have to do with bondage, domination, sadism, and masochism?

Focusing on the masochistic pole of a relationship, the provocative thesis Ghent explores is that seeking out submission, pain, and adversity in BDSM sometimes—and he is careful to say sometimes, not always—springs from a spiritual longing. There is another dimension, "often deeply buried," he says, to masochistic erotic desire. The *apparent* wish is to be controlled, dominated, and disciplined by another person, and this wish is enacted physically by allowing oneself to be ordered about and punished, put in restraints, humiliated; even physical pain is not out of bounds. The core desire in this dynamic is the desire to cede control completely. Even the submissive's power to disobey the dominant is exercised only in order to be disciplined back into powerlessness. The submissive acts autonomously in order to abdicate autonomy. And why? Because the desire is for giving oneself over, not for taking oneself back.

This "giving oneself over" is the clue to the link between this masochistic dynamic and ecstatic spiritual experience. The true longing, deeply buried, may be for authentic surrender, *bitul yeish,* a breaking free of the boundaries of individuality. Such experience is hard to come by, however, so a substitute for surrender can be very enticing. In allowing oneself to be dominated and controlled, afflicted and punished, a substitute is found, a shortcut: the normal boundary between self and other is crossed, encroached upon in a way that the survival instinct normally precludes. It is like storming the walled city of the ego so as to smash its ramparts. The resulting breakdown of the boundary between self and other is experienced by some as liberating. It is, as Esther Perel notes, delight in the "abandon that comes with the sense of powerlessness."

Ghent calls such masochistic enactment a "defensive mutant of surrender." This substitute, this ersatz spiritual experience, Ghent calls *submission,* in contrast to surrender. "Submission, losing oneself in the power of the other, becoming enslaved in one or other way to the master, is the ever available lookalike to surrender."

The look-alike nature of submission to surrender is all the more vivid when we consider that similarities between sexual submission and some Jewish mystical states are not limited to the mental-emotional-spiritual levels, but extend to the physical as well. For instance, some mystical experiences include a letting go or even a vanquishing of physical autonomy. "When a man attains to the stage of self-annihilation he can thus be said to have reached the world of the divine Nothingness. Emptied of selfhood his soul has now become attached to the true reality, the divine Nothingness. . . . *All his physical powers are annihilated."* There can be very specific kinds of dissociation from one's physical being. "Sometimes [a] voice emerges from within the mystic, who then is heard speaking in a different voice from his usual one. Another variation of this phenomenon is the belief that a celestial power is guiding the hand of the writing mystic." In other words, physical defeat, spiritual victory. Given these co-occurring phenomena of spiritual openness and physical "annihilation," it is not hard to see how "submission, losing oneself in the power of the other, becoming enslaved in one or other way to the master, is the ever available lookalike to surrender."

This act of substituting one experience for another might be compared to the search for spirit in "spirits"—that is, in alcohol, in recreational drugs, or in other reckless or dangerous behavior, all involving a giving up of control and a concomitant transformation of the feeling state. We speak colloquially of going to a party and "letting go," "letting loose," "losing inhibitions." Ghent notes the wide spectrum of behavior that partakes of some degree of masochism, from unhealthy and self-injuring forms, to others such as running a marathon, riding a roller coaster, or, we might add, even the child's twirling round and round to the point of collapsing in dizziness. However we may judge the activity, Ghent is focusing us away from the pain or self-injuring behavior itself, and instead on what makes the pain feel worthwhile. We can see in all of these examples the common goal (not the only goal) of changing one's state of consciousness—in a word, getting high. More than one marathon runner speaks of the spiritual high of extreme exertion; it is a common experience among athletes. BDSM, because it occurs in the sexual realm, is in a class of its own, however, because of the special nature of sexuality. "The closest most of us come to the experience of surrender is in the moment of orgasm with a loved one," writes Ghent. "Little surprise it should be then for the sexual scene to be the desired focus for such letting-go." Being "known in one's nakedness" is the "ultimate longed-for goal of self-surrender."

How Ghent reaches his conclusions from a clinical perspective is outside our scope here, but we have begun to see that the thrust of his insight—the linking of masochistic behaviors with spiritual strivings or, more broadly, the linking of suffering with spirit—is not as bizarre as it might at first appear. BDSM can contain spiritual longings of which Judaism has a profound and highly developed understanding, including a recognition of the dangers of spiritual exploration. The classic story of the perils of the mystic journey tells of the four rabbis, Ben Azzai, Ben Zoma, Acher, and Rabbi Akiva, who entered the *pardes,* the mystic garden. One died, one went insane, and one "cut down the plantings," a puzzling phrase perhaps meaning he became a heretic. Only Rabbi Akiva exited with all his faculties intact—the same Rabbi Akiva, in fact, who so recognized the spiritual core, with all its fearsome majesty, in the erotic poetry of Song of Songs that he declared it the holiest of all books in the *Tanach.*

Sanctity and self-imposed suffering have long been coupled in religious traditions. Christian practices of flagellation, for example (Latin *flagellum* means "whip"), go at least as far back as the fourth century and grew to "a huge scale in the second half of the thirteenth century, after which it spread all over Europe and became endemic." Flagellants, sometimes including both men and women, processed through village streets lashing themselves for hours. The word "passion" as in "passion of Christ," encodes the twinship of suffering and spirituality, as does "Muslim," meaning "one who surrenders and submits." In Zen Buddhism, too, the pain of sitting for extended periods of zazen meditation may be experienced as a gateway or vehicle to a less dualistic state of being, and some forms of Zen include being hit with a switch as a spur to awakening.

In Judaism, the spiritualization of suffering is less overt than in some religions, but it is hardly ancillary. Fasting on Yom Kippur derives from the commandment in Leviticus 23:32, "you shall *afflict* [*v'initem*] your souls." Indeed, the word we translate as "fast," *taanit,* derives from the same root letters—*ayin, nun, bei*—as do a variety of other words with meanings such as "torment," "suffering," "humility," "self-abasement," and "submission." One such word, *inui,* means "torture." The self-mortification (Latin *mors/mortis* means "death") accomplished through the affliction of fasting is part of the enactment of death on Yom Kippur, along with the four other "afflictions" prohibiting washing, anointing with any oils or cosmetics, wearing leather shoes, and sex. On our most solemn day, when we meditate on all the ways we have fallen short of our own standards and ideals and confront the shame of our wrongdoing, we perform a set of rituals that is not meant to buoy us up, but that rather brings us even lower, down into our earthy humble vulnerability. "The antidote to humiliation is not pride, or a reassertion of self-respect or virtues or positive qualities," writes psychotherapist Lyn Cowan. "It is humility. There are occasions of fault, failure, exposures of shameful weakness, which can be borne only by yielding completely to the feeling of them." In Jewish tradition as in others, we descend in order to ascend. *M'chayeih hameitim*: God brings renewed life to that which has touched death.

Perhaps one reason for *choosing* adversity, humiliation, and self-abasement is that we recognize the spiritual power that can be wrested from pain and suffering. Would Nelson Mandela have had the inner fortitude and the world's respect necessary for leading his nation through political and spiritual transformation had he not lived for twenty-seven years as a prisoner on Robben Island? Elie Wiesel's searing works were formed in the earthly hell he lived through. Oprah Winfrey's gracious stature is inseparable from her struggles. Whether we look at the character-building mission of an army boot camp, the collective calamity of centuries in slavery, or the inevitable hardships of negotiating puberty or a first job, trial and tribulation are necessary conditions for reaching some stages of maturity.

One of our tradition's most dramatic tales is of Rabbi Akiva insisting on teaching Torah publicly, against the decree of Hadrian. He was to be executed as punishment, and as the Romans were raking his flesh with iron combs, Akiva recited the *Sh'ma*. His students were amazed. How at this moment could he bring himself to praise God? Akiva said that he had always wondered what loving God "with all your soul" meant in the *V'ahavta*. (BT *B'rachot* 61b) He was grateful now at last to be able to fulfill that mitzvah. In *Midrash Rabbah*, righteous souls are said to endure severe trials, and this is compared with the owner of flax who will beat it often and severely so as to make it more pure. Even the most abject suffering may be occasion for transcendence.

A phenomenon in contemporary Israel sheds unique light on experiences of affliction and responses to them. Some children and grandchildren of Holocaust survivors have chosen to get tattooed with the numbers their relatives had branded on their forearms by the Nazis. This has of course shocked and appalled many people who see it. How could they possibly do to *themselves* what was done so horrifically to their family and their people? Why would anyone choose to replicate and carry into yet another generation such a graphic and permanent sign of what Primo Levi called part of the demolition of a human being? When Oded Ravek, the fifty-six-year-old son of survivor Livia Ravek, first showed his tattoo to his mother, "she was really upset about it. When I explained the reasons for why I did it, we cried together. I said, 'You're always with me.'" Mr. Ravek's son, Daniel Philosoph, also chose to be tattooed with his grandmother's number. All the descendants interviewed by journalist Jodi Rudoren echoed Ravek's sentiments. "They wanted to be intimately, eternally bonded to their survivor-relative." For a documentary film about the survivors and their self-tattooing descendants, filmmaker Dana Doron interviewed about fifty Holocaust survivors. She asked them whether lovers kissed their numbers as they might a scar. "Some of them looked at me like, 'What are you, nuts?' and some of them said, 'Of course.'"

There are clusters and knots of meanings here. Suffering and trauma are not pushed away, covered over with a long-sleeved shirt. They are drawn close and exposed. The gotesqueness of branded human beings, the beauty of family bonds, somehow interwoven. Grief/suffering/intimacy/satisfaction/bad/good: the words are separate but the experiences are not. Reasonable questions seeking reasonable answers—*Why would someone want to do a thing like that?*—presume a level of logic and singular causality better suited to other domains. Such queries are going to the ocean with a thimble. In these areas of the psyche, unlike in the material world, two things and many more do occupy the same space at the same time. Suffering and sanctity appear to be attached by a double-pointed arrow, like the antirational power of biblical sacrifice. *Sacri-fice*: a *making sacred*—through? in? of? with? pain, destruction, death, blood, suffering. A whole burnt offering, a *holocaust*. A *drawing close,* the literal meaning of *korban,* Hebrew for "offering" or "sacrifice." Pain and suffering, chosen and unchosen, one's own or that of another to whom one is bound by love, hold a special susceptibility to sanctity.

In the heart of Jerusalem was the Temple, and in the heart of the Temple, sacrifice was performed. In the heart of Judaism is an extraordinary genius for holding the kinds of clashing meanings we have been exploring. It is a genius for ambivalence—defined not as uncertainty or indecisiveness, but as the coexistence of opposing attitudes or feelings.

Explosions of paradox happen everywhere in Judaism. In ritual: the breaking of the glass at a wedding—burst of joy, remembrance of destruction; Yom Kippur—most solemn day of the year while also a *Shabbat Shabbaton,* "Sabbath of Sabbaths"— the "fast is a feast," in Philo's words. In story: Abraham is breathtakingly *chutzpadik* on behalf of those at Sodom, while infuriatingly submissive in bringing Isaac up the mountain as sacrifice; Moses is the greatest prophet and also a murderer; the tribe he comes from, Levi, savagely brutalizes the Shechemites, then becomes the tribe of priests. In theology: God is immaterial, beyond all picturing, and full of *chesed* and *rachamim,* compassion and loving-kindness, while also a "Warrior" (Exod. 15:3). God is, in the same breath, Isaiah's "Maker of peace and Creator of bad/evil" (*oseh shalom u'vorei ra,* Isa. 45:7). Examples could be multiplied endlessly.

In BDSM, the union of seeming irreconcilables may be pushed to the nth degree. Life-invigorating eros may vibrate to very nearly the same frequency as life-injuring violence. This is terrifying territory. It is like a dark corridor that leads to we know not what—a place we might prefer to believe does not exist. Indeed, walking by a sex shop in the East Village of Manhattan, seeing the dog collars, the gags and muzzles, the hoods and blindfolds, the whips and paddles, it is impossible not to recall the photos of the abuse at Abu Ghraib. No matter how much one may domesticate BDSM and normalize it with best-selling novels and major motion pictures—"it is a flavor of erotica, just as chocolate (and vanilla) are flavors of ice cream"—it cannot be denied that it sits along a continuum of sexualized violence and violent sex that includes the most horrifying of human behavior.

With BDSM, we are looking, then, at a cluster of psychodynamics that may come to life horrifically, in murderous earnest, in torture chambers and concentration camps, and also in consensual sensual play in the privacy of a bedroom. The dissonance is even more shrill if there is any truth at all to the idea we have explored, that there is a spiritual aspiration motivating some BDSM behavior, an actual striving toward an experience of God. These are the clanging, clashing meanings that BDSM challenges us to hold at one and the same time. It reminds us that spiritual zones may be the farthest things from cozy safety. The High Priest on Yom Kippur risked death, so a rope was tied around him just in case, lest somebody else need to enter the Holy of Holies to retrieve his body. When we do encounter God, injury may result: Jacob's becoming Israel left him with a limp.

Looking at BDSM from the point of view of Judaism, it is tempting to take up a seat in a perch of moral judgment. Religion is prone to be used this way, to survey things dangerous and bad from up behind the crenellated safety of the Old City walls. But ancient Jerusalem drew its water, and thus its life, from outside those walls, from a region down below that could be unpredictable and uncontrollable and dangerously violent. Judaism challenges us with the terribly disturbing teaching of monotheism. We may wish to envision it as a grand magnificent harmony, and such it may be on some ultimate level. But closer to earth, it means that if everything is linked up together, then nothing human is alien to any one of us. The *Tanach* is relentless in driving the point home. It looks at the worst of human behavior and says: That is us. It looks at lust and murder and says: That is us (King David). It looks at deceit and fraud and says: That is us (Jacob and Rebekah in league against Esau and Isaac). It looks at berserk, heedless vengefulness and says: That is us (Simeon and Levi at Shechem). It looks even at genocide and says: That is us (the Book of Joshua). If we had judged BDSM from the beginning, we would immediately have set up a contrast between it and us, the result of which is the quiet premise: it is different from us. Are we, instead, willing to think without being scared? Are we brave enough to look at some parts of ourselves that are even crazier than irrational, that are antirational? Torah reminds us each week who we are. We go to it again and again, seeking a vision of what we would like to be, if only we could be, and surely ought to be. And what Torah gives us again and again is not the Ought but the Is—what we really are—and this turns out to sustain us more than what we came for, because it's true.

9

Nakedness, Nonviolence, and Brahmacharya:

Gandhi's Experiments in Celibate Sexuality

VINAY LAL

Vinay Lal is a scholar of South and Southeast Asia. The excerpt from his article "Nakedness, Nonviolence, and Brahmacharya: Gandhi's experiments in Celibate Sexuality" examines the Indian reformer Mahatma Gandhi's controversial practice of lying naked in his bed with three young women. In it, Lal challenges the view that Gandhi exploited young girls on the basis of his pseudo-scientific views of sexuality. Instead, Lal reads Gandhi's experiments with nudity in terms of his pursuit of brahmacharya, celibacy, or more broadly the eradication of desire. For Lal these experiments must be understood to correspond with Gandhi's politics, which, at center, offered a critique of power and violence. His celibate experiments, asserts Lal, did not negate the sexual. Their goal was to make Gandhi a (near) androgynous subject no longer constrained by the limits of finite, carnal desire. Lal's analysis points to the intersections between gender performance and erotic desire. His conclusions also reveal that gender performances can (and perhaps often do) give rise to conflicting responses.

I Continence and the blot of lust

Gandhi's experiment in "sexual celibacy" or "celibate sexuality" paves the way, as I shall argue, for an enhanced understanding of his relations with women, his simultaneous reliance on, and defiance of, Indian traditions of sexuality and sexual potency, his advocacy of androgyny, and his articulation of the relationship of nonviolence to sexual conduct. Though it would be wholly erroneous to speak of the sexlessness of Gandhi, who appeared to many of his friends, associates, and visitors as possessed of a "strong sexuality," it is quite clear that he sought to cultivate the ideal of brahmacharya, and more specifically its component of celibacy—understood as voluntary abstinence from sex—while decrying the tendency, particularly pronounced among those with spiritual aspirations, to segregate the sexes. Gandhi evidently relished the company of women, and his life and writings are a striking testimony to his emphatic willingness to reject varying standards of sexual mores for men and women and to persuade women to give up false standards of modesty which ironically undermined the true capacities of feminine power. Gandhi's brahmacharya experiment also enables us to pose some questions, which have been most inadequately addressed, about Gandhi's renunciation of power, his understanding of the nature of political power in the twentieth century, and his view that the ontology of the female is superior to that of the male.

"The core of the Gandhian teaching," wrote T. K. Mahadevan in a seminal piece on Gandhi's political philosophy, "consists of one piece—and no other. It is truth." The primacy of satya, or truth, in Gandhi's thinking is widely accepted, and Mahadevan was surely right in pointing to the folly of ascribing greater interpretive importance to ahimsa, or nonviolence. Gandhi is, in the popular conception, the Prophet of Nonviolence, and it is the various nonviolent campaigns which he waged in the struggle to free India from British rule that have won him a place in the popular imagination. But Gandhi himself termed his movement of nonviolent resistance satyagraha, the force of truth, and as Mahadevan has so persuasively argued, he can be located within an Indian tradition which has accorded an extraordinarily privileged place to the quest for truth. "He is a satyagrahi," Gandhi was to say, "who has resolved to practice nothing but truth, and such a one will know the right way every time." Though the cardinal principle in Gandhi's thought may well be satya, it is nonetheless revealing that Mahadevan should not have considered the place of brahmacharya, alongside satya and ahimsa, in Gandhi's conception of the ethical and political life. To a very large extent, his views on sexuality and brahmacharya have been an embarrassment to his admirers, while provoking outrage among his detractors. "I cannot imagine a thing as ugly as the intercourse of man and woman," averred Gandhi with scarcely a trace of any misgiving, and such frequently voiced sentiments, though less harshly expressed in his later years, were not calculated to earn him the goodwill of those who took a more 'modern' and 'healthy' view of sex. Having taken the vow of brahmacharya, which is commonly understood as abstinence from sex, Gandhi counseled others to become celibate as well; moreover, celibacy was to be observed, not merely by the young and the unmarried, but also by married couples. Though sexual intercourse outside marriage was unpardonable, even within marriage it had no place, in Gandhi's view, except as a regrettably unavoidable means to create progeny. The observance of celibacy among the unmarried was scarcely a matter for congratulation, for Gandhi held that the true meaning of celibacy could only be realized within a marriage. The institution of marriage provided a legal sanction to the sexual intercourse of man and woman, husband and wife, and celibacy could only be constituted as a worthy sacrifice when sexual intercourse, though construed as a natural right and a pleasure in which indulgence could legitimately be sought, was forsaken. Brahmacharya commanded married people to behave as though they were unmarried.

Insofar as Gandhi's espousal of brahmacharya has been taken seriously, it is deemed to be nothing more than a zealous advocacy of celibacy, and Gandhi's insistence on recommending celibacy even to married couples is construed as evidence of his irrational and almost monstrously insensitive view of "human nature."

Gandhi had, almost from the outset, found the narrow and widely accepted conception of brahmacharya as the abstinence from sexual intercourse woefully inadequate, and he did not think that the practitioner of brahmacharya could be judged by the moral conventions of the day. No one who desired but merely failed to realize the desire could be considered celibate: "So long as the desire for intercourse is there, one cannot be said to have attained brahmacharya. Only he who has burned away the sexual desire in its entirety may be said to have attained control over his sexual organ." As Gandhi was to stress repeatedly over the course of many years, "Brahmacharya means control of the senses in thought, word and deed." Brahmacharya did not mean that one could not touch a woman "in any circumstances whatsoever." But, in so touching a woman, it was not implied "that one's state of mind should be as calm and unruffled during such contact as when one touches, say, a piece of paper. . . . He [the brahmachari] has to be as free from excitement in case of contact with the fairest damsel on earth, as in contact with a dead body." Gandhi had so averred in 1926, but this formulation late in his life must have appeared to him as somewhat tentative, for in a letter to his female friend Amrit Kaur on March 18, 1947, the capacity to partake of the private company of naked women was to constitute an integral part of his definition of brahmacharya. Gandhi now described the "meaning of brahmacharya" thus: "One who never has any lustful intention, who by constant attendance upon God has become proof against conscious or unconscious emissions, who is capable of lying naked with naked women, however beautiful they may be, without being in any manner whatsoever sexually excited." The richer meaning of being able to lie "naked with naked women" without having any sexual thoughts would then flower into the more sublime teachings of the scriptures: a "full brahmachari," Gandhi noted, is "incapable of lying, incapable of intending or doing harm to a single man or woman in the whole world," and such a person remained "free from anger and malice and detached in the sense of the Bhagavadgita." Gandhi's definition of brahmacharya in an instant takes us away from celibacy towards self-realization, and a brahmachari correspondingly is described as a "person who is making daily and steady progress towards God and whose every act is done in pursuance of that end and no other."

No less important than that dark night of his youth when Gandhi abandoned his dying father for his pregnant wife (and so, on a different reading, embraced life over death) was an experience from the eve of his life where he was awakened to the possibility that his spiritual discipline was seriously wanting. One evening in 1936, as he was recovering from a physical breakdown induced by long hours of work, Gandhi was given a jolting and painful reminder of the inadequacy of his brahmacharya, which he said he had been "trying to follow . . . consciously and deliberately since 1899." He dreamt of a woman and, as a consequence, experienced an erection which caused a seminal emission. There had been only "one lapse" previously in his "thirty-six years' constant and conscious effort" to remain pure in thought and deed, he wrote, and only on that occasion had he experienced such "mental disturbance." He felt utterly "disgusted" with himself, and at once acquainted his "attendants and the medical friends" with his "condition." But this was a matter where others could only be sympathetic listeners: "They could give no help. I expected none." Nonetheless, he adds, "the confession of the wretched experience brought relief to me. I felt as if a great load had been raised from over me. It enabled me to pull myself together before any harm could be done." Gandhi doubtless took the view, not uncommon in India, that a true brahmachari experiences no sexual passion even in the dream state. Towards the end of the year, he was to advert to this matter again in his weekly newspaper, *Harijan,* this time in more characteristically ominous and even apocalyptic tones. He says that his "darkest hour" came to him when, in his sleep, he felt as though he wanted to experience the body of a woman. That was not pleasing to him, for

> a man who had tried to rise superior to the instinct for nearly forty years was bound to be intensely pained when he had this frightful experience. I ultimately conquered the feeling, but I was face to face with the blackest moment of my life and if I had succumbed to it, it would have been my absolute undoing.

The "path of self-purification," as Gandhi would readily concede in his autobiography, is "hard and steep," and from his own standpoint he had faltered once too often. His political triumphs seemed rather easier than the conquest of "subtle passions," and he acknowledged that since his return to India he had had "experiences of the dormant passions lying hidden within [him]." In May 1924, Gandhi had reported having had "bad dreams," but the intensity of his wet dream of 1936, a recurrence of which on April 14, 1938, once again left him shocked and repulsed, gave him other reasons for alarm. Many commentators hold that Gandhi ascribed to the view, said to be especially prominent in India, that a man must preserve his 'vital fluid', most particularly because, as common wisdom had it, semen is not easily formed: indeed, as the anthropologist Morris Carstairs framed the widely-held belief of his informants, "it takes forty days, and forty drops of blood to make one drop of semen." The "ascetic longings of Yogis who seek to conquer and transform" sexuality "into spiritual power," opines Kakar, "has been a perennial preoccupation of Hindu culture," and Erik Erikson thought that Gandhi's conduct late in his life could be reasonably rooted in a "deeply Indian preconception with seminal continence and mental potency." Writing on sexual matters for his newspaper, *Harijan,* in 1936, pursuant to his own nocturnal troubles, Gandhi himself adverted to a discussion of the "vital fluid," insisting that any expenditure of it other than for the purpose of procreation constituted a "criminal waste," the "consequent excitement caused to man and woman" being an "equally criminal waste of precious energy." "It is now easy to understand," wrote Gandhi, "why the scientists of old have put such great value upon the vital fluid and why they have insisted upon its strong transmutation into the highest form of energy for the benefit of society." "If a man controls his semen except on the occasion of such purposeful cohabitation," Gandhi wrote elsewhere, "he is as good as an avowed brahmachari," but for "an avowed brahmachari" of his aspirations no such indulgence was permitted. To this one can add the observation, whose more extended and ripe meanings cannot here be explored, that in both mythological and folkloric Indian traditions, the semen retained by a yogi is thought to turn into milk, and such a yogi is said to develop breasts. "The yogi thus becomes," writes Wendy O'Flaherty, "like a productive female when he reverses the flow of his male fluids."

II Gandhi's vagina: A political account of semen

Whatever Gandhi's own pronouncements about the imperative to preserve the "vital fluid," any interpretation which fixates on this aspect of his thought, or on what is taken to be his troubled view of the body as an obstacle to spiritual enlightenment, does not offer a compelling insight into the more striking relationship between Gandhi's advocacy of brahmacharya, his political life, and his espousal of femininity. For even as enthusiastic and careful a student of Gandhi's life as the Indian political scientist Bhikhu Parekh, the whole matter of Gandhi's "bizarre" sexual life can virtually be dismissed with the observation that his "theory of sexuality rested on a primitive approach to semen." Working almost entirely within a positivist framework, Parekh has nothing much to say except that Gandhi's ideas about the "production and accumulation" of semen were "untrue," and that the old man was "wrong" to "mystify" semen by ascribing it with "life-giving power," just as he was "wrong to associate it with energy"; indeed, "the very concept of *ojas* or spiritual energy is largely mystical and almost certainly false." Yet, as is amply clear, there are innumerable mystical traditions and sexual practices around the world for which there is no "evidence" or "basis in facts," and this ought not to compel us to confine our explorations to the most common forms of heterosexual love. Likewise, the supposition that to Gandhi his own body was a "foreign" object, for which any person of intense spiritual inclination could have nothing but fear and loathing, can scarcely be reconciled with everything else we know about Gandhi's relation to his body. Few men could have been as finely attuned to the rhythms of their bodies as Gandhi was with his, and accounts of ashram life suggest his remarkable ease with his nakedness. Far from avoiding all contact with women, as we have previously observed, Gandhi reveled in their company, and it is preeminently through the sense of touch that he consorted with the men and women around him. He would dictate letters to his secretaries or conduct other important business while his body was being massaged, and he thought nothing of putting his arms around the shoulders of friends, associates, and even visitors. He kept a careful record of the food he ingested, and his bowel movements were of as much concern to him as were the negotiations for Indian independence. Gandhi's attentiveness to matters of sexuality, hygiene, nutrition, and the presentation of the body was his way of injecting the body into the body politic, and no-where does he show the Brahmin's disdain for the polluting body or the modesty regarding one's own body which he decried in the Indian female

If the physiological account of semen loss has little to commend to our attention, can we profitably render what we might call a political account of semen? In his next life, Gandhi had often said, he would like to be reborn as an untouchable, the most exploited element of Indian society, and numerous times he gave the impression of wanting to be reborn as a woman. In either case, one would be positioned to gain a more complex phenomenological understanding of the nature of oppression. In his arduous quest for mastery over his sexual desires, *Gandhi appears to have found masculinity a nearly insuperable obstacle,* and he may have thought that women had, in this respect, an enviable advantage. It is almost plausible to speak of *Gandhi's vulva envy.* Among Indian renunciates, as the psychoanalytical investigations of one Indian brahmachari's dreams suggest, the idea is prevalent that "as long as the penis remains, one cannot be a true ascetic." It is not sufficient to curtail the activities of the penis or to prevent it from achieving a state of excitability; it must be made to disappear within the body. When the sexual passions are subdued, and the mind is prepared by means of a rigorous discipline for the exercise of abstinence, the penis begins to shrink; gradually it becomes inverted and "draws itself within the body in such a way that its very root enters into the body. By this process its appearance becomes that of a female sexual organ, while really it is the disappearance of the male sexual organ from outside the body." In their own perverse way, Gandhi's militant detractors—such as his assassin and members of the Hindu paramilitary organization Rashtriya Swayamsevak Sangh (RSS), who held him responsible for India's partition and the inability of the Indian government to protect Hindus even in the nation's capital—may have been signifying their fear that Gandhi was not quite a man when they threw at him the epithet *hijra,* which in common parlance stands for a castrated or intersexed man who takes on the identity of a woman.

Though it cannot be known how the women who partook in Gandhi's experiment "experienced" his body, the preponderant portion of the biographical and anecdotal literature suggests that the women who were intimate with him may have ceased to think of Gandhi as a man. Manu's aptly named book, *Bapu—My Mother,* points to that as much as the frequently noted observation that women felt entirely at ease in his company. Consequently, when Manu, Abha, and Sushila Nayyar agreed at various times to share Gandhi's bed with him, there is no reason to suppose that they felt they were lying besides anyone other than a woman, sharing as Indian women commonly do a bed amongst themselves.

In his aspiration to embody femininity, then, Gandhi may have been relying upon familiar idioms of Indian thought, though it is instructive how far he departed from Indian textual and customary traditions as well. He roundly ignored those traditions which enjoined upon their male followers to keep at a physical remove from women. "A brahmachari, it is said," wrote Gandhi in 1938, "should never see, much less touch a woman. Doubtless a brahmachari may not think of, speak of, see or touch a woman lustfully. But the prohibition one finds in books on brahmacharya is mentioned without the important adverb," that is "lustfully." Recognizing that observance of brahmacharya was difficult "when one freely mixes with the world," Gandhi nonetheless added that "it is not of much value if it is attainable only by retirement from the world." In all domains of life, Gandhi rejected the segregation of the sexes, even preferring (unusual for Indians of his time) coeducational schools to single-sex schools. He thought that Indian women's refusal to be attended by male gynecologists or surgeons originated from a false sense of shame, though he recognized that there were "unscrupulous doctor[s]" who took advantage of their patients. Writing to the young Muslim daughter of a friend on the subject of an enema, in whose efficacy Gandhi reposed much trust, he put the matter quite candidly: "Whether the person who helps you with the enema is a man or a woman, it should make, and I am sure it will make, no difference to you at all." To a brahmachari, in the event, this could be no important consideration.

Most tellingly, though, Gandhi appears to have found some sustenance in certain strands of Vaishnava theology and literature. During the course of one long exposition of his views on brahmacharya, Gandhi had remarked: "When the Gopis were stripped of their clothes by Krishna, the legend says, they showed no sign of embarrassment or sex-consciousness but stood before the Lord in rapt devotion." Subsequent to disclosures about his experiment, this story was to find its way into his public speeches. The reference here is to a famous scene in Krishna's life where the gopis or cowherdesses, having stripped at the banks of the river Yamuna to take a bath, are about to emerge from the water when they find their garments missing. When they look around them, they find Krishna dangling them from a tree upon which he is perched; the gopis implore him to return their clothes, while Krishna reminds them that since each of them had set their hearts on him, uttering a prayer that would grant them Krishna as their husband, they should be prepared to walk into his presence without a trace of shame.

The *Bhagavata Purana*, the preeminent text of Krishna devotion, states explicitly that "bashfully they [the gopis] looked at each other and smiled, but none came out of the water." When eventually they do so, notwithstanding their most earnest pleas that they should be spared this indignity, they cover "their private parts with the palms of their hands." But Krishna is not so easily appeased: since in entering the water in a naked state after taking a religious vow the gopis had committed a transgression, they were to expiate their sin by raising their folded palms to their heads and prostrating themselves on the ground. Each gopi attempts to comply with Krishna's injunction by raising one of her hands, while her other hand continues to cover her genitals; this only provokes Krishna to the observation that such a mode of rendering obeisance constitutes a gross violation of the ethics of worship, and that the Lord cannot be satisfied other than by a complete fulfillment of religious observances. In this manner the gopis, now aware of the nature of their transgression, submit in a state of complete nudity, and their clothes are returned to them. Their obeisance has been rendered, and now they can reasonably await its fulfillment: it is also characteristic of Krishna that, recognizing the longing each gopi has for him, the longing that each one of us has to be merged into the absolute and to receive the favors of the divine lover, he exercises the power within him to satisfy each gopi. Thus, in the received versions of the Krishna legend, he can be with nearly 20,000 gopis simultaneously, though each lives in the illusory state that she alone is the object of his affections. Yet this "satisfaction" has no necessary, or even any, referent to sexual intercourse: indeed, one of Krishna's myriad names is *Acyuta*, "the one whose seed does not fall," since once sexual orgasm has been achieved, the erotic play is over. This interpretation is unequivocally echoed in a Hindi proverb, where it is said of Krishna, *"Solah sahasra nari phir bhi brahmachari"* [He has sixteen thousand women but still remains a celibate.] It is perhaps against this backdrop that we should view Gandhi's comment to his disciple Vinoba Bhave: "My mind daily sleeps in an innocent manner with millions of women, and Manu also, who is a blood relation to me, sleeps with me as one of these millions."

Whatever liberty Gandhi appears to have taken in suggesting that the gopis showed no embarrassment in appearing before Krishna in a state of nakedness, what is particularly illustrative is the manner in which Gandhi sought to deploy the trope of nakedness in the service of a philosophical and political conception of "truth." Though no detailed thoughts can be entertained here over Gandhi's sartorial politics, it is germane that over the course of a lifetime Gandhi came increasingly to shed clothes. In the early years of his youth, as a law student in Britain, he had endeavored to dress as an English gentleman, and it was not until he thrust himself into the struggle to procure Indians' political rights in South Africa that he simplified his dress. It was around the time of the noncooperation movement of 1920–1922, by which time Gandhi had already initiated a daily regimen of spinning and also urged it upon the nation as part of a program of national rejuvenation, that he further shed his clothes, choosing to move around only in a simple loincloth, a shawl thrown over his chest during the winter months. This is the image with which he would henceforth be associated, captured perhaps nowhere better than in his remark to an English reporter in 1930, as he was questioned about whether he proposed to go dressed in this manner to have tea with His Royal Highness at Buckingham Palace, that the King-Emperor was wearing enough for both of them. In a similar vein, while taking note of Churchill's insulting remark that the prospect of direct negotiations between the British government and a "half-naked seditious fakir of a type well known in the Orient" was too nauseating to be contemplated, Gandhi had expressed the hope that he might become completely naked.

III Naked before God: The infinite play of sexuality

Gandhi had set for himself the ambition to appear naked before God, which for him was nothing other than Truth, and consequently come face to face with the "Truth." At this particular juncture, when India was almost on the verge of independence, he was tormented by the awareness that his teachings on ahimsa had been less successful than he had hoped. The tone of his statement released to the press on November 20, 1946, as he was to proceed to the village of Srirampur in Noakhali district, reveals his deep foreboding: "I find myself in the midst of exaggeration and falsity. I am unable to discover the truth. . . . Truth and ahimsa by which I swear, and which have, to my knowledge, sustained me for sixty years, seem to fail to show the attributes I have ascribed to them." He had striven to maintain Hindu-Muslim harmony, even fasted (oftentimes with grave consequences to his health) whenever there had been a major recrudescence of communal violence, and no issue since the mid-1920s had occupied more of his attention; and yet, well more than twenty years after his attainment of Mahatmahood, he now seemed to have little control over the unfolding of events. This is scarcely to say that Gandhi believed that his Mahatmahood conferred on him powers which were rightfully his, or that his word should have had, as it apparently once did, the force of law. If his utterances no longer commanded obedience, that was a sure sign that his voice did not carry very far into the public sphere. However, everything in Gandhi's own philosophical leanings, and most particularly his conception of truth, disposed him to the belief that the violence and untruth which pervaded the public domain were reflections of some profound shortcomings in his own practice of ahimsa and brahmacharya. Satyagraha implies that the individual carries within himself or herself the burden of social failings, and that one reads from social developments as from a mirror the history of one's own thought and practices. "Ever since my coming to Noakhali," Gandhi reported to Bapa Thakkar in 1947, in his endeavor to explain why he commenced upon his experiment, "I have been asking myself the question 'What is it that is choking the action of my ahimsa? Why does not the spell work?' May not be because I have temporized in the matter of brahmacharya." If his teachings of ahimsa had failed to avert communal rioting, Gandhi was prone to think that there was something profoundly amiss in his own practice of ahimsa. "There must be some serious flaw deep down in me which I am unable to discover," he wrote, and again he added with insistent, even compulsive force: "There must be something terribly lacking in my ahimsa and faith which is responsible for all this."

That "serious flaw" deep down inside him which he had "failed to discover" might have set Gandhi on the trajectory of the last great—albeit troubled—experiment of his life, but in this trajectory of reasoning there appears at first sight to be more than a faint trace of an almost furtive attempt to recoup the power that he had exercised with unrivaled authority for over two decades. While profoundly committed to the democratic ethos, to the point where he refused to distinguish between intellectual elites and common workers, much as he thought the labor of the hands to be at least as productive and worthy as the labor of the mind, Gandhi's methods were nonetheless often autocratic. In 1939, for example, he had suffered an unprecedented defeat when his candidate for the presidency of the Congress received fewer votes than Subhas Chandra Bose, who was later to flee India and offer Germany and Japan the services of the Indian National Army. Not accustomed to having his wishes defied, Gandhi made it impossible for Bose to function as president and within a few months had procured his resignation. When he commenced his experiments in brahmacharya sometime after his release from jail in mid-1944, he had to make some effort to reestablish his preeminent presence on the Indian political scene, and in the negotiations for independence he was only one of several leaders with whom the British parleyed; at the same time, witnessing the communal carnage—which would accelerate greatly in the last year before his death—his loss of moral authority must have struck him with even greater force. In consonance with Indian teachings, one of his biographers suggests, Gandhi was under the circumstances particularly prone to accept the view that his power to influence events would be enhanced if he could test himself as a brahmachari. Stretching this argument yet further, it appears not unreasonable to conclude that, forsaking the position that Gandhi had advocated since his early days in South Africa that the ends never justify the means, he was even prepared to make the young women who idolized him the instrument of his quest for political power.

Any such interpretation, as I have throughout been endeavoring to argue, cannot really be sustained. That Gandhi would now resort to the vulgar, not to mention reprehensible, notion that any means were permissible in order to enhance his political fortunes can scarcely be reconciled with anything we know of Gandhi's political philosophy, his decisive rejection of instrumental rationality, his practices of satyagraha, and—as even his critics concede—his willingness to endure the most dangerous risks to his own life in his resolve to bring the violence to an end. Alone among Indian leaders, Gandhi entirely repudiated the trappings of power and understood that in the visible sovereignty and display of power reside the seeds of its destruction. He was more attuned to the nature of power in the modern age than the politicians who more than fifty years after his death consider the number of security guards attached to them as the index of their power and prestige. By this yardstick, Gandhi, who refused protection even after an attempt on his life, was a mere commoner. It is instructive that he never held office after having established a decisive moral authority over the Congress in 1920, and that from the mid-1920s onwards he was not even a member of the party over whose destiny he presided and which had been charged with liberating India from British rule. Gandhi was most certainly perturbed, indeed mortified, by the communal violence that had broken out, but this in no manner leads inescapably to the conclusion that unable to accept the loss of his influence, he was now prepared to abandon his convictions and the principles of satyagraha in the pursuit of his political ambitions. He had committed, in his own language, "Himalayan blunders" before, most particularly during the 1920–1922 noncooperation movement which he had felt compelled to suspend when it had degenerated into violence, and his political difficulties from 1945 to 1947 can easily be overstated. Then, in 1922, he had faced with remarkable equanimity a prison term designed to prevent him from preaching sedition, and had so embraced a form of powerlessness that would have the curative and rejuvenative effect of launching him into the next stage of the struggle for India's spiritual, political, and social revival. In the last years of his life, Gandhi again seems to have been seized with the desire to be stripped clean, and such was his disdain for power that he was altogether prepared to face calumny and opprobrium. As a brahmachari, he had put limits upon himself with respect to "contacts with the opposite sex," but these limits now struck him as unacceptable, as constraints placed upon his constant engagement with the truth.

On more than one occasion Gandhi had described his life's endeavor as nothing but a concerted effort to reduce himself to "zero." This is the note on which he concludes his autobiography of the mid-1920s, and a year before his death he was to put the matter in similar terms in a letter to Mirabehn: "If I succeed in emptying myself utterly, God will possess me. Then I know that everything will come true but it is a serious question when I shall have reduced myself to zero. Think of 'I' and 'O' in juxtaposition and you have the whole problem of life in two signs." To empty oneself is not only to render oneself a vehicle for something else, to become capable of being possessed, but to lead life to the fullest. Gandhi's nakedness needed no adornment, and any adornment would have been an effrontery to his nakedness. Appearing naked before the world, Gandhi would yet scarcely have championed nudity: he had no "private parts," not even, despite his (near) androgyny, a penis-vagina. Having renounced sex, Gandhi had by no means abjured sexuality; quite to the contrary, he was to embrace it in the amplest measure. In the language of James Carse, Gandhi was an exponent of infinite rather than finite sexuality. Where players at the finite game of sexuality view persons as the expressions of sexuality, Gandhi was interested in sexuality as the expression of persons; and where finite players relate to the body, infinite players relate to the person in the body. "Finite sexuality is a form of theater in which the distance between persons is regularly reduced to zero," writes Carse with extraordinary prescience, "but in which neither touches the other." Gandhi had not the power of touch, for he was no miracle-maker, but he had the vision of touch: "Finite players play within boundaries," adds Carse, but "infinite players play with boundaries"; infinite players of sexuality play not *within* sexual boundaries, as do heterosexuals, bisexuals, lesbians, and homosexuals, but *with* sexual boundaries. Gandhi, who abhorred sex, was yet the most consummate player at the game of sexuality.

10

Discussion Questions

1 Based on the familiarity with your own religious tradition or with the religious traditions of others, discuss how sexual or erotic desire might be framed and regulated therein. Does that tradition seek to erect a firm barrier between religious and sexual desire? Why, or why not?

2 What does it mean to say that gender is "performed?" Do you think that one can claim the same thing about religion? Why, or why not?

3 Can you think of religious rituals whose purpose it is to "perform" gender or to put it on display? What sorts of gendered scripts or messages are being enacted or conveyed? Are these being put forward in order to reaffirm or control normative gender patterns, or rather to raise questions about them?

4 Scholars have argued that femininity and masculinity are performed gendered categories, as opposed to being biologically given or determined. Give examples from the readings, or from your own religious knowledge, which support this argument. Why do humans so often have difficulty in viewing gender this way?

5 Do you agree that bondage and discipline or sadomasochistic practices can be sources of religious and spiritual enlightenment? Why, or why not?

6 Institutionalized religions do not have a great deal to say about transsexual issues. Why might that be? In his text, Jakob Hero argues that the transsexual experience can be understood positively from the theological perspective of human flourishing. How might this view help religions develop a more accepting outlook on trans issues and concerns?

7 The reading by Karen McCarthy Brown raises questions about the ways in which women practitioners of Haitian Vodou use ritual as a means of "performing" or expressing their gendered identities. Did you find the reading compelling? What did you especially like about it? More broadly, what might it teach us about how women's religious lives differ from those of men, if they do?

8　In the two readings from the Hindu tradition (Lal and Reddy), can one say that gender and sexuality are performed differently? Compare and contrast the readings.

9　How do you "perform" gender or sexuality in your own religious or spiritual life, or how do you see it being "performed" in the religious or spiritual lives of others?

10　A number of the texts in this reader suggest that the boundaries between people's erotic or sexual desires and their religious experience can be, in fact, rather porous and unstable. Discuss, using examples from some of these readings.

Glossary

Ahimsa A Sanskrit term referring to a concept developed in Jainism, Hinduism, and Buddhism that can be translated as "do no harm" or "injury." Appropriated by Gandhi in his revolutionary efforts, the term indicated nonviolent demonstration as a means to resist political oppression and institute social change.

Al-Sarakshi An influential Sunni Muslim jurist from the majority Hanafi branch of legal schools. He lived in twelfth century C.E. Transoxania (modern day Turkistan in Central Asia).

Androgyny Possessing masculine and feminine characteristics. It can be said of persons and of such things as clothing and hairstyles, but also of types of behavior.

Asexuality A lack of, or a low or absent interest in, erotic attraction. Asexuality is seen as a legitimate erotic choice.

Bridal mysticism In the Christian mystical tradition, the use of bridal imagery to refer to the union of the mystic or the soul with God. Almost always, God is cast in the role of the husband. This imagery draws heavily from the book, *Song of Songs*, found in the Christian Old Testament.

Catholic devotionalism Forms of piety specific to Roman Catholic culture, such as devotion to the saints or to Mary, the rosary, the crucifix, and other similar persons or objects.

Cisgender Where gender and sex are in accord. It is seen as complementary to the term "transgender."

Divination The religious belief that through some ritualized use of creatures or objects, insight can be gained into the future or the deeper workings of reality.

Etrog A citrus fruit used especially during the Jewish fall festival of Sukkot.

Evangelical Member of a Protestant Christian movement that emphasizes missionary activity, the necessity of accepting Jesus Christ for salvation, and the authority of the Bible. This movement grew out of the religious revivals of the eighteenth and nineteenth centuries in North America. Evangelicals commonly employ personal and intimate language to describe their relationship with Jesus and God.

Galenic-Hippocratic Refers to a classical Greek medical tradition that held both men and women provided "seeds" that joined together in utero to produce a child, in contrast to the view of Aristotle that men provided "seed" and women only matter.

Genitocentric Said of a theology or an understanding of sexuality that is excessively focused on genital activity.

Hallah, niddah, hadlaqah Indicates the three commandments (*mitzvot*) especially associated with women in rabbinic Judaism. *Hallah* refers to a woman's knowledge and observance of Jewish dietary laws in the preparation of food; *niddah*, her observance of protocols of separation from her husband during menstruation and after childbirth; *hadlaqah*, to lighting the Sabbath candles, and more generally to the performance of domestic rituals associated with Jewish festivals and holy days.

Hermaphrodite Someone who possesses the reproductive organs of both sexes.

Heteronormative The supposition that heterosexuality is the normative sexual/gender paradigm, but also that it is superior to other forms of sexual choice and behavior.

Holy Ghost In Christian theology, the third person of the Trinity. The first person is the Father or God, and the second person is the Son or Jesus Christ. The Holy Ghost is also often called the Holy Spirit.

Izzat A Hindi term meaning respect or honor.

Kadā-cātla kōti A *koti* who wears male clothing, does not have an official kinship link with *hijras*, and does not have the *nirvan* operation.

Karmic law From the Sanskrit, meaning "action" or "doing." It is the belief that good or bad actions will have equally good or bad effects in this life or in the next.

Koti A "female-identified" man who desires and engages in receptive (same-sex) intercourse and adopts "feminine" mannerisms of discourse and practice.

Krishna The eighth incarnation of the God Vishnu, Krishna became the subject of numerous devotional cults across India. Mythological accounts of Lord Krishna often represent him as an amorous and playful figure, notably in his sexual exploits with the gopis, female cow-herders.

Laïcité A concept developed during the French Revolution, and codified in French law in the early twentieth century. The term derives from the French for "laity" (lay people as opposed to clergy). It indicates that citizens have the freedom of religion and prohibits the influence of religion in public institutions.

Lexiography Encyclopedic writing concerned with the meaning of, and connection between, particular words.

LGBTIQ An acronym which refers to *L*esbian, *G*ay, *B*isexual, *T*rans, *I*ntersexed (or *I*nquiring), and *Q*ueer or *Q*uestioning. Sometimes, *TS* is added to refer to *T*wo-*S*pirited, an indigenous designation.

Midrash Tanhuma Midrash refers to a form of rabbinic interpretation that attempts to fill in gaps in biblical materials and includes both narrative (*aggadah*) and legal (*halakha*) materials. Midrash Tanhuma is a particular midrashic collection, named after Rabbi Tanhuma who is cited in it.

Niddah A Hebrew term that refers to a menstruating woman; it can also indicate the commandment that a woman maintain separation from her husband during menstruation and after childbirth as well as use a ritual bath (*mikvah*) to cleanse herself after these events.

Nirvan Literally, "spiritual rebirth"; used among *hijras* to connote the physical excision of male genitalia.

Psychoanalytic theory Employed in both academic studies and in therapeutic contexts, this theory is informed by, and responding to, the work of Sigmund Freud. It emphasizes childhood experiences and the role of the unconscious in the development of the personality.

Queer Originally a pejorative term for homosexuals, it has been reclaimed to designate those who reject a specific sexual label or identity. More generally, it refers to any destabilizing or nonnormative political or cultural activist strategy and similar forms of intellectual inquiry.

Rapture A particular Christian understanding of eschatology (or end-times) where the elect or the saved, both living and dead, will be pulled upward to meet Jesus during his Second Coming.

Renunciant One who renounces or gives up some worldly gain for religious or spiritual reasons. The term is especially relevant to Hinduism, where such renunciation is expected in later life.

Relic Body parts or objects which belonged to a holy person, and which are believed to contain special powers. Relics are notably found in Roman Catholicism and in Buddhism.

Sacrament In Christian theology, a sacrament is a ritual that is believed to be a manifestation or a source of grace. Roman Catholics believe that there are seven sacraments: baptism, confirmation, the Eucharist (or Mass), confession, marriage, holy orders or ordination, and the anointing of the sick or extreme unction. Generally, Protestants believe in only two "Bible-based" sacraments: baptism and the Eucharist.

Saint Found in many religious traditions, saints are holy persons who are emblematic of the faith. In the Roman Catholic Church, such individuals are formally recognized and declared to be saints by the Pope.

Satyagraha A Sanskrit word that indicates a philosophical approach to the truth. For Gandhi, this truth is obtained by observing nonviolence and self-scrutiny so as to exist in harmonious relationship with the Infinite.

Shabbat Hebrew term for "rest" or "cessation." It goes from Friday sunset to Saturday sunset, and is marked by a variety of religious rituals and observances.

Shi'i jurist A legal scholar from the Shi'a community (as opposed to the Sunni community), who maintain that Muhammad's son-in-law, Ali, was the prophet's legitimate successor (or Caliph).

Spirit possession The religious belief that some transcendent power (god, spirit, force) can take possession of the body of a person, for either beneficial or harmful purposes.

Vaishnava A variety of Hinduism in which the deity Vishnu (or one of his avatars/ incarnations, often Krishna) is venerated as the highest God.

White culture Indicates racist beliefs about and actions promoting the superior value of "whiteness," and the denigration of "nonwhite" people. As a culture, it is something that is taught and perpetuated, not something one possesses by virtue of a racial or ethnic background. It also represents values that can be challenged and changed through education.

Zenāna a male (koti) dancer who adopts "feminine" gestures and mannerisms; wears female clothing only when performing; has a kinship network distinct from that of the *hijras*. Also, domestic space reserved for women.

Index